LANGUAGE AND HISTORY IN VIKING AGE ENGLAND

Linguistic Relations between
Speakers of Old Norse and Old English

STUDIES IN THE EARLY MIDDLE AGES

EDITORIAL BOARD UNDER THE AUSPICES OF THE

CENTRE FOR MEDIEVAL STUDIES
UNIVERSITY OF YORK

Elizabeth M. Tyler (University of York)
Julian D. Richards (University of York)
Ross Balzaretti (University of Nottingham)

VOLUME 6

LANGUAGE AND HISTORY IN VIKING AGE ENGLAND

Linguistic Relations between
Speakers of Old Norse and Old English

by

Matthew Townend

BREPOLS

British Library Cataloguing in Publication Data

Townend, Matthew
Language and history in Viking age England : linguistic relations between speakers of Old Norse and Old English. – (Studies in the early middle ages ; v. 6)
1.English language – Old English, ca. 450-1100 – Social aspects 2.Old Norse language – England – Social aspects 3.English language - Old English, ca. 450-1100 – History 4.Old Norse language – Influence on English
I.Title
429

ISBN 2503518419

©2002, Brepols Publishers n.v., Turnhout, Belgium

All rights reserved. No part of this publication may be reproduced, stored in a retrieval system, or transmitted, in any form or by any means, electronic, mechanical, photocopying, recording, or otherwise, without the prior permission of the publisher.

D/2002/0095/62
ISBN: 2-503-51841-9

Printed in the E.U. on acid-free paper.

For my mother and father

Contents

Acknowledgements	ix
Abbreviations	xi
Bibliographical Abbreviations	xiii
Terminology and Conventions	xv

Chapter 1. Introduction: Anglo-Norse Language Contact — 1

Chapter 2. The Languages: Viking Age Norse and English — 19
The Evolution of Viking Age Norse and English — 20
A Phonological Comparison of Viking Age Norse and English — 31

Chapter 3. The Scandinavianisation of Old English Place-Names — 43
Theories of Intelligibility: Two Models — 43
Norse Speakers and English Place-Names — 47
Analysis and Discussion — 57

Appendix 3.1. Corpus of Scandinavianised Place-Names — 69

Chapter 4. Anglo-Norse Contact in Anglo-Saxon Sources — 89
'The Voyages of Ohthere and Wulfstan' in the Old English Orosius — 90
Æthelweard's *Chronicle* — 110
Ælfric and Wulfstan: *De Falsis Diis* — 128

Chapter 5. Literary Accounts and Anecdotal Evidence 145
Old Norse: The Witness of the Sagas 145
Old English and Anglo-Latin: Interpreters in Anglo-Saxon England 161
The Old English *Carta Dominica* Homilies 171

Chapter 6. Old Norse in England: Towards a Linguistic History 181
Review: Evidence for Intelligibility 181
Societal Bilingualism in Viking Age England 185
Old Norse Literacy in England 189
Inflexional Loss in Old English and Old Norse 196
Norse Loans in English and Old Norse Language Death 201
Concluding Remarks 210

Bibliography 213

Index 239

Acknowledgements

This book originally began life as a doctoral thesis, and I am above all deeply indebted to my former supervisor, Heather O'Donoghue, for longstanding encouragement and guidance. For help of various kinds, and at various stages, I am also grateful to Malcolm Godden, Deborah A. Oosterhouse, Christine Rauer, Clinton Robinson, Elizabeth Tyler, and the anonymous readers who commented on the manuscript. Particular thanks are due to Richard Dance, who read various sections in draft and with whom I have enjoyed many conversations on the subject of Anglo-Norse contact. Finally, the dedicatees of this book have not read a word of it, but it could not have been written without them.

Abbreviations

acc. = accusative
AM = Arnamagnæan Institute, Copenhagen / Stofnun Árna Magnússonar, Reykjavík
Bd = Bedfordshire
BL = British Library
Brk = Berkshire
C = century (e.g. C12 = twelfth century)
CCCC = Corpus Christi College, Cambridge
Ch = Cheshire
Cu = Cumberland
D = Devon
dat. = dative
Db = Derbyshire
DB = Domesday Book
Do = Dorset
Du = Durham
EETS = Early English Text Society
    NS = New Series
    OS = Ordinary Series
    SS = Supplementary Series
EPNS = English Place-Name Society
fem. = feminine
gen. = genitive
Gl = Gloucestershire
Gmc = Germanic
ind. = indicative
K = Kent
L = Lincolnshire
La = Lancashire
Lei = Leicestershire
masc. = masculine
ME = Middle English

MnE = Modern English
neut. = neuter
nom. = nominative
NOWELE = North-Western European Language Evolution
Nt = Nottinghamshire
Nth = Northamptonshire
O = Oxfordshire
OE = Old English
OEN = Old East Norse
OHG = Old High German
ON = Old Norse
OWN = Old West Norse
pers. = person
pres. = present tense
pl. = plural
S = reference number in Sawyer 1968
sg. = singular
So = Somerset
SIL = Summer Institute of Linguistics
St = Staffordshire
STUAGNL = Samfund til Udgivelse af Gammel Nordisk Litteratur
VAN = Viking Age Norse
W = Wiltshire
Wa = Warwickshire
We = Westmorland
Wo = Worcestershire
WS = West Saxon
YE = East Riding of Yorkshire
YN = North Riding of Yorkshire
YW = West Riding of Yorkshire

Bibliographical Abbreviations

For ease of reference, especially in Appendix 3.1, standard works on place-names are designated as follows (full details are to be found in the Bibliography):

DEPN = Ekwall 1960
PNCh = Dodgson 1970–97
PNCu = Armstrong and others 1950–52
PNDb = Cameron 1959
PNL = Cameron 1989–
PNLa = Ekwall 1922
PNNt = Gover, Mawer, and Stenton 1940
PNNth = Gover, Mawer, and Stenton 1933
PNW = Gover, Mawer, and Stenton 1939
PNWa = Gover and others 1936
PNWe = Smith 1967
PNYE = Smith 1937
PNYN = Smith 1928
PNYW = Smith 1961–63
SSNEM = Fellows-Jensen 1978
SSNNW = Fellows-Jensen 1985
SSNY = Fellows-Jensen 1972

Terminology and Conventions

A number of points of terminology and other practice should be noted:

(1) The term 'Old Norse' is used to designate the language spoken by Scandinavians in the Viking Age: it does not mean 'Norwegian'. Some writers choose to speak of 'Old Scandinavian' for this period, but since 'Old Norse' is the usual English term for the language in the later Middle Ages I have retained it for the earlier period as well. Inconsistently, however, I have preferred the common term 'Scandinavianisation' to the much rarer 'Norsification'.

(2) I have not been consistent in designating Norse and English as either 'languages' or 'dialects', but use both terms at different times. The distinction is an impossible one to maintain, and the most common criterion for regarding two speech varieties as dialects rather than languages — the criterion of mutual intelligibility — is one of the central issues which this work investigates.

(3) While 'Norse' is used as a linguistic term, 'Scandinavian' is employed with cultural or historical reference; in many ways this parallels the distinction between '(Old) English' and 'Anglo-Saxon'.

(4) Except where discussing philological details, I usually refer to well-known figures by their most familiar name-form in Modern English (for example, Alfred, Cnut, Harold Godwineson).

(5) Principles of transcription are as follows. In citing linguistic forms I employ the convention of italics, although phonemic slanted brackets // are sometimes used, especially for consonants. Graphemic angled brackets ◇ are used when discussing purely orthographic issues, and bold type is used for the transcription of runic text.

(6) Unless otherwise stated, all translations are my own.

CHAPTER 1

Introduction:
Anglo-Norse Language Contact

The Vikings in England

AN..dcclxxxvii. Her nom Beorhtric cyning Offan dohtor Eadburge. ⁊ on his dagum cuomon ærest .iii. scipu, ⁊ þa se gerefa þærto rad ⁊ hie wolde drifan to þæs cyninges tune þy he nyste hwæt hie wæron, ⁊ hiene mon ofslog. Þæt wæron þa ærestan scipu deniscra monna þe Angelcynnes lond gesohton.

(787. In this year King Beorhtric married Offa's daughter Eadburg. And in his days three ships came for the first time; and then the reeve rode there and wanted to take them to the king's vill because he did not know what they were; and he was killed. They were the first ships of Danish men that came to the land of the English people.)

In these familiar words (Bately 1986, 39), in the entry six years prior to that recording the more famous sack of Lindisfarne, the Vikings make their first appearance in the *Anglo-Saxon Chronicle*, and so in English history; and as the years go by this initial trickle of Norsemen becomes a stream, and the stream an irresistible flood (Bately 1986, 42, 44, 47):

AN..dcccxxxv. Her cuom micel sciphere on Westwalas, ⁊ hie to anum gecierdon, ⁊ wiþ Ecgbryht Westseaxna cyning winnende wæron.

(835. In this year a great Viking fleet came to the Cornish Britons, and the two peoples united, and waged war against King Ecgbryht of the West Saxons.)

AN..dcccli [. . .] ⁊ hęþne men ærest ofer winter sæton.

(851 [. . .] And for the first time the heathens remained over the winter.)

> AN..dccclxvi. Her feng Æþered Æþelbryhtes broþur to Wesseaxna rice. ⁊ þy ilcan geare cuom micel here on Angelcynnes lond, ⁊ wintersetl namon on Eastenglum ⁊ þær gehorsude wurdon, ⁊ hie him friþ <wiþ> namon.
>
> (866. In this year Æþelbryht's brother Æþered succeeded to the kingdom of the West Saxons. And in the same year a great army came to the land of the English people, and took winter quarters in the land of the East Angles, and there they were provided with horses, and the East Angles made peace with them.)

This *micel here* ('great army') is that of the Viking leaders who in later traditions became known as the sons of Ragnarr loðbrók (see Smyth 1977). After the wars and treaties come the settlements (Bately 1986, 50, 51):

> AN..dccclxxvi. [. . .] ⁊ þy geare Healfdene Norþanhymbra lond gedęlde ⁊ ergende wæron ⁊ hiera tilgende.
>
> (876. [. . .] And in the same year Halfdan shared out the land of the Northumbrians, and they turned to ploughing and making a living for themselves.)
>
> AN..dccclxxvii. [. . .] ⁊ þa on hærfeste gefor se here on Miercna lond ⁊ hit gedęldon sum ⁊ sum Ceolwulfe saldon.
>
> (877. [. . .] And then in the autumn the Viking army went into the land of the Mercians, and they shared some of it out and gave some to Ceolwulf.)
>
> AN..dccclxxx. Her for se here of Cirenceastre on Eastengle ⁊ gesæt þæt lond ⁊ gedęlde.
>
> (880. In this year the Viking army went from Cirencester into the land of the East Angles, and they occupied that land and shared it out.)

Thus the Vikings become the Vikings in England; and it seems clear from the great weight of place-name evidence that the Scandinavian settlement of the area later known as the Danelaw was large-scale and profound, and most probably involved some form of secondary, continuing migration from Scandinavia (see pp 47–48 below). But it is also clear that the native Anglo-Saxon population in the areas of Scandinavian settlement was by no means driven out or otherwise suppressed; and so in the tenth and eleventh centuries Anglo-Saxon England is more properly to be regarded as Anglo-Scandinavian England, with the two peoples, similar but distinctive, in close and persistent contact.

Sir Frank Stenton, in his classic review of Anglo-Scandinavian relations and the settlement of what he termed 'the essential Danelaw' (that is, between the Tees and the Welland), concluded as follows (1927, 241, 246):

> [W]e begin to discern two races in pre-Conquest England, differing in language, law, and social order, held together by little more than common acquiescence in the role of a king whose authority was narrowly limited by custom. We are driven, in fact, towards the

conclusion that the superficial unity of the Old English state concealed a racial cleavage which was none the less real because it was taken for granted by contemporaries. [. . .] All lines of investigation — linguistic, legal, and economic — point to the reality of the difference between Danes and English in the tenth century.

The terms of Stenton's discussion ('two races') are now, of course, out of favour, and recent publications by, in particular, Dawn Hadley (1997; 2000a, 298–341; 2000b; 2001) have queried whether the difference between Danes and English was at all as simple and straightforward as Stenton suggested. It is possible to explore the question of Anglo-Danish interaction in Viking Age England with reference to various types of evidence — for example, law, sculpture, and land-holding — but the area to be considered in this work is that of language, and, as will be seen, the distinctiveness of Old Norse and Old English is in itself a factor in favour of Stenton's position (see Townend 2000a). The crucial concept here is that of the 'speech community': speech communities may or may not correlate with other types of social community (see Hudson 1996, 24–30; Weinreich 1953, 89–99), but at the very least one can easily distinguish the Old Norse and Old English speech communities in Viking Age England, and it is for this reason that linguists have been more hesitant than, say, archaeologists and historians to embrace those contemporary ideas about 'ethnicity' which substantially downplay the importance of linguistic factors in the creation and maintenance of group identities. There is no need for a full rehearsal of the issues at this preliminary stage; but as will become clear, one of the outcomes of this book will be to uphold broadly Stentonian perspectives on the reality of the English/Danish distinction in Viking Age England.

Anglo-Norse Contact in Viking Age England

Angus McIntosh articulates the following principle: 'Fundamentally, what we mean by "languages in contact" is "users of language in contact" and to insist upon this is much more than a mere terminological quibble and has far from trivial consequences' (1994, 137; see also Milroy 1997, 311). It is therefore instructive to begin this introduction not with some of the well-known examples of Old Norse influence on the English language, but rather with some of the ample evidence from Anglo-Saxon records for situations of contact between users of English and users of Norse in Viking Age England. Leaving aside military confrontations, Anglo-Saxon texts from the ninth to eleventh centuries record many more peaceful encounters between English speakers and Norse speakers, inevitably prompting the question, amongst others, of the language or languages in which such encounters were conducted. Did the Anglo-Saxons learn to speak Norse or the Scandinavians learn to speak English; or was there something of both? If so, was such bilingualism widespread, or were negotiations conducted via a few specialist interpreters? Or was it the case, as has often been suggested, that speakers of the two languages enjoyed adequate mutual intelligibility for each side to be understood by the other while speaking their own language?

A selection of representative encounters, with this linguistic question hanging over them, might be as follows (presented in roughly chronological order):

(1) In the mid-ninth century, early in the course of the Viking raids, and possibly before the arrival of the great army, the eighth-century gospel-book now known as the Stockholm Codex Aureus fell into the hands of a Viking warband (presumably along with some other manuscripts). A contemporary Canterbury inscription tells how it was recovered (Whitelock 1967, 205; see further Brooks 1984, 151):

In nomine Domini nostri Ihesu Christi. Ic Aelfred aldormon ond Wērburg mīn gefēra begētan ðās bēc æt hāeðnum herge mid uncre clāene fēo; ðæt ðonne wæs mid clǣne golde. Ond ðæt wit deodan for Godes lufan ond for uncre sāule ðearf[e], ond for ðon ðe wit noldan ðæt ðās hālgan bēoc lencg in ðǣre hāeðenesse wunaden, ond nū willað hēo gesellan inn tō Crīstes circan Gode tō lofe ond tō wuldre ond tō weorðunga.

(*In the name of Our Lord Jesus Christ.* I, Ealdorman Ælfred, and Werburg my wife acquired these books from the heathen army with our pure money; that was, with pure gold. And we two did that for the love of God and the need of our souls; and because we did not wish these holy books to remain any longer in heathen possession; and now we wish to give them into the keeping of Christ Church [Canterbury], to the praise and honour and glory of God.)

What, therefore, were the linguistic means by which Ealdorman Ælfred negotiated with the Vikings for the recovery of the gospel-book?

(2) In 878, after the battle of Edington, Alfred and Guthrum came to terms. One of the conditions of their reconciliation was that the Scandinavian king should become a Christian, and the *Anglo-Saxon Chronicle* MS 'A' for this year accordingly recounts how the two kings spent a considerable amount of time together (Bately 1986, 51):

þa salde se here him foregislas ⁊ micle aþas, þæt hie of his rice uuoldon ⁊ him eac geheton þæt hiera kyning fulwihte onfon wolde, ⁊ hie þæt gelæston swa, ⁊ þæs ymb .iii. wiecan com se cyning to him Godrum þritiga sum þara monna þe in þam here weorþuste wæron æt Alre, ⁊ þæt is wiþ Eþelinggaeige, ⁊ his se cyning þær onfeng æt fulwihte, ⁊ his crismlising was æt Weþmor, ⁊ he was .xii. niht mid þam cyninge, ⁊ he hine miclum ⁊ his geferan mid feo weorðude.

(Then the Viking army gave him hostages and solemn oaths that they intended to leave his kingdom, and they also promised him that their king would receive baptism; and they carried out their word, and after three weeks King Guthrum came to him at Aller, which is near Athelney, with twenty-nine of the worthiest men who were in the army; and the king received him there in baptism, and the removal of his baptismal robes was at Wedmore, and he passed twelve nights with the king, who greatly honoured him and his men with gifts.)

As Christine Fell wrote twenty years ago, 'We still, I think, do not have an adequate understanding of the degree to which these two peoples were mutually intelligible, or what language and languages were involved every time Alfred and the Danes (and possibly some Swedes and Norwegians) sat down together to sort out yet another treaty'

Introduction: Anglo-Norse Language Contact

(1982–83, 88) (on Alfredian treaties see Lund 1987, 256–57, 261–63; Kershaw 2000). Indeed, not only to sort out a treaty, but also, in this instance, to discuss the rudiments of the Christian faith and to pass almost a fortnight of hospitality together.

(3) It is clear from a number of charters that Edward the Elder, and afterwards Athelstan, favoured a policy of buying back land that had passed into Scandinavian control (first noted by Stenton 1910, 74–75; see most recently Hadley 2000a, 155–58; Keynes 2001, 56). Two of Athelstan's charters from 926 record grants to those who had earlier engaged in this West Saxon repurchase of the Danelaw. The first of these (Birch 1885–93, II, 334–36 (No. 659), S396) grants to the minister Ealdred 'terram que nuncupatur CEALHGRÆFAN ꝸ TEOBBANÞYRþe . v . manentium quam propria condignaque pecunia id est . x . libras inter aurum ꝸ argentum a paganis emerat jubente Eadwardo rege' (Birch 1885–93, II, 335) ('the land of five hides which is called Chalgrave and Tebworth [i.e. in Bedfordshire], which he bought with sufficient money of his own, namely ten pounds of gold and silver, from the pagans by the order of King Edward': Whitelock 1979, 546 (No. 103)). The second 926 charter (Birch 1885–93, II, 333–34 (No. 658), S397), employing identical wording to the clause quoted above, grants to Uhtred land at Ashford and Hope, Derbyshire (on the contents of this charter see further Sawyer 1975, 31–34). A third Athelstan charter from the early 930s (Birch 1885–93, II, 405–07 (No. 703), S407) grants to the church of St Peter, York, land in Amounderness, Lancashire, of which the king declares that 'propria et non modica emi pecunia' (Birch 1885–93, II, 406) ('I bought [it] with no little money of my own': Whitelock 1979, 549 (No. 104)).[1] Although not explicitly stated in the charter, this too is presumably a purchase from the Scandinavians, and a later version of the charter in the *Chronicle of the Archbishops of York* (Raine 1879–94, II, 339) does indeed add the detail that the purchase was made *a paganis* ('from the pagans'). It is furthermore likely that a similar purchase is commemorated in the Cumberland district-name Copeland (*Caupalandia c*. 1125 < ON *kaupaland* ('bought land')) (for place-name forms see *PNCu* 2; *SSNNW* 115; *DEPN* 121). Stenton argued that the name 'suggests that it was brought under English rule by purchase from the Scandinavian armies which occupied this country in the tenth century' (1936, xlviii), whereas the aptly named Copeland (1983) would instead see the name as indicating purchase by, rather than from, the Scandinavians.[2] This seems less likely, however, in the light of the other evidence for repurchase as a deliberate West Saxon policy; but whichever the direction of purchase, clearly all of these Anglo-Scandinavian transactions will have involved considerable negotiation.

(4) The *Anglo-Saxon Chronicle* MS 'D' contains the following entry for the year 925 (Cubbin 1996, 41):

Her Æþelstan cyning ꝸ Sih\t/ric Norðhymbra cyng heo gesamnodon æt Tameweorðþige .iii. kalendas Februarius, ꝸ Æþelstan his sweostor him forgeaf.

---

[1]Another version of the charter is given in Birch 1885–93, III, 684–86 (No. 1344 (703B)); the phrase quoted above appears in identical form.

[2]The same place-name is also found in County Durham: see Watts 1988–89, 28, 40.

(In this year King Athelstan and King Sigtryggr of the Northumbrians met together at Tamworth on 30 January, and Athelstan gave him his sister in marriage.)

This sister was Eadgyth (on whose later history see Thacker 2001, 257–58), and it is noteworthy that Athelstan's apparent settlement with the Scandinavian king of York was one of his first actions on succeeding his father Edward. But what were the means of communication when, as A. P. Smyth puts it, '[t]he grandson of Ívarr met the grandson of Alfred' (1987, II, 3)? A further question is of course the language or languages involved in such an Anglo-Scandinavian mixed marriage.

(5) The treaty known as II Æthelred, which probably dates from 994, stipulates various penalties and processes for settling disputes between individual Anglo-Saxons and Scandinavians (see Lund 1987, 264–68; Keynes 1991, 103–07; Wormald 1999a, 320–21), and a number of its clauses refer to situations in which speakers of both languages would be required to plead their cause. For example, Clause 7 specifies (Keynes 1991, 105),

⁊ gif man secge on landesmann, þæt he orf stæle oððon man sloge, ⁊ hit secge an sceiðman ⁊ an landesman, ðonne ne beo he nane[s] andsæces wyrðe.

(And if a man of this country should be accused of stealing cattle or killing a man, and a Viking and a man of this country make the accusation, then he is not entitled to denial.)

While it is unclear whether the *sceiðman* and the *landesman* need to bring their charge at the same time, it is nevertheless evident that this clause envisages speakers of the two languages being both obliged and able to present their claims before the same authority.[3] Again, no suggestion is given as to the linguistic means whereby this is to be done. Is this a situation involving interpreters, bilingualism, or mutual intelligibility?

(6) The charter of King Æthelred in support of the will of Æthelric of Bocking (S939) explains how the king's confirmation was granted at a council at Cookham, and was there witnessed by a number of named churchmen and noblemen as well as by 'ealle ða ðegnas ðe þær widan gegæderode wæron ægðer. ge of Westsexan. ge of Myrcean. ge of Denon. ge of Englon' ('all the thegns who were gathered there from far and wide, both from the West Saxons and Mercians, and from the Danes and English') (Whitelock 1930, 44–47). This occurred sometime between 995 and 999 (Whitelock 1930, 147). Stenton draws attention to the 'national character of the assembly' and comments that '[t]he reference to the "Danes" is important in view of the rarity of Danish names in witness-lists of the period' (1971, 551 n.1; on this assembly see further Keynes 1980, 161–62; Innes 2000, 83). Did this very 'national character' pose any problems for communication?

---

[3]In passing it is interesting to note that a loanword (or, more strictly, a new formation based on a loan) should be used in this clause to designate the Scandinavian involved (the first element of *sceiðman* being from ON *skeið*, a type of war-ship). The meeting of Norse speaker and English speaker is thus mirrored in the phrase 'an sceiðman ⁊ an landesman'.

Introduction: Anglo-Norse Language Contact

(7) In 1016, after a conclusive Danish victory, Edmund Ironside and Cnut met near Deerhurst on an island in the Severn in order to fix terms for a division of the country. As the *Anglo-Saxon Chronicle* MS 'D' records (Cubbin 1996, 62),

coman begen þa cyningas togædre æt Olanige wið Deorhyrste, ⁊ wurdon feolagan ⁊ wedbroðra, ⁊ þæt gefæstnadan ægðer mid wedde ⁊ eac mid aðan, ⁊ þæt gyld gesettan wið þone here, ⁊ hi seoððan tohwurfon. ⁊ feng þa EADMUND cyng to Westsexan ⁊ Cnut to þam norðdæle.

(The two kings came together at Alney near Deerhurst, and became comrades and sworn brothers, and secured that with both pledges and oaths, and settled the geld to be paid to the Viking army; and afterwards they parted. And then King Edmund succeeded to Wessex and Cnut to the north.)

Precisely how did the two kings convey to one another that they were prepared to become *feolagan ⁊ wedbroðra* ('comrades and sworn brothers')?[4]

(8) Two years later in 1018, shortly after Cnut succeeded to the throne of all England, a meeting between Danes and English was held in Oxford. The entry in the *Anglo-Saxon Chronicle* MS 'D' for that year reads as follows (Cubbin 1996, 63):[5]

On þisum geare wæs þæt gafol gelæst ofer eall Angelcynn — þæt wæs ealles twa ⁊ hundseofonti þusend punda, butan þam þe seo burhwaru on Lundene geald, endlifte healf þusend punda. ⁊ se here þa ferde sum to Denmarcon, ⁊ .xl. scypa belifon mid þam cynge Cnute. ⁊ Dene ⁊ Engle wurdon sammæle æt Oxanaforda to Eadgares lage.

(In this year a tribute was paid throughout England which was seventy-two thousand pounds in all, not counting that which the citizens of London paid (ten and a half thousand pounds). And then some of the Viking army went to Denmark, and forty ships remained with King Cnut. And Danes and English reached an agreement at Oxford to observe Edgar's law.)

The precise details of this reconciliation are unclear (see Lawson 1993, 88–89), but its importance is indicated by Archbishop Wulfstan's opening reference in Cnut's 1018 law code. According to its most recent editor, the version of this code preserved in MS CCCC 201 represents 'legislative pronouncements compiled by Wulfstan and issued in consequence of the meeting between Danes and Englishmen at Oxford in 1018' (Kennedy 1983, 58; see further Wormald 1999a, 129–33, 346–47). Chapter 1 of the code

---

[4]It is interesting that this phrase also consists of one native term and one loanword (< ON *félagi*): might it represent a record of the very formula used, acceptable to both sides? (See also Cubbin 1996, lxviii, on the possibility that it is Worcester traditions that have preserved this phrase.)

[5]And again, one notes in this entry the occurrence of a legal loanword, *sammæle* (< ON *sammála*), as well, of course, as *lage*.

also refers to the resolution 'eadgares lagan. geornlice folgian' (Kennedy 1983, 72) ('to eagerly follow Edgar's law'), and its introduction is as follows (Kennedy 1983, 72):

> IN NOMINE DOMINI Ðis is seo geræednes þe witan geræddon. ⁊ be manegum godum bisnum. asmeadon. And þæt wæs geworden sona swa cnút cyngc. mid his witena geþeahte. frið ⁊ freondscipe. betweox denum ⁊ englum. fullice gefæstnode ⁊ heora ærran saca. ealle getwæmde.
>
> (*In the Name of the Lord.* This is the course which the counsellors determined and settled on with many good precedents. And that happened as soon as King Cnut, with the advice of his counsellors, fully established peace and friendship between the Danes and English and completely put an end to their earlier enmity.)

Again, the question of the means of communication at this important council is an issue, especially since a number of writers have assumed that members of Cnut's Anglo-Scandinavian court must have been bilingual (see for example Lawson 1993, 219 n.15).

(9) All of the preceding meetings, with the exception of (4), occurred at what one might term the diplomatic level. But of course in this period contact and interaction must have been frequent or even daily between certain Anglo-Saxons and Scandinavians, either individually or in groups, perhaps at market or on the land or in the towns — as well as in many a home.[6] Such Anglo-Norse contact must in particular have been a quotidian reality in areas of the Danelaw, since it is apparent from place-name and other evidence that the native population was by no means submerged or expelled when such regions came under Scandinavian control; and Dawn Hadley (1997) has recently emphasized the degree of immediate integration in such areas. Specific examples of this sort of lower-level, non-diplomatic interaction can naturally not be cited from the *Chronicle* or major historical sources, but a representative example of contact through trade may be adduced to complete this catalogue. Audrey Meaney has assembled various records of Anglo-Norse trading relations in Viking Age England, in particular for Scandinavian merchants from Northumbria making journeys into southern England, and she draws attention to an iron-bound chest, containing a hundred or so coins, found near Shaftesbury (1970, 127):

> They [i.e. the coins] were all of Æthelred's 'Long Cross' issue, which was current only between about September 997 and September 1003. Although more than twenty mints were represented, 28 of the coins were from York, 13 from Lincoln, 12 from London and 8 from Chester. [. . .] [It has been suggested] that they formed the capital of a Danelaw merchant, who concealed it before taking lodging for the night in the town, and who was never able to recover it.

This last, non-literary example poses the same question as the various passages quoted above. How did this Danelaw merchant conduct with his Anglo-Saxon counterparts the

---

[6] See, for example, the evidence for a Danish community in late Anglo-Saxon Oxford (Blair 1994, 167–70).

Introduction: Anglo-Norse Language Contact

negotiations on which his livelihood depended? In all of these instances of Anglo-Norse encounters, were the linguistic channels those of a few specialist interpreters, or of widespread bilingualism, or of adequate intelligibility between speakers of the two languages? Stated in crude terms, these are the three alternatives, and members of the two speech communities must have communicated somehow.

Problems and Opinions

Let us turn, then, to a consideration of earlier studies of Anglo-Norse language contact — the opinions offered and the types of evidence employed in the formulation of such opinions. Confining attention at this stage to the premier question of the means of linguistic communication, it is easy enough to draw up a roll-call of distinguished scholars who have commented on this, even though the focus of their studies has almost without exception been on the product of language contact (that is, loanwords, and sometimes place-names) rather than the process; and one can begin with those who have attempted to relate Anglo-Norse contact to the larger history of the English language. So, for example, Otto Jespersen, in his influential *Growth and Structure of the English Language*, writes as follows (1956, 60, 75):

> An enormous number of words were then identical in the two languages. [. . .] The consequence is that an Englishman would have no great difficulty in understanding a viking — nay, we have positive evidence that Norse people looked upon the English language as one with their own. [. . .] The Scandinavians and the English could understand one another without much difficulty.

In many ways Jespersen stands at the head of a whole sequence of textbooks on the history of the English language. Turning to two of the publications most often used in undergraduate teaching, one finds Baugh and Cable pronouncing as follows (1978, 95 (§71)):

> The Anglian dialect resembled the language of the Northmen in a number of particulars in which West Saxon showed divergence. The two may even have been mutually intelligible to a limited extent.

And Barbara Strang says (1970, 282),

> Danish and Norwegian were not widely separated at that date [*c.* 970], nor would either have been mutually incomprehensible with English. Our evidence on this is literary, but it is strong and inherently plausible.

Even from such a limited survey, certain phrases become familiar in their recurrence, and one can detect the echo of the earlier writers in the later. Evidently there is something of a consensus among canonical historians of the language, and since little supporting evidence tends to be offered one suspects that this orthodoxy is rather a self-perpetuating one. Coming to the 1990s, it is therefore no surprise to find Richard Hogg stating in volume I of the *Cambridge History of the English Language* that 'the Danes and the Anglo-Saxons [. . .] must have been to some extent mutually comprehensible' (1992b, 7), and Norman Blake seconding this in volume II with the assertion that '[t]he languages spoken by the Viking invaders [. . .] were not only mutually intelligible but were also largely comprehensible to speakers of Old English' (1992a, 11).

Turning to those who have specifically devoted themselves to aspects of the Old Norse language in England, and whose views are presumably underpinning those of the general historians of the English language, prime deference must properly be paid to the opinions of Erik Björkman in the field of loanwords, and of Gillian Fellows-Jensen in the field of place-names and personal names. Björkman's turn-of-the-century study, *Scandinavian Loan-Words in Middle English*, not only pioneered the field, but still remains the standard analysis of Norse loans in the later medieval period. Björkman's view of linguistic relations was simply that '[t]he English and the Northmen could very easily understand each other in their own languages' (1900–02, 8), but he gave little in the way of discussion on the issue. However, Gillian Fellows-Jensen, whose long sequence of publications has done so much to catalogue and clarify Norse place- and personal names in England, writes as follows in the piece in which she most directly addresses the question of Anglo-Norse communication (1975b, 201–02; see also Fellows-Jensen 1975a, 8–9):

> Any study of the Scandinavian place-names in England is complicated by uncertainty as to the degree of mutual intelligibility of Scandinavian and English and as to how long the Scandinavian language survived in use in England. I consider that it is hardly likely that the ninth-century Northumbrians, speaking a West Germanic language, would easily be able to understand Danes and Norwegians speaking a North Germanic one. This is not, however, to say that communication would have been impossible without the acquisition of bilingualism.

As a complement to this one may also quote the view of the distinguished Danish onomastician John Kousgård Sørensen (1982, 14):

> How did the two groups communicate with each other? Were the English and Scandinavians able to talk to each other, to understand each other's words and sentences? [. . .] A reasonable guess would seem to be that the more linguistically-gifted members of the two population-groups would, after a period of acclimatisation, have been able to understand each other's language. The basic elements in the two vocabularies were identical and would have been recognisable, even when there had been different phonetic developments.

However, by no means have all commentators wished to tolerate the notion of intelligibility, of whatever degree: Bente Hyldegaard Hansen, in an important methodological survey from 1984, rejects any such possibility, declaring that 'If we exclude immediate mutual intelligibility — and that seems reasonable — we shall have to work with bilingualism as part of the cause of the many borrowings, probably combined with the affinity between the two languages' (1984, 88–89).

Introduction: Anglo-Norse Language Contact

In the 1980s the whole question of Anglo-Norse language contact received a renewed impetus from an enthusiasm among academic linguists for pidgins and creoles. In this more or less exhausted debate on the possible creole origins of early Middle English (see further pp 198–99 below), much — if not all — of the plausibility of the thesis turns on how intelligible or otherwise Norse and English naturally were, and yet this is one of the areas that has received least attention. As Michael Barnes writes in his illuminating survey of some of the recent literature on the subject (1993a, 72), 'Difficult though it is, the question of the degree of mutual comprehensibility between Norse and English does, I think, require serious discussion, not least because it has loomed so large in the debate about Norse-English language contact in the Danelaw and elsewhere in England'.

The only sustained attempt to seriously address the issue of possible intelligibility that is known to me is William Moulton's 1988 paper, 'Mutual Intelligibility among Speakers of Early Germanic Dialects' (see also Christophersen 1992).[7] As his title indicates, Moulton is casting his net wider than just Old Norse and Old English, drawing in Gothic, Old Saxon, and Old High German also. His paper is in three parts: the first part attempts to identify the mechanisms whereby intelligibility operates, drawing on the evidence of communication between speakers of different modern Swiss German dialects; the second part reviews a number of passages from medieval writings which describe or imply intelligibility between speakers of different Germanic dialects; and the third part compares texts of the Lord's Prayer in the five dialects under scrutiny in order to gain some idea of which aspects of dialectal divergence (phonological, morphological, lexical) would have been likely to cause comprehension difficulties for speakers of the other dialects. Moulton (1988, 26) concludes that the evidence under review suggests that linguistically

> there was indeed for many centuries a Germania that was 'unified at the core, with several particular branches.' It was unified linguistically because many speakers of different dialects could, and did, easily learn how to talk with one another.

Moulton's enquiry is refreshingly purposeful, and admirably eclectic in its approach, but it cannot be said that his conclusions are anything more than suggestive. One must therefore ask how exactly one might make a systematic attempt at intelligibility testing in historical linguistics. That is, what are the methods linguists currently employ in testing intelligibility between modern languages and dialects, and how far are these methods applicable to an historical situation?

Methods of Intelligibility Testing

Angus McIntosh's dictum that one must think not of 'languages in contact' but rather of 'users of language in contact' was quoted earlier. In other words, any investigation

---

[7] An article by Bengt Odenstedt specifically on intelligibility as it relates to the Norwegian seafarer Ohthere at King Alfred's court is discussed below at pp 98–101.

into a situation of language contact must be broadly sociolinguistic in conception, and one must not fall into the habit, however unconsciously, of thinking of languages as disembodied entities that can exist apart from those who speak and write them. As a discipline sociolinguistics attempts to relate the variability of language (especially spoken language) to non-linguistic variables such as age, sex, and position in social networks (as well as register); such observation brings with it the possibility of observing language change in progress, and this has been an important part of the discipline ever since its major origins in William Labov's 1960s research in New York (see Labov 1966; 1972; Bynon 1977, 198–215). The British sociolinguist James Milroy has recently given an important reminder that 'although linguistic changes are observed to take place in *linguistic systems*, they must necessarily come about as a result of the activities of *speakers*' (1992, 22). In other words, as Milroy states (1992, 221 (and see also 195–200)),

> linguistic change is a social phenomenon. It is negotiated by speakers in face-to-face encounters, and an innovation in a speaker's output is not a linguistic change until it has been agreed on and adopted by some community of speakers, however small the community may be.

Of course, many features of linguistic usage are not directly observable for historical linguistics, as the extant 'database' is limited and uncontrollable, and the tape-recording of a spoken corpus is obviously impossible; nonetheless, attempts to reconstruct linguistic history from the material that is available must still be governed by sociolinguistic principles (see further Milroy 1992, 45–47; Thomason 1998).

The modern study of 'languages in contact' derives substantially from Uriel Weinreich's 1953 book of that title: Weinreich is mostly concerned with contact between mutually unintelligible varieties of language, and so places his emphasis on the role of the bilingual speaker. As noted above, however, there have been repeated suggestions that speakers of Norse and English did not, in fact, find themselves in this situation; so one may be grateful for Peter Trudgill's 1986 study which is complementary to Weinreich's. As Trudgill (1986, 1) explains in his introduction, his book

> deals not with languages but with *dialects in contact*, by which is meant contact between varieties of language that are mutually intelligible at least to some degree. In this type of contact situation, many of the linguistic developments that may take place are not strictly speaking necessary from a purely communicative point of view, although of course comprehension difficulties may occur. Nevertheless, it can readily be observed that related, mutually intelligible dialects do have an effect on one another in contact situations, with or without the development of individual bidialectalism.

In particular Trudgill explores what is commonly known as 'accommodation theory'; that is, the strategies speakers employ in face-to-face communication in order to make themselves understood and/or in order not to appear too different (see further Giles and Smith 1979). In addition to this work by sociolinguists such as Labov, Milroy, and

Trudgill, other recent studies of language contact which will be drawn on in the present work include those by Frans van Coetsem (1988) and by Sarah Grey Thomason and Terrence Kaufman (1988).

It is a curious fact that research, both theoretical and practical, into the phenomenon of mutual intelligibility is substantially under-developed in comparison with research into the related issue of bilingualism, and this is particularly true in mainstream academic linguistics. In contrast, where intelligibility questions are of great practical importance, considerable strides have been and are being made, for understanding and measuring intelligibility are above all of pressing importance for literacy programmes in the developing world — that is, in Africa and Asia, where 'dialect extendibility' is one of the key issues involved in attempting to select a variety of language for diffusion as a standard. Does one variety have a wider currency than another, being understood by more surrounding peoples of differing dialects? If one has resources to translate a text into only, say, three out of twelve dialects spoken in an area (whether for reading aloud or teaching people to read for themselves), one obviously wants to know which three have the greatest currency. Hence the literacy programmes of many countries involve thorough dialect surveys, investigating (amongst other things) the degree of intelligibility enjoyed by speakers of dialects in contact. It is through this fieldwork being done by governments and the agencies employed by them that insights into the phenomenon of intelligibility are especially being gained.

The methods used in contemporary attempts to measure intelligibility are essentially fourfold, namely (1) 'Test-the-informant' approaches, (2) 'Ask-the-informant' approaches, (3) linguistic comparison, and (4) analysis of social relations. Gary Simons points out, however, that none of these four possible approaches — broadly speaking, empirical, anecdotal, philological, and social — is necessarily entirely accurate in isolation, and that rather they should be combined to create a reliable overall picture (for surveys of the evolution of methods of intelligibility testing see Casad 1974, 52–66; Simons 1979, 12–18). These four methods will therefore be reviewed in more detail.

(1) 'Test-the-informant' or Recorded Text Tests. In Recorded Text Tests (RTTs) sentences and passages spoken by a speaker of dialect A are recorded and subsequently played back to a speaker of dialect B. Various questions are then asked of the speaker of dialect B to ascertain how well he or she understood the test text; these questions are either asked and answered in the listener's own dialect, or else the listener is required to demonstrate their understanding by translating parts of the test text into a neutral third language or dialect. This approach was first advocated by Voegelin and Harris (1951) and was refined through practice over the following two decades, culminating in a standard handbook by Eugene Casad (1974). RTTs have, however, received criticism on the grounds that their results are likely to be distorted, firstly by such elements as the intelligence and education of the listener, and secondly by the listener's attitude to speakers of the dialect they are listening to and also to the testing machinery itself — this final problem being what is sometimes termed the 'Observer's Paradox' in sociolinguistics (for such criticism see Wolff 1959; on the Observer's Paradox see Labov 1972, 209–10). Furthermore, RTTs do not enable one 'to distinguish between

intelligibility due to linguistic proximity alone and that which is due to some kind of learning process' (Simons 1979, 13). Nevertheless, they remain the main source for empirical evidence of intelligibility.

(2) 'Ask-the-informant'. Here fieldworkers deliberately elicit opinions concerning intelligibility from those involved. So, for example, they will ask, 'How well do you understand the speech of the people from village C or region D? How well do the people from those areas understand your own speech?' The value of the answers received has, naturally, been queried; indeed, of the various approaches to intelligibility testing, Voegelin and Harris (1951) suggested that 'Ask-the-informant' is probably the least informative. However, others have argued that the method is not only valid, but provides sociolinguistic information unavailable through other methods (see for example Yamagiwa 1967; Callister 1977): since anthropologists generally employ and trust in 'Ask-the-informant' approaches on such issues as kinship, marriage, and environment, there seems no reason why linguists should not do so on the issues of dialect difference and intelligibility. 'Ask-the-informant' was also the method employed by Einar Haugen in his well-known survey of modern inter-Scandinavian intelligibility (1966; see also Haugen 1976, 61–62), and his results have been generally accepted as reliable. The major objection to 'Ask-the-informant' testing has been that opinions regarding intelligibility are influenced by cultural attitudes towards the speakers of other dialects. But since, as will be seen below, it is clear that intelligibility itself is directly affected by such attitudes this objection loses its validity: the underlying attitudes are likely to lead to a consonance, not a discrepancy, between intelligibility and opinion.

(3) Linguistic comparison. This attempts to establish the degree of linguistic similarity and genetic relationship between two languages or dialects, and it can be of at least three types: traditional comparative linguistics, lexicostatistics, and phonostatistics. The first of these, most obviously, involves comparison of the structures of as many corresponding language subsystems as possible, in phonology, morphology, syntax, lexis, and suprasegmental features; and in such comparative work exhaustiveness is clearly the ideal. However, as will be seen below in Chapters 2 and 3, it is the phonological systems of languages which seem to be most important in determining the degree of intelligibility enjoyed by speakers of closely related languages.

Lexicostatistics and phonostatistics on the other hand represent an attempt to measure and quantify relationships between languages in a numerical fashion. While the resultant figures are unlikely to have any absolute value, they can be of utility in relative terms for the various aspects of language planning sketched above. Diachronic lexicostatistics, also known as glottochronology, uses the proportion of shared cognates in the so-called 'core vocabulary' to calculate the duration of time since two speech varieties diverged, and is generally regarded with a good degree of scepticism (see Bynon 1977, 266–72). There is little need, however, for synchronic lexicostatistics to be held in quite such suspicion: this approach attempts to quantify the degree of similarity between speech varieties by comparing word-lists (say, of 100, 200, or 300 words) and calculating the percentage of shared cognates. The similarity that is being measured is of course simply and purely lexical similarity, and while Simons has argued that lexical similarity 'is a good predictor of intelligibility and thus must be viewed as a useful approximation to a measure of linguistic similarity' (1979, 68), others have doubted this, or at least have wondered whether a better guide to linguistic similarity is available than lexicostatistics.

Phonostatistics is one result of this. It represents the same principle of calculating cognates from a word-list, but is applied to phonology rather than lexis. Proponents of phonostatistics argue that it is a more trustworthy indicator than lexicostatistics of both the degree of similarity between speech varieties and also the intelligibility enjoyed by speakers of those two varieties. That is, they argue that, within certain limits, phonological similarities or divergences permit or hinder intelligibility more than lexical ones; and phonostatistic figures are reached by calculating the number of cognate sounds in cognate words and the number of differences in articulation between cognate sounds (for example, voiced/voiceless, position of tongue, openness of mouth, etc.). However, while phonostaticians are agreed on the value of their approach, there is as yet no agreed method for the measurement and quantification of their data, and it is thus true to say that so far phonostatistics is more a principle than a technique (see Simons 1977, who explains and assesses various approaches).

(4) Analysis of social relations. This represents indirect but essential evidence for intelligibility. The extralinguistic, social relations between speakers of different dialects and their attitudes towards one another are universally agreed to be highly important for the degree of intelligibility enjoyed; Casad, for instance, affirms simply that 'intelligibility is determined by degree of linguistic similarity and by sociolinguistic factors such as the degree of contact between a pair of language groups' (1974, 5). In particular, social relations are likely to be a key factor in non-reciprocal intelligibility: this was first stated strongly by Hans Wolff in a 1959 paper in which he argued that intelligibility is not dependent primarily on linguistic similarity but rather on 'inter-cultural or interethnic trends and relationships' (1959, 37). Thus, Wolff asserted (1959, 39),

> In a given area, interlingual communication — involving any one of different types of intelligibility — takes place, when cultural factors are favorable to such communication. Linguistic comparability, although it may play a limiting or boosting role, is not a decisive factor. The phrase 'cultural factors favorable . . .' is deliberately vague. Obviously, a great variety of factors and circumstances come into play.

Indeed, Wolff goes so far as to argue, in almost paradoxical fashion, that one can either study intelligibility in order to determine social relations, or study social relations to determine intelligibility.

How far, then, can these four contemporary methods of intelligibility testing be reapplied to an historical situation of language contact, and in particular to that between speakers of Norse and English in Viking Age England? The approaches will be reviewed in reverse order.

The evidence for cultural interaction between the two peoples is of course very substantial and diverse, covering such fields as law, sculpture, metalwork, land-holding, and religion; and these are in addition to the more obvious power-based confrontations in military and political terms (see for example Ashdown 1928–29; Arngart 1947–48; Morris 1981; Hadley 1997; 2000a, 298–351; 2000b; Hadley and Richards 2000; for a brief review of possible models of Anglo-Norse integration see Keynes 1997, 68–69). The nature of the relations between the two peoples remains a subject of intense ongoing debate and cannot properly be considered apart from the linguistic evidence of place-names and loanwords; but in spite of the absence of a universal orthodoxy on the subject, the potential socio-cultural data relevant to an investigation of intelligibility is enormous. Indeed, it seems likely that some of the rather general assertions that have been made concerning a 'mixed' or 'fused' Anglo-Norse language have been motivated by an automatic analogy with the mixture or fusion that can be seen, say, in Anglo-Norse coinage or, in particular, Anglo-Norse sculpture.

Linguistic comparison is likewise possible. Old Norse and Old English have been subjected to decades of comparative scrutiny for the purposes of establishing groupings among the family of Germanic languages, quite apart from centuries of individual study. Lexicostatistical investigations have in the past been attempted, and in theory a phonostatistical approach is also viable. Colloquial and suprasegmental features are of course the areas for which evidence is lacking, and much of our knowledge of Norse in the Viking Age must be projected back from later sources; but as with the previous category, there is in principle an abundance of potential evidence.

'Ask-the-informant' evidence is also available for Anglo-Norse contact, although not of course via the practices used by contemporary fieldworkers. A number of Anglo-Saxon texts have anecdotal information, both explicit and implicit, to offer on the subject, and the witness of Old Norse texts is very considerable, albeit from a later period. Indeed, it is a passage in one of the Icelandic sagas which effectively lies behind the majority of previous opinions in favour of Anglo-Norse intelligibility, some of which were quoted above; it will be recalled that Barbara Strang declared the evidence to be 'literary, but [...] strong and inherently plausible'. This is the well-known observation in Chapter 7 of *Gunnlaugs saga ormstungu*. The Icelandic poet Gunnlaugr Illugason has ended up at the court of Æthelred, and the saga-author remarks of the country at that time (Nordal and Guðni Jónsson 1938, 70),

> Ein var þá tunga á Englandi sem í Nóregi ok í Danmǫrku. En þá skiptusk tungur í Englandi, er Vilhjálmr bastarðr vann England; gekk þaðan af í Englandi valska, er hann var þaðan ættaðr.

> (The language in England then was the same as in Norway and Denmark. But the languages changed in England when William the bastard conquered it; from then on French became current in England, because he was from France.)

The basic claim, then, of the author of *Gunnlaugs saga* is that the English and Norse languages were the same — *ein tunga* — in about the year 1000. But although this passage from *Gunnlaugs saga* is by far the most celebrated saga-witness to a supposed Anglo-Norse intelligibility, it is by no means the only one, and so these texts provide a fruitful source for an historical equivalent of 'Ask-the-informant' testing.

The use of Recorded Text Tests is clearly the one method of testing not available to an historical investigation, but the principles underlying them may be observable in another form. This relates to the actual mechanisms of intelligibility, to precisely how it is that speakers of one dialect process and understand speech in another dialect. It will be argued that the Scandinavianisation of English place-names and personal names, and the Anglicisation of Norse ones, gives the same sort of evidence as RTTs; that is, empirical evidence of the ability to understand (and translate) heard speech in another dialect. Indeed, while one of the objections raised against RTTs is that they test only under artificial conditions, the treatment of place-names in the Danelaw is evidence of real practice.

All four of these methods will be discussed more fully in subsequent chapters; what is argued here is simply that all the major methods of intelligibility testing can, with certain adaptations, be applied to an historical investigation, and in particular to an investigation into Anglo-Norse contact in the Viking Age. The remainder of this book, then, seeks to investigate as thoroughly as possible the nature of the linguistic relations between speakers of Norse and English in Viking Age England, and in particular the likelihood of the two speech communities being mutually intelligible. This has not been done before in any sustained fashion but, as Michael Barnes points out, seems to be essential if the study of Anglo-Norse contact is to make progress. Chapter 2 therefore assesses the degree of linguistic distance between Viking Age Norse and English by considering the closeness of their historical evolution and comparing the phonological systems of the two languages. Chapter 3 analyses the Scandinavianisation of Old English place-names and relates this to the processes involved in dialect intelligibility. Chapter 4 considers aspects of Anglo-Norse contact as reflected in three Anglo-Saxon sources, and Chapter 5 assesses the more anecdotal witness of literary texts — Old Norse, Old English, and Anglo-Latin, and an important statement in Old English homilies based on the apocryphal *Carta Dominica*. These four chapters represent the main substance of the investigation, employing different lines of approach towards the same issue, and necessarily proceeding in at least a partly piecemeal manner: therefore Chapter 6 finally co-ordinates the findings of these preceding chapters, draws some general conclusions, and explores certain implications in an attempt to begin reconstructing the linguistic history of the Old Norse language in England.

CHAPTER 2

The Languages:
Viking Age Norse and English

The date at which Old English and Old Norse began to diverge from one another as dialects of Germanic and the degree to which they did so are crucial issues for the question of Anglo-Norse intelligibility. Thus a further opinion on Viking Age contact can be offered to exemplify this, namely that of Dieter Kastovsky (1992, 329):

> Given that at ca 900 at least 400 to 500 years had passed since the two languages had been direct neighbours and probably mutually intelligible in the same way as two not too distant dialects of the same language, it is indeed likely that the degree of mutual intelligibility now had become rather limited, though certainly not zero.

For Kastovsky, in other words, the prime factors in assessing Anglo-Norse intelligibility are the related ones of chronological separation and linguistic divergence. Although, as noted in the previous chapter, these are in fact only two of the factors relevant for the determining of intelligibility, they are of course foundational ones, and so this present chapter will seek, first, to establish the position of Norse and English within the groupings of the Germanic languages and so to assess the closeness of the genetic relationship between the two and, second, to supply a linguistic comparison of the two languages as they existed at the time of contact in Viking Age England. Of course, these are both subjects which have received an enormous amount of attention in the past, and indeed continue to do so. With regard to the evolution of the Germanic dialects there is no possibility, therefore, that the present account can hope to do much more than to review some of the dominant issues and arguments, while being careful to orientate the question towards the specific context of Anglo-Norse contact. Similarly, with regard to the linguistic comparison of Norse and English, the discussion will necessarily confine itself to those features that are most important for possible intelligibility — in particular, it will be argued, the degree of regularity in the divergent phonologies of the two languages.

The Evolution of Viking Age Norse and English

As a language-group, Germanic is customarily distinguished from its antecedent Indo-European state by a number of key changes of which the foremost are the Germanic Consonant Shift (commonly known as Grimm's Law), the fixing of primary stress on the first syllable of each word, the development of a 'weak' type of verb which forms its past tense by a dental suffix, and the development of a second or 'weak' form of the adjective. Foremost vocalic changes are the merger of *a* with *o* and the vocalisation of the Indo-European syllabic consonants *l, r, m, n* to Gmc *ul, ur, um, un*. Taken together, these changes constitute a package of features that are conventionally held to demarcate Germanic from the other Indo-European language-groups (see further Prokosch 1939; Nielsen 1989, 15–33; Bammesberger 1992). As to the chronology of these changes, dating must necessarily be tentative, but if one of the latest developments (the fixing of primary stress on the first syllable) occurred as recently as the beginning of the Christian era, it is also thought that movement towards a distinctively Germanic variety of Indo-European had certainly begun by the beginning of the second millennium BC and was reached by or during the Bronze Age (for summaries and reasons for this dating see Haugen 1976, 97–102 (§§8.1–2); Keller 1978, 46–48). As to geographical locality, the Germanic language-group was of course formed in the region of what is now southern Scandinavia and northern Germany and later spread some distance in most directions.

Historically, the Germanic period is usually held to have ended with the so-called Age of Migrations (AD *c*. 350–550), but the linguistic entity of 'Germanic' which existed up to that point should not be conceived of as a monolithically static and unified language. It has long been a linguistic commonplace that every variety of language is in a continuous state of evolution, and that a synchronic description only represents, as it were, a single still frame from a moving picture (that is, in Saussurean terms, a bisection of the axis of succession by the axis of simultaneity (Saussure 1983, 80)). Furthermore, and as noted in the previous chapter, sociolinguistic observation reveals that all languages and dialects are marked by a great 'variational pool' in the domains of phonology, grammar, and lexis, with linguistic variation often correlating with extralinguistic (social) variables. Plainly this must also have been the case for past languages and dialects, even those which we can now only reconstruct (to a very limited degree) at the level of 'asterisk-reality'. So even though the details are largely irrecoverable, we must nonetheless conceive of Germanic as a variety of language which was, like every variety, subject to continuous change and permeated by sociolinguistic variation.

Similarly, dialect geography teaches that every language varies diatopically as well as diachronically and socially. Every linguistic feature has its own geographical boundary or isogloss, and although the occurrence of bundles of major isoglosses along roughly the same line may permit us to make some helpful divisions, nevertheless it is clear that such divisions are often artificial and conventional, and that one should think in terms of continua rather than discrete delimitations. It is therefore again evident that we must conceive of Germanic as a language showing geographical variations, some of which must have been substantial and significant. The linguistic commonplaces expressed in this and the previous paragraph therefore amount to R. E. Keller's observation that 'Germanic is thus a linguistic phase and a linguistic complex with the usual dimensions of language rather than a uniform parent language ideally existing at a given point of time prior to the "break-up" and the emergence of "daughter languages" ' (1978, 45).

Germanic Dialect Groupings

One must therefore ask at what point divergent features become sufficiently discernible in early Germanic for one to be able to speak meaningfully of the differentiation of dialects, and how far different dialects of Germanic enjoy a shared evolution. In other words, one must confront the question of the groupings of the Germanic dialects, and this is a deeply contentious issue. As stated above, in the present context one can only reasonably hope to survey some of the dominant schools of thought, and to relate them to the particular issue of Anglo-Norse contact and intelligibility (for a helpful review of some of the key issues and opinions see Robinson 1992, 247–64); but it is essential to do this in order to address the questions of linguistic distance and similarity.

It should be stated at once that archaeological evidence will not be invoked here for the pre-migration period (for a critique of extralinguistic approaches to Germanic dialect grouping, and a fuller analysis of possible linguistic approaches, see Nielsen 1989, 109–51); and any linguistic discussion must of course depend on datable and localisable texts. With the exception of Germanic names occurring in earlier classical writings, linguistic records for Germanic are available from perhaps the third century AD in the shape of runic inscriptions written in the twenty-four-letter older *fuþark*. Excluding those on bracteates, from the period AD *c*. 200–500 there are approximately 125 inscriptions; these are found mostly in southern Scandinavia (for a distribution map see Haugen 1976, 114) and are characteristically brief and difficult to interpret. However, as far as interpretation is possible, their language seems to be surprisingly uniform, and it can thus be compared with the other main textual source for this early period, namely the surviving sections of the Gothic Bible. The main translation by Wulfila was made in the mid-fourth century, although it is now extant only in manuscripts of later periods (on Wulfila's activities see Fletcher 1997, 66–77). We therefore have two early sources of Germanic available for comparison, one from northern regions (the runic inscriptions) and the other from eastern ones (the Gothic Bible).

Study of these sources reveals that we appear to be dealing with two distinct varieties of Germanic. The language of the runic inscriptions is in some ways the more conservative of the two, showing, for example, a fuller preservation of vowels in unaccented syllables (see Antonsen 1975; Syrett 1994; and for summaries see Haugen 1976, 123–27 (§8.8); Nielsen 1989, 6–11); whereas Gothic, while still more conservative than Germanic dialects recorded later, shows a considerable range of particular developments (see Wright 1910). Although the question of the relations between Gothic and other Germanic dialects is inevitably much more complicated than this summary statement suggests, what is important here is simply the point that the Gothic Bible indicates that by the fourth century AD discernible divisions within the Germanic complex had arisen, and northern and eastern varieties can be readily distinguished — conventionally termed North Germanic and East Germanic.[1]

Some of these early inscriptions are found in eastern Jutland, either close to or even in regions from which many of the Anglo-Saxon settlers are traditionally held to have come, but otherwise there is a shortage of texts from this period with a geographical provenance which would obviously qualify them to be regarded as the direct antecedents of recorded West Germanic dialects; this is obviously of importance for attempting to observe the process of differentiation between North Germanic dialects and West Germanic ones. However, the post-war period saw a reassessment of the language of the early runic inscriptions, and in particular of its dialectal status. The language of the inscriptions has been traditionally known as *urnordisk* (or *urnordisch* or *Primitive* or *Proto-Norse*), for the related reasons that the inscriptions occur predominantly in Scandinavia, and their language is undeniably the antecedent of later Norse. However, in 1955 Hans Kuhn asserted that there is no form in the runic language that could not equally well be the ancestor of later West Germanic — that is, that the runic language represents not only the antecedent state of later North Germanic dialects, but also of later West Germanic ones (for recent discussion see Nielsen 1998). This language has therefore come to be known as 'North-West Germanic', and recent decades have indeed witnessed 'the growing popularity of the theory of a common Northwest Germanic dialect group' (Syrett 1994, 34 (§2.1.2)), to the point where it may in fact be regarded as a canonical view. That is not to claim, of course, that the antecedents of speakers of the later West Germanic dialects all came from the Scandinavian regions of the inscriptions (although the eastern Jutland connections are to be borne in mind), but rather that between AD *c.* 200 and *c.* 500 (the period of the inscriptions) 'the Germanic language area was largely uniform if we disregard the language spoken by the Gothic emigrants' (Nielsen 1989, 5). The qualification 'largely' here is important, since, as noted above, no language or dialect can possibly be variation-free; in rejecting the idea that the relative uniformity of the runic language is due to the use of a written *koine*, however, Martin Syrett observes that 'there is no need to argue for a pan-dialectal *koine* if it is assumed that any dialectal differences that existed were marginal enough not to be indicated by the orthography' (1994, 31 (§2.1.1)).

---

[1] A number of earlier scholars did in fact propound the theory that there were special links between the two dialect groups: for a review of such opinions see Nielsen 1989, 17–21.

The Languages: Viking Age Norse and English

One thus arrives at the concept of North-West Germanic as a dialect group in contradistinction to East Germanic, existing certainly until the beginning of the Migration Period in the fifth century AD; as Robinson therefore notes, 'many take the runic inscriptions from before about 550 as evidence for a surprisingly late breakup of Common Germanic (excluding East Germanic) into North and West Germanic, and thence into the various dialects' (1992, 97).[2] This concept of North-West Germanic is also supported by the findings of those scholars who have attempted to group the Germanic dialects on the basis of later linguistic resemblances (primarily phonological and morphological); that is, by surveying correspondences in terms of common retentions and, more significantly, common innovations. If two Germanic dialects share a large number of features which other dialects lack, then one is justified in assuming a particular closeness or period of shared development for those two dialects. Naturally, the potential shortcomings of such an approach should be noted: first, the earliest attestations for the different dialects vary widely (for example, the earliest Old English manuscripts are from the eighth century but the earliest Old Frisian from the eleventh); second, it may only be due to the vagaries of loss and survival that no instances of a certain feature are to be found in certain dialects; and third, what appears to be a common innovation may in fact be an independent and purely coincidental selection of the same variant from the range that must have existed in Germanic. But even granting such qualifications (and the significance of the third point is disputable), the contribution of this approach to the grouping of the Germanic dialects is absolutely central.

In the years since Kuhn's 1955 article, the notion of especial links between North and East Germanic has generally lost acceptance, as has that of a concurrent tripartite split into North, East, and West Germanic; instead there has been widespread acceptance of the proposal that the break between North and West Germanic was considerably later than that between Gothic and the rest of the Germanic language-group. Antonsen, for example, traces the development of the Germanic vowel system and concludes that following the lowering of $ē^1$ to $ā$ one reaches 'a stage of development which, in its entirety, is common to the North and West Germanic languages and foreign to Gothic' (1965, 30); Voyles propounds the same thesis, proclaiming his conviction unequivocally (1968, 738):

[I]t is the task of this paper to demonstrate that, in deriving the various daughter-languages from Proto-Germanic, North and West Germanic share more rules than do North and East Germanic (as represented by Gothic). One may assume that while these sound changes common to North and West Germanic were going on, these two dialects had not yet separated and were still a single language; and further, that East Germanic (Gothic) had by this time already split off from North-West Germanic.

---

[2] A counter-argument for a continental runic language showing specifically West Germanic traits is Hines and Odenstedt 1987 (restated in Odenstedt 2000); for runological scepticism in response see for example Page 1991, 24–26, and for archaeological scepticism see Hills 1991, 54–59.

To this end, and forming his analysis in generative terms, Voyles adduces thirteen sound-changes which are 'shared by North and West Germanic to the exclusion of Gothic' and which 'must have occurred when North and West Germanic were a single dialect' (1968, 743, 744).

The criteria of Antonsen and Voyles are exclusively phonological; Markey (1976) advances morphological parallels as well, and his conclusions are a further reinforcement of the North-West Germanic consensus. An entirely different, and more controversial, approach is that of Arndt (1959), who employs lexicostatistical techniques of glottochronology in his attempt to establish Germanic dialect groupings. Although, as noted in the previous chapter, the precision claimed in glottochronology is highly doubtful, Arndt's findings are nonetheless interesting, in that his conclusion is that 'the data do not support a West Germanic unity of (say) AD 300 that was not shared in part by North Germanic also' and that '[t]he parent dialects of Old English [. . .] had hardly begun to set themselves off against early Norse [. . .] when large sections of them were transferred to Britain' (1959, 186, 188).

It is, however, Hans Frede Nielsen's 1985 book, *Old English and the Continental Germanic Languages*, that may be regarded as, at present, the most definitive survey available of the phonological and morphological parallels which cast light on the position of English within, and the nature of its proximity to, the other Germanic dialects (an earlier study, Nielsen 1975, was restricted to Old English and Old Norse). In his discussion of the relations between Old English and Old Norse Nielsen lists no fewer than forty-five parallels (1985, 187–212): after rejecting six of these as coincidental, Nielsen subdivides the evidence into (in increasing order of importance) common retentions, common selections of the same variant, and common innovations, and explains that of these parallels about half are shared by Old Norse, Old English, Old Frisian, and Old Saxon, and a further dozen are restricted to Old Norse, Old English, and Old Frisian.[3] Few similarities link Old Norse, Old English, and Old Saxon; but (most significantly) there are six parallels that are shared only by Old Norse and Old English, and these represent either common selections of the same Indo-European variant[4] or common innovations.[5]

In Nielsen's view this corpus of parallels is both substantial and significant, and in his summing-up he concludes that 'there can be no doubt that our investigation represents a relative substantiation of the North-West Gmc. hypothesis' (1985, 257), a conclusion based on a thorough consideration of the similarities linking Old

---

[3]Of these, the early (that is, pre-migration) and significant parallels are, in his listing, Nos (4) nom.pl.masc. of *n*-stem nouns, (12) formation of ordinal numbers 13–19, (16) dat.sg.masc. and neut. of demonstrative and interrogative pronouns, (17) gen. and dat.sg.fem. of demonstrative pronoun, and (31) Gmc long $\bar{o}$ to $\bar{u}$ in final and accented position.

[4]Nos (5) acc.sg. of *r*-stem nouns, (6) gen.sg. of *r*-stem nouns, and (27) *er/*or in pres.ind. paradigm.

[5]Nos (9) nom. and acc.neut. forms for 'two', (30) lowering of *i* and *u* before tautosyllabic *z*, and (44) loss of medial *þ* before *l* with compensatory lengthening.

English to all the Germanic dialects (individually and in groups), not simply to Old Norse. More specifically, Nielsen goes on to say (1985, 257–58),

> The concept of a North-West Gmc. macro-group would also explain why English is heavily connected with not only the other so-called W[est]G[ermanic] languages, but also with ON. [...] If the geographical position of pre-OE were intermediate in relation to both north and south within Gmc., this would account for links in either direction. Alternatively, the Gmc. speaking invaders of Britain may be supposed to have been of mixed origin. In any case, OE had more exclusive (and active) parallels in common with ON than with any of the other languages except O[ld]Fris[ian], which suggests that pre-ON and pre-OE were once in immediate contact (or that there was a Scandinavian element among the fifth-and-sixth century invaders).

Thus one can conclude that the evidence of both dialect grouping and the runic language supports the notion of a North-West Germanic continuum which contained (in proximity) speakers of the antecedents of both Norse and English.[6] Furthermore, the likely date at which this continuum split and distinct dialects began to emerge has already become evident: the runic language, as has been seen, maintained its relative uniformity until AD *c.* 500, and by that time, of course, the so-called Age of Migrations had begun — a period which saw, amongst much else, the departure of the Anglo-Saxon tribes from their continental homes and the cross-channel invasion of Britain.

While the precise chronology and progress of the *Adventus Saxonum* are disputed, the general patterns are clear enough (for standard accounts see for example Salway 1981, 413–501; Campbell 1982, 8–44). Bede famously assigns the date 449 to the *Adventus*, but there are good reasons for believing that this is on the late side, as archaeological evidence is thought to testify to the presence of Germanic incomers in the first half of the fifth century. Nonetheless, if one gives the approximate dates AD *c.* 400–500 for the process of migration, one can see that the possible dissolution of the North-West Germanic continuum is some three hundred to four hundred years prior to the later onset of Scandinavian raiding and settlement in England. The evolution of major and distinctive changes, which in time differentiated Old Norse and Old English, must therefore have begun with the severance and separation that the Anglo-Saxon migrations entailed; or rather, it was severance and separation that permitted the possibility of dialectal divergence — for one must not regard the Anglo-Saxon migrations as inevitably unleashing some sort of linguistic centrifugal force, hitherto held in check. It seems clear, for example, that the distinctive phonological changes held to mark out Old Norse began later than those held to mark out Old English: while some early Old English sound-changes are dated to the sixth century or possibly even earlier, it is thought that the distinctive Old Norse changes date

---

[6]David Parsons comments also on the significance of a shared runic script (1996, 151): 'If a reasonable linguistic case can be made for a dialect continuum without a sharp break between "West Germanic" Anglian and "North Germanic" Scandinavian, then the existence of a writing-system that spans the potential boundary appears to support the idea.'

from after 600. Indeed (and as will be seen), in some aspects of its phonological system (such as the preservation of Germanic diphthongs) Old Norse continued to be more conservative and less innovative than Old English. In other words, the Anglo-Saxon migration does not mean, from the point of view of linguistic history, that the North-West Germanic group was instantly broken and that the antecedents of Old Norse and of Old English immediately began to develop in opposite directions; it simply means that the centripetal force of geographical proximity was removed, and the evolution of divergent dialects became more of a possibility.

The Evolution of the Old English Dialects

At this point, therefore, it is important also to consider whether certain dialects of Old English exhibit closer links to Norse than others. Since such links (in terms of linguistic parallels) must have largely originated in the pre-migration period, this raises the further question as to whether the differences between Old English dialects preserve pre-migration differences, or whether they arose after the invasion of Britain; if the latter were the case, one would naturally not expect to find any pre-migration parallels between particular dialects and continental Germanic languages (including Old Norse). This is, of course, a very well-worn subject, and a host of adherents can be found for both schools of thought; the following discussion will again mention only a few names.[7]

For example, Richard Jordan (1906) held that Anglian showed a particular closeness to Norse, owing, he believed, to the geographical proximity of the two on the continent. His evidence for this was almost entirely lexical, but he also drew attention to the similarity between Old Norse Fracture and Anglian Back Mutation. Back Mutation is found even more fully in Kentish than in Anglian (and least of all in West Saxon), and so in 1971 M. L. Samuels followed Jordan in arguing that the relative distribution of Back Mutation in Kentish, Anglian, and West Saxon 'mirrors exactly the varying degrees of connection between North Germanic and the Jutes, Angles and Saxons that might be expected from the historical evidence for their original positions' (1971, 7); he also cited the similar development of rising diphthongs in Old Norse (*-já-, -jó-, -jú-*, etc.) and Middle Kentish. Samuels is therefore in no doubt that the English dialects reflect earlier continental dialect divisions, and the late development of some of these parallels (for example, rising diphthongs in Old Norse and Middle Kentish) is not for him an objection. As he explains (1971, 4),

---

[7]For a history of opinions on the subject see Nielsen 1989, 65–70. A third view, plausibly argued by John Hines, is that pre-existent differences were lost in the early settlement period as the language-varieties of the Anglo-Saxon migrants converged on a focused 'Primitive Old English', and therefore the evolution of the major recorded dialect differences is a process subsequent to this (see Hines 1990, 29–33; 1994, 56–57; 1995a, 44–49; this notion is also explored in Parsons 1996, 152–53).

The late appearance of [phonological] correspondences does not prove that there was no original connection. Phonetic change is determined largely by the suprasegmental features of juncture, stress, pitch and intonation, which are never recorded in early writings. The same change may appear, therefore, centuries after the two groups of speakers have separated, yet be the result of the same conditioning factors that have been operating ever since the separation.

This is certainly possible, but it is not the only explanation for later correspondences; for, as Nielsen points out, Samuels has underplayed the possibility that the same variational pool was available for all Germanic dialects, and therefore that 'the actual phonemicisation of allophones may have been more or less coincidental — that phonemicisation in some Gmc. dialects and not in others does not necessarily prove that the same suprasegmental and subphonemic features were not present in all dialects' (Nielsen 1985, 70). On the other hand, to elevate this argument to a firm principle would seem to militate against Nielsen's own technique of grouping the Germanic dialects on the basis of shared features.

As is clear, Nielsen is himself of the opposing school to Samuels, believing that the language of the Anglo-Saxon invaders was largely undifferentiated and that dialectal differences arose after settlement. In the early part of the century this view was affirmed by Jordan's contemporary, H. M. Chadwick (1907, 57–69, basing his argument on phonological evidence),[8] and for the post-war period it is epitomised by Alistair Campbell (1959, 3–4 (§5)):

[A]t an early date linguistic differentiation seems not to have been sharp among these [i.e. the Germanic settlers of Britain], and would seem to have been practically limited to matters of vocabulary. Accordingly, while there is no objection to the designation of the two main Old English dialect types as Anglian and West Saxon, the distinctions between them mostly developed in England, owing to the considerable isolation of the various parts of the country from one another in early times. Similarly, the differentiation of Kentish from other dialects is due to the isolation of the area rather than to the descent of the inhabitants from the Jutes.

This position is reinforced by Nielsen's survey of morphological and phonological parallels which exist between continental Germanic languages and particular Old English dialects (1985, 223–52). Most interestingly, he asserts that there is 'no pattern on the basis of which a special relationship between Angl[ian] and N[orth]G[ermanic] can be assumed' (1985, 252), and concludes (1985, 258),

[T]he pre-invasion correspondences between the OE dialects and the continental languages are few and even contradictory, and there is nothing in the evidence to suggest that the OE dialects were the direct successors of ancient tribal dialects transferred

---

[8]Chadwick was also an early believer in the essential unity of the post-Gothic North-West Germanic language-group (1907, 60).

from the Continent. In the case of the Angl[ian] dialect, e.g., our investigation has revealed features that have counterparts in different sections of the entire N[orth]G[ermanic]/W[est]G[ermanic] *Sprachraum*. [...] In other words, it is the (pre-invasion) agreements between continental Gmc. and OE as a language that are important (and of which the general tendency is clear) and not the sporadic (random) deviations exhibited by the dialects.

Accepting this to be the case, its significance for the present investigation would seem to be twofold. First, it is both a corollary and apparent confirmation of the prevailing unity of the North-West Germanic group before its dissolution; and second, it demonstrates that the language of the ninth-century Scandinavian settlers did not, historically speaking, share particular links with or show especial closeness to any particular Old English dialect. There is no reason therefore why speakers of the two languages in contact should have been more mutually intelligible in one part of the country than in another. It should be noted, though, that this statement is meant historically, as certain developments in certain dialects did indeed have the effect, favourable to intelligibility, of rendering that dialect more similar to Norse in some respect (for example, Back Mutation in Anglian and Kentish). Contrariwise, particular developments could have the effect of rendering a dialect less similar to Norse in some respect (for example, Palatal Diphthongisation in West Saxon). But these similarities should be regarded as either coincidental or (bearing in mind Nielsen's response to Samuels quoted above) as a shared selection from a common variational pool.

Naturally, a word should also be said here about the evolution of the Old Norse dialects, although this is less of an issue since — again indicating the conservatism of North Germanic — the appearance of discernibly distinct dialects in Old Norse occurs considerably later than in Old English (although to some degree this must be a trick of the evidence, most of which is also considerably later, as of course no language can be variation-free: for discussion see Barnes 1997; also Bibire 2001, 92–93). Einar Haugen suggests that some differences between Old East Norse and Old West Norse may date back as far as *c.* 800, even though the earliest extant texts postdate such a point by some centuries (1993, 131); but on the whole the classic diagnostic features of the Norse dialects are thought to be tenth or eleventh century in origin (such as West Norse Assimilation and East Norse Monophthongisation), and thus largely arose after the establishment of the Norse language in England.[9]

Anglo-Norse Contact between the Migration Period and the Viking Age

There are, however, two further questions which require attention. The first is whether there might not have been a significant Scandinavian presence among the

---

[9]On the extreme paucity of phonological dialect markers in Old Norse place-names in England see *SSNY* 237–39; *SSNEM* 269–71; *SSNNW* 323–24.

Germanic settlers of Britain, and if so, what the linguistic significance of this might be. The second is how far post-migration contact between the two peoples continued in the Vendel Period (*c.* 550–750), and whether the North Sea (or, indeed, any sea) should be regarded as an effective linguistic barrier.

Both of these issues receive discussion in John Hines's 1984 book, *The Scandinavian Character of Anglian England in the pre-Viking Period*. Regarding the first point, Hines argues that finds of a certain type of wrist-clasp in Anglian England are most easily explained by postulating a relatively small-scale migration from western Norway to Humberside and Norfolk in AD *c.* 475 (Hines 1984, 35–109, 273–76; reasserted in Hines 1992, 315–17). If one accepts this migration hypothesis, then it is worth returning to a possibility raised by H. F. Nielsen (quoted in his conclusion above), and asking whether these postulated settlers from western Norway might be responsible for at least some of the Old Norse-Old English parallels listed earlier. The presumed smallness of the number of settlers is not necessarily an objection to breadth of influence, since the archaeological evidence suggests a high prestige factor. However, the distribution of finds is restricted to areas which are culturally 'Anglian', whereas the linguistic parallels cited by Nielsen are not restricted to Anglian dialects. Unless further evidence for a heavier Scandinavian involvement in the so-called Anglo-Saxon invasions becomes available, it therefore seems reasonable to conclude that features shared between Old English and Old Norse should not be substantially attributed to the presence of Scandinavians amongst the Germanic settlers of England; furthermore the opposite conclusion would, of course, go against the evidence of the runic language discussed earlier. This does not mean, however, that such a presence cannot have played a part (however small) in preserving common features, whether retentions or earlier (pre-invasion) innovations.

In any case, the areas from which the Anglo-Saxon migrants are primarily held to have come are not, of course, in the region of Norway but rather Jutland and localities to the east — that is, areas of which some at least later came to be regarded as 'Danish' (and so if one wishes to classify such settlers as 'Scandinavian' there is arguably no falsehood in doing so, but such a term does invite an anachronistic perspective). In this context it is therefore worth reviving the intriguing notion, enthusiastically developed by scholars in the early part of the twentieth century, that Anglo-Saxon origins in areas later held to be 'Danish' would seem to indicate an especial closeness between (the antecedents of) the two peoples. R. W. Chambers argued that it is this that accounts for the Old English interest in Danish legendary history, as evidenced in *Beowulf* and *Widsith* (1912, 75–79, 158–59; see also Chadwick 1907, 272–77), and so, for example, 'that the English should have felt an interest in the fate of Heorot is, after all, natural, when we remember that the ground on which it stood had perhaps been theirs' (1912, 78). Is it possible that this did indeed contribute to some sort of continuing closeness between speakers of Norse and English, either in the post-migration period or (once recognition had occurred) in the Viking Age itself? The notion is at least worth bearing in mind.

On the other hand, the issue of continued contact through trade and exchange in the post-migration (but pre-Viking) period is one that has received increasing attention in recent years, to the degree that for some scholars the onset of the Viking Age is by no means seen as the sharp line of demarcation it once was; the most famous articulation of this is probably Peter Sawyer's statement that the so-called 'Viking outburst' should rather be seen as 'an extension of normal Dark Age activity made possible and profitable by special circumstances' (1962, 194). For the immediately postmigration period Hines gathers archaeological evidence to indicate that considerable trade between Scandinavia and Anglian England continued into the early sixth century, while investigations of other linguistic situations have suggested that seas and rivers present no barrier to the preservation or spread of linguistic features between speech communities, provided those waterways constitute a major route for persistent contact. For example, Samuels (1971) considers linguistic relations between Kent and the Low Countries and concludes that the twelfth and thirteenth centuries saw the spread of linguistic features across the Channel from Flanders, via trade and other contacts (but see Voss 1995). Thus in the present situation the continued trade contacts which are archaeologically attested for the fifth and early sixth centuries may be assumed to have preserved some degree of linguistic exposure, and so potentially to have permitted the spread of innovations; hence in his corpus Nielsen posits three parallels as having arisen after the Anglo-Saxon invasions.[10]

The question whether trade contacts between England and Scandinavia in the pre-Viking period were ever broken is more controversial (for helpful reviews see Carver 1990; Myhre 1993, 188–92). Certainly there can be no doubt of their diminution: according to Hines, Anglo-Scandinavian links disappear quickly towards the end of the Migration Period, and by the time of Sutton Hoo (conventionally AD *c*. 625) they are represented only by aristocratic artefacts of the highest quality from the Uppland region of Sweden. Ulf Näsman's influential study of glass imports into Scandinavia during the Vendel Period emphasizes that, perhaps surprisingly, England represents the main manufacturing source for glass found in Scandinavia at this time, supplying between five and seven of the eight types found there (1984, 85): this clearly indicates the existence of Anglo-Scandinavian trade contacts of some sort in the centuries between the Migration Period and the Viking Age. However, two of Näsman's other points are crucial in this context: first, that glass falls within the category of luxury wares (like, say, gold), and that there is evidence only for trade in luxury goods at this time and not for more basic commodities; and second, that trade distances in this period appear to have been traversed in a sequence of 'steps' rather than through direct contact — most obviously along the Frisian coast (see Bakka 1971, 49–51). In other words, in the Vendel Period 'long distance trade was limited to luxury goods distributed by stages through the social network which linked together all the leading families of the Germanic region' (Näsman 1984, 105).

Hines, however, also argues that 'documentary evidence of the 8th. century, when carefully read, provides persuasive contemporary witness of some form of continuing

---

[10]Nos (13) 3rd pers.masc.sg. personal pronoun in *h*-, (35) rising diphthongs in ON and Kentish ME, and (45) loss of final -*n* in ON and Northumbrian OE.

Anglo-Scandinavian contacts over the North Sea' (1984, 292). Unfortunately, the documents require very careful reading indeed if one is to reach this conclusion. With the exception of Alcuin's well-known familiarity with the *tonsura* of *pagani*, the passages cited by Hines all seem to require either an ingenious interpretation or the assumption of some sort of authorial or scribal misunderstanding if one is genuinely to regard them as a 'persuasive contemporary witness'. So, for example, Hines cites the famous 787 *Anglo-Saxon Chronicle* entry ('Þæt wæron þa ærestan scipu deniscra monna þe Angelcynnes lond gesohton') and argues that the verb *gesēcan* should here be taken as meaning 'to attack' rather than simply 'to seek, to come to', and that therefore what was new and noteworthy 'was that the Scandinavians were no longer traders, but raiders' (1984, 294; see also Bibire 2001, 90). But the Chronicler makes it clear that to the Anglo-Saxon *gerēfa* the mariners were generically unfamiliar figures ('he nyste hwæt hie wæron'), and the Latin writer of the bilingual MS 'F' of the *Chronicle* seems to be in no doubt of the meaning of *gesohton* when he renders it as *uenerunt* (Garmonsway 1972, 54; for further discussion see Page 1987, 21–25).

What matters in the present context is simply the linguistic significance of the evidence (or lack of it) for Anglo-Scandinavian contact in the period between the Age of Migrations and that of the Vikings; and the obvious conclusion would seem to be that its linguistic significance is in fact negligible. Neither the archaeological record nor (if one believes Hines) the historical indicate more than, at best, occasional trade contact (leaving no archaeological trace in England) or, at worst, no direct contact at all (with transport of luxury goods occurring via continental intermediaries). Not even a best-case scenario permits belief in an Anglo-Scandinavian intimacy sufficient to prevent or limit linguistic divergence between the two speech communities; for the Anglo-Saxons, seventh- and eighth-century contact can have meant, at most, only the familiarity of Norse speech to a few coastal ears. As will be seen, the incontrovertible evidence is that language contact in Viking Age England constitutes contact between speakers of discernibly divergent varieties of language; and of course linguistic divergence is dominantly due to a lack of contact between speakers.

A Phonological Comparison of Viking Age Norse and English

As A. C. Gimson declared, 'The state of a given language at any (synchronic) moment must be seen against the background of its historical (diachronic) evolution' (1980, 7). The preceding section traced the evolution of Norse and English up to the time of their recontact in Viking Age England, in order to establish, in broad terms, the length of divergence and degree of linguistic distance between the two. The present section now supplies an account and comparison of some of the major similarities and differences between the two languages at the time of recontact. Naturally, the review that follows cannot represent an exhaustive attempt to compare and contrast Viking Age Norse and English in all their fullness, nor to condense the grammars of the two languages into the space of a few pages (for a brief survey of major phonological and morphological differences see Blake 1996, 78–81). Rather, attention will be confined to the phonologies of the two languages since (as will be argued in the next chapter) it appears to be these which are of primary importance in determining intelligibility between speakers of closely related languages, and to a large degree it is such phonological questions which will receive repeated emphasis in the rest of this book. A summary will therefore be given of the major changes which occurred in the phonological systems of the two languages between the Migration Period and the Viking Age, and mention will also be made of certain Viking Age developments as well as some important dialectal variations.

There are of course a number of substantial difficulties in any such account — difficulties which obtain in all discussions of Viking Age Norse and English. Firstly, and most obviously, there is a shortage of unquestionably contemporary evidence for Viking Age Norse, since the traditions of Scandinavian literacy in the Roman alphabet began a century or two later: contemporary runic inscriptions, although crucial, are a limited resource and are often problematic with regard to graphemic-phonemic correlations, while contemporary Norse poetry (skaldic and Eddic) is preserved only in much later manuscripts and following a lengthy period of oral transmission (on the question of sources see Haugen 1976, 137–42 (§9.2); Barnes 1993c, 376). Secondly, in addition to general problems in dating Norse sound-changes, it is often difficult (and sometimes impossible) to ascertain the state of development of the Norse language specifically in England, at the time of the Scandinavian settlements and later. And thirdly, of course, the perennial question of historical linguistics remains as to how well the extant written 'database' represents or reflects the spoken language, and how we can know this. Inevitably, all available evidence is written, and yet in an investigation of possible intelligibility it is the spoken language with which one is ultimately concerned. However, one may suggest that since primarily it is the subsystem of phonology which is under consideration here, this is not necessarily such a great problem as it would be for other linguistic subsystems (such as syntax or suprasegmental features): the phonemic systems of Viking Age Norse and English — and, even more importantly, the correspondences between them — are by and large clear enough, and it is at the phonemic level, rather than the narrowly phonetic, that much of the analysis of subsequent chapters will be conducted. What follows, therefore, represents a fairly standard account of the phonologies of the two languages, with full recognition of the degree of idealisation and simplification that this inevitably involves.[11]

---

[11] As a final preliminary it should also be noted that in general one's appreciation of the degree of (dis)similarity between the two phonological systems may have been profoundly obscured by the contemporary habit of reading Old Norse with a Modern Icelandic pronunciation, according to which certain divergences will appear very great indeed (for example, ON *æ*, *au*, and geminate consonants).

Vowels

During the period when North-West Germanic formed 'a reasonably unified dialect complex' (Robinson 1992, 259), the Germanic vowel system appears to have been as follows (see Wright and Wright 1925, 19–26 (§§16–38); Campbell 1959, 38–40 (§§99–104); Hogg 1992a, 53–54 (§§3.2–3)):

Short Vowels	a	e	i		u
Long Vowels	ǣ	ē	ī	ō	ū
Diphthongs	ai	au	eu		

Normally, when in accented position and in circumstances where they were not subject to conditioned changes, these vowels developed as follows (see Wright and Wright 1925, 26–31 (§§39–45)):[12]

Gmc	OE	ON
a	æ (Kentish e)	a
e	e	e
i	i	i
u	u	u
ǣ	ǣ¹ (nonWS ē)	á
ē	ē	é
ī	ī	í
ō	ō	ó
ū	ū	ú
ai	ā	ei
au	ēa	au
eu	ēo	jó

However, the centuries between the Migration Period and the Viking Age saw a good deal of vocalic divergence between Norse and English through conditioned changes in stressed syllables. Although some of these changes (most obviously *i*-mutation) are common to both languages, many others are found only in one. The following, therefore, are the major Old English sound-changes:

(1) Breaking (see Luick 1914–40, I.i, 138–44 (§§133–43); Campbell 1959, 54–60 (§§139–56); Hogg 1992a, 84–95 (§§5.16–34)). Before certain velar consonants or consonant-clusters, front vowels were diphthongised by the development of a back glide vowel. So *i* > *io*, *e* > *eo*, *æ* > *ea* (all long and short) before *h*, *h* + consonant, *r* + consonant (short vowels only), and *l* + consonant (in certain cases). However, in

---

[12] In the terms of Milliken and Milliken (1993), these are all entirely congruent changes (see Chapter 3 below). The table of phonemic correspondences given here is of central importance and will frequently be referred to, especially in Chapter 3.

Anglian *æ* was not broken to *ea* before *l* + consonant, but underwent Retraction to *a* (e.g. Anglian *aldor*, WS *ealdor* ('life')), thereby resembling Norse (ON *aldr*) (see Luick 1914–40, I.i, 145–48 (§§144–53); Campbell 1959, 55–56 (§143); and Hogg 1992a, 80–84 (§§5.10–15), who is, however, doubtful of the reality of Retraction as a genuine sound-change).

(2) Palatal Diphthongisation (see Luick 1914–40, I.i, 160–64 (§§171–77); Campbell 1959, 69–71 (§§185–89); Hogg 1992a, 106–21 (§§5.47–73)). After palatal *g*, *c*, or *sc* the front vowels *e* and *æ* were diphthongised to *ie* and *ea* respectively (long and short); in Old English these developments are more or less restricted to West Saxon and are without regular parallels in Old Norse (e.g. OE *giefan*, ON *gefa* ('to give')). (The status of Palatal Diphthongisation as a genuine sound-change has, of course, been challenged, but is generally accepted.)

(3) *i*-mutation (see Luick 1914–40, I.i, 166–86 (§§182–202); Campbell 1959, 71–85 (§§190–204); Hogg 1992a, 121–38 (§§5.74–86)). When followed by *i* or *j* in the next syllable, front vowels were raised and back vowels were fronted. So in the monophthongs (short only) *æ* > *e*, (long and short) *a* > *æ* (short > *e* before nasals), *o* > *œ* (> *e*), and *u* > *y*; and in the diphthongs (long and short, West Saxon only) *io* > *ie* and *ea* > *ie* (nonWS *ea* > *e*). Examples are OE *dēman*, Gothic *dōmjan* ('to judge'); OE *cynn*, Gothic *kuni* ('kindred'); OE *hīehsta*, Gothic *háuhista* ('highest'). This phenomenon is found in Old Norse as well as in Old English (see below; on attempts to account for this parallelism see Nielsen 1989, 134–38).

(4) Back Mutation (see Luick 1914–40, I.i, 205–13 (§§224–34); Campbell 1959, 85–93 (§§205–21); Hogg 1992a, 152–66 (§§5.103–12)). When followed by a single consonant and a back vowel, short front vowels were diphthongised: so *i* > *io* (> *eo*) and *e* > *eo*. For various reasons this change was rare in West Saxon, but in Anglian Back Mutation took place before all consonants except *c* and *g*, and in Kentish even before these (e.g. WS *fela*, Anglian, Kentish *feola* ('many')). Possible resemblances between Back Mutation and Old Norse Fracture will be discussed below.

(5) Anglian Smoothing (see Luick 1914–40, I.i, 213–18 (§§235–41); Campbell 1959, 93–98 (§§222–33); Hogg 1992a, 142–52 (§§5.93–102)). In Anglian all diphthongs were monophthongised before the consonants *c*, *g*, and *h*, and the consonant-clusters *r* or *l* + *c*, *g*, or *h*. So long and short *ea* > *æ* ($\bar{æ}$ later > $\bar{e}$), *eo* > *e*, and *io* > *i* (e.g. Anglian *werc*, WS *weorc* ('work'); Anglian *ēc*, WS *ēac* ('also')).

(6) 'Unstable *i*' (see Luick 1914–40, I.i, 238–39 (§263); Campbell 1959, 127–28 (§§300–01); Hogg 1992a, 194–99 (§§5.163–69); see also Quirk and Wrenn 1955, 140–41 (§193)). Early WS *ie* (long and short) was monophthongised to so-called 'unstable *i*' and was later rounded to *y* (e.g. early WS *hīe*, late WS *hȳ* ('they')).

(7) Late West Saxon Smoothing (see Luick 1914–40, I.i, 251–53 (§§278–80); Campbell 1959, 131 (§§312–14); Hogg 1992a, 170–73 (§§5.119–23)). In late West Saxon there was monophthongisation of *ea* > *e* (long and short) before *c*, *g*, and *h* and after *c*, *g*, and *sc* (e.g. early WS *eahta*, late WS *ehta* ('eight')).

(8) Labialisation and Delabialisation (see Luick 1914–40, I.i, 253–55, 256–58 (§§281, 283–85); Campbell 1959, 132–33 (§§315–19); Hogg 1992a, 199–202

(§§5.170–75); see also Gradon 1962). In late WS *i* > *y* (long and short) in proximity to labial consonants (e.g. early WS *clipian*, late WS *clypian* ('to call')), and *y* > *i* (long and short) in proximity to palatal consonants (e.g. early WS *dryhten*, late WS *drihten* ('lord')).

Taking these and other lesser changes together, one therefore arrives at the following vowel system for Old English (where the diphthong *ie* (long and short) is found only in early West Saxon):

Short Vowels	a	æ	e	i	o	u	y
Long Vowels	ā	ǣ	ē	ī	ō	ū	ȳ
Short Diphthongs	ea	eo	ie				
Long Diphthongs	ēa	ēo	īe				

We can now turn to Old Norse. D. A. Seip states of the period 600–800 that 'språket i Norden i denne tiden ble sterkt forandret, ja, så sterkt at ingen periode i nordisk språkhistorie kan vise maken til det' (1955, 22) ('the language in Scandinavia became greatly changed in that period; indeed, so greatly changed that no period in Scandinavian linguistic history can compare with it'). In particular, the language was dominated by the changes wrought by the processes of syncope and umlaut, resulting in a number of new vowels and a much more complex vowel system. One can in fact see the two processes as being connected, since together they constitute 'a transfer of information from the syncopated vowels of the suffixes to the more complex umlaut vowels of the roots' (Haugen 1976, 151 (§9.4)). That is, some of the functions performed by the grammatical suffixes were taken over by the root vowels, thereby reorganizing both phonology and morphology. Syncope of unaccented vowels, and consequent assimilations, will be discussed below. In terms of vowels in accented syllables, the most important changes in Old Norse are briefly as follows:

(1) *a*-umlaut (see Noreen 1923, 53–54 (§§59–60); Brøndum-Nielsen 1950, 104–05 (§§74–75); see also Hald 1978). When followed by *a*, *o*, or *æ* in the next syllable, *i* was lowered to *e* (e.g.*miðal > *meðal* ('middle'); OE *middel*). This constitutes part of the general tendency towards vowel harmony in early Germanic (such as *u* > *o* in comparable conditions), but *i* > *e* in these circumstances is not usually found in Old English (see for example Hogg 1992a, 54–56 (§§3.5–12, esp. 3.9)).

(2) *i*-umlaut (that is, *i*-mutation, also known as Front Mutation) (see Noreen 1923, 57–65 (§§63–69); Brøndum-Nielsen 1950, 113–32 (§§78–81)). The general operation of this was the same as in Old English, but a number of differences should be noted: *a* > *e* and *á* > *æ*; *o* > *ø* and *ó* > *œ*; and *au* > *ey*.

(3) Labial Umlaut, customarily subdivided into *u*-umlaut and *w*-umlaut (see Noreen 1923, 69–85 (§§77–84); Brøndum-Nielsen 1950, 136–48 (§§84–92)). When followed by *u* or *w* in the next syllable, unrounded vowels (long and short) were rounded: so *a* > *ǫ*, *e* > *ø*, *i* > *y*, and *ei* > *ey* (e.g. ON *hǫll*, OE *h(e)all* ('hall'); ON *Yngvi*, OE *Ing* (personal name)). However, although Labial Umlaut is usually dated to the Viking Age (or even earlier: Barnes 1993c, 376, suggests that *u*-umlaut may

have been completed by 700 but subsequently reversed), there is in fact little or no evidence for the sound-change among the Norse loans in English or the Norse place- or personal names preserved in English documents (so, for example, OE *laga* ('law') must derive from VAN **lagu*, a pre-umlaut stage antecedent to later ON *lǫg*). While this may be partly due to the sound-change being rare in Old East Norse, this is unlikely to be the sole explanation, as other distinctive Old West Norse changes do feature in Norse loans in English (for instance, certain consonant assimilations).[13]

(4) Fracture (see Noreen 1923, 86–92 (§§87–96); Brøndum-Nielsen 1950, 148–61 (§§93–97)). When followed by *a* or *u* in the next syllable *e* was broken to *ea*, unless preceded by *w*, *l*, or *r* or followed by *h*. The similarity of such a sound-change to Old English Back Mutation is readily apparent. However, in addition to its relative lateness, Nielsen (1985, 239–43) has given a number of reasons why Fracture should not be linked to Back Mutation and so be regarded as a common innovation, and these are as follows: (a) Back Mutation occurs only before single consonants, Fracture before consonant-clusters as well; (b) Back Mutation occurs before all consonants only in Kentish, whereas in the other Old English dialects (especially West Saxon) its operation is severely restricted; (c) Fracture affects only *e*, but Back Mutation *i*, *e*, and *æ*; (d) in Back Mutation the nature of the following back vowel is not usually significant, whereas in Fracture *u* causes additional Labial Umlaut while *a* does not; and (e) the effect of Back Mutation is strengthened when the mutating vowel is preceded by *w*, whereas in Old Norse a preceding *w* prevents Fracture.

(5) Rising Diphthongs (see Noreen 1923, 94–95 (§§100–01); Brøndum-Nielsen 1950, 148, 184 (§§93, 114); see also Ross 1939–40; Sandahl 1964). From the ninth or tenth century onwards the stress began to be shifted in Norse diphthongs from the first element to the second, thus creating rising rather than falling diphthongs (e.g. ON *sjóðr* < **séoðr*; compare OE *sēod* ('(money-)bag')). This change appears to have occurred earliest in word-initial position.

Again, taking these and other lesser changes together, one arrives at the following vowel system for Old Norse:[14]

Short Vowels	a	e	i	o	u	y	ø	ǫ	
Long Vowels	á	é	í	ó	ú	ý	œ	ǫ́	œ
Diphthongs	au	ei	ey						
	ja	já	jó	jú	jǫ				

A word should also be said here about the development of vowels in unstressed syllables. Prokosch states the general trend: 'The strong stress accent on the stem (or first syllable) [...] caused in Germanic a progressive weakening of unaccented

---

[13] Another factor may be the question of what Old English graph might be used to represent the umlauted form *ǫ*.

[14] It should be noted, however, that this represents the classic Old Norse vowel system at the close of, or shortly after, the Viking Age, and hence includes the results of some changes rarely (if at all) evidenced in Viking Age Norse in England (such as Labial Umlaut).

syllables, which is particularly marked in the case of final syllables' (1939, 133). This 'progressive weakening' in unaccented syllables involved the loss of final consonants, the monophthongisation of diphthongs, the shortening of long vowels, and the centralisation and disappearance of short vowels. There is therefore a reduction in the repertoire of vowels found in unaccented position: for example, final *-æ* is no longer found by the close of the Old English period, and in Old Norse (or at least, in classical Old West Norse) only *a*, *u*, and *i* are found in unaccented syllables. The tendency for unaccented vowels is thus a gradual centralisation to schwa, and this was particularly the case in late Old English. The consequences of this centralisation are grammatical and not merely phonological, since it leads to the loss of many inflexional distinctions.

Between the Migration Period and the Viking Age, all short unaccented vowels were lost in Norse (unless protected by final *m*, *n*, or *r*), and those bearing secondary stress were weakened (see Noreen 1923, 132–40 (§§153–60); Brøndum-Nielsen 1950, 191–95 (§§121–23)). The medial loss of short vowels (that is, syncope) is thus one of the most distinctive Norse sound-changes in this period and led to considerable contraction. In words of three syllables the weakest syllable was lost: thus, for example, the development of **katilaR* > **katilR*, later *ketill* ('kettle'), and **katiloR* > **katlaR*, later *katlar* ('kettles'). This loss of vowels in unaccented syllables also entailed the loss of a number of verbal prefixes in Old Norse, most importantly Gmc **ga-* (OE *ge-*), of which consonantal traces survive in the adjectives *glíkr* ('like'; OE *gelīc*) and *gnógr* ('enough'; OE *genōh*). As will be seen below, one of the results of syncope in Old Norse was that new consonant-clusters were formed, subsequently leading to some unique assimilations.

Consonants

After the so-called Germanic Consonant Shift (that is, Grimm's Law) the Germanic consonant system was as follows (see Wright and Wright 1925, 111–34 (§§229–51); Campbell 1959, 163–64 (§398); Hogg 1992a, 251–52 (§§7.1–3)):[15]

	Bilabial	Labio-dental	Dental	Alveolar	Palatal	Velar	Guttural
Stops:							
voiceless	p			t		k	
voiced	b			d		g	
Fricatives:							
voiceless		f		s	þ	ɣ	h
voiced		v		z	ð		
Nasals	m			n			
Liquids				l, r			
Semivowels	w				j		

---

[15]It is uncertain whether the consonants here represented as *b*, *d*, and *g* should be regarded as voiced stops or voiced fricatives in the Germanic period.

Consonantal developments into Old English and Old Norse, especially divergent developments, were fewer than vocalic developments; again, the following account will list the major changes, and on this occasion the two languages will be treated together rather than successively:

(1) Rhotacism (see Luick 1914–40, I.ii, 818–20 (§629); Campbell 1959, 166 (§404); Hogg 1992a, 74 (§4.15); Noreen 1923, 163–64 (§224); Brøndum-Nielsen 1957, 7–9, 12 (§§227.4, 230(a))). In both Norse and English the process commonly known as Rhotacism meant that Gmc *z* (derived from *s* through Verner's Law) became *r*. In early Norse this *r* < *z* is distinct from original Gmc *r*, is expressed by a different rune (transcribed *R*), and causes so-called *R*-mutation (e.g. ON *ker*, Gothic *kas* ('goblet')) (see Noreen 1923, 66–67 (§§71–72); Brøndum-Nielsen 1950, 132–34 (§82)). However, in both Old English and later Norse there is no distinction between original *r* and *r* through Rhotacism, the two having fallen together. It should also be noted here that the suggestion has sometimes been made that early ON *-R* had not yet become *-r* at the time of the Scandinavian settlements in England but retained an articulation closer to *-z*, and hence, in its appearance in the verb inflexion *-aR*, was the cause of the 3rd pers.sg.pres.ind. ending *-es* in northern Middle English. This was argued by Keller (1925a; for a critical contemporary review see Tolkien 1927, 45–46), revived by Samuels (1985, 275–76), and recently endorsed by Smith (1996, 144). However, although runic inscriptions in eastern Scandinavia continue to distinguish the two sounds into the tenth and eleventh centuries, no Norse loan in Old or Middle English, or Norse place- or personal name recorded in an English document, shows *-s* for original *-R*: all show *-r* (see Björkman 1900–02, 17–19, 167–68; Barnes (1977, 470) has also noted that the change *-R* > *-r* seems to have occurred much earlier in Norway and the western colonies than elsewhere in Scandinavia).

(2) Loss of nasals (see Luick 1914–40, I.ii, 817–18 (§627); Campbell 1959, 47 (§121); Hogg 1992a, 57 (§3.14); Noreen 1923, 168 (§233); Brøndum-Nielsen 1957, 56 (§268.1)). Old English shows the loss of nasal consonants before the voiceless fricatives *f*, *þ*, and *s*, with compensatory lengthening of the preceding vowel (e.g. OE *fīf*, Gothic *fimf* ('five')); as a comparable change, in Old Norse *n* is only lost before *s* (e.g. ON *gás*, OE *gōs*, OHG *gans* ('goose')).

(3) Gemination (see Luick 1914–40, I.ii, 823–27 (§631); Campbell 1959, 167–68 (§§407–08); Hogg 1992a, 73–74 (§§64.11–14); Noreen 1923, 203–04 (§279); Brøndum-Nielsen 1957, 66–69 (§274)). Both languages show consonant gemination to a greater or lesser extent. In Old English all consonants except *r* were doubled between a short vowel and following *j*, and often between a short vowel and following *r* or *l* (e.g. OE *biddan*, Gothic *bidjan* ('to request')); in Old Norse, on the other hand, only *g* and *k* were doubled between a short vowel and following *j*, and sometimes between a short vowel and following *w* (e.g. ON *hyggja*, Gothic *hugjan* ('to think')). Thus gemination is found in a large number of Old English words where it is lacking in their Norse cognates (e.g. OE *sittan*, ON *sitja* ('to sit'); OE *bitter*, ON *bitr* ('bitter')).

(4) Gmc *ð* > *d* (see Luick 1914–40, I.ii, 827–30 (§632); Campbell 1959, 168 (§409); Hogg 1992a, 74 (§4.17); Noreen 1923, 174–75 (§238.1); Brøndum-Nielsen

1957, 22 (§243)). In all positions Gmc *ð* becomes *d* in Old English (e.g. OE *geard*, ON *garðr* ('enclosure')), whereas in Old Norse this change occurs only after *l* or *n* (e.g. ON *halda*, OE *healdan* ('to hold')).

(5) OE Palatalisation and Assibilation (see Luick 1914–40, I.ii, 835–41 (§637); Campbell 1959, 173–79 (§§426–43); Hogg 1992a, 257–76 (§§7.15–43)). The dual process of palatalisation and assibilation which affected *k* and *g* is without question the most distinctive innovation in the Old English consonant system; it is a development that occurred only in Old English and Old Frisian amongst the Germanic languages, and in Old English most consistently in West Saxon (it can also be found in some Scandinavian languages at a later period: see for example Haugen 1976, 268–72 (§11.3.18)). Briefly, one may say that in primitive Old English an allophonic distinction arose between palatal and velar *k* and *g*: palatal *k* and *g* developed before and sometimes after front vowels or diphthongs with a front first element, whereas velar *k* and *g* remained before back vowels and all consonants; thus the allophones were in complementary distribution. Chronologically, the palatalisation of *k* and *g* before front vowels occurred before *i*-mutation, but when back vowels were fronted through that later process the new front vowels produced did not cause palatalisation, and so a phonemic split occurred through the establishment of certain minimal pairs, at least for *k*.[16] The subsequent process of assibilation meant that in many instances (and always in initial position) palatalised *k* ultimately became /tʃ/ (e.g. OE *cirice* ('church')); somewhat less frequently palatalised *g* became /dʒ/ (most commonly after a nasal or in gemination, where it is usually spelt <cg> in Old English: e.g. OE *ecg* ('edge')). The consonant-cluster *sk* underwent palatalisation and assibilation even more regularly than *k* in Old English, often before back vowels as well as front ones, resulting in /ʃ/ (e.g. OE *scip* ('ship'), *disc* ('dish')). These palatalised and assibilated sounds are unknown in Old Norse, which preserves the Germanic velar stops, and thus they constitute a major (and regular) divergence in the consonant systems of the two languages. As noted above, these developments in Old English are found most fully and pervasively in West Saxon, and so in this respect Anglian dialects may to some degree preserve the Germanic system and thereby resemble Old Norse (see for example Hogg 1992a, 305 (§§7.98–99)).

(6) Metathesis (see Luick 1914–40, I.ii, 917–20 (§693); Campbell 1959, 184–86 (§§459–60); Hogg 1992a, 302–04 (§§7.93–97); Noreen 1923, 226–29 (§§313–16); Brøndum-Nielsen 1957, 47 (§260)). *r*-metathesis is a feature that Old English only shares to any extent with Old Frisian (e.g. OE *hors*, ON *hross* ('horse')), although it is found in a very few words in Old Norse (e.g. the doublet ON *argr-ragr* ('cowardly')); and Old English also demonstrates *s*-metathesis. However, *l*-metathesis is found in both languages, where it occurs in the combinations *fl*, *sl*, and *þl* (or *dl*) becoming *lf*, *ls*, and *ld* (e.g. the personal name element OE, ON *-gils*; compare OE *gīsl*, ON *gísl* ('hostage')).

---

[16]For example *cēn* ('torch'; with palatalised *k*) and *cēne* ('bold'; with velar *k*, and *ē* fronted through *i*-mutation) (see further Penzl 1947). There was no phonemic split with *g* because palatalised *g* fell together with inherited /j/.

(7) ON Sharpening (see Noreen 1923, 165–66 (§227); Brøndum-Nielsen 1957, 14–15 (§233)). This is the first of a series of distinctive consonantal developments in Old Norse. By the process commonly known as Sharpening (or Holtzmann's Law), medial *jj* and *ww* become *ggj* and *ggv* respectively (e.g. ON gen. *beggja*, OE *bēgen* ('both'); ON *tryggr*, OE *trēow* ('trustworthy')); elsewhere this process is found only in Gothic, and with different results.

(8) ON loss of /j/ (see Noreen 1923, 168 (§231); Brøndum-Nielsen 1957, 54 (§265)). Overall one sees in Viking Age Norse that '[t]he trend in the consonant system was one of reduction through loss and assimilation' (Haugen 1976, 154 (§9.4.1)): an early loss was that of the semi-vowel *j* in initial position, and medially except before back vowels (e.g. ON *ár*, OE *gēar* ('year')).

(9) ON loss of /w/ (see Noreen 1923, 169–71 (§235.1); Brøndum-Nielsen 1957, 49–54 (§264)). Similarly the semi-vowel *w* was lost in Old Norse in all positions except before non-rounded vowels or before *r* followed by a non-rounded vowel (e.g. ON *orð*, OE *word* ('word')).[17]

(10) ON Assimilation (see Noreen 1923, 192–203 (§§266–78); Brøndum-Nielsen 1957, 29–46 (§§249–59); see also Kolb 1962 and 1969).[18] Assimilation of consonants was extremely common in Old Norse, more so than in any other Germanic language, and this is largely a consequence of the syncope of unaccented medial syllables in the seventh and eighth centuries. Thus the subsequent assimilations represent an attempt to simplify the new consonant-clusters that arise, presumably for greater ease of articulation. Nasals, *R* (< Gmc *z*), *h*, and *ð* were the chief consonants to be assimilated, and details are as follows: progressive assimilations are *mp > pp*, *nk > kk*, and *nt > tt* (e.g. ON *brattr*, OE *brant* ('steep')); *Rd > dd*, and *Rn > nn* (e.g. ON *oddr*, OE *ord* ('point')); *ht > tt* (e.g. ON *þótti*, OE *þūhte* ('it seemed')); *ðl > ll*, and *dt* and *ðt > tt* (e.g. ON *fritt*, nom.neut.sg. of *friðr* ('beautiful')). Regressive assimilations are *lþ > ll* and *nþ > nn* (e.g. ON *sannr* ('true'); compare OE *sōð*, where there has been loss of nasal with compensatory lengthening). These assimilations occurred largely within the Viking Age itself and, as is obvious, led to a high number of doubled consonants in Old Norse in circumstances where they were not found in Old English.

(11) Finally, there was in both languages considerable loss of consonants in final unaccented syllables, and on the whole this loss was more advanced in Old Norse than in Old English; certainly, Norse shows losses that are not found in Old English, most obviously the loss of final *-n* which is still preserved, for example, in the infinitive in Old English, but not in Old Norse (e.g. OE *beran*, ON *bera* ('to bear')). However, the Northumbrian dialect of Old English does show this loss, thus rendering it in this respect similar to Old Norse.

---

[17] These two changes — loss of /j/ and /w/ — can be seen reflected in the runic alphabet, whereby two of the runes (No. 8 and No. 12 in the older *fuþark*) alter their value upon the loss of their initial semi-vowels (see further Liestøl 1981; Barnes 1987).

[18] Not all assimilations are evidenced in the Norse language in England, and some represent dialectal differences between Old West Norse and Old East Norse.

Conclusion

In this chapter it has been seen that the antecedents of Old English and Old Norse were participants in a North-West Germanic continuum which at the time of the early runic inscriptions had not yet evolved into discernibly distinct dialects; and dialect grouping studies suggest that there may have been particularly close links between the two. This relationship was broken in the fifth century by the events of the Migration Period, and in particular by the Anglo-Saxon invasion of Britain. Increasing linguistic divergence followed this separation, even though for a time isolation was not total, since there appear to have been considerable trade contacts in the fifth and early sixth centuries. Nevertheless, the quantity of contact must have diminished massively from the time of the migrations and the end of geographical proximity, and in time all overseas contact dwindled. Some slight contact evidently persisted into the first quarter of the seventh century, but after that the separation between speakers of Norse and English seems to have been more or less complete, and innovations in the one language would not normally have been shared with the other.

Thus by the time they came into recontact at the beginning of the Viking Age, speakers of Norse and English had been isolated from one another for approximately two hundred to two hundred and fifty years. During that period, as the table given above indicates (p 33), the phonological systems of the two languages had remained remarkably similar when not affected by conditioned sound-changes; and many of the divergent sound-changes that had occurred were of a regular, and therefore potentially predictable, nature. In the next chapter this degree of regularity in the differences between the phonological systems of Norse and English will be termed dialect congruity, and it will be suggested that it is a factor of the very greatest importance for determining the degree of intelligibility enjoyed by speakers of the two languages in Viking Age England.

CHAPTER 3

The Scandinavianisation of Old English Place-Names

Theories of Intelligibility: Two Models

In this chapter it will be argued that the principles of dialect intelligibility, as observed and defined in recent linguistic studies, can also be traced in the Scandinavianisation of Old English place-names by the Norse speech community in Viking Age England, and that this phenomenon represents the best empirical evidence available for Anglo-Norse intelligibility. Before proceeding to a consideration of this place-name evidence, therefore, some helpful terminology will be adopted from two recent studies of the passive intelligibility of heard speech, namely those of C. F. Hockett and of Margaret and Stuart Milliken.

Hockett's 'Switching-Code'

In his 1987 book *Refurbishing Our Foundations*, C. F. Hockett considers language and its use from the standpoint not of the speaker but of the hearer, and he endeavours to do so in a relatively informal manner. Thus for Hockett the fundamental communicative question is 'when we hear someone say something in a language we know, how do we know what is said?' (1987, 2). Or, to put this somewhat more expansively (1987, 15), 'What is the nature of the collusion between the structure of utterances and the strategy of listeners by virtue of which correct interpretation and understanding are possible?'

Hockett's fourth chapter ('Hearing Words') analyses the strategies hearers appear to employ for understanding — that is, parsing and construing — what they hear, and in Hockett's view these are of two modes, namely *listening for word identity* and *listening for word shape*. The former, he claims, is by far the commoner and involves at least three devices which are used under different circumstances: these he terms *implicit motor-matching, gestalt perception*, and the operation of a *switching-code*.

The first of these, implicit motor-matching, is by far the least persuasive, and in any case hardly relevant to the present investigation. Turning to the second of his three strategies for understanding, Hockett points out that in reading a piece of text one habitually recognises words as wholes, rather than a letter at a time in linear fashion; despite the variations of typeface or handwriting, one recognises 'the same holistic pattern or GESTALT, and it is this overall pattern that identifies the word for us' (1987, 41). This same principle, he argues, applies to speech (1987, 41):

> A spoken word is a perceptual gestalt. In listening we register the overall pattern and ignore — or set aside for separate handling — the finer details. We understand heard speech despite great variations in dialect, voice quality, and superimposed paralinguistic effects, because all these changes are rung on an almost invariant skeletal pattern.

Hockett's third strategy is the one that especially concerns us here, and it develops from the recognition that one is usually able to parse and construe words spoken by the speaker of a different dialect from one's own. As Hockett explains (1987, 43),

> Gestalt perception [...] is probably not enough to account for some of our more remarkable feats of understanding. The third proposal is that as, say, Chicagoans get more and more practice at listening to British English, or Danes at dealing with Norwegian, they build up a SWITCHING-CODE: certain sounds or arrangements of sound in the alien dialect come to be coded automatically into the proper sounds or combinations of sounds in the listener's own dialect, and the intended word is recognized by assembling the latter.

Thus, in Hockett's terminology, one understands words spoken in another dialect by the operation of a switching-code, and, as he points out, this proposal does not conflict with the notion of the gestalt perception of whole words; indeed, it seems likely that the two strategies are complementary, and it is important also to stress that the deployment of these strategies need not be conscious or deliberate on the part of the hearer (though of course it may be). Hockett goes on to give a personal and anecdotal example of the co-operation of these two strategies, explaining how as a mid-Westerner he is able to understand the speech of those from the southern states on account of an awareness of what vowel sounds in his own dialect correspond to those in a southerner's (1987, 43):

> What I am not sure of is how much I call on my knowledge of this correspondence when dealing with southern speech. My impression is that usually I don't need to — I simply recognize the word as a whole (gestalt perception). But how would I handle an unfamiliar word, presented in a context that made its meaning clear? If subsequently,

in using the word myself, I replaced the southern vowel by my regular equivalent, I think that would be evidence for the code-switching hypothesis.

This last point, I will argue, is the central principle according to which we can trace in the Scandinavianisation of English names (and vice versa) evidence for dialect intelligibility between speakers of Norse and English in Viking Age England.

Milliken and Milliken's 'Dialect Congruity'

In a 1993 paper entitled 'System Relationships in Dialect Intelligibility', Margaret and Stuart Milliken present a brief formulation or summary of their ideas about the operation of intelligibility between dialects, ideas which represent a development from certain phonostatistic approaches to intelligibility study. Margaret Milliken's 1988 Cornell dissertation contains some of these ideas at an earlier stage, testing (and confirming) the hypothesis that 'the degree of intelligibility between any two dialects correlates with the system of phonological correspondences that exists between cognate lexical items in those dialects' (1988, 1).

It was noted in Chapter 1 that so far phonostatistics is more a principle than a technique. Milliken and Milliken also believe that phonostatistics is potentially a better guide to linguistic similarity and intelligibility than lexicostatistics, but they argue that the focus of study should be changed. Hitherto phonostatistic methods have largely endeavoured to measure phonetic similarity between speech varieties. The foundation of their thesis, however, is that intelligibility is not dependent on *phonetic* similarity in itself, but rather on the ability of hearers to make *phonemic* correspondences. That is, for phonostatistic purposes sounds must be considered within the context of the phonological system to which they belong, and not simply compared in isolation. This claim that intelligibility is dependent on the ability of the hearer to make the correct phonemic correspondences is of course simply Hockett's switching-code couched in different terms; in explication of the notion Milliken and Milliken identify three elements involved in dialect intelligibility, which they term respectively *initial intelligibility, inherent learnability*, and *dialect congruity*.

Initial intelligibility is, naturally, concerned with the first acquaintance between two dialects: if two dialects were in fact identical, initial intelligibility would be total and there would be no call for any further strategies of understanding. But if two varieties are not identical, such strategies are necessary, and inherent learnability therefore represents the ease or difficulty with which intelligibility between two dialects can be achieved. Learnability is thus a property of the dialects themselves (or more precisely, a property of the relationship between the phonological systems of the dialects), and not of the speakers and hearers of those dialects. Furthermore, the importance of this property is paramount, since it is at the heart of dialect intelligibility (Milliken and Milliken 1993, 2):

> For practical applications, inherent learnability is the crucial aspect of intelligibility. For purposes of both everyday communication and high-level language planning, the

important issue is not simply the initial degree of intelligibility, but rather how quickly and easily listeners can adjust to or 'catch on to' the other dialect. If it is easy for listeners to adjust to the other dialect, then for practical purposes intelligibility will be high even if at first hearing initial intelligibility is rather low. On the other hand, if it is very difficult for listeners to adjust to the other dialect, intelligibility may remain at the initial level and listeners may have to study the dialect as they would a foreign language in order to achieve effective communication.

Milliken and Milliken's third notion, that of dialect congruity, really constitutes an aspect of inherent learnability — indeed, the key aspect. It is concerned with (1993, 3)

whether or not an actual correspondence can be expressed as an exceptionless generalization from the point of view of the listener, i.e., 'Their [b] always corresponds to our /p/.' Those correspondences that permit exceptionless generalizations we call 'congruent' correspondences; those that do not we refer to as 'incongruent' correspondences. A dialect may be more or less congruent with another depending on the nature and number of incongruent correspondences existing between it and the other dialect.

In Margaret Milliken's 1988 doctoral dissertation ('Phonological Divergence and Intelligibility: A Case Study of English and Scots') this hypothesis is therefore tested as follows: (1) intelligibility between speakers of different Scots and American English dialects is tested using Recorded Text Tests; (2) the degree of (in)congruity between the phonological systems of the dialects is calculated in phonostatistic terms; and (3) the results of (1) and (2) are compared to see how well they correlate (which turns out to be very well indeed, especially in the demonstration that it is incongruent correspondences that hinder intelligibility).

Such, in summary, is Milliken and Milliken's argument in their 1993 paper. They offer no suggestions as to how such system relationships might be quantified numerically; hence, valuably, their work contributes to intelligibility theory rather than phonostatistic computation. And as such their central thesis — that intelligibility is dependent not on simple phonetic similarity but rather on the ability to make correct phonemic correspondences — ties in very productively with Hockett's notion of the switching-code.

The value of Hockett's and Milliken and Milliken's work, therefore, is that they consider communication and dialect intelligibility from the standpoint of the hearer; and the present study is substantially concerned with how well Norse speakers were able to understand the English speech which they heard (and vice versa), beginning with the intelligibility of Old English place-names to the Norse-speaking population of the Danelaw.

Norse Speakers and English Place-Names

Scandinavian Settlers and Place-Names in England

When the Scandinavians settled in England from the late ninth century onwards, they naturally used their own language to give names to settlements and to topographical features (for introductory summaries of the Norse element in English place-names see Reaney 1960, 162–91; Gelling 1988, 215–36, 261–63; Cameron 1996a, 73–87). That the Old Norse element in the place-nomenclature of England is extremely heavy in certain parts of the country indicates that the linguistic influence of the settlers was heavy, and this in turn implies that the settlement itself was heavy also, although of course this has been disputed (most famously in Sawyer 1962). There is no necessity here to enter into a full rehearsal of the issues involved in this well-known debate about Viking numbers and whether the great quantity of Old Norse place-names in England are to be attributed to a genuine large-scale migration (for resumés see Fellows-Jensen 1975b; Wormald 1982, 134–37; Hadley 2000a, 17–22; while the essential place-name papers answering Sawyer are collected in Cameron 1975, 115–71). Linguistically, the main points are simply as follows: (1) In terms of case studies of language contact it would probably be impossible to find a parallel for ascribing such exceptionally heavy influence on lexis and nomenclature solely to a small elite group. (2) Since a speech community's lexicon and its onomasticon are discrete entities, and since language learning customarily involves a much greater appropriation of the lexicon of the target language than of its onomasticon, it is much more difficult to attribute widespread onomastic influence to a small elite than widespread lexical influence: this is supremely seen in the contrast between the relatively restricted repertoire of Norman personal names which are found in England and the much more diverse repertoire of Norse personal names, importantly including women's names and those which appear to be archaic or distinctive to the Danelaw (for the classic formulation of this point see Stenton 1927, 227–33). In other words, it is not the number of different people bearing Norse (or Norman) names that is significant, but rather the number of different names. As Gillian Fellows-Jensen remarks of the situation in Yorkshire and Lincolnshire: 'The Scandinavian names are not only numerous but also varied in type, and the vitality of the Scandinavian nomenclature must reflect the name-giving customs of a Scandinavian-speaking community of some considerable size and not merely the influence of a trend-setting aristocratic minority' (1975b, 193). (3) The real proof of the intensity of Norse influence on English place-nomenclature is to be found not so much in the major settlement names as in the minor names and field-names, as such a profound effect on microtoponymy is again wholly absent from the Norman influence on English nomenclature (for a recent re-demonstration of this see Cameron 1996b). For these (albeit briefly stated) reasons I therefore subscribe, in broad terms, to the traditional philological view that the sheer scale of the Norse linguistic influence in England can only be explained on the assumption of substantial Scandinavian settlement (see further Townend 2000a; for an impressive exemplification of these principles in one particular area, see F. T. Wainwright's study of Scandinavian settlement in Lancashire (1975, 181–227)).

But when the Norse-speaking Scandinavians settled in northern and eastern England the country around them was not, as it were, toponymically virgin territory: the pre-resident Anglo-Saxons already had a sufficiently developed nomenclature to refer to the places they needed to refer to. One must consider, therefore, the reaction of the Scandinavian settlers to the pre-existing Old English place-names they heard around them — and 'heard' is of course the key word here, as the illiterate Vikings can only have learnt of them through direct face-to-face contact, from the lips of the English-speaking Anglo-Saxons. Did the Norse speech community appropriate the English names and use them themselves, and if so how?

In situations where speakers of two languages are in contact over an extended period of time, three possible relationships between the place-names of one language and the other may develop: speakers of the incoming language may appropriate and use unchanged the names they encounter; or they may coin their own names, entirely unrelated to the pre-existent ones; or they may in some way adapt the names they encounter in order to make them more congenial to their own speech habits.

To argue for the first possibility is to suggest that the Scandinavian settlers made no changes to the Old English names they encountered since they either found no phonological difficulties in the native names or else were able to mimic perfectly the phonological features whereby Old English diverged from Old Norse. If such were the case one might expect to find areas of undoubted Scandinavian settlement in which no recorded place-name forms show traces of Norse influence; and Gillian Fellows-Jensen, drawing on work by Kristian Hald, has pointed out that in certain areas of Lincolnshire a number of field-names show traces of Norse inflexions (and so must have been given by a Norse-speaking population) while the major names of the villages around show no signs at all of Norse influence (*SSNY* 117–18; see also Cameron 1973; 1996b). This might initially appear to support this first possibility, but a more likely explanation is that the non-preservation of Scandinavianised forms does not mean that such Scandinavianised forms never existed, but rather that sufficient English speakers survived to pass on the English name to the present day, while a Scandinavianised variant, originating with the Viking settlers, was also current (perhaps to the eleventh or twelfth century) but has not survived or even been recorded. The treatment of Old English loanwords in Old Norse emphatically supports this interpretation, as it is clear that certain sounds in Old English did indeed cause pronunciation difficulties for Norse speakers (for lists of Old English loans in Old Norse see for example Fischer 1909, 20–25, 46–55; de Vries 1961, xxvii). This can be seen especially plainly with assibilated consonants: Campbell remarks on the 'complete failure to assibilate by Scandinavian settlers' (1959, 177 (§438)), and on entering Old Norse assibilated /ʃ/ in English-derived loans was replaced by the more congenial consonant-cluster /sk/ (for example, OE *biscop* ('bishop') > ON *biskup*, OE *disc* ('dish') > ON *diskr*, and OE *scrūd* ('shroud') > ON *skrúð*). Hence, with the obvious exception of those names whose English forms would have been identical with their Norse equivalent, I do not believe, as Gillian Fellows-Jensen does, that the Scandinavian settlers sometimes 'left the English names unchanged' (*SSNY* 251) (see further pp 187–89 below).

The second possibility listed above is that the settlers may have ignored the English names entirely and independently coined their own. There might be a number of reasons for this: lack of contact so that a Norse name was established among the Norse speech community before the native one had been learnt; apparent meaninglessness in the native name (perhaps especially likely where the first element was an unfamiliar personal name); or simply a different attitude to the place designated (since the received wisdom is that names customarily originate as descriptions given by neighbours). The difficulty is in supplying examples of this second option, since we can never know whether a Norse name has replaced an earlier English one unless the earlier name itself is also recorded, and our early sources for the northern counties (especially the north-west) are extremely scarce. We know the Vikings coined their own names for places in Ireland and Wales, unrelated to the pre-existing Celtic ones (see for example Loyn 1976, 9 n.1; Greene 1978, 122; Fellows-Jensen 1975b, 196; 1992, 31–32), but the linguistic relationship between Norse and Celtic is profoundly different to that between Norse and English: in the former case linguistic distance would seem to preclude all possibility of intelligibility. We do, however, have a couple of famous examples from England of an unrelated Norse name displacing an earlier English one to illustrate that the Scandinavians did sometimes employ this practice in the Danelaw: Whitby YN (ON *Hvítabý*, *Witebi* DB) was earlier OE *Streoneshalh* (*PNYN* 126; *SSNEM* 4; on this much-discussed name see further Coates 1980–81; Fell 1981b, 82–85; Blair 1985, 9–12; Townend 1998, 42–44; Styles 1998), and Derby Db (ON *Djúrabý*) was earlier OE *Norðworðig* (*PNDb* 446; *SSNEM* 43; *DEPN* 142; concerning this change of name see further Fellows-Jensen 1981, 141–42; 1991, 347; Hall 1989, 161–62), although in both of these examples it has been queried whether precisely the same spot was designated by the two names.[1] It has also been plausibly suggested that the many examples of the name *Kir(k)by* (< ON *kirkjubý*) 'are almost certainly instances of appellatival names that were given by the Vikings to pre-existing nucleated settlements with a church, in replacement of earlier English names' (Fellows-Jensen 1981, 138; see further Fellows-Jensen 1987a, 298–99). Beyond noting that it evidently occurred at times in Scandinavian England, however, there is little more one can say about this second possibility; in particular its frequency must remain unknown, though the fact that we can only point to a few instances with certainty suggests that it cannot have been the dominant practice of the settlers.

---

[1] With regard to the latter case see Hall 1989, 155–57, who argues that it is indeed the same place that is being referred to by the two names, and not different sites, and suggests that the central area around St Alkmund's church was that known as *Norðworðig*.

The third possibility for the Scandinavian settlers was in some way to adapt the English names so as to make them more congenial to their own speech habits, and this is the phenomenon which requires fuller consideration here.

Processes of Scandinavianisation

When speakers of one language or dialect appropriate and use a name from another, the possibilities for adaptation are the same as for when a loanword is borrowed, and are basically twofold (excluding, that is, the option of no change, even if this means adding a new sound to one's language): the speakers may make the foreign name approximate phonetically to sounds in their own; or they may translate the foreign name sound-by-sound or element-by-element into their own language by substituting cognate forms. W. F. H. Nicolaisen characterises the first of these processes as follows (1975, 170):

> The name in one language is a phonological adaptation of the name in the other language; by definition such a name becomes instantly meaningless in the receiving language. (It may, of course, also have been without lexical meaning in the donor language.) Phonological adaptation may be called the prototype of onomastic transfer; it clearly is the most common toponymic phenomenon in linguistic contact.

And the second process (1975, 169):

> The name in one language is a translation or part-translation of the name in the other language; this appears to be the result of the closest contact between speakers of the two languages concerned, with the incoming language usually being required to do the translating.

As Scottish examples of the first process Nicolaisen cites *Beinn Liath* > *Ben Lee* (Uist) and *Sleibhte* > *Sleat* (Skye), and of the second *An t-Eilean Dubh* > *Black Isle* (Ross-shire) and *Coit Garten* > *Boat of Garten* (Inverness-shire, part-translation). All these are of course instances of contact between Gaelic and Scots English.

However, although many names begin as words, one might argue that an important difference between the English lexicon and the English onomasticon is that there is a higher proportion of compound names than of compound words. The importance of this is that, in Saussurean terms, compounds are motivated signs; that is, they comprise two or more meaningful elements combined in a meaningful manner, and hence are more like a short burst of speech or descriptive phrase than simply an arbitrary string of sounds (see Saussure 1983, 130–32). As Nicolaisen puts it in his discussion of 'Words as Names' (1976, 142),

> [Names] in many ways never cease to be what most of them originally started out as — words. While playing new roles in the process of communication, they therefore still share many grammatical properties with other, non-onomastic, lexical items and,

especially in syntactic environments, are frequently indistinguishable from these, particularly in the spoken language.

I would therefore argue that a study of the Scandinavianisation of Old English place-names represents the best available evidence for how well the Viking settlers were able to understand the English words and speech they heard from the lips of the native Anglo-Saxons. To approach the question in the terms of Milliken and Milliken, does the adaptation of place-names show that the settlers were able to make the correct phonemic correspondences between Old English and Old Norse? In the terms of Hockett, does it demonstrate the operation of an adequate switching-code on the part of the Norse-speaking population? One of Hockett's central points was that if when using a word previously heard from the speaker of a different dialect, one were to substitute one's own equivalent sounds or elements, this would be persuasive evidence for the switching-code hypothesis (1987, 43). The Scandinavianised place-names to be examined here indicate what substitutions or adaptations the Viking settlers made when they themselves subsequently used the names and descriptive phrases they heard from the Anglo-Saxons, and hence they provide an empirical indication of the intelligibility of Old English speech and names to the Norse-speaking population of the Danelaw; they are the closest one is likely to come to an equivalent of the Recorded Text Test in an historical study of dialect intelligibility.

There is an additional reason for valuing the material examined here which becomes evident when one compares it with the other potential source for the treatment of heard Old English names by speakers of Old Norse, namely skaldic verse. A good number of such names (personal names as well as place-names) are to be found in skaldic verse celebrating events in England, especially the conquest and reign of Cnut (see Townend 1997; 1998). However, one might argue that the evidence of English names in skaldic verse only indicates the ability of one particular Norse speaker to understand Old English and hence may be misleading: that speaker may have been Anglicised by residence at court, or unrepresentative in some other way; and indeed, skalds can hardly have been linguistically typical of the general population. As Eugene Casad observes, 'An informant's ability to understand a given dialect may be very different from the general ability of the population viewed as a whole' (1974, 123). Furthermore, and very importantly, the evidence of an individual cannot indicate whether we are dealing with a situation of dialect intelligibility or with one of bilingualism. Unlike the names recorded in skaldic verse, however, those used in general circulation and recorded in native documents from the medieval period and later (often continuing to the present day) are likely to reflect the usage of the general population. That is to say, the Scandinavianised forms of English place-names found in native English documents, often in considerable number, show that place-names in England were affected by the whole Norse-speaking population.

The obvious qualification to this is to acknowledge the possibility of scribal influence. Gillian Fellows-Jensen adduces two examples (namely the so-called Lindsey Survey and the Domesday Book accounts of the Bruce fief) where she believes the recorded forms showing Scandinavianisation probably derive 'from the scribes or from the man who provided the information, either orally or in written form, about the vills in question' and therefore 'probably reflect the linguistic usage of these men and not the normal local form of the p[lace-]n[ame]s' (*SSNEM* 199–200; see further Fellows-Jensen 1969; 1969–70; *SSNY* 132, 207). Names showing Scandinavianisation only in such sources should therefore be excluded from an analysis of Anglo-Norse intelligibility.

Another important contrast is therefore with the Norman-French layer in English place-names. These were very often imposed from above, deliberately bestowed by a ruling aristocracy speaking a different language from its subjects (*DEPN* xxviii; for introductory studies of the Norman-French element see Reaney 1960, 192–202; Gelling 1988, 236–40; Cameron 1996a, 88–94). But the Scandinavian layer in English toponymy — including the Scandinavianisation of pre-existing Old English names — does not derive from such a tiny elite; and hence, I would again suggest, Scandinavianised place-names in England reflect how Norse speakers more generally understood and adapted the English place-names they heard.

The phenomenon of Scandinavianisation has of course been noted and discussed before, in particular by Ekwall and Fellows-Jensen (see *DEPN* xxv–xxvi; *SSNY* 131–68; *SSNEM* 199–230; *SSNNW* 192–259). However, the Scandinavianisation of English place-names has not been purposefully or systematically considered in the context of linguistic relations and possible intelligibility. That is, the phenomenon and much of the material has been noted, but it has not been greatly interpreted; or if it has, it has been used as an indicator of Scandinavian influence for the purposes of measuring breadth and depth of settlement, rather than for what it can tell us about linguistic relations between the two speech communities. Indeed, in discussions of possible intelligibility, it is Margaret Ashdown who, in an old but important study, has probably come closest to emphasising the potential importance of the process of Scandinavianisation (and the reverse process of Anglicisation), though she is clearly thinking primarily of loanwords rather than place-names: 'With regard to language, it has to be remembered that, while the mere fact of borrowing is little to the present purpose, the fact that the Scandinavian settlers and English inhabitants were evidently able partially to understand each other, as the occasional substitution of native sounds in borrowed words suggests, must have been a constant reminder of their common origin' (1928–29, 82; see also Bibire 2001, 97–101).

The Present Material

The material illustrating Scandinavianisation that is analysed here is taken from Gillian Fellows-Jensen's three great regional studies: *Scandinavian Settlement Names in Yorkshire* (1972), *Scandinavian Settlement Names in the East Midlands* (1978), and *Scandinavian Settlement Names in the North-West* (1985). This corpus of material, presented in Appendix 3.1, therefore makes no pretence of being a comprehensive catalogue of all instances of the Scandinavianisation of English place-names: this is not the purpose of the present chapter, which is rather the investigation of possible intelligibility, and nor would such an exhaustive listing be either possible or desirable until every county has been covered by the English Place-Name Society's survey, and the pre-war volumes have been revised and augmented in detail, especially with regard to minor names; needless to say, there are also too many uncertain cases to permit a definitive listing. Fellows-Jensen's three volumes, however, provide ample and readily accessible material for study, though one should note the deliberate restrictions of their scope: first, they examine names of settlements only, and so names for topographical features such as mountains and rivers are not detailed unless they have subsequently been transferred to settlements (and microtoponymy such as field-names is similarly excluded); and second, the Yorkshire and East Midlands volumes are confined only to those settlements mentioned in Domesday Book or earlier.[2]

The listing in Appendix 3.1 therefore records all convincing examples, drawn from Fellows-Jensen's three volumes, of lexical substitution in Old English place-names for which we have both pre- and post-Scandinavianisation forms; the preservation of both forms means that we can see precisely what the Old English form was and precisely how the Scandinavian settlers adapted it. This point is an important one, as a great number of names survive only in a post-Scandinavianisation form, since, as has been noted, pre-Conquest documents are a rarity for the northern counties, and much of the north-west was not included in Domesday Book; for many of these names there can be no doubt that they are genuine cases of Scandinavianisation and not young formations, but since no pre-Scandinavianisation form exists, one cannot know what the original English element was for which a Norse element has been substituted. Fellows-Jensen assumes that an Old Norse element will always have been substituted for its Old English cognate ('Where a cognate OE word exists [. . .] it is reasonable to assume that it was this word the Scandinavian element replaced and not some entirely unrelated word' (*SSNY* 119)), but it is the very frequency of this phenomenon that the present chapter seeks to establish: a 100% success rate for cognate substitution cannot be assumed, as this would be circular reasoning.

Since the earliest form for some names may be post-Conquest, and for other names pre-Scandinavianisation forms may survive only in documents later than those containing post-Scandinavianisation forms, and since furthermore the two forms could evidently coexist over a long period (see further p 187 below), it might be objected that what we have are not Scandinavianisations of English names at all but rather young formations from the Middle English period or even Anglicisations of Norse names. There are, however, various factors which indicate that this is not the case, and it is important to rehearse these here; in fact, the likelihood of uncertainty as to whether a name shows Scandinavianisation or Anglicisation is minimal, as these two phenomena are primarily concerned with phonological form.

---

[2]The vast majority of Fellows-Jensen's data comes from the volumes of the English Place-Name Society and other earlier studies such as *PNLa*.

One may distinguish three sorts of Scandinavianised name, each of which requires slightly different arguments in this regard. First, there are hybrids; that is, compound names where one element is Norse and the other English, and where (for reasons given below) one would argue that the Norse element has replaced an earlier English one. Second, there are simplex names where one would argue that a Norse element has replaced a cognate or phonetically similar English one (of course, were the two elements neither cognate nor phonetically similar one would not have a case of Scandinavianisation, but rather an English name simply being replaced by an unrelated Norse one, as in the compound example of *Norðworðig - Derby*). And third, there are names (both simplex and compound) where a Norse sound has replaced an English one, resulting in a name without semantic content (of course, the English name may already have lost its semantic content due to sound-changes or other processes).

This third category is the most straightforward. Where one finds a name composed of Norse sounds but not amounting to a Norse word, one is evidently justified in suspecting phonological adaptation of an earlier English name, especially when the English form (postulated or recorded) would be semantically and toponymically plausible. It will be seen for instance that, where Norse lacks a cognate of the English word, substitution of ON /k/ and /sk/ for cognate OE /tʃ/ and /ʃ/ is especially prone to lead to meaningless names (see *SSNY* 131; *SSNEM* 180): examples of this type are given separately in an important Note at the end of Appendix 3.1, and are discussed further below (and as will be seen, this body of material also poses some problems of classification with regard to the question of 'semantic content').

The situation with hybrids is more complex. A place-name comprising one English element and one Norse element could represent either an originally English name with Norse lexical substitution in one element, or an originally Norse name with English lexical substitution in one element, or a later Middle English formation, coined at a time when Norse loanwords (or loan-elements) had entered the English active onomasticon (obvious examples would be elements such as *beck, fell, gill,* and so on). No doubt this third option is the correct explanation for a good number of names, especially minor ones (see for example Wainwright's study of Amounderness field-names (1975, 257–66)), but certain other factors often indicate that this cannot be the case. Date is only the most obvious of these: the earlier the first recorded occurrence of a name is, by definition the less likely it is that it represents a young formation from the Middle English period. More importantly, the preservation of distinctively Norse inflexions in any recorded form indicates that at some point speakers of Norse have been involved in the naming process.

The nature of the Old English element is arguably a more important factor still, especially when it is the name's generic (that is, its second element, according to the Germanic pattern of name-formation). When the generic is one which other sources confirm as no longer being current as a name-forming element after, say, the eighth or ninth century, then clearly the name cannot be a young hybrid formation but must rather be an originally Old English formation with later Norse substitution in one element. Elements that fall into this category (of being obsolete by the ninth or tenth century) include *hām*, *-ingas*, and *worþ* (*SSNNW* 195). Similarly the possibility of Anglicisation is excluded when the Old Norse generic is one that was no longer current in the Viking Age (for example, *heimr*, *tún*). Thus, for instance, a name showing *-hām/-heimr* variation can only be explained as the Scandinavianisation of an older (pre-Viking Age) English name. It cannot be a Norse formation that has been Anglicised, because ON *heimr* was not a name-forming element in the Viking Age; and it cannot be a young formation, because OE *hām* was similarly no longer functional.

One particular sort of hybrid that has received considerable attention are those commonly known as 'Grimston hybrids'; that is, hybrids whose specific is an Old Norse personal name and whose generic is the Old English place-name element *-tūn*. These were first studied in detail by Kenneth Cameron (1975, 157–71), and Fellows-Jensen devotes a chapter to them in each of her three regional volumes, suggesting that they should be considered in conjunction with what she terms 'Carlton hybrids'; that is, hybrids whose generic is *-tūn* but whose specific is a Norse word rather than a Norse personal name (*SSNY* 109–30; *SSNEM* 174–98; *SSNNW* 180–91; for a later reappraisal of this material see Fellows-Jensen 1995b, 172–75). As a place-name element *tún* is found also in Scandinavia, but as an active element in the Viking Age it occurs only in Norway to any degree, and so (as noted above) Danish settlers cannot have brought it over with them in their name-giving onomasticon; however, the element would not, perhaps, have been unfamiliar to them when they encountered it in England (see *SSNNW* 180–82). Fellows-Jensen furthermore explains (*SSNNW* 181),

> The main reason for assuming that the names are partial adaptations by the Danes of English names of pre-existing settlements is that most of the Grimston- and Carlton-type names are borne by settlements whose situation and status are in no way distinguishable from those of neighbouring settlements with purely English names. They are thus not likely to be young settlements squeezed in by Danes on hitherto vacant land in English-dominated areas nor settlements established long after the Scandinavian invasions, when a growing population may have made it necessary to bring less favourable land under cultivation.

It should be noted therefore that in the present investigation the argument is simply that Grimston hybrids represent originally English names; the significance of the Old Norse personal name in the first element is not in fact an issue here.

With the Grimston and Carlton hybrids we have moved on to extralinguistic criteria for determining whether a hybrid name represents Scandinavianisation, Anglicisation, or a young formation; and five criteria of such a type can be cited, all of which serve to demonstrate that a settlement is old, since pre-Viking Age origin must mean that a hybrid settlement name is most reasonably explained as a Norse adaptation of a pre-existing English name (on these general principles of dating place-names see further Sørensen 1979):

(1) The evidence of distribution patterns in relation to geology (alluded to in the quotation above concerning Grimston and Carlton hybrids). Broadly speaking, this assumes that the best land will be the first to be used for settlement and cultivation; since many hybrids are situated on high quality sites, or at least on sites in no way inferior to those occupied by settlements with purely Old English names, one may conclude that they were pre-existing Anglo-Saxon settlements with Old English names: it is unlikely that such premium sites would still have been unoccupied by the late ninth century or later.

The other four criteria for helping to establish that a hybrid was an older settlement with an originally English name are various reflections of this first one, since they all serve to indicate that a settlement was in a prosperous situation and hence likely to be established early:

(2) The presence of stone sculpture is an important indicator because of the expense involved in its production. As Richard Bailey states, 'Put simply, the relationship between sculpture and settlements [. . .] is this: the quality of the land provides the wealth which ultimately finances the production of sculpture' (1980, 213). Hence where a settlement with a hybrid name possesses some stone sculpture (whether Viking Age or Anglian period), it is reasonable to assume that Scandinavianisation of one element has occurred (for discussion and supplementation of Bailey's arguments see *SSNNW* 401–09; Fellows-Jensen 1995b, 175–78 (revisiting *SSNY* 218–21)).

(3) Fiscal evidence reflects the same principle, and involves calculating the yields and tax assessments for the different genres of place-name (purely Old English, purely Old Norse, hybrid, etc.), in order to establish which were most prosperous. Where such calculation is possible (employing the data of Domesday Book), the evidence of tax assessments supports the interpretation that many of the hybrid names, and especially the Grimston and Carlton hybrids, arose through partial Scandinavianisation of older purely English names (see *SSNEM* 337, 341).

(4) Administrative evidence involves calculating what proportion of each genre of place-name became the centre of some sort of administrative division (essentially, hundreds and wapentakes, and parishes). The argument once more is that such roles are likely to have been played by the more important and prosperous (and therefore long-established) settlements, and again Fellows-Jensen's findings, particularly with regard to the parish-names, support those of the other types of evidence (*SSNEM* 353–55):

> The hybrid *tūn*s have practically the same proportion of parishes as the English *tūn*s, an indication that they are likely to be English vills with scandinavianised names. The proportion of vills with miscellaneous hybrid names that are parishes is so high that most of these names must have been borne by old-established vills.

(5) The final type of external evidence is that of continuity. This criterion assumes that it is the smaller and less well-established settlements that are likely to have

suffered depopulation and desertion in the medieval period; and again settlements with hybrid names are among those most likely to show vitality and continuity (see *SSNEM* 362–63; *SSNNW* 397).

Cumulatively, these various external reasons combine with the earlier linguistic ones to form a very strong probability that one can say, in any particular case, whether a hybrid name has arisen through Scandinavianisation or Anglicisation or later Middle English coinage. As a result of this, Fellows-Jensen's view is that 'the majority of the hybrid and scandinavianised names are borne by English vills whose names were partly altered by the invading Scandinavians' (*SSNEM* 368).

As mentioned above, the third type of Scandinavianised place-name is that in which a simplex name has undergone substitution of a Norse cognate for its original English form. Names like these therefore have purely Norse forms which are semantically meaningful, and are thus more like hybrids than those names in which substitution of a Norse sound has resulted in a meaningless form; the same criteria therefore apply to these names as to the hybrids.

For reasons of brevity these various criteria have all been treated here in general and rather simplified terms, without illustrative examples, but it is according to these criteria that the place-names listed in Appendix 3.1, and analysed below, can be deemed to qualify as examples of Scandinavianisation; hence it has been important to rehearse, albeit in summary fashion, the methodology according to which one can assemble such a list.

Analysis and Discussion

Appendix 3.1 lists a total of 228 examples (in 220 different place-names) of lexical substitution of an Old Norse element for an Old English element.[3] Of these 228 examples, 192 show cognate substitution and 36 non-cognate: this amounts to a success rate for cognate substitution of 84.2%.[4] As to the range of vocabulary involved, this represents 76 different words or names being replaced, of which 61 undergo cognate substitution, and 15 non-cognate. The cognate substitutions, and their frequency of occurrence, are as follows:

---

[3]The eight place-names showing two lexical substitutions are as follows: Beckwith YW (*bēce - bekkr* and *widu, wudu - viðr*), Brisco Cu (*birce, bircen - birki, birkinn* and *sc(e)aga - skógr*), Conisbrough YW (*burh - borg* and *cyning - konungr*), Eastburn YE (*burna - brunnr* and *ēast - austr*), Kirkham La (*cirice - kirkja* and *hām - heimr*), Stenwith L (*stān - steinn* and *wald - vað*), Stonegrave YN (*græf - gryfja* and *stān - steinn*), and Swanscoe Ch (*hōh - skógr* and *swān - sveinn*).

[4]This figure will be revised below. I have, perhaps unjustifiably, classified a number of cases of related substitutions as cognate (e.g. *æsc - eski*).

Old English	Old Norse	No.
āc	eik	5
æsc	askr	4
æsc	eski	1
alor	elri	2
ān(a)	einn	3
bece, bæce	bekkr	5
birce, bircen	birki, birkinn	5
brād	breiðr	7
brycg	bryggja	4
burh	borg	2
burna	brunnr	12
busc	buskr	1
ceorl	karl	2
cirice	kirkja	9
cyning	konungr	1
Dene	Danir	1
dræg	drag	4
ēa	á	2
ēast	austr	2
ef(e)n	jafn	1
ēl	ál	1
eofor	*jórr	1
fisc	fiskr	1
fiscere	fiskari	2
gæt	gata	1
gāra	geiri	1
gāt	geit	3
god	guð	2
hǣð	heiðr	1
hæsel	hesli	4
hām	heimr	17
hēafod	*haufuð	1
heorde	hjǫrð	1
hrycg	hryggr	1
hwǣte	hveiti	2
*lece	lækr	4
lȳtel	lítill	1
midd	miðr	2
middel	meðal	7
rēad	rauðr	2
salh	selja	1
sc(e)acol	skǫkull	1

The Scandinavianisation of Old English Place-Names

Old English	Old Norse	No.
sc(e)aft	skapt	1
sc(e)aga	skógr	2
sc(e)ard	skarð	1
sc(e)arn	skarn	1
scēla	skáli	1
sceld	skjǫldr	1
scelf	skjálf	7
scīr	skirr	3
scīte	skítr	1
*scor(a)	skor	1
spōn	spánn	1
stān	steinn	30
stede	staðr	2
swān	sveinn	1
tord	torth	1
þorn	þyrnir	1
ward	varða	1
wēt	vátr	1
widu, wudu	viðr	4
wurm, wyrm	urm	1
	TOTAL	192

The non-cognate substitutions, and their frequency of occurrence, are as follows:

Old English	Old Norse	No.
ald	jalda	1
bēce	bekkr	1
brōc	bekkr	2
byrig	bý	8
byrig	bøli	1
cot	toft	1
denu	dalr	5
ears	ey(jar)	1
gāra	garðr	1
gāra	gata	1
græf	gryfja	1
Hōc	haukr	2
hōh	skógr	1
-um	heimr	1
wald	vað	2
wīc	viðr	6
Winuc	Víkingr	1
	TOTAL	36

The quantity of cognate substitutions which this corpus yields is impressive, both in terms of the number of different words and the number of occurrences. It will be recalled that the essence of Hockett's switching-code is the replacement of a sound in another dialect with the corresponding sound in one's own dialect, and that the evidence for this would be the employment of that corresponding sound when subsequently using the word involved oneself (1987, 43). Clearly more than one sound may be replaced by its equivalent in any one word: the number depends on the number of phonological divergences between the two dialects evidenced in that word.

I would argue that the evidence of cognate substitutions assembled above indicates the operation of just such a switching-code on the part of Norse-speaking settlers in England. When they heard English words and names spoken, they recognised and understood those words and names and inwardly transposed them into their own dialect. It is the subsequent use of the Scandinavianised forms of the place-names that proves that this was the case. And since this Scandinavianising switching-code has affected the forms of place-names so pervasively, it seems that it must have been employed by the Norse-speaking community as a whole, and not simply by a handful of influential linguists. This in turn suggests that in the contact of speakers of Norse and English in Viking Age England we primarily appear to be dealing with a situation of dialect intelligibility rather than one of bilingualism.

Although couching their discussion in different terms, the argument of Milliken and Milliken is the same as that of Hockett, pointing out that intelligibility depends not on phonetic similarity per se but on the ability of hearers to make correct phonemic correspondences. Hence the list of cognate substitutions given above can be analysed in terms of the range of correctly posited phonemic correspondences evidenced therein, and the congruity (to use Milliken and Milliken's term) of those correspondences. Before doing this, however, an acknowledgement must be made that these cognate substitutions have been described as lexical rather than phonemic. Strictly speaking, they are of course both, and this is an important point, bearing in mind Hockett's assertion that the two strategies of a switching-code and 'gestalt perception' can and do operate in tandem (1987, 43). This will be discussed further below under the question of 'contextual clues'.

The correctly posited phonemic correspondences will now be listed, beginning with consonants and then proceeding to vowels, together with an estimation of the congruity or otherwise of each correspondence — that is, 'whether or not an actual correspondence can be expressed as an exceptionless generalization from the point of view of the listener' (Milliken and Milliken 1993, 3).[5]

---

[5]I have not included Old English palatal diphthongisation in the following list of divergences, as this appears not to have occurred in Anglian dialect areas (whence most of the Scandinavianised place-names derive). Substituted Old English elements which would show palatal diphthongisation in West Saxon are *gæt*, *sc(e)acol*, *sc(e)aft*, *sc(e)aga*, *sc(e)ard*, *sc(e)arn*, *scēla*, *sceld*, and *scelf*.

(1) OE *d* - ON *ð*
This is a highly regular correspondence: Germanic *ð* became *d* in all positions in Old English, but only after *l* or *n* in Old Norse (see above pp 38–39). Twelve substitutions show this correspondence:[6] *brād - breiðr, god - guð, hēafod - *haufuð, heorde - hjǫrð, midd - miðr, middel - meðal, rēad - rauðr, sc(e)ard - skarð, stede - staðr, tord - torth, ward - varða, widu/wudu - viðr.*

(2) OE /j/ - ON /g/
Before a front vowel Germanic velar /g/ was palatalised in Old English to /j/, while retaining its velar quality in Old Norse (see above p 39). One substitution shows this correspondence:[7] *gæt - gata.*

(3) OE /dʒ/ - ON /g/
Through the twin processes of palatalisation and assibilation Germanic /g/ regularly became /dʒ/ in Old English in positions where it remained /g/ in Old Norse (see above p 39). Two substitutions show this correspondence: *brycg - bryggja, hrycg - hryggr.*

(4) OE /tʃ/ - ON /k/
As with /g/, /k/ in Old English regularly underwent palatalisation and assibilation in positions where Old Norse retained the Germanic velar stop (see above p 39). Five substitutions show this correspondence:[8] *bece/bæce - bekkr, birce/bircen - birki/birkinn, ceorl - karl, cirice - kirkja* (both initial and final), **lece - lækr.*

(5) OE /ʃ/ - ON /sk/
Again, the Germanic consonant-cluster /sk/ regularly underwent palatalisation and assibilation in Old English while retaining its velar quality in Old Norse (see above p 39). Fifteen substitutions show this correspondence:[9] *æsc - askr/eski, busc - buskr, fisc - fiskr, fiscere - fiskari, sc(e)acol - skǫkull, sc(e)aft - skapt, sc(e)aga - skógr, sc(e)ard - skarð, sc(e)arn - skarn, scēla - skáli, sceld - skjǫldr, scelf - skjálf, scīr - skírr, scīte - skítr, *scor(a) - skor.*

(6) OE *r*-metathesis
Metathesis of *r* is found very frequently in Old English but only in a very few words in Old Norse (see above p 39). One substitution shows this correspondence: *burna - brunnr.*

---

[6] As well as those Old English words without Old Norse cognates listed as examples of phonemic substitution in the Note at the end of Appendix 3.1.

[7] As well as the two names listed as examples of phonemic substitution.

[8] As well as those listed as examples of phonemic substitution.

[9] As well as the many words listed as examples of phonemic substitution.

(7) ON loss of initial /w/

In Old Norse /w/ was lost initially before rounded vowels (and often in other positions also), while Old English preserved its Germanic distribution (see above p 40). One substitution shows this correspondence: *wurm, wyrm - urm*.

(8) OE *æ* - ON *a*

The regular (unconditioned) development of Germanic *a* was to *æ* in Old English, *a* in Old Norse (see above p 33). Three substitutions show this correspondence: *æsc - askr, dræg - drag, gæt - gata*.

(9) OE *ǣ, ē* - ON *á*

The regular development of Germanic *ǣ* was to *ǣ, ē* in Old English (WS *ǣ¹*, nonWS *ē*), *á* in Old Norse (see above p 33). Three substitutions show this correspondence:[10] *ēl - ál, scēla - skáli, wēt - vátr*.

(10) OE *ā* - ON *ei*

The regular development of the Germanic diphthong *ai* was to *ā* in Old English, *ei* in Old Norse (see above p 33). Ten substitutions show this correspondence: *āc - eik, ān(a) - einn, brād - breiðr, gāra - geiri, gāt - geit, hǣð* (with subsequent *i*-mutation) *- heiðr, hām - heimr, hwǣte* (with *i*-mutation) *- hveiti, stān - steinn, swān - sveinn*.

(11) OE *ēa* - ON *au*

The regular development of the Germanic diphthong *au* was to *ēa* in Old English, *au* in Old Norse (see above p 33). Three substitutions show this correspondence: *ēast - austr, hēafod - *haufuð, rēad - rauðr*.

(12) *i*-mutation

Both Old English and Old Norse were affected by *i*-mutation, but owing to such factors as syncope or different inflexional endings the phenomenon is not always found in the same circumstances or same words in the two languages (see above pp 34, 35). In addition to the two instances of OE *ǣ²* (mutated from *ā* < Gmc *ai*) - ON *ei* (unmutated < Gmc *ai*) listed above under (10), there are also the following:

(a) two substitutions showing the correspondence OE *a* (unmutated) - ON *e* (mutated): *alor - elri, salh - selja*;

(b) two substitutions showing the correspondence OE *e* (mutated) - ON *a* (unmutated): *Dene - Danir, stede - staðr*;

(c) one substitution showing the correspondence OE *æ* (unmutated) - ON *e* (mutated): *hæsel - hesli*.

Clearly the distribution of *i*-mutation between the two languages was not always such as to permit 'exceptionless generalizations', but equally clearly the nature of the correspondences was predictable.

---

[10] As well as that listed as an example of phonemic substitution.

(13) ON *a*-umlaut

This Old Norse sound-change led inter alia to the lowering of *i* to *e* when followed by *a* in the next syllable (see above p 35). One substitution shows this correspondence: *middel - meðal*.

(14) ON Fracture

When followed by *a* or *u* in the next syllable *e* was broken in Old Norse to *ea*, and this new diphthong was then potentially subject to *u*-umlaut (a post-Viking Age development, not certainly found in Old Norse in England). Though Back Mutation shows certain similarities, this sound-change is not found in Old English (see above p 36). Two substitutions show this correspondence: *sceld - skjǫldr, scelf - skjálf*.

(15) ON Rising Diphthongs

While Old English diphthongs remained falling (that is, with greater stress on the first element), during the Viking Age Old Norse diphthongs underwent a shift of stress and thus became rising. This change occurred earliest in word-initial position (see above p 36). Two substitutions show this correspondence: *ef(e)n - jafn, eofor - *jórr*.

These are the chief phonemic correspondences evidenced in the words known to have been substituted in Scandinavianised place-names. Certain phonological divergences in some of these words have not been noted, namely those which are not examples of regular developments but rather represent particular developments in specific words (that is, individual cases or examples influenced by analogy). And even in cases like these where distribution is irregular and regular rules cannot be readily formulated (that is, where congruity is low), often the nature of the divergences will have been familiar (for example, *o - u* variation found in such substitutions as *burh - borg, god - guð*).

These, however, are very much the exception. The purpose of giving the above analysis of correspondences was to demonstrate, first, that more or less all the important phonological divergences between Old English and Old Norse are highly congruent and predictable and, second, that they are all found in the recorded range of substitutions. The substitution of cognate sounds even where no cognate word existed, listed in the Note at the end of Appendix 3.1 and discussed further below, would seem to confirm this. The conclusion to be drawn is therefore that, since all the important divergences are evidenced, there is no reason to imagine that words other than those found in the recorded place-names should have caused any problems. That is, speakers of Norse were clearly able to make correct phonemic correspondences when hearing English speech; they performed admirably the function required to understand another dialect. It is the repertoire of substituted correspondences that demonstrates this, rather than the vocabulary of substituted words; that is, the recorded instances of lexical substitution reveal an ability to make every important phonemic substitution.

Some of the recorded words do of course require more than one phonemic correspondence to be made, and the substitutions falling into this category are as follows (references are to the list of correspondences above):

Substitution	Correspondences involved
æsc - askr	(5), (8)
brād - breiðr	(1), (10)
gæt - gata	(2), (8)
hǣð - heiðr	(10), (12)
hēafod - *haufuð	(1), (11)
hwǣte - hveiti	(10), (12)
middel - meðal	(1), (13)
rēad - rauðr	(1), (11)
sc(e)ard - skarð	(1), (5)
scēla - skáli	(5), (9)
sceld - skjǫldr	(5), (14)
scelf - skjálf	(5), (14)
stede - staðr	(1), (12)

This brings us back, therefore, to the question of the difference between lexical and phonemic substitution, and whether it is meaningful to attempt to distinguish the two. Should one regard substitutions involving only one correspondence as phonemic rather than lexical? Should one regard substitutions involving two correspondences as a single lexical example rather than two phonemic examples within the same word? Such questions are, I think, misleading or even irrelevant, especially if one is concerned, as here, with empirical evidence for pragmatic intelligibility. As Hockett remarks, there is no reason to doubt that the two mechanisms of a switching-code and 'gestalt perception' can and do operate concurrently. An important factor that prevents the strict disentanglement of the two must therefore be the degree to which any speech-situation provides guidance as to what is being said — what Milliken and Milliken call 'contextual clues'. What they term their 'Interpretation Principle' is that 'Members of one dialect will interpret a sound in another dialect as corresponding to the most similar eligible phoneme in their own dialect, in the absence of sufficient contextual clues to otherwise bias their decision' (Milliken and Milliken 1993, 4). This is certainly unexceptionable as far as it goes, but of course outside of a language laboratory it is hard to imagine any situation of linguistic contact in which some sort of contextual clues won't be present. Quite the reverse — the whole field of pragmatics is devoted to elucidating the myriad ways in which extralinguistic factors assist, or even render redundant, communication by language. In other words, communication and miscommunication are emphatically sociolinguistic phenomena, and not simply linguistic ones (see further L. Milroy 1984; J. Milroy 1992, 33–45), and in discussing interdialectal intelligibility Peter Trudgill has in fact suggested that context 'plays a much greater role in the comprehension of other varieties [of language] than it does in the comprehension of one's own' (1983, 22). This is an important point, as Milliken and Milliken develop their theoretical model by positing a series of hypothesis-revisions, until the correct phonemic correspondence is reached. But considering both the pragmatics of context and the inherent redundancy of language, one may wonder whether in the vast majority of cases hypothesis-revision would be necessary: a combination of a switching-code and 'gestalt perception' would probably be adequate.

Furthermore, Hockett points out how strict grammatical and syntactic coherence is rarely necessary for the purposes of communication (1987, 63):

> The redundancy of the total communicative package also explains why we can often understand even an 'imparsible' utterance: one whose parts just can't be fitted together by our syntactic patterns to make a coherent whole. [...] Handling such material is like trying to assemble a jigsaw puzzle with a few pieces missing, or with a few extras, or both. Given sufficient context, we can supply the missing pieces or discard the extras, and thus get the picture, or something enough like it as usually to make no practical difference.

Clearly this is pertinent to an investigation into the degree of intelligibility enjoyed by two closely related speech varieties between which one of the chief differences is in inflexional endings (see further pp 196–201 below); but it is also an issue that requires fuller discussion. What is being stressed here is simply that a consideration of both the value of 'contextual clues' and the inherent redundancy of language confirms the conclusion that speakers of Norse were able to recognise and understand English words and names, presumably through a combination of a switching-code and 'gestalt perception'; and the evidence for the successful operation of a switching-code indicates that we seem to be dealing with a situation of dialect intelligibility rather than one of bilingualism.

Something must also be said, however, about the instances of non-cognate substitution.[11] These have been listed above, and as can been seen they are much fewer, both in the overall number of cases and in the number of different words substituted. What is most striking is that of the 36 examples, 31 involve substitution of the second element and only 5 of the first. This would appear to confirm Gillian Fellows-Jensen's suggestion that the Vikings found the first elements of Old English place-names easier to recognise and understand because they received the main stress (*SSNY* 140). By the Viking Age unstressed syllables in Old English were in the process of being centralised to schwa, and so it is not surprising to find Norse speakers less successful in recognising second elements.

---

[11]Of these non-cognate substitutions *byrig - bý* and *wīc - viðr* should be picked out on account of their especial frequency: on the latter see further Ekwall 1964, 58–60, and Townend 1998, 46 n.43, where it is suggested that the substitution of cognate ON /k/ for OE /tʃ/ may have been resisted or reinterpreted on the grounds that the resultant Old Norse word *vík* 'coastal inlet' would be topographically inappropriate in a good number of cases.

In fact, as far we can tell from our incomplete knowledge of the two languages, only five of the Old English words undergoing non-cognate substitution have Old Norse cognates (or 15 out of the 36 examples); and three of these — *byrig*, *hōh*, and *wald* — have extenuating circumstances that render the expected cognate substitution somewhat less likely (the two exceptions are *ald* and *gāra*, which has in one name at least been replaced by its cognate *geiri*):[12] there are two examples of Norse speakers recognising the nominative form of *byrig* (in the substitution *burh - borg*), although none of the mutated oblique form; in the substitution *hōh - skógr* there has been mistaken (though understandable) delimitation of element-boundaries;[13] and semantic shift has obscured the relationship between OE (Anglian) *wald* ('woodland') and cognate ON *vǫllr* ('field, plain'), as well as therefore causing it to be a topographically inappropriate substitution. The other ten Old English words do not have cognates in Old Norse: in some cases they have been replaced by topographically equivalent terms (for example, *brōc - bekkr*, *denu - dalr*), either on account of a shared perception of the landscape, or possibly an appreciation of the semantic content of these non-cognate English terms; in other cases the substitution is due to similarity in sound rather than meaning (for example, *Hōc - haukr*). Thus the earlier figure of 84.2% for cognate substitutions can be reviewed, and if one calculates only cognate substitutions where they could actually be made (that is, where an Old Norse cognate existed), the figure goes up to a success rate of 92.8% (192 out of 207). If one confines the calculation to cognate substitutions in the stressed first element and where an Old Norse cognate existed, one arrives at a figure of 99.2% (128 out of 129), indicating near-perfect operation of a switching-code.[14]

The names listed in the Note to Appendix 3.1, exemplifying phonemic substitution rather than lexical, also require discussion. First, they indicate, at the very least, an awareness of cognate correspondences between the phonological systems of the two languages, and thus support the case for the successful operation of a switching-code. Second, they would seem to argue against widespread active bilingualism on the part of Norse speakers, since in that case one might have expected the lexical substitution of semantically equivalent terms (as has happened in the topographical examples noted above of *brōc - bekkr* and *denu - dalr*). A third point relates to the few instances noted above of non-cognate substitution on account of similarity in sound rather than meaning (for example, *Hōc - haukr*). These might perhaps suggest that Norse speakers did not usually regard the Old English names they heard as mere meaningless strings of sounds, but rather endeavoured to construe and understand

---

[12]The absence in Old English of an inflexional ending containing a consonant may be why Norse speakers failed to make the cognate substitution *ald - aldinn*.

[13]The name in question is Swanscoe Ch (*Swanneshogh* 1357, *Swanescough* 1611): Norse speakers appear to have construed the medial *-s-* as belonging to the second rather than the first element (that is, *-shogh* rather than *Swannes-*).

[14]The exception is *ald - jalda*.

them: one could argue that not even non-cognate substitution would have occurred if the Scandinavians had habitually regarded the English names as semantically meaningless. The examples listed in the Note might argue against this, but alternatively they might indicate that Norse speakers generally recognised when an Old English name or word was without an Old Norse equivalent, and so did not attempt to reanalyse them by the process of folk etymology; it is noteworthy that very few of the Old English elements undergoing phonemic substitution in the Note to Appendix 3.1 had Old Norse cognates. The process of phonemic substitution in these examples should therefore be thought of as simply the reproduction of English names with a Norse 'accent': it was stressed above that the operation of a switching-code should not necessarily be conceived of as conscious or deliberate.

On the other hand, a number of the examples might give cause for thought with regard to the question of semantic comprehension. Could one claim that in the examples involving OE *scīr* ('shire'), Norse speakers have re-construed this element as ON *skírr* ('bright')? This would then be an example of Old English homophones causing problems for Norse hearers (OE *scīr* ('shire') and OE *scīr* ('bright')), as only one of them had an Old Norse cognate (ON *skírr* ('bright')). Similarly it is not impossible that (notwithstanding the question of vowel length) some of the examples involving OE *scīp* ('sheep') have been re-construed as ON *skip* ('ship'). This is probably an insoluble dilemma, as in such examples (especially OE *scīr*) it is formally impossible to distinguish between non-cognate lexical substitution and cognate phonemic substitution. One could certainly argue that my placing of these names in the Note (as cognate phonemic substitutions) represents a form of etymological fallacy, and that they should instead have been listed (as non-cognate lexical substitutions) among the main body of substitutions in Appendix 3.1. In other words, since Norse speakers habitually substituted cognate /sk/ for OE /ʃ/, there is an element of chance as to whether the resultant form is a recognisable (that is, semantically meaningful) word in Old Norse, as some phonemic substitutions do result in such (for instance, OE *scīr* ('shire') > ON *skírr* ('bright')). The examples listed in the Note to Appendix 3.1 therefore raise some important questions about the nature of the semantic comprehension involved in cognate substitutions (and are arguably not unrelated to the issue of 'contextual clues' discussed above); but in the regularity of their substitutions they do not militate against — indeed, they unanimously support — the central point concerning the operation of a phonological switching-code.

To conclude: this chapter has sought to demonstrate that the Scandinavianisation of Old English place-names indicates the reliable operation of a switching-code on the part of Norse-speaking settlers in England. The substitution of cognate sounds and words suggests that, by and large, Norse speakers recognised and understood the words they heard in the place-names used by their English neighbours. Only where no cognate word existed did they understandably encounter difficulties. Otherwise the substitutions show that they were able to make all the correct phonemic correspondences, covering the whole repertoire of major phonological divergences between Norse and English, and so there are few grounds for believing that other cognate words need have caused problems of intelligibility. As the forms in the Note indicate, however, the situation with regard to non-cognate words is considerably less clear.

The essence of what has been attempted in this chapter is therefore very simple — to juxtapose the mechanism of dialect intelligibility with the treatment of place-names by an incoming speech community — but as far as I am aware it has not been done before. Having made such a juxtaposition, it may at once seem obvious that the processes of intelligibility and the processes of cognate substitution are one and the same — but again, as far as I am aware it has not been pointed out before, even though each has received a good deal of attention individually. If one wishes to make some sort of attempt at empirical intelligibility testing for an historical situation (as one must if the study of Anglo-Norse contact is to make progress), then I would suggest that this is a plausible way of doing so, and indeed that no better alternative has yet been proposed.

APPENDIX 3.1

Corpus of Scandinavianised Place-Names

The following corpus of Old English place-names which have undergone Scandinavianisation represents the material analysed in the preceding chapter; as explained there, it is based on Gillian Fellows-Jensen's three regional studies. The material is set out as follows. The recorded lexical substitutions are listed by alphabetical order of the English element being replaced (including personal names), and for each element an alphabetical list is given of the place-names showing that particular substitution. Place-names which are now lost are printed in italic. For each of the place-names documentary forms are cited illustrating the substitution, and, when available, page references are given to the full details to be found in the volumes of the English Place-Name Society, Ekwall's *Oxford Dictionary of English Place-Names*, and Fellows-Jensen's three regional studies. (Where a county has not yet been covered by the English Place-Name Society survey (for example, Lancashire), reference is sometimes given to other standard works (for example, *PNLa*).) For each place-name pre-Scandinavianisation forms are given under (i) and post-Scandinavianisation forms under (ii): consequently, not all citations occur in chronological order, since, as was pointed out earlier, pre-Scandinavianisation forms sometimes survive only in documents later than those containing post-Scandinavianisation forms. I have selected for citation those forms which most clearly demonstrate the process of Scandinavianisation, and therefore have not felt obliged always to give a name's Domesday Book form. Regnal dates for illustrative forms have been expanded, and for texts surviving only in late copies, original dates of composition are given in square brackets.

Finally, in order to make sense of some of the forms some knowledge of the intricacies of Domesday Book and Anglo-Norman orthography is required; this is especially the case for those names containing /tʃ/ or /k/ and /ʃ/ or /sk/. The following principles are therefore as accurate as is possible (see further Zachrisson 1909,

24–36; von Feilitzen 1937, 107–12 (§§113–25); for a reassessment of post-Conquest spelling, however, see Clark 1995, 144–76):

In Domesday Book orthography:
(1) Word-initial, before front vowels, the graph <c> represents /tʃ/ and the graphs <ch> represents /k/ (so DB <cerce> = OE *cirice* and <cherche> = ON *kirkja*). Word-initial, before back vowels, <ch> represents /tʃ/ and <c> represents /k/. Word-final, post-vocalic, <ch> usually represents /k/. In other positions in the word, though, <c> and <ch> are ambiguous, so (for example) DB <bec> could represent either OE *bece* or ON *bekkr*.
(2) Word-initial, before front vowels, the graphs <s, ss, sc> represent /ʃ/ and the graphs <sch> represents /sk/ (so DB <scelf> = OE *scelf* and <schelf> = ON *skjálf*). In other word-positions, though, <sc> and <sch> are ambiguous, so (for example) DB <asc> could represent either OE *æsc* or ON *askr*.

However, in later Anglo-Norman orthography (from the twelfth century onwards):
(1) The graphs <ch> represents /tʃ/ and the graphs <k, c> represent <k> (so C12 <cherch> = OE *cirice* and <kirk> = ON *kirkja*).
(2) The graphs <sch, sh> represent /ʃ/ and the graphs <sk, sc> represent /sk/ (so C12 <schelf> = OE *scelf* and <skelf> = ON *skjálf*).

OE *āc* ('oak') replaced by cognate ON *eik*
  Ackton YW (*PNYW* 2.85; *SSNY* 114; *DEPN* 2)
    i. *Acitone* DB ii. *Aitone* DB, *Aicton* C12
  Akefrith La (*PNLa* 180; *SSNNW* 193)
    i. *Okes[f]rith* 1246, *Akefrith* 1529 ii. *Eichefrid* 1154–89
  Aughton YE (*PNYE* 237; *SSNY* 138; *DEPN* 19)
    i. *Actun* DB, *Acton* 1230 ii. *Ayketon* 1298
  Eagle L (*SSNEM* 216; *DEPN* 155)
    i. *Aclei, Acley* DB ii. *Eicla* 1135–39, *Aycle* 1254
  Skyrack YW (*PNYW* 4.88–89; *SSNY* 139)
    i. *Siraches* DB, *Scirac* 1166 ii. *Skiraik* 1219

OE *æsc* ('ash-tree') replaced by cognate ON *askr*
  Ashford Db (*PNDb* 27; *SSNEM* 207; *DEPN* 15)
    i. *æt Æscforda* [926] C13, *Aisseford* DB ii. *Askeford'* 1265
  Aske YN (*PNYN* 286; *SSNY* 138; *DEPN* 16)
    i. *Hasse* DB ii. *Ask* 1157
  Askham Nt (*PNNt* 44; *SSNEM* 212; *DEPN* 16)
    i. *Ascham* 1167 ii. *Askham* 1329
  Aspatria Cu (*PNCu* 261–62; *SSNNW* 214; *DEPN* 16)
    i. *Aspatric c.* 1160, *Espatric* 1171–75 ii. *Askpatri(c)k* 1291

OE *æsc* replaced by related ON *eski* ('place growing with ash-trees')
  Louthesk L (*SSNEM* 219)
    i. *Lvdes* DB ii. *Luddeske* 1200

OE (Anglian) *ald* ('old') replaced by ON *jalda* ('mare')
  Aldoth Cu (*PNCu* 289; *SSNNW* 201; *DEPN* 5)
    i. *Aldelathe* 1292 ii. *Ialdlathyt, Ialdelathyt* 1292

OE *alor* ('alder-tree') (gen.pl. *alra*) replaced by related ON *elri* ('alders')
  Ellerton YE (*PNYE* 238; *SSNY* 114; *DEPN* 163)
    i. *Alreton* 1206 ii. *Elreton* DB, *Elretuna c.* 1190
  Ellerton on Swale YN (*PNYN* 277; *SSNY* 138; *DEPN* 163)
    i. *Alreton* DB ii. *Ellerton* 1184

OE *ān(a)* ('one, solitary') replaced by cognate ON *einn*
  Ainsty YW (*PNYW* 4.235; *SSNY* 151)[1]
    i. *Anestig* ii. *Ainesti, Einesti* DB
  Ancoats La (*PNLa* 35; *SSNNW* 193; *DEPN* 9)
    i. *Ancoates* 1240–59, *Ancotes* 1322 ii. *Einecote* 1212
  Ayntrepot Cu (*PNCu* 292; *SSNNW* 214)
    i. *Antrepot* 1189 ii. *Aintrepot* 1285, *Ayntrepot'* 1292

OE *bece, bæce* ('stream') replaced by cognate ON *bekkr*
  Beighton Db (*PNDb* 210; *SSNEM* 207; *DEPN* 35)
    i. *æt Bectune* [c. 1002] C11 ii. *Becktone* 1258
  Cotesbach Lei (*SSNEM* 207; *DEPN* 125)
    i. *Cotesbece* DB ii. *Catisbek* 1285
  Holbeach L (*SSNEM* 218; *DEPN* 244)
    i. *Holebeche* [810] C17 ii. *Holebech* DB
  Howbeck Ch (*PNCh* 3.71; *SSNNW* 193)
    i. *Holebagge* 1259 ii. *Hollebeke* 1304
  Welbeck Nt (*PNNt* 103; *SSNEM* 229; *DEPN* 504)
    i. *Wellebech c.* 1161 ii. *Welebec* 1201–12, *Welebek* 1226

OE *bēce* ('beech') replaced by ON *bekkr* ('stream')
  Beckwith YW (*PNYW* 5.116; *SSNY* 153; *DEPN* 34)
    i. *bec wudu* [972] C11 ii. *Beck(e)with* 1301 etc.

---

[1] In OE *ānstig*, traditionally taken to mean 'path wide enough for one man'. However, the meaning of this compound has recently been disputed (see Gelling 1984, 63–64; Parsons and Styles 1997, 18; Gelling and Cole 2000, 66–67).

OE *birce* ('birch') and *bircen* ('birchen') replaced by cognate ON *birki, birkinn*
  Birkenhead Ch (*PNCh* 4.313–14; *SSNNW* 216; *DEPN* 45)
    i. *Bircheveth* 1190–1216, *Birchinheuid* 1294   ii. *Byrkeheveht* (sic) 1259, *Birkenhed* 1278
  Birkenshaw La (*PNLa* 47; *SSNNW* 216)
    i. *Byrcheneshaghe* 1278   ii. *Byrkeneshawe* 1277
  Birkin YW (*PNYW* 4.16–17; *SSNY* 153; *DEPN* 45)
    i. *Byrcene* c. 1030   ii. *Berchine* DB
  Birkwood L (*SSNEM* 225)
    i. *Birchewda* 1158, *Birchewud'* 1199–1216   ii. *Birkewude* 1210
  Brisco Cu (*PNCu* 148; *SSNNW* 219; *DEPN* 66)
    i. *Byrchsawe* 1279   ii. *Byrkscawe* 1231, *Birkscagh* 1290

OE *brād* ('broad') replaced by cognate ON *breiðr*
  Bradley L (*PNL* 5.6–7; *SSNEM* 207; *DEPN* 58)
    i. *Bradela* 1163   ii. *Braidela* 1175–81, *Braithela* C13
  Bradleyfield We (*PNWe* 1.101; *SSNNW* 355–56; *DEPN* 58)
    i. *Bradeley, -lay* 1292, 1393   ii. *Braithlagh* 1324
  Bradleys Both YW (*PNYW* 6.11; *SSNY* 139; *DEPN* 58)
    i. *Bradelei* DB   ii. *Brathelay* 1246, *Braydlay* 1379
  Braithwell YW (*PNYW* 1.132–33; *SSNY* 139; *DEPN* 59)
    i. *Bradeuuelle* DB   ii. *Breithwelle* 1196–1201
  Braybrooke Nth (*PNNth* 110; *SSNEM* 216; *DEPN* 61–62)
    i. *Bradebroc* DB   ii. *Braybroke* C12, *Breibroc* 1215
  Braystones Cu (*PNCu* 413; *SSNNW* 218; *DEPN* 62)
    i. *Bradestanes* 1247   ii. *Braythestanes* 1294, *Breithstanes* 1300
  Brayton YW (*PNYW* 4.24; *SSNY* 116; *DEPN* 62)
    i. *Brattona* 1078–85   ii. *Breiðetun* c. 1030, *Braiþatun* [c. 1050] C11

OE *brōc* ('stream') replaced by ON *bekkr* ('stream')
  Holbeck Farm Nt (*PNNt* 176; *SSNEM* 208; *DEPN* 244)
    i. *on holan broc* [958] C14   ii. *Holebek* 1180 etc.
  Sherbrook Lodge Db (*PNDb* 372; *SSNEM* 208)
    i. *Sirebroch* 1101–08   ii. *Scirebec* 1207

OE *brycg* ('bridge') replaced by cognate ON *bryggja*[2]
  Agbrigg YW (*PNYW* 2.117; *SSNY* 151)
    i. *Agebrvge* DB   ii. *Aggebrigg(e)* 1277 etc.
  Brigham Cu (*PNCu* 355; *SSNNW* 193; *DEPN* 64)
    i. *Bricgaham* 1185   ii. *Briggham* c. 1175

---

[2]On the difficulties of distinguishing these two elements see Styles 2001, 292–96.

Brigsley L (*PNL* 4.60–62; *SSNEM* 207; *DEPN* 65)
    i. *Brigeslai* DB ii. *Briggele* 1202
Winnibriggs L (*SSNEM* 207)
    i. *Winegebrige, Winebruge* DB ii. *Winierbrigg'* 1199

OE *burh* ('stronghold') replaced by cognate ON *borg*
Brandesburton YE (*PNYE* 74; *SSNY* 143; *DEPN* 78)
    i. *Bvrtvn, Brantisburtune* DB ii. *Bortun, Branzbortune* DB
Conisbrough YW (*PNYW* 1.125; *SSNY* 144; *DEPN* 120)
    i. *æt Cunugesburg* [1002–04] *c.* 1100 ii. *Coningesborc* DB

OE *burna* ('spring, stream') replaced by cognate ON *brunnr*[3]
Bourne L (*SSNEM* 152)
    i. *into Burnan* [971–83] C14 ii. *Brune* DB, *Brunna* 1163
Brindle La (*PNLa* 134; *SSNNW* 219; *DEPN* 65)
    i. *Burnhull* 1206, 1246 ii. *Brunhull* 1254
Cliburn We (*PNWe* 2.136; *SSNNW* 193; *DEPN* 112)
    i. *Clibburn(e)* 1204, 1235 ii. *Clibbrun* 1133–47
Eastburn YE (*PNYE* 166; *SSNY* 155; *DEPN* 279)
    i. *Austburne* DB ii. *Estbrunne* 1274
Eastburn YW (*PNYW* 6.24; *SSNY* 155; *DEPN* 156)
    i. *Est(e)burn(e)* C12 etc. ii. *Estbrune* DB
Kilburn YN (*PNYN* 195; *SSNY* 139; *DEPN* 275)
    i. *Chilebvrne* DB ii. *Killebrun(na)* C12
King's Meaburn We (*PNWe* 2.141; *SSNNW* 239; *DEPN* 319)
    i. *Meburn(e)* 1200 ii. *Meabruna* C12, *Mebrun(n)* 1158–66
Leyburn YN (*PNYN* 257; *SSNY* 139; *DEPN* 297)
    i. *Leborne* DB ii. *Laibrunn* 1208
Maulds Meaburn We (*PNWe* 2.156; *SSNNW* 239; *DEPN* 319)
    i. *Mayburne c.* 1200 ii. *Mebrun(e)* 1153–82, *Medbrunne* C13
Roeburndale La (*PNLa* 181; *SSNNW* 247; *DEPN* 391)
    i. *Reburndale* 1285 ii. *Rebrundale, Reynbrundale* 1301
Welbourn L (*SSNEM* 222; *DEPN* 504)
    i. *Weleburne* [*c.* 1080] C13 ii. *Wellebrvne* DB
Welburn (Bulmer) YN (*PNYN* 40; *SSNY* 167; *DEPN* 504)
    i. *Welleburn(e)* 1167 etc. ii. *Wellebrune* DB, *Welbrun* 1243

OE *busc* ('bush') replaced by cognate ON *buskr*
Antrobus Ch (*PNCh* 2.127–28; *SSNNW* 193; *DEPN* 11)
    i. *Entrebus* DB ii. *Anderbusk(e)* 1297

---

[3]It is however possible that some of the forms listed here as Old Norse substitutions are in fact Old English variants without *r*-metathesis.

OE *byrig* ('stronghold') (dat.sg. of *burh*) replaced by ON *bý* ('settlement')
   Badby Nth (*PNNth* 13; *SSNEM* 34; *DEPN* 21)
      i. *baddan byrig* 944 ii. *baddan by* 944, *Badebi* [1020] C12
   Dalbury Lees Db (*PNDb* 548; *SSNEM* 208; *DEPN* 138)[4]
      i. *Dellingeberie* DB, *Dalebiry c.* 1141 ii. *Delbebi* DB
   Greasby Ch (*PNCh* 4.291; *SSNNW* 194; *DEPN* 203)
      i. *Gravesberie* DB ii. *Grauisby* [1096–1101] 1280
   Naseby Nth (*PNNth* 73; *SSNEM* 14; *DEPN* 336)
      i. *Navesberie* DB ii. *Navesbya* C12, *Nauesbi* 1166
   Quenby Lei (*SSNEM* 14; *DEPN* 377)
      i. *Qveneberie* DB ii. *Quenebia c.* 1130
   Rugby Wa (*PNWa* 143; *SSNEM* 14; *DEPN* 396)
      i. *Rocheberie* DB ii. *Rochebi c.* 1155–90 etc.
   Shoby Lei (*SSNEM* 14; *DEPN* 419)
      i. *Seoldesberie* DB ii. *Siwaldebia c.* 1130, *Siwoldebi c.* 1240
   Thornby Nth (*PNNth* 74–75; *SSNEM* 14; *DEPN* 467)
      i. *Torneberie* DB ii. *Thirnebi c.* 1160

OE *byrig* replaced by Old Danish *bøli* ('homestead')
   Newball L (*SSNEM* 214; *DEPN* 339)
      i. *Nevberie* DB ii. *Neubele c.* 1110, *Neobole* 1115–18

OE *ceorl* ('peasant') replaced by cognate ON *karl* (in gen.pl.)
   Carlton Curlieu Lei (*SSNEM* 182–83; *DEPN* 87)
      i. *Cherletona* [*c.* 1055] C13 ii. *Carletone* DB
   Carlton in Lindrick Nt (*PNNt* 72; *SSNEM* 182–83; *DEPN* 87)
      i. *Charleton'* 1182 ii. *Carletone* DB, *Carleton* 1212

OE *cirice* ('church') replaced by cognate ON *kirkja*
   Achurch Nth (*PNNth* 219; *SSNEM* 211–12; *DEPN* 2)
      i. *æt Asencircan, Asecyrcan* [*c.* 980] *c.* 1200 ii. *Asechirche* DB, *Asekirke* 1209–18
   Algarkirk L (*SSNEM* 206–07; *DEPN* 6)
      i. *Algarescherche* 1194 ii. *Algarkyrk* 1209–12
   Anderchurch Lei (*SSNEM* 212)
      i. *Andreschirch(e)* [1175–95] C15 ii. *Andreskirka* [1132–66] C14
   Gosberton L (*SSNEM* 213; *DEPN* 201)
      i. *Goseberdeschirche* 1167 ii. *Gosberkirke* 1212
   Kirkham La (*PNLa* 152; *SSNNW* 203–04; *DEPN* 280)
      i. *Chircheham c.* 1130 ii. *Chercheham* DB, *Kyrkham* 1094

---

[4] A 1555 citation gives both forms: *Dalby als Dalbury*.

Corpus of Scandinavianised Place-Names 75

Kirkham YE (*PNYE* 143–44; *SSNY* 148; *DEPN* 280)
    i. *Chercheham c.* 1125 ii. *Chirchan* DB, *Kirkaham c.* 1200
Kirton in Lindsey L (*SSNEM* 184; *DEPN* 281)
    i. *Circeton* DB ii. *Chircheton* DB, *Kirketune* 1155–60
Peakirk Nth (*PNNth* 241; *SSNEM* 214; *DEPN* 360)
    i. *æt Pegecyrcan* [1016] C12 ii. *Peikirke* 1198
Romaldkirk YN (*PNYN* 309; *SSNY* 149; *DEPN* 391)
    i. *Rumoldescerce* DB ii. *Rumbald(e)kirke* 1184 etc.

OE *cot* ('cottage') replaced by ON *toft* ('curtilage')
  Yelvertoft Nth (*PNNth* 77; *SSNEM* 215–16; *DEPN* 544)
    i. *Gelvrecote* DB ii. *Givertost* (sic) DB, *Gelvertoft* C12

OE *cyning* ('king') replaced by cognate ON *konungr*
  Conisbrough YW (*PNYW* 1.125; *SSNY* 144; *DEPN* 120)
    i. *æt Cunugesburg* [1002–04] *c.* 1100 ii. *Coningesborc* DB

OE *Dene* ('Danes') replaced by cognate ON *Danir*
  Denhall Ch (*PNCh* 4.221; *SSNNW* 225)
    i. *Denewell* [*c.* 1240] 1293 ii. *Danewell* 1184, 1238

OE *denu* ('valley') replaced by ON *dalr* ('valley')
  Bakestonedale Ch (*PNCh* 1.131; *SSNNW* 194)
    i. *Blakesstonisdene* C13 ii. *Baxendale* 1620
  Chippingdale La (*PNLa* 143; *SSNNW* 194; *DEPN* 105)
    i. *Chipinden* DB ii. *Cepndela* 1102, *Chippendal* 1256
  Figdale Ch (*PNCh* 4.150; *SSNNW* 194)
    i. *Fikedene* 1296 ii. *Figdale* 1481
  Langdale (Orton) We (*PNWe* 2.43; *SSNNW* 236)
    i. *Langedena* 1179 ii. *Langedal(a)*, *-dale* 1178, 1199, etc.
  Langdales We (*PNWe* 1.203; *SSNNW* 194; *DEPN* 286)
    i. *Langedene* 1157–63 ii. *Langdale* 1578

OE *dræg* ('portage') replaced by cognate ON *drag*
  Draughton Nth (*PNNth* 112; *SSNEM* 183; *DEPN* 150)
    i. *Drayton'* C12 ii. *Dractone* DB
  Draughton YW (*PNYW* 6.65; *SSNY* 114; *DEPN* 150)
    i. *Draython* 1285 ii. *Dractone* DB, *Drahton* 1275
  Drax YW (*PNYW* 4.8–9; *SSNY* 155; *DEPN* 150)
    i. *æt Ealdedrege* [959] *c.* 1200 ii. *Drac* DB
  Dundraw Cu (*PNCu* 139–40; *SSNNW* 226; *DEPN* 153)
    i. *Drumdraye* 1292 ii. *Dundrag* 1230

OE *ēa* ('river') replaced by cognate ON *á*
    Ayton (Great and Little) YN (*PNYN* 165–66; *SSNY* 113; *DEPN* 21)
        i. *Etona c.* 1162 ii. *Atune* DB
    Eamont We (*PNWe* 2.205; *SSNNW* 193; *DEPN* 155)
        i. *æt Ea motum c.* 1100 ii. *Amot* 1279

OE *ears* ('buttock') replaced by ON *ey(jar)* ('island(s)')
    Caldy Ch (*PNCh* 4.283; *SSNNW* 194; *DEPN* 82)
        i. *Calders* DB ii. *Caldei* 1182

OE *ēast* ('east') replaced by cognate ON *austr*
    Austwick YW (*PNYW* 6.229; *SSNY* 142; *DEPN* 19)
        i. *Estwich* 1175 ii. *Ovstevvic* DB, *Austwich* 1175
    Eastburn YE (*PNYE* 166; *SSNY* 155; *DEPN* 279)
        i. *Estbrunne* 1274 ii. *Austburne* DB

OE *ef(e)n* ('flat, even') replaced by cognate ON *jafn*
    Yanwath We (*PNWe* 2.204–05; *SSNNW* 259; *DEPN* 542)
        i. *Euenewit* 1150–62, *Euenwith c.* 1270 ii. *Yau-, Yavenwith(e) c.* 1200, 1242, *Iawenwyth* C13

OE (Anglian) *ēl* ('eel') replaced by cognate ON *áll*
    Auburn YE (*PNYE* 87; *SSNY* 138; *DEPN* 18)
        i. *Eleburne* DB ii. *Alburn(e)* C12

OE *eofor* ('boar') replaced by cognate ON *jǫfurr* (in OWN form **jórr*)
    York YE (*PNYE* 275–80; *SSNY* 138; *DEPN* 545)[5]
        i. *Eoforwic* 1053–66 ii. *3(e)orc, York(e)* C13

OE *fisc* ('fish') replaced by ON *fiskr*
    Fishlake YW (*PNYW* 1.14; *SSNY* 138; *DEPN* 180)
        i. *Fischelake* 1194–99 ii. *Fiskelak* 1230

OE *fiscere* ('fisherman') replaced by cognate ON *fiskari*
    Fiskerton L (*SSNEM* 183; *DEPN* 180)
        i. *Fischertune* 1115–18 ii. *Fiskertuna* [1060] C12
    Fiskerton Nt (*PNNt* 164; *SSNEM* 183; *DEPN* 180)
        i. *Fiscertune* [956] C14 ii. *Fiskerton* 1236

OE (Anglian) *gæt* ('opening, gap') replaced by related ON *gata* ('road, street')
    Yatehouse Ch (*PNCh* 2.233; *SSNNW* 193)
        i. *(Byleych)yathuses* C14 ii. *(Byuele)gate* 1310–30

---

[5] For discussion of this name see Fellows-Jensen 1987b; Townend 1998, 44–46.

OE *gāra* ('gore, triangular piece of land') replaced by ON *garðr* ('enclosure')
Plungar Lei (*SSNEM* 214–15; *DEPN* 369)
   i. *Plungar c.* 1130 ii. *Plumgard c.* 1130, *Plumgard* 1187

OE *gāra* replaced by ON *gata* ('street, road')
Walmsgate L (*SSNEM* 208; *DEPN* 494)
   i. *Walmesgar* DB, *Walmeresgara* 1115–18 ii. *Walmesgate* 1196

OE *gāra* replaced by cognate ON *geiri*
Gargrave YW (*PNYW* 6.53; *SSNY* 156; *DEPN* 192)
   i. *Geregraue* DB, *Gargrave* 1182–85 ii. *Gairgrava c.* 1160

OE *gāt* ('goat') replaced by cognate ON *geit*
Gateforth YW (*PNYW* 4.27; *SSNY* 156; *DEPN* 193)
   i. *Gateford* 1316 ii. *Gæiteford c.* 1030, *Geiteford* 1166
Gayton le Wold L (*SSNEM* 183–84; *DEPN* 194)
   i. *Gattunasoca c.* 1154 ii. *Gaituna c.* 1155
Geddington Nth (*PNNth* 166; *SSNEM* 184; *DEPN* 194–95)
   i. *Gadintone* DB, *Gatinton* 1159 ii. *Geitentone* DB, *Geytington* C12

OE *god* ('god, God') (as element in OE personal name *Godmund*) replaced by cognate ON *guð*
Goodmanham YE (*PNYE* 230–31; *SSNY* 146; *DEPN* 200)
   i.*Godmunddingaham c.* 730 (Bede) ii. *Gudmundha'* DB
Gumley Lei (*SSNEM* 217; *DEPN* 207)
   i. *Godmundeslaech* [749] C12, *Godmundesleah* 779 ii. *Gvtmvndeslea* DB, *Guthmvndel(e)(y)* 1109, *c.* 1200, etc.

OE *græf* ('pit') replaced by ON *gryfja* ('steep-sided valley')
Stonegrave YN (*PNYN* 55; *SSNY* 166; *DEPN* 446)[6]
   i. *Staningagraue* [757–58] C11 ii. *Steinegrif* DB

OE *hǣð* ('heath') replaced by cognate ON *heiðr*
Hatfield YW (*PNYW* 1.7; *SSNY* 138; *DEPN* 224)
   i. *Hæðfeld c.* 890, *Hedfeld* DB ii. *Heitfeld* 1175–90

OE *hæsel* ('hazel-tree') replaced by related ON *hesli* ('place growing with hazel-trees')
Haselbech Nth (*PNNth* 115; *SSNEM* 217–18; *DEPN* 223)
   i. *Haselbech* C12 ii. *Heselbech(e) c.* 1220 etc.

---

[6]Fellows-Jensen notes that the meaning of the substituted element 'steep-sided valley' is not appropriate for this location.

Hazlebadge Db (*PNDb* 118; *SSNEM* 218; *DEPN* 228)
    i. *Haselbech(e)* 1251 etc. ii. *Heselbache* 1367
Hessle YE (*PNYE* 215; *SSNY* 139; *DEPN* 237)
    i. *Hase* DB ii. *Hesel* C12
Hessle YW (*PNYW* 2.89; *SSNY* 139; *DEPN* 237)[7]
    i. *Hasele* DB ii. *Hesal* 1119–35

OE *hām* ('homestead, dwelling') replaced by cognate ON *heimr*
Bentham YW (*PNYW* 6.237; *SSNY* 142–43; *DEPN* 37)
    i. *Benetham* C13 ii. *Benethaim* 1202–08
Bispham La (*PNLa* 136; *SSNNW* 193; *DEPN* 46)
    i. *Bispam* 1219, *Bispham* 1332 ii. *Bispaim* 1268
Bispham with Norbreck La (*PNLa* 156; *SSNNW* 193; *DEPN* 46)
    i. *Biscopham* DB, *Biscopeham* 1094 ii. *Biscopheyma* 1216
Brigham YE (*PNYE* 90; *SSNY* 139; *DEPN* 64–65)
    i. *Bringeha'* DB, *Brigham* 1226–28 ii. *Brigheym* 1259
Clapham YW (*PNYW* 6.232; *SSNY* 139; *DEPN* 109)
    i. *Clapeham* DB ii. *Claphaim* 1165–77
Cockerham La (*PNLa* 170; *SSNNW* 193; *DEPN* 114)
    i. *Cocreham* DB, *Kokerham* 1190 ii. *Cokerheim c.* 1155
Coverham YN (*PNYN* 254; *SSNY* 139; *DEPN* 126)
    i. *Coureha'* DB ii. *Couerhaim* 1177
Fosham YE (*PNYE* 60; *SSNY* 139; *DEPN* 185)
    i. *Fosham* DB ii. *Fosseym* 1285
Gressingham La (*PNLa* 178; *SSNNW* 193; *DEPN* 205)
    i. *Gersingeham* 1183, 1194 ii. *Gersinghaim* 1204–12
Heversham We (*PNWe* 1.87; *SSNNW* 193; *DEPN* 237)
    i. *Hefresham c.* 1050, *Heveresham* 1090–97 ii. *Eureshaim* DB
Heysham La (*PNLa* 178; *SSNNW* 193; *DEPN* 238)
    i. *Hessam* DB, *Hesham c.* 1190 ii. *Hesseim* 1094, *Hesheim* 1180–99
Kirkham La (*PNLa* 152; *SSNNW* 203–04; *DEPN* 280)
    i. *Chicheham* DB, *Chercheham* 1094 ii. *Kirkeheim* 1196, *Kyrkheym* 1246
Levisham YN (*PNYN* 92; *SSNY* 139; *DEPN* 296)
    i. *Levesham* 1234 ii. *Leueshaim c.* 1250
Middleham YN (*PNYN* 252; *SSNY* 149; *DEPN* 324)
    i. *Mid(d)elham* 1184 ii. *Midelhaym* 1240
Mortham YN (*PNYN* 301; *SSNY* 139; *DEPN* 331)
    i. *Mortham* DB ii. *Morthaim c.* 1150

---

[7]Fellows-Jensen points out that Hessle YW lies on the Northumbrian / Mercian dialect border, and so one may have to reckon with the influence of Mercian *hesel* (showing Second Fronting).

Tatham La (*PNLa* 182; *SSNNW* 206; *DEPN* 461)
    i. *Tateham* 1202, *Tatham* 1226 ii. *Tathaim* DB, *Tathaim* 1215
Wintringham YE (*PNYE* 136; *SSNY* 139; *DEPN* 525)
    i. *Wentrigha'* DB ii. *Winteringeheim* 1190

OE *hēafod* ('head, headland') replaced by cognate ON **haufuð* (OWN *hǫfuð*, OEN *howuth*)
    Howden YE (*PNYE* 243; *SSNY* 158; *DEPN* 254)
        i. *æt Heafuddene* [959] *c.* 1200 ii. *Hovedene* DB

OE *heorde* ('herd') replaced by cognate ON *hjǫrð*
    Hardwick Nt (*PNNt* 107; *SSNEM* 223; *DEPN* 218)
        i. *Herdewic* 1316 ii. *Herthewik* [*c.* 1155–90] C17

OE personal name *Hōc* replaced by ON *haukr* ('hawk') or personal name *Haukr*
    Hawkswick YW (*PNYW* 6.124; *SSNY* 146; *DEPN* 227)
        i. *Hochesuuic* DB ii. *Houkeswyk* 1226
    Hawksworth Nt (*PNNt* 226; *SSNEM* 208; *DEPN* 227)
        i. *Hochesuuorde* DB ii. *Houkeswrda* 1179

OE *hōh* ('spur') replaced by ON *skógr* ('wood')
    Swanscoe Ch (*PNCh* 1.107; *SSNNW* 194)
        i. *Swanneshogh* 1357 ii. *Swanescough* 1611

OE *hrycg* ('ridge') replaced by cognate ON *hryggr*
    Marrick YN (*PNYN* 294; *SSNY* 139; *DEPN* 316)
        i. *Marige* DB ii. *Marrich c.* 1150

OE *hwǣte* ('wheat') replaced by cognate ON *hveiti*
    Wheatcroft YW (*PNYW* 4.104; *SSNY* 138)
        i. *Watecroft* DB ii. *Wai(te)croft* 1219
    Wheatley YW (*PNYW* 1.36; *SSNY* 138; *DEPN* 512)
        i. *Watelag* DB ii. *Weytelay* 1246

OE **lece* ('brook') replaced by cognate ON *lækr*[8]
    Leake L (*SSNEM* 157; *DEPN* 292)
        i. *Lech c.* 1185 ii. *Leke* 1212
    Leake YN (*PNYN* 207; *SSNY* 99; *DEPN* 292)
        i. *Lece* DB, *Leche* 1088 ii. *Leke* 1231

---

[8] Gelling, however, is sceptical that postulated OE **lece* ever existed (1984, 25).

Leek St (*SSNEM* 157; *DEPN* 294)
 i. *Lech c.* 1100 ii. *Leke* 1247
Legbourne L (*SSNEM* 219; *DEPN* 294)
 i. *Lecheburna* 1115–18 ii. *Lekeburne* [*c.* 1150] 1409

OE *lȳtel* ('little') replaced by cognate ON *lítill*
Littledale La (*PNLa* 177; *SSNNW* 237)[9]
 i *Luteldale* 1226 ii. *Liteldale* 1251

OE *midd* ('middle') replaced by cognate ON *mið̄r*
Meathop We (*PNWe* 1.76; *SSNNW* 240; *DEPN* 319)
 i. *Midhop(e), -hopp* 1184–90 ii. *Mithehop* 1190–1210
Mythop La (*PNLa* 153; *SSNNW* 240; *DEPN* 335)
 i. *Midehope* DB ii. *Mithop* 1212

OE *middel* ('middle') replaced by cognate ON *með̄al*
High Melton YW (*PNYW* 1.76; *SSNY* 116; *DEPN* 321)
 i. *Middeltvn* DB ii. *Medeltone* DB
Melbourne YE (*PNYE* 236; *SSNY* 139; *DEPN* 320)
 i. *Middelbvrne* DB ii. *Methel(e)burn'* 1230
Middleham YN (*PNYN* 252; *SSNY* 149; *DEPN* 324)
 i. *Mid(d)elham* 1184 ii. *Medelai* DB
Middleton YW (*PNYW* 5.65; *SSNY* 137, 139; *DEPN* 325)
 i. *Middeltune* [*c.* 972] C11, *Middeltune* DB ii. *on Með̄eltune c.* 1030
Milton Db (*PNDb* 654; *SSNEM* 208; *DEPN* 326)
 i. *Middeltune* DB ii. *Meelton c.* 1162, *Melton c.* 1227
Stony Middleton Db (*PNDb* 147; *SSNEM* 208; *DEPN* 324)
 i. *Middeltone* DB ii. *Medilton* 1265
West Melton YW (*PNYW* 1.114; *SSNY* 116; *DEPN* 321)
 i. *Middeltvn* DB ii. *Medeltone* DB, *Metheltona* 1208–37

OE *rēad* ('red') replaced by cognate ON *rauð̄r*
Rawcliff Bank YN (*PNYN* 146; *SSNY* 162; *DEPN* 382)
 i. *in Readeclive* [1043–60] 1104–08 ii. *Roudeclif* DB
Rockcliffe Cu (*PNCu* 146; *SSNNW* 246; *DEPN* 390)
 i. *Redeclive* 1203 ii. *Roudecliua* 1185

---

[9]Insley, however, rejects Fellows-Jensen's idea that substitution has occurred in this name (1986, 175): 'This explanation is needlessly involved, because the first element is OE *lytel* and the ME variation <u> - <i> represented in the forms *Luteldale* 1226 and *Liteldale* 1251 merely reflects overlap in North Lancs. between West-Midland and Northern reflexes of OE /y:/'.

OE (Anglian) *salh* ('willow') replaced by cognate ON *selja*
　Silecroft Cu (*PNCu* 444; *SSNNW* 249; *DEPN* 422)
　　　i. *Salcroft* 1292 ii. *Selecroft* (sic) c. 1205, *Selecroft* 1211

OE *sc(e)acol* ('pole; tethering yard') replaced by cognate ON *skǫkull* (VAN *skakull*)
　Shallcross Manor Db (*SSNEM* 207; *PNDb* 99)
　　　i. *Sachalcros* 1101–08 ii. *Skakelcros* C13

OE *sc(e)aft* ('shaft, pole') replaced by cognate ON *skapt*
　Skeffington Lei (*SSNEM* 207; *DEPN* 424)
　　　i. *Sciftitone* DB ii. *Skeftintone* 1165 etc.

OE *sc(e)aga* ('wood') replaced by cognate ON *skógr*
　Barnskew We (*PNWe* 2.154; *SSNNW* 214)
　　　i. *Barnesthagh* (sic, for *-schagh*) C13 ii. *Barnesco* c. 1240
　Brisco Cu (*PNCu* 148; *SSNNW* 219; *DEPN* 66)
　　　i. *Byrkscawe* 1231, *Briscagh* 1352 ii. *Briscowe* 1393

OE *sc(e)ard* ('gap, notch') replaced by cognate ON *skarð*
　Wainscarre Nt (*PNNt* 69; *SSNEM* 229)
　　　i. *Wayneschard, -scart* 1274 ii. *Waynstarthe* (sic) C13,

OE *sc(e)arn* ('dung, muck') replaced by cognate ON *skarn*
　Scarrington Nt (*PNNt* 228–29; *SSNEM* 185; *DEPN* 407)
　　　i. *Scherninton'* 1166 ii. *Scarintone* DB, *Skeryngton* c. 1270–1310

OE (Anglian) *scēla* ('shieling') replaced by cognate OWN *skáli*
　Skelbrooke YW (*PNYW* 2.43; *SSNY* 164–65; *DEPN* 424)
　　　i. *Schelebrok* 1230 ii. *Scalebro* DB, *Skelebrok* 1253

OE (Anglian) *sceld* ('shield') replaced by cognate ON *skjǫldr*
　Skellingthorpe L (*SSNEM* 221; *DEPN* 424)
　　　i. *Scheldinghop* 1141 ii. *Scheldinchope* DB, *Skeldinghop* 1238

OE (Anglian) *scelf* ('shelf, ledge') replaced by cognate ON *skjálf*
　Bashall YW (*PNYW* 6.192–93; *SSNY* 153; *DEPN* 29)
　　　i. *Bacshelf* 1251 ii. *Baschelf* DB, *Bacskalf* 1276
　Shelley YW (*PNYW* 2.248; *SSNY* 138; *DEPN* 415)
　　　i. *Scelneleie* (sic, with *n* for *u*) DB ii. *Skelflay* 1243
　Skelton Cu (*PNCu* 239; *SSNNW* 188; *DEPN* 424)
　　　i. *Sheltone* c. 1160 ii. *Skelton* 1271
　Skelton YE (*PNYE* 255; *SSNY* 116; *DEPN* 424)
　　　i. *Scilton* DB ii. *Schilton* DB, *Skeltun* 1199

Skelton (Bulmer) YN (*PNYN* 16–17; *SSNY* 116; *DEPN* 424)
    i. *Sceltun* DB   ii. *Scheltun* DB, *Skelton* 1181–84
Skelton (Langbargh East) YN (*PNYN* 145; *SSNY* 116; *DEPN* 424)
    i. *Sceltun* DB   ii. *Scheltun* DB
Skelton (Skyrack) YW (*PNYW* 4.120; *SSNY* 117; *DEPN* 424)
    i. *Sceltune* DB   ii. *Skeltun* 1185

OE *scīr* ('bright') replaced by cognate ON *skirr*
  Sherburn in Elmet YW (*PNYW* 4.60; *SSNY* 138; *DEPN* 416)
    i. *Scireburnan* 963, *Scireburne* DB   ii. *Skireburne* C12
  Skirbeck L (*SSNEM* 160; *DEPN* 425)
    i. *Scirebec* DB   ii. *Schirebec* DB, *Skirbec* 1202
  Skirlaugh (North and South) YE (*PNYE* 49; *SSNY* 165; *DEPN* 425)
    i. *Scirlai* DB   ii. *Schirelai* DB

OE *scīte* ('dirt, dung') replaced by cognate ON *skitr*
  Skidbrooke L (*SSNEM* 221; *DEPN* 425)
    i. *Scitebroc* DB   ii. *Skydbrok* 1328

OE **scor(a)* ('river-bank, precipitous slope') replaced by cognate ON *skor* ('ravine')
  Scorton YN (*PNYN* 278; *SSNY* 113; *DEPN* 408)
    i. *Schorton* 1184   ii. *Scortone* DB, *Scorton* 1231

OE *spōn* ('chip, shaving') replaced by cognate ON *spánn*
  Spondon Db (*PNDb* 605; *SSNEM* 208; *DEPN* 434)
    i. *Spondune* DB   ii. *Spandon* 1177, 1233

OE *stān* ('stone') replaced by cognate ON *steinn*
  Allerston YN (*PNYN* 93; *SSNY* 152; *DEPN* 6)
    i. *Alurestan* DB   ii. *Alurestain* DB
  Beston YW (*PNYW* 5.122; *SSNY* 153)[10]
    i. *Beston* 1386   ii. *Bestaine* 1301, *Bestayne* 1342
  Elstronwick YE (*PNYE* 53; *SSNY* 139; *DEPN* 165)[11]
    i. *Alstanewich* DB   ii. *Elstainnewic* C12
  Featherstone YW (*PNYW* 2.86; *SSNY* 139; *DEPN* 176)
    i. *Fredestan* DB   ii. *Fethestain* c. 1130–40
  Humberston(e) L (*PNL* 5.116–17; *SSNEM* 207; *DEPN* 256–57)
    i. *Humbrestone* DB   ii. *Humberstein* 1180

---

[10]The Domesday Book forms also show confusion with OE *hām*, ON *heimr*: i. *Bestham* ii. *Besthaim*.

[11]The first element here is the OE personal name *Ælfstān*.

North Stainley YW (*PNYW* 5.159; *SSNY* 138–39; *DEPN* 436)
    i. *Nordstanlai* DB ii. *Northstainle* 1246
Radstone Nth (*PNNth* 57; *SSNEM* 207; *DEPN* 379)
    i. *Rodestone* DB ii. *Rodestayn* 1295
Ravenstonedale We (*PNWe* 2.30–31; *SSNNW* 246; *DEPN* 382)
    i. *Rau-*, *Ravenstandal(e)* 1251, 1292 ii. *Rau-*, *Raven(e)steindal(e)* 1223 etc.
Ribston (Great and Little) YW (*PNYW* 5.20, 32; *SSNY* 162–63; *DEPN* 386)
    i. *Ripestan* DB ii. *Ripestain* DB, *Ribbestein* C12
Rudston YE (*PNYE* 98–99; *SSNY* 163; *DEPN* 395)
    i. *Rodestan* DB, *Ruddestan* 1100–22 ii. *Rodestain* DB, *Rudestain* C12
South Stainley YW (*PNYW* 5.95; *SSNY* 139; *DEPN* 436)
    i. *Stanlei* DB ii. *Steinlei* C12
Stainborough YW (*PNYW* 1.312–13; *SSNY* 150; *DEPN* 435)
    i. *Stanburg* DB ii. *Stainbvrg* DB, *Steinburgh c.* 1165
Stainburn Cu (*PNCu* 435–36; *SSNNW* 251; *DEPN* 435)
    i. *Stanburn'* 1279 ii. *Steinburn c.* 1135, *Stainburn* 1227
Stainburn YW (*PNYW* 5.48–49; *SSNY* 165; *DEPN* 435)
    i. *Stanburne* [*c.* 972] C11, *Stanburne* DB ii. *Stainburne* DB
Stainforth (Lower Strafforth) YW (*PNYW* 1.12; *SSNY* 165; *DEPN* 436)
    i. *Stenforde* DB ii. *Steinforde* DB
Stainforth (West Staincliffe) YW (*PNYW* 6.154; *SSNY* 165; *DEPN* 436)
    i. *Stranforde* (sic) DB ii. *Stainforde* DB
Staining La (*PNLa* 156; *SSNNW* 206; *DEPN* 436)
    i. *Stanynggas* 1211–40 ii. *Staininghe* DB, *Steyninges* 1211–40
Stainland YW (*PNYW* 3.49; *SSNY* 138; *DEPN* 436)
    i. *Stanland* DB ii. *Staineland* C13
Stainmore We (*PNWe* 2.71; *SSNNW* 193; *DEPN* 436)
    i. *Stanmoir c.* 990 ii. *Steinmor(e) c.* 1230, 1279
Stainton L (*PNL* 6.110–11; *SSNEM* 187; *DEPN* 436)
    i. *Stantone* DB ii. *Staintone* DB, *Steintuna* 1115–18
Stainton (Upper Strafforth) YW (*PNYW* 1.130; *SSNY* 113; *DEPN* 436)
    i. *Stantone* DB ii. *Staintone* DB
Stainton by Langworth L (*SSNEM* 187; *DEPN* 436)
    i. *Stantone c.* 1125 ii. *Staintvne* DB, *Steintuna* 1115–18
Stancill YW (*PNYW* 1.60; *SSNY* 89)
    i. *Stansale* [1199] 1232 ii. *Steineshale* DB
Standroyd La (*PNLa* 87; *SSNNW* 193)
    i. *Stanrede* 1465, *Stanrode* 1539 ii. *Staynrode* 1540
Stansfield YW (*PNYW* 3.177; *SSNY* 139; *DEPN* 438)
    i. *Stanesfelt* DB ii. *Staynsfeld* 1246
Staunton Harold Lei (*SSNEM* 207; *DEPN* 440)
    i. *Stantone* DB ii. *Stainton c.* 1291
Stenigot L (*SSNEM* 207; *DEPN* 441)
    i. *Stangehou* DB, *Staningho* 1185 ii. *Stainigot* 1212, *Steiningho* 1234

Stenwith L (*SSNEM* 207; *DEPN* 441)
    i. *Stanuuald* DB   ii. *Steinwad* 1185–86, *Steinwath* 1212
Stonegrave YN (*PNYN* 55; *SSNY* 166; *DEPN* 446)
    i. *Staningagraue* [757–58] C11, *Stanegrif* DB   ii. *Steinegrif* DB
Wigston Parva Lei (*SSNEM* 207; *DEPN* 518)
    i. *Wicgestane* [c. 1002] C11, *Wicestan* DB   ii. *Wiggestain* 1195

OE *stede* ('place, farm') replaced by cognate ON *staðr*
  Ganstead YE (*PNYE* 48; *SSNY* 145; *DEPN* 192)
    i. *Gaunstede* 1150–60, *Gagenstede* C13   ii. *Gagenestad* DB
  Winestead YE (*PNYE* 29; *SSNY* 150; *DEPN* 523)
    i. *Wifestede* DB   ii. *Wifestad* DB

OE *swān* ('herdsman') replaced by cognate ON *sveinn*
  Swanscoe Ch (*PNCh* 1.107; *SSNNW* 193)
    i. *Swanneshogh* 1357   ii. *Swainnehooh* [1357] 1620

OE *tord* ('dung') replaced by cognate Old Danish *torth*
  Torworth Nt (*PNNt* 100; *SSNEM* 215; *DEPN* 478)[12]
    i. *Tvrdeworde* DB, *Tordewrth* C13   ii. *Torthewrthe* 1209

OE *þorn* ('thorn') replaced by related ON *þyrnir*
  Thornby Nth (*PNNth* 74–75; *SSNEM* 14; *DEPN* 467)
    i. *Torneberie* DB   ii. *Thirnebi* c. 1160, *Turneby* 1220

OE dat.pl. -*um* confused with OE *hām* and replaced by cognate ON *heimr*
  Holtham L (*SSNEM* 208)
    i. *Odham* [c. 1150] 1409   ii. *Odheim* [c. 1150] 1409

OE (Anglian) *wald* ('woodland') replaced by ON *vað* ('ford')
  Prestwold Lei (*SSNEM* 209; *DEPN* 374)
    i. *Presteuuald* DB   ii. *Presteswad* c. 1155–90
  Stenwith L (*SSNEM* 207, 208–09; *DEPN* 441)
    i. *Stanuuald* DB   ii. *Steinwad* 1185–86

OE *ward* ('beacon') replaced by cognate ON *varða*
  Warthill YN (*PNYN* 11; *SSNY* 259; *DEPN* 499)
    i. *Wardhille* DB   ii. *Warthehill* 1295

---

[12]Some forms also suggest confusion with the Old Norse personal name *Þórðr*: e.g. *Thordeswrð* 1200, *Thordworth* 1232.

OE (Anglian) *wēt* ('wet') replaced by cognate ON *vátr*
    Watton YE (*PNYE* 158; *SSNY* 167; *DEPN* 501)
        i. *Wæta dun* [*c*. 890] C11 ii. *Wattvne, Watun* DB

OE *wīc* ('farm') replaced by ON *viðr* ('wood')
    Barwick YW (*PNYW* 4.106; *SSNY* 142; *DEPN* 29)
        i. *Baruica* 1137–39, *Berewic* C13 ii. *Bereuuith* DB
    Bubwith YE (*PNYE* 239; *SSNY* 144; *DEPN* 71)
        i. *Bubbewych* 1279–81 ii. *Bubvid* DB, *Bobewyth* [1066–69] *c*. 1300
    Butterwick YE (*PNYE* 114; *SSNY* 144; DEPN 79)
        i. *Butreuic* C12 ii. *Butruid* DB
    Cottingwith YE (*PNYE* 237; *SSNY* 144; *DEPN* 125)
        i. *Cottingwic* 1157 ii. *Coteuuid* DB, *Cotingwith* 1100–15
    Kilnwick YE (*PNYE* 160; *SSNY* 148; *DEPN* 276)
        i. *Killingwic* C12, *Kilnewic* 1226 ii. *Chilewid* DB
    Skipwith YE (*PNYE* 262; *SSNY* 138, 149; *DEPN* 425)
        i. *Schipewic* DB ii. *Schipwyth* C12, *Skipwith* 1291

OE *widu, wudu* ('wood') replaced by cognate ON *viðr*
    Beckwith YW (*PNYW* 5.116; *SSNY* 153; *DEPN* 34)
        i. *bec wudu* [972] C11 ii. *Beck(e)with* 1301 etc.
    South Bramwith YW (*PNYW* 1.13; *SSNY* 154; *DEPN* 60)
        i. *Branuuode* DB ii. *Branuuithe* DB
    Withcall L (*SSNEM* 162–63; *DEPN* 527)
        i. *Widcale* DB ii. *Wythecalla* [*c*. 1155] 1409
    Withern L (*SSNEM* 215; *DEPN* 527)
        i. *Widerne* DB ii. *Withern* 1210

OE personal name *Winuc* replaced by ON personal name *Vikingr*
    Winksley YW (*PNYW* 5.195; *SSNY* 168; *DEPN* 524)
        i. *Wincheslaie* DB ii. *Wichingeslei* DB

OE *wurm, wyrm* ('serpent') or personal name *Wurm* replaced by cognate ON *urm* or personal name *Urm*, a side-form of *ormr*
    Urmston La (*PNLa* 37; *SSNNW* 191; *DEPN* 488)
        i. *Wermeston* 1194, *Wurmeston* 1219 ii. *Urmeston* 1212

Note

In addition to the above instances of lexical substitution, a number of place-names show cognate phonemic substitution in one phoneme, usually where an Old English word is without an Old Norse cognate. The following phonemic substitutions are therefore evidenced in the following names (pre- as well as post-Scandinavianisation forms are not extant for all these names, and hence citations have not been given, but there can be no doubt of the substitution involved as a semantically meaningless name is usually the result):

(1) OE (Anglian) *ē* replaced by ON *á*
   OE (Anglian) *cēse* ('cheese'): Casewick L (*SSNEM* 213; *DEPN* 89)

(2) OE /d/ replaced by ON /ð/
   OE *brād* ('broad'): Bradley Cu (*PNCu* 229; *SSNNW* 193)
   OE **clūder* ('mass of rocks or debris'): Clotherholme YW (*PNYW* 5.163; *SSNY* 138; *DEPN* 113)
   OE *hod* ('shelter'): Hotham YE (*PNYE* 225–26; *SSNY* 147; *DEPN* 252)
   OE *loddere* ('beggar'): Lothersdale YW (*PNYW* 6.31; *SSNY* 138; *DEPN* 305)
   OE *mǣd* ('meadow'): Fonaby L (*PNL* 2.88–89; *SSNEM* 46–47)
   OE *tāde, tadde* ('frog, toad'): Tathwell L (*SSNEM* 222; *DEPN* 461)

(3) OE /j/ replaced by ON /g/
   OE people-name **Gētlingas* (< OE personal name **Gētla*): Gilling YN (*PNYN* 288–89; *SSNY* 146; *DEPN* 196)
   OE personal name *Gikel* (< biblical name *Judichael*): Giggleswick YW (*PNYW* 6.144; *SSNY* 145–46; *DEPN* 195)

(4) OE /ʃ/ replaced by ON /sk/
   OE *biscop* ('bishop'): Biscathorpe L (*SSNEM* 103–04; *DEPN* 45), Bustabeck Cu (*PNCu* 244–45; *SSNNW* 221)
   OE *(ge)mǣnscipe* ('community'): Minskip YW (*PNYW* 5.85; *SSNY* 138; *DEPN* 327)
   OE *mersc* ('marsh'): Saltmarske YE (*PNYE* 254; *SSNY* 138; *DEPN* 403)
   OE *riscen, ryscen* ('rushy'): Riskenton L (*SSNEM* 185), Ruskington L (*SSNEM* 185; *DEPN* 397)
   OE *sc(e)ald* ('shallow'): Scaldwell Nth (*PNNth* 131; *SSNEM* 220; *DEPN* 406), Scalford Lei (*SSNEM* 220; *DEPN* 406)
   OE *sc(e)amol* ('bench, stall; shelf of land, ledge on river-bank'): Scamblesby L (*SSNEM* 66–67; *DEPN* 406)
   OE (Anglian) *scēp* ('sheep'): Scopwick L (*SSNEM* 215; *DEPN* 408)
   OE *scēat* ('corner of land, projecting piece of land'): Sketteclyff Lei (*SSNEM* 227–28)
   OE (Anglian) **scēne-helde* ('beautiful slope'): Skendleby L (*SSNEM* 69; *DEPN* 424)
   OE *scinna* ('demon'): Skinburness Cu (*PNCu* 294; *SSNNW* 249–50; *DEPN* 425)
   OE (Northumbrian) *scīp* ('sheep'): Skibeden YW (*PNYW* 6.73; *SSNY* 165; *DEPN* 230), Skiprigg Cu (*PNCu* 135; *SSNNW* 250), Skipton YW (*PNYW* 6.71; *SSNY* 138; *DEPN* 425), Skipton on Swale YN (*PNYN* 186; *SSNY* 117; *DEPN* 425), Skipwith YE (*PNYE* 263; *SSNY* 138, 149; *DEPN* 425)

OE *scipen* ('cow-shed'): Shippen YW (*PNYW* 4.109; *SSNY* 138; *DEPN* 418)
OE *scīr* ('shire'): Shirley Db (*PNDb* 599; *SSNEM* 207; *DEPN* 418), Skirlington YE (*PNYE* 80; *SSNY* 117; *DEPN* 425), Skirwith Cu (*PNCu* 242–43; *SSNNW* 250; *DEPN* 425), Skyrack YW (*PNYW* 4.88–89; *SSNY* 138)
OE *scīr-gerēfa* ('sheriff'): Screveton Nt (*PNNt* 229; *SSNEM* 186; *DEPN* 409)
OE people-name **Scīrhēahingas* (< OE personal name **Scīrhēah*): Scrayingham YE (*PNYE* 147; *SSNY* 149; *DEPN* 408)
OE *scræf* ('cave'): West Scrafton YN (*PNYN* 255; *SSNY* 117; *DEPN* 408)
OE *scrēad* ('shred'): Scredington L (*SSNEM* 186; *DEPN* 408–09)
OE **screfen* ('hollow place with pits'): Scriven YW (*PNYW* 5.114; *SSNY* 163; *DEPN* 409)
OE *scrīc* ('missel-thrush'): Shrigley Park Ch (*PNCh* 1.130–31; *SSNNW* 193; *DEPN* 420)
OE *scrōf* ('hollow, side of hollow, cutting'): Scrooby Nt (*PNNt* 96; *SSNEM* 67–68; *DEPN* 409)
OE personal name **Scyttel*: Shitlington YW (*PNYW* 2.205; *SSNY* 117; *DEPN* 419)

(5) OE /tʃ/ replaced by ON /k/
OE *brēc* ('breaking up, land broken up for cultivation'): Breaks We (*PNWe* 2.89; *SSNNW* 218)
OE (Anglian) *cælc*, *celc* ('cup') (< Latin *calix*): Kelfield L (*SSNEM* 226–27; *DEPN* 270), Kelfield YE (*PNYE* 266; *SSNY* 159; *DEPN* 270)
OE (Anglian) **celc* ('chalk'): Kelk (Great and Little) YE (*PNYE* 92; *SSNY* 159; *DEPN* 270)
OE (Anglian) *celf* ('calf'): Kilpin YE (*PNYE* 252; *SSNY* 148; *DEPN* 276)
OE personal name *Ceolla*: Kellington YW (*PNYW* 2.59; *SSNY* 116; *DEPN* 270)
OE (Anglian) *cēse* ('cheese'): Casewick L (*SSNEM* 213; *DEPN* 89), Dunkeswick YW (*PNYW* 5.50–51; *SSNY* 147; *DEPN* 153), East Keswick YW (*PNYW* 4.184; *SSNY* 147; *DEPN* 273), Keswick Cu (*PNCu* 301; *SSNNW* 203; *DEPN* 273)
OE *cild* ('child, young man'): Kilby Lei (*SSNEM* 56; *DEPN* 275), Kildwick YW (*PNYW* 6.18; *SSNY* 148; *DEPN* 275), Kilsby Nth (*PNNth* 25; *SSNEM* 56–57; *DEPN* 276), Kilton YN (*PNYN* 143; *SSNY* 116; *DEPN* 276)

CHAPTER 4

Anglo-Norse Contact in Anglo-Saxon Sources

The previous chapter examined the Scandinavianisation of Old English place-names and, drawing on Hockett's concept of a 'switching-code' in dialect intelligibility, concluded that this material suggests that, on the whole, English words and names were consistently intelligible to Norse speakers in England. Arguably, therefore, this should now be complemented by a corresponding study of the Anglicisation of Norse names, employing a similarly substantial, and coherent, body of evidence. However, this will not be attempted here in any systematic manner, for the simple reason that no such comparable corpus is readily available. With regard to place-names, records show a far greater frequency of English names being Scandinavianised than vice versa. This is no doubt due to the fact that such processes tend to occur only when a new speech community arrives and adapts to its own uses the pre-existing nomenclature of another speech community; and therefore in Viking Age England the changes, naturally enough, are in the direction of Scandinavianisation. With regard to personal names, on the other hand, there has already been considerable study of the Norse names recorded in English documents, and part of such study necessarily involves a consideration of phonological and morphological form. The important landmarks in the study of Norse anthroponymy in England are basically three: Erik Björkman's ground-breaking work of 1910, Gillian Fellows-Jensen's 1968 study of Norse personal names in Lincolnshire and Yorkshire, and John Insley's 1994 corpus of Norse personal names in Norfolk. Especially important in the present context is Fellows-Jensen's systematic analysis of the phonology and morphology of the Norse names in the English sources from which she draws her corpus (1968, lxvii–cviii); reference should also be made here to Olof von Feilitzen's study of the Domesday Book material (1937, esp. 18–26).

It is of course also true that the Norse loanwords in English have received a good deal of detailed attention, especially those from the Old English period (that is, at the time of Anglo-Norse contact); but for the most part discussion of this material will be postponed until Chapter 6. In contrast to the previous one, therefore, this chapter will approach the subject in a manner that is text-specific rather than topic-specific, and will concern itself with the whole range of issues involved in 'Anglo-Norse language contact', rather than just the narrower question of possible intelligibility; this seems the most profitable line of approach from the English-speaking side. Inevitably, therefore, the study of language contact will at various points shade into that of cultural contact more generally. For this purpose three Anglo-Saxon texts have been selected which are conspicuously fertile ground for investigating Anglo-Norse contact, namely 'The Voyages of Ohthere and Wulfstan' in the Old English Orosius, Æthelweard's Latin *Chronicle*, and Ælfric's homily *De Falsis Diis*, later adapted by Wulfstan. In terms of date, therefore, the Orosius derives from the reign of Alfred in the late ninth century, while the other two works are from the reign of Æthelred in the late tenth; other Anglo-Saxon texts which would no doubt repay similar study include Aldred's glosses to the Lindisfarne Gospels and the *Historia de Sancto Cuthberto* (for discussion of Norse-derived features in Aldred's work see Ross 1940; Hofmann 1955, 167–81 (§§232–54); Stanley 1988, 320–23; Hines 1991, 409–13; Pons Sanz 2000). These three works will therefore be successively combed as closely as possible for information relating to Anglo-Norse language contact; in particular it is information of a philological type which will be considered most closely in this chapter, while more purely anecdotal evidence will be treated later in Chapter 5.

'The Voyages of Ohthere and Wulfstan' in the Old English Orosius

The seafaring additions made to the first, geographical chapter of the Old English translation of Orosius's *Historiarum adversum Paganos Libri Septem* are, of course, among the best-known passages of Old English prose. Customarily known as 'The Voyages of Ohthere and Wulfstan', the text has received an extraordinary amount of attention, and as Eric Stanley observed over twenty years ago, 'whoever is foolhardy enough to attempt a reconsideration of even a small part of this text must labour under the great weight of accumulated scholarship dealing with it' (1977, 2). These seafaring additions have been analysed for all sorts of different purposes, and many of the explicatory publications make beguiling reading, as distinguished medievalists pore over Admiralty charts, thumb the pages of the *White Sea Pilot*, and submit their theories to the higher wisdom of Hull fishermen (best of all are the expeditions recorded in Ross 1954). In other words, the great majority of publications on 'The Voyages of Ohthere and Wulfstan' are on matters extraliterary and extralinguistic. For present purposes, however, the passage is to be approached with one relatively narrow object alone: what can this text reveal about Anglo-Norse language contact in the reign of Alfred? Fortunately, as Tolkien noted in his O'Donnell Lecture of 1955, it is clear that an interest in linguistic issues was in fact one of the enthusiasms that prompted Alfred in his discussion with Ohthere (1963, 22 n.1), and also that some degree of linguistic aptitude was one of Ohthere's talents. Thus during his stay with the *Beormas*, Ohthere evidently learnt enough of their language to listen to stories and to make philological assessments of neighbouring languages (Bately 1980, 14.27–30 (references are to page and line)):

> Fela spella him sædon þa Beormas ægþer ge of hiera agnum lande ge of þæm landum þe ymb hie utan wæron, ac he nyste hwæt þæs soþes wæs, for þæm he hit self ne geseah. Þa Finnas, him þuhte, ⁊ þa Beormas spræcon neah an geþeode.

> (The *Beormas* told him many stories both about their own land and about the lands which surrounded them, but he did not know how much of it was true, because he did not see for himself. It seemed to him that the *Finnas* and the *Beormas* spoke almost the same language.)

In terms of Anglo-Norse language contact, the first thing to note is that the usual conception of the passage as a single item, 'The Voyages of Ohthere and Wulfstan', disguises the fact that we are dealing with two distinct situations. The Ohthere section concerns a Scandinavian in England, whereas the Wulfstan section concerns an Englishman in Scandinavia. And although the reports of these two seafarers are presented together, there is nothing in the text to suggest that both of them came before Alfred at the same time — indeed, it is never stated that Wulfstan came before Alfred at all, and it is conceivable that his information could have been derived via someone else in the king's circle (and hence it was able to be incorporated in the Orosius at a relevant point in its composition or editing). Furthermore, linguistic differences between the two accounts would indeed seem to indicate that these passages have been worked into the Orosius from separate sources. That Ohthere's account concludes in Hedeby, and Wulfstan's commences there, does not mean that one long voyage is being described in two parts, nor that Ohthere and Wulfstan encountered one another in Hedeby, and there handed over the baton in some sort of geographical relay. Ohthere's nightly anchorage between *Hālgoland* and *Scīringesheal* contrasts with Wulfstan's continuous sailing from *Scīringesheal* to *Trūsō*, and indicates that the two voyages were undertaken in different types of vessel (see Crumlin-Pedersen 1984), and Wulfstan's account takes over from Ohthere's at Hedeby simply in order to give an encyclopaedic record of trade routes in that part of northern Europe. It is for this very purpose that the two accounts have been brought together in the first, geographical chapter of the Old English Orosius, and there is no duplication between the two for the same reason. We thus have two separate sources juxtaposed, from seafarers of two different nationalities.

Ohthere himself tells us that he was Norwegian, from the area of Hålogaland: 'Ohthere sæde þæt sio scir hatte Halgoland þe he on bude' (Bately 1980, 16.1) ('Ohthere said that the region in which he lived was called *Hālgoland*'). The form of his name, *Ōhthere*, represents the usual Old English form of *Óttarr*, a fairly common Old Norse personal name (see Lind 1905–15, 824–25). The *Anglo-Saxon Chronicle*, for example, records two jarls of that name as having fought in Mercia in the early tenth century (MSS 'BCD' *sub annis* 911, 915, MS 'A' *sub anno* 914; see Björkman 1910, 104; Lehiste 1958, 15; for the occurrence of the name in other, later English sources see also Fellows-Jensen 1968, 207–08). The name also features five times in *Beowulf*, where it is borne by the son of the Swedish king Ongenþēow, and therefore it is possible that the familiarity of this name to the Anglo-Saxons may have influenced the form it takes here. The etymology of ON *Óttarr* seems to be *óhta-herr 'fear + army' ('terrifying army'?). According to Noreen (1923, 195 (§267)), the assimilation *ht* > *tt* had occurred by 900 in Old West Norse, and Seip dates it to before 800 (1955, 28), but Eduard Kolb has used the evidence of Norse loanwords in English (such as OE *saht* < ON *sátt* ('reconciliation'), and OE *ridesoht* < ON *riðusótt* ('fever')) to argue that these datings are too early: in his view the change 'cannot have been general in Scandinavia before the middle of the 10th century' (1962, 310). It is therefore probable that the English and Norse forms of the first element of the name would have been identical at the time of Alfred; while in the second element OE *Ōhthere* shows substitution of cognate OE *here* for ON *herr*.[1]

As a Norwegian, Ohthere's presence at Alfred's court can therefore be profitably viewed in the light of Asser's well-known passage on the kindness of the English king towards foreigners who submitted to him:[2]

> Eleemosynarum quoque *studio et largitati indigenis et advenis omnium gentium, ac maxima et incomparabili contra omnes homines* affabilitate atque iocunditate, *et* ignotarum rerum investigationi solerter *se iungebat*. Franci autem multi, Frisones, Galli, pagani, Britones, et Scotti, Armorici sponte se suo dominio subdiderant, nobiles scilicet et ignobiles. (Stevenson 1904, 59–60 (Chapter 76))

> (He similarly applied himself attentively to charity and distribution of alms to the native population and to foreign visitors of all races, showing immense and incomparable kindness and generosity to all men, as well as to the investigation of things unknown. Wherefore many Franks, Frisians, Gauls, Vikings, Welshmen, Irishmen and Bretons subjected themselves willingly to his lordship, nobles and commoners alike. (Keynes and Lapidge 1983, 91))

Alfred's *dominium* is of course the very note on which Ohthere's account begins: 'Ohthere sæde his hlaforde, Ælfrede cyninge' (Bately 1980, 13.29) ('Ohthere said to his lord, King Alfred').[3] And from the statement that 'þa teð hie brohton sume þæm

---

[1] A number of the *Anglo-Saxon Chronicle* forms, however, show in their second element assimilation of the *h* to the preceding *t*, resulting in *Ohter*.

[2] The opprobrious term here for Scandinavians, *pagani*, is the usual one among Anglo-Latin writers, corresponding to OE *hǣðen* (see further pp 173–74 below).

[3] For a discussion of precisely what kind of relationship this term might indicate see Lund 1987, 260, and 1984, 13; as Whiting drily notes, it is not likely to be 'a polite expression of gratitude for temporary hospitality' (1945, 221).

cyninge' (Bately 1980, 14.32–15.1) ('They brought some teeth [of the walrus] to the king') it is clear — as one would expect — that Ohthere did not come to Alfred's court as a solitary Norwegian, but that others of his compatriots (retainers?) came with him.[4]

The nationality of Wulfstan is not so obvious, as his origins are not announced in the way that Ohthere's are. The seemingly automatic assumption in the late nineteenth and early twentieth century was that he was a Scandinavian, like Ohthere (see for example Stevenson 1904, 300–01; Collingwood 1908, 100), and OE *Wulfstān* might indeed represent an Anglicisation of ON *Úlfsteinn*. But although ON *úlfr* and *steinn* are both common name elements, the personal name *Úlfsteinn* is not in fact found in Norse records.[5] As an Old English name, on the other hand, *Wulfstān* is extremely common and was borne by a number of (very) distinguished Anglo-Saxons (Searle 1897, 518–19). Furthermore, as W. A. Craigie (1925) pointed out, the account of Wulfstan's voyage (present only in London, BL, MS Cotton Tiberius B.i) contains a conspicuous number of Anglian dialect features otherwise absent from the early West Saxon of the Orosius. The most important of these are uncontracted forms of the 3rd person singular present tense (for example, *cymeð*, *hafað*, *rideð*, as against West Saxon *cymð*, *hæfð*, *ritt*) and Back Mutation in the place-name *Weonodland* (four occurrences; West Saxon *Winodland* only once).[6] Craigie further argues that the use in Wulfstan's account of the 1st person plural pronoun, absent in Ohthere's account, suggests verbatim copying by a scribe, rather than the slightly stilted recording due to a question-and-answer format that seems to have been the case with Ohthere. In examining this issue more recently, Christine Fell has also commented on the much greater fluency of Wulfstan's account, suggesting, she believes, a native speaker of Old English (1984, 57). In other words, there seems now to be a consensus that the evidence points to Wulfstan being an Anglo-Saxon rather than a Scandinavian, and probably an Anglian at that.[7] The following discussion accepts this conclusion.

---

[4]As to the possible year in which Ohthere came to Alfred's court, see in particular Malone 1930a; Whiting 1945; and (summing up) Bately 1980, lxxxvii–lxxxix. The question must be left open.

[5]Lind 1905–15, 957, lists Old Norse compound names with -*steinn* as their second element: *Úlfsteinn* does not feature. In English sources one finds one occurrence each of *Ulstan* and *Wulstain* (Searle 1897, 468, 520; Fellows-Jensen 1968, 327): these would therefore seem to be distinctively Anglo-Scandinavian forms (that is, perhaps, examples of an Old English name appropriated by Norse speakers in England).

[6]However, for a rather lukewarm response to Craigie's theory see Gordon 1927b, 81. For a number of further linguistic features which differentiate the accounts of Ohthere and Wulfstan see Bately 1980, lxxii; Cuesta and Silva 2000, 20–22.

[7]Thus Alan Binns, for example, characterises him as 'probably a northern Englishman' (1980, 41). Only Alan Ross in recent years has argued for a Scandinavian origin for Wulfstan. He points out that the name is recorded once in Danish sources as *Ulstanus* (a twelfth-century priest in Lund; see also Odenstedt 1994, 156–57 n.2), and that the form in the Orosius of OE

In terms of Anglo-Norse contact, therefore, Ohthere's account gives us a Scandinavian in England, in conversation with an English king; Wulfstan's account, on the other hand, gives us an Englishman in Scandinavia, later retelling his experiences to an English audience (either Alfred himself or another of his circle). If one predicates the notion that speakers of Norse and English were adequately intelligible in the Viking Age, then Ohthere's account in the Old English Orosius represents an English record of a Norse exposition; Wulfstan's account remains an English record of an English exposition. Developing this further, one could therefore say that in Ohthere's account all aspects of the language are potentially informative on the question of Anglo-Norse contact; in Wulfstan's account this is true only of aspects in which the earlier Anglo-Norse contact (that is, in Scandinavia) is likely to have been encoded or preserved — specifically, perhaps, terminology for unfamiliar items and (most of all) names.

How far are we justified in regarding the Orosius accounts as dependable records of what Ohthere and Wulfstan actually said? The answer one gives to this question effectively turns on the faith of the investigator, since, beyond certain obvious generalities, little can be said either way. The fact that some form of editing has occurred is indicated by the structure of the passage, with Ohthere's account ending at Hedeby, and Wulfstan's beginning there; and Christine Fell has demonstrated persuasively that what we have in Ohthere's account is only one half of a question-and-answer interview (1982–83, 95, and 1984).[8] But even bearing in mind these facts, it remains true that the language of Ohthere and Wulfstan's accounts differs conspicuously not only from each other, but also from the language of the rest of the Orosius (for a list and discussion of these distinguishing features see Bately 1980, lxxii). Furthermore, both passages begin with the claim to represent indirect speech.[9] So while the notion of an 'undoctored transcript' (Cassidy and Ringler 1971, 191) is clearly going much too far (the very switch from 1st to 3rd person narrative would indicate as much), it seems reasonable to believe that the passages are honest and dependable attempts by one or more scribes to record what was said, and that at least some distinctive linguistic features may plausibly be attributed to the speech of Ohthere and Wulfstan.

This brings us to the central question: how did Ohthere say to his lord, King Alfred, what he did say? Did he speak Norse or English, or was an interpreter used? (And indeed, in what language was Ohthere addressed?) At this point, I shall

---

Este is best explained by the assumption 'that Wulfstan was a Dane' (1978, 102). However, he at once goes on to acknowledge, 'Of course other hypotheses are possible. For instance, Wulfstan may have been English and may have heard the name from Danes.'

[8]Janet Bately agrees, but would also — mistakenly, I think — regard Wulfstan's account in the same way (1988, 119).

[9]'Ohthere sæde his hlaforde, Ælfrede cyninge, þæt [. . .]' (Bately 1980, 13.29) ('Ohthere said to his lord, King Alfred, that [. . .]'); 'Wulfstan sæde þæt [. . .]' (Bately 1980, 16.21) ('Wulfstan said that [. . .]').

observe simply that no interpreter is mentioned,[10] and that the many Norse features found in the English of Ohthere's account (see below) must mean either that he was speaking Norse, or that, if speaking English, his English was influenced by his native language. Full discussion of this must be postponed for the moment, and ultimately it needs to be fitted into a general model of Anglo-Norse communication; however, it is worth noting here the opinions of the two most important commentators on the language of the Ohthere and Wulfstan passages. Janet Bately writes (1980, lxxi), 'Whether he [i.e. Ohthere] spoke English or used the services of an interpreter is uncertain, though in the ninth century comprehension between Anglo-Saxon and Norseman should have provided no great difficulty'. And Christine Fell comments (1984, 56–57),

> The two languages were at this date still moderately close, close enough for a number of simple words and constructions to sound fairly similar. [...] Clearly Ohthere may have been using an interpreter, but the evidence of the text is I think against it. [...] The text carries in itself the implications both of the questions behind the answers, and of the occasional fumbling for words which hesitant communication would necessitate.

Norse Influence on the Language of Ohthere's Account

A number of linguistic features in Ohthere's account require notice, as the text contains several loans, loan-translations, and semantic loans from Old Norse. Fell's 1984 study is by far the most important discussion of these 'questions of language', and a number of her observations will simply be relayed here:

(1) *Hranas* (both as a simplex and as the second element of the obscure *stælhranas*) represents a loan from ON *hreinar* 'reindeer (pl.)' (Bately 1980, 15.9, 10, 11, 15),[11] while the manner in which the word is introduced indicates its unfamiliarity to an English audience ('Þa deor hi hatað hranas' (Bately 1980, 15.9) ('They call those animals *hrānas*')). *Hrānas* shows phonemic substitution of cognate OE *ā* for ON *ei*, suggesting that even at this early point of contact an adequate switching-code had been established: this might serve to confirm Asser's statement concerning the frequency of Scandinavians at Alfred's court, or else perhaps that Ohthere's sojourn there was not of a fleeting nature.

(2) *Horshwæl* (Bately 1980, 14.31) almost certainly represents a loan-translation from ON *hrosshvalr* ('walrus'), though conceivably it could be a loan-translation based on a mishearing (in the first element) of ON *rosmhvalr*. Again the unfamiliarity of the word to an English audience is indicated by Ohthere's gloss that 'Se hwæl bið micle læssa þonne oðre hwalas: ne bið he lengra ðonne syfan elna lang' (Bately 1980, 15.2–3) ('This whale is much smaller than other whales: it is no larger than seven ells in length'); and again *horshwæl*, like *hranas*, passes Hockett's test

---

[10] On references to interpreters in Anglo-Saxon England see pp 161–71 below.

[11] ME *raynedere* is a later borrowing (see Björkman 1900–02, 48).

for the evidence of a switching-code (1987, 43), showing as it does cognate lexical substitution of OE *hors* ('horse') for ON *hross* and OE *hwæl* ('whale') for ON *hvalr*.

(3) *Unfriþ* (Bately 1980, 14.19) is likely to be a loan-translation from ON *ófrið* ('lack of permission'), though arguably the two words would have been identical in the Viking Age.[12] Fell (1982-83) has discussed this word in detail, and the translation is hers.

(4) *Æþele* is likely to be a semantic loan in this context ('hie habbað swiþe æþele ban on hiora toþum' (Bately 1980, 14.32) ('They [i.e. walruses] have very *æþele* bone in their teeth')). Fell argues that OE *æþele* 'is most commonly used of people in the sense 'noble', and is more rarely used of inanimate things', whereas ON *aðal* 'is used as the first element of many compounds where its implication is "foremost" or "most important" and it is possible that the implication of Ohthere's statement is that he had located the best quality material' (1984, 61).

(5) *Kyrtel* (Bately 1980, 15.19) is probably another semantic loan (or misunderstanding), since in Old English the word most frequently indicates a full-length woman's dress, whereas in Old Norse a *kyrtill* is a short jacket worn by men; it is this latter meaning which is applicable here (see further Fell 1984, 62).

(6) In Fell's view there is also some evidence of the need for Ohthere to employ circumlocutions in order to clarify his use of Old Norse words which did not have cognates in Old English; in particular it is suggested that the second alternative in 'þa beag þæt land þær eastryhte, oþþe seo sæ in on þæt lond, he nysse hwæðer' (Bately 1980, 14.11-12; see also 14.16) ('Then the land turned due east there, or the sea in on the land, he did not know which') is Ohthere's attempt at explaining the meaning of ON *fjǫrðr* ('inlet, fjord') — as Fell notes, this is indeed 'a word without which Norwegians would be at a considerable loss in describing their own environment' (1984, 57).

Other observations on the language of Ohthere's account can be added:[13]

(7) *Eastewe(a)rd* (Bately 1980, 15.25, 26) has also been suggested as a semantic loan or misunderstood term (see Craigie 1917, 201). Part of Ohthere's description of Norway is as follows (Bately 1980, 15.24-29):

---

[12] Denasalisation in the Old Norse negative prefix (*un- > ú- > ó-*) appears to have occurred post-1000.

[13] In the following catalogue I have rejected *ambyrne* as a possible loan from Old Norse (Bately 1980, 16.5; presumed nominative *ambyre*). While some older commentators have connected it with a Modern Icelandic *andbyrr* ('contrary wind') (and Binns 1980, 39, also seems to entertain the idea), it is clear from its context (and also from the one other occurrence of a related word in Ælfric) that the meaning must be 'favourable' rather than 'unfavourable', and that the word is a native one, with intensifying *an-* prefix (see further Bately 1980, 193; Ekwall 1943; Bammesberger 1983). However, since OE **ambyre* is thus without an Old Norse cognate, it must be regarded as a word introduced by the Orosius scribe/editor, in clarification of what Ohthere said: but this is not a problem, as there are undoubtedly a number of other words like this, such as *hryðera* ('cattle'), and *scir* ('district') (Bately 1980, 15.12, 16.1).

On þæm morum eardiað Finnas. ꝛ þæt byne land is easteweard bradost ꝛ symle swa norðor swa smælre; eastewerd hit mæg bion syxtig mila brad oþþe hwene brædre, ꝛ middewerd þritig oððe bradre; ꝛ norðeweard, he cwæð, þær hit smalost wære, þæt hit mihte beon þreora mila brad.

(The *Finnas* live in the mountains; and the cultivated land is widest *easteweard*, and progressively narrower the further north; *eastewerd* it may be sixty miles wide or a little wider, and in the middle thirty or wider; and in the north, he said, it was the narrowest, so that it might be three miles wide.)

This description, though, only makes sense if *eastewe(a)rd* here means not 'in the east (of Norway)' but rather 'in the south (of Norway)' — in other words, if it has the same meaning as the Old Norse phrase *austr í Vík*.

(8) The usual Old English verb 'to sail' is *(ge)seglian*, and this is found four times in Ohthere's account (Bately 1980, 16.4, 6, 13, 15). However, one also finds *(ge)siglan* six times (Bately 1980, 14.11, 13, 14, 16, 17, 19). Bately, in her Orosius glossary, classifies *siglan* and *gesiglan* as Class 1 weak verbs, and *seglian* and *geseglian* as Class 2. This is plausible, but in fact *(ge)siglan* is found nowhere else in Old English, and so an alternative explanation is that the verb's form has been influenced by the cognate Old Norse verb *sigla*. It is certainly curious that all the *(ge)siglan* forms should come in one section of the account (the voyage to the land of the *Beormas*), and all the *(ge)seglian* forms in another (the voyage from *Halgoland* to *Sciringesheal*). Perhaps the English scribe changed his practice, switching from the Norse-influenced form to the normal Old English cognate; perhaps even this is evidence that we have the reports of two separate interviews brought together here.[14] (The verb 'to sail' does not occur in Wulfstan's account, and so no comparison can be made.)

(9) Though only an impression, it seems possible that there is a more frequent use of adverbial prepositions in Ohthere's account than in Wulfstan's, including in the form of phrasal verbs: for example, 'Ða læg þær an micel ea up in on þæt land' (Bately 1980, 14.17–18; see also 14.18–19, 16.10) ('Then a great river stretched up into the land there'), 'hy foð þa wildan hranas mid' (Bately 1980, 15.11) ('They catch the wild reindeer with [them]'). Old Norse of course had a much greater repertoire of phrasal verbs than Old English on account of early loss of prefixes, and many of those which one finds in Middle English are loans or loan-translations; it is therefore possible we may have reflections here of Ohthere's usage.

(10) It seems generally agreed among commentators on this passage that Ohthere's sailing directions and his specification of the points of the compass are based on Old Norse usage rather than Old English; what is not agreed is how exactly this

---

[14]It is noteworthy that each of the two voyages is introduced by the formula *Ohthere sæde*, just as Wulfstan's account is introduced by *Wulfstan sæde*. These are the only three occurrences of the personal names in the text.

works out in practice. The issue has generated a great deal of (often highly technical) literature; all that is important here is to note the agreed fact of Old Norse usage (to follow the discussion, see Malone 1930b; 1933; Ekblom 1939–40; 1960; Stokoe 1957; Binns 1961; 1980, 35–40; Derolez 1971; Jørgensen 1985; and (especially) Bately 1980, 179–99 (commentary on individual points)).

As noted earlier, the two possible explanations for this heavy Norse influence on the language of Ohthere's account are either that Ohthere had learned English and spoke a form of English influenced by his native Norse, or else that Ohthere spoke Norse at Alfred's court, and that the scribe, in making his notes, was at times influenced in his English by the Norwegian's language. Of the ten points enumerated above, several could be accounted for by either hypothesis, but a good number are probably more plausibly explained by the idea that Ohthere was speaking in his own native Norse: in particular (7), and also (4) and (5), would seem to be due to a mishearing or misunderstanding by Ohthere's scribal audience, and the cognate substitutions involved in (1) and (2) are better attributed to the Anglicising tendencies of scribes or hearers. In particular, the phonemic substitution in *hrānas* seems to demonstrate the phenomenon which was observed in the reverse English-to-Norse direction in Chapter 3, and which in Chapter 6 below will be termed 'recipient language agentivity'. At any rate, there is certainly no feature which cannot be satisfactorily accounted for by the 'intelligibility' hypothesis rather than the 'bilingualism' one, and the semantic misunderstandings would seem to preclude the idea of an interpreter being at work; as noted above, though, the interpretation of Ohthere's usage must ultimately be dependent on the overall picture of Anglo-Norse communication which emerges in the rest of this book.

At this stage, however, it is necessary to dwell further on the rejected possibility that an interpreter was employed in the course of Ohthere's account, and to engage at some length with a recent article that argues precisely this; for in 1994 Bengt Odenstedt presented a radically new theory concerning Ohthere and Wulfstan. Odenstedt's argument is essentially twofold, namely (1) that speakers of Norse and English in the Viking Age were mutually unintelligible, and so required interpreters to communicate, and (2) that Wulfstan was in fact Ohthere's interpreter. Odenstedt states his case as follows (1994, 148; unless otherwise stated, all italics are his):

> My theory implies that Wulfstan was not a sea-captain but *an interpreter who translated Ohthere's story* (which was of course in O[ld]Norw[egian]) *into OE*. I take the passage *Wulfstān sǣde þæt he gefōre of Hǣðum*, ... to mean 'Wulfstan (*the interpreter*) said that he (*Ohthere*) travelled from Hedeby, ...' I assume that during Ohthere's account at Alfred's court somebody took notes of the interpreter's translations. At one point this person made a mistake: instead of writing *Ohthere sǣde þæt he gefōre* ... (as he had done before) he happened to write *Wulfstān sǣde þæt he gefōre*, ... This is a very natural mistake — he was after all listening to the interpreter's, Wulfstan's, version of the story. He then carried on by referring to Ohthere as *he*, as he had done before. The scribe's mistake was not discovered by the 'editor' of the two stories; he might have thought (as modern people have done) that Wulfstan was another sea-captain!

In other words: If my theory is correct, what has generally been referred to as 'Wulfstan's voyage' is really the second part of Ohthere's voyage, from Hedeby to Estland.

This argument turns on a strange assumption, namely that the scribe of this passage never re-read his work or realised his error, and that no-one else who subsequently read or heard the translation of Orosius — including, one assumes, Alfred himself — was aware of this error, that Wulfstan was not a second seafarer. This is hard to believe, but even if one sets it to one side (for the sake of argument), there are a number of objections that must be made to Odenstedt's reasoning, and also various presuppositions which need querying and correcting in the light of the evidence assembled in the present work (for another response to Odenstedt, see Cuesta and Silva 2000):

(1) As noted above, it is clear that the voyage to Hedeby (by Ohthere), and the voyage from Hedeby (traditionally ascribed to Wulfstan) were undertaken in ships of different types, whereas Odenstedt assumes one continuous voyage.

(2) Odenstedt says nothing concerning Ohthere's designation of Alfred as his *hlāford*; as has been pointed out, though, this would seem to indicate that Ohthere had been at Alfred's court for some time, whereas Odenstedt's argument assumes a foreigner who is wholly unfamiliar with Old English and whose own language Alfred's Anglo-Saxon court is in turn wholly unfamiliar with.

(3) Odenstedt rejects the linguistic differences between the Old English of Ohthere's account and the Old English of Wulfstan's account, as catalogued by Craigie, Bately, and Fell. Rather he argues that so many stages must have intervened between mouth and manuscript that '[u]nder these circumstances it would be dangerous to claim that the differences we might find in the surviving versions of "O" [i.e. Ohthere's account] and "W" [i.e. Wulfstan's account] reflect differences in the original, oral versions' (Odenstedt 1994, 154). However, this fails to explain why errors or dialectal differences should consistently creep into one section and not the other, if (as Odenstedt argues) both texts come from the same source — are, in fact, only one text. Nor does it explain why one finds loans from Old Norse (as catalogued above) clustering in Ohthere's account, but not in Wulfstan's.

(4) As was also noted above, both Craigie and Fell remark on how the Ohthere passage seems to give us only one side of a question-and-answer style discussion (implying a slow, even stilted, probing for information from Ohthere), whereas the Wulfstan passage seems to be more fluent, and therefore a continuous discourse, presumably from a native speaker. Odenstedt does not observe this stylistic difference.

(5) One of the grounds cited by Craigie and Fell for their belief in (4) above is the presence of 1st person plural pronouns in the Wulfstan passage (as well as 3rd person singular), suggesting verbatim copying by a scribe, whereas one only finds 3rd person pronouns (singular and plural) in the Ohthere passage, suggesting a certain distance in the recording. Odenstedt notes that both passages employ both singular and plural pronouns and regards this as indicating their common origin

(1994, 154–55); he overlooks the fact that 1st person pronouns are found only in the Wulfstan passage.

(6) The main evidence that Odenstedt proffers in support of his belief that speakers of Norse and English were mutually unintelligible is a translation of ten lines of Ohthere's account into reconstructed Runic Swedish (1994, 149–52; for the ten lines selected see Bately 1980, 15.7–17). He compares the vocabulary of the two texts, and concludes that 'out of the 119 words in the OE text 50 [...] would not have been understood by a Scandinavian' (1994, 152). There are serious problems with this exercise, however. Firstly, it is clear that Odenstedt's reconstructed Norse text has no authority, in that as we do not know what exactly Ohthere said to Alfred, it seems unwise to argue a case on the basis of what one thinks he might have said. The Orosius text as we have it is in Old English and has clearly been edited by an Anglo-Saxon; not even the keenest proponent of Anglo-Norse intelligibility would want to argue that we have Ohthere's unadulterated *ipsissima verba* — for they would be Old Norse, not Old English. Secondly, Odenstedt is arguing the wrong way round: what his comparison is really testing is how much of the Old English Orosius passage would be immediately intelligible to a Scandinavian. Furthermore, the possibility that intelligibility may be non-reciprocal has clearly not been considered, as the quotation given above (counting 50 out of 119 words) continues thus: 'From this it follows *of course* that an Anglo-Saxon would not have understood the corresponding Scand[inavian] words' (1994, 152 (my italics)).

(7) In fact, Odenstedt's whole handling of the comparison of texts is faulty, as his criterion for what words would or would not be intelligible appears to be solely his own intuition. So, for example, he believes (for no stated reason) that Norse *ne hafði* would be unintelligible to an English speaker, whose own form would be *næfde*, and proceeds to calculate his figures on this basis. Most serious of all, though, is Odenstedt's wholesale neglect of the phenomenon of phonemic substitution — what is being termed in this book the operation of a switching-code. Therefore Odenstedt believes, for example, that English speakers would have been hard pressed to recognise ON *skip* ('ship') as corresponding to their own *scip*, or ON *konungr* ('king') to their own *cyning*, and would certainly not have recognised ON *húð* ('hide') as corresponding to their own *hȳde*. Odenstedt does note that OE *hrānas* must derive from ON *hreinar* ('reindeer'), thus indicating an awareness of the phonemic correspondence ON *ei* - OE *ā*, but he takes this as a sign that there must have been 'a clever interpreter at work' who 'had a good knowledge of both languages' (1994, 153). For Odenstedt, in other words, sounds must be identical to permit intelligibility, not cognate, whereas the thrust of the present investigation (and of contemporary intelligibility testing) is that intelligibility is likely to occur precisely when sounds are regularly cognate. This failure to appreciate the mechanisms of intelligibility largely invalidates Odenstedt's comparison of texts; and since this comparison is the main body of evidence to be offered, it would therefore seem to invalidate his case as a whole.

For all these reasons, therefore, Odenstedt's interpretation seems unpersuasive and even at times incoherent — both in the specific claim that Wulfstan was really

Ohthere's interpreter, and in the more important general claim that speakers of Norse and English were normally in need of interpreters in order to communicate. Therefore, there seem to be no reasonable grounds to reject the conclusion reached in the above discussion of Ohthere's language, namely that Ohthere was speaking Old Norse when he gave his geographical account at Alfred's court, and in doing so was, for the most part, effectively understood by his English-speaking audience.

Place- and People Names in Ohthere and Wulfstan's Accounts

Both Ohthere and Wulfstan's accounts are rich in the names of peoples and places; these will be listed and analysed here to see what patterns of adoption or adaptation emerge in the treatment of such names in the Old English text. All the names in Ohthere's account are of interest, since they must all derive from Ohthere himself; that is, these are names spoken by a Scandinavian and consequently written down by an Englishman. In Wulfstan's account, however, only Norse names are of potential evidential value, as it seems reasonable to assume — at least as a provisional theory — that the Englishman learnt these from the lips of native speakers during his travels in Scandinavia. It also seems likely that at least some of the names in the geography of Europe that precedes the seafarers' accounts have been derived from, or corroborated by, Ohthere and/or Wulfstan, and so these will be noted for comparison when the same name features in one of the two accounts (the geography is to be found in Bately 1980, 12.14–13.28). Presented alphabetically, the following gazetteer, then, is concerned solely with linguistic issues, and specifically with Anglo-Norse contact; ample guidance on geographical and historical issues has been provided elsewhere by Janet Bately and Niels Lund (see the Commentary in Bately 1980, 179–200, and the Notes in Lund 1984, 64–69).

(1) Names in Ohthere's account
Angle (Bately 1980, 16.14). In Ohthere's account this must be the region (Angeln) rather than the people: firstly, because it is in the dative following *betuh* (and so the people name would be *Anglum*, like the preceding *Winedum* and *Seaxum*); and secondly, because of course the Angles were no longer to be found on the continent, or at least not under such a name.[15] The Old Norse name for the region was *Ǫngul* (VAN *Angul, Old Danish *Angul*). In Old English, however, the name was *Angel*, and so the English and Norse forms were hardly to be differentiated at this time; either could lie behind the Orosius form.
Beormas (Bately 1980, 14.24, 27, 30). This name has been subject to immense scrutiny, both historical and philological (see in particular Ross 1981). All that

---

[15]As is asserted only shortly afterwards, in what must be an insertion into Ohthere's narrative by a Bede-reading editor: 'on þæm landum eardodon Engle, ær hi hider on land coman' (Bately 1980, 16.18–19) ('The Angles dwelt in that land before they came here into this country'). *Engle* is the normal Old English form of the people name, though *Angle* is also found frequently.

matters here is that the Old Norse form of their name was *Bjarmar*, VAN **Biarmar*, and OE *Beormas* is thus a close phonological reproduction of the Old Norse form with morphological substitution in the plural inflexion. In fact, *-eo-* in *Beormas* is an unusually exact reproduction of the Norse diphthong, as customarily ON *-ja-* (Viking Age *-ia-*) appears as *-e-* in English sources (see further Ross 1939–40).

Cwena land (Bately 1980, 15.34), *Cwenas* (Bately 1980, 15.34, 36). The Norse form of this people name — *Kvenir* — is derived from the first element of the Finnish form *Kainulaiset* (see Ross 1981, 82–83); phonologically, the Old English form is thus an exact reproduction of the Norse form (ON /w/ > /v/ being a post-Viking Age change), with morphological substitution in its inflexional ending (on the pattern of a masculine *a*-stem noun).[16]

Dene, Denamearc, Denemearce (Bately 1980, 16.15, 16, 20). Although as a people the Danes are named in poetic texts such as *Beowulf* and *Widsith*, this is the first occurrence of the place-name *Denemearc* in Old English (all other occurrences are in the *Anglo-Saxon Chronicle*, and mostly from the early eleventh century).[17] In Old Norse the name was *Danmark* (later *Danmǫrk*), as seen on the smaller Jelling stone from the mid tenth century (see Lund 1991); the Orosius form therefore shows cognate lexical substitution in both elements, with OE *Dene* ('Danes') for ON *Dan-*, and OE *mearc* ('boundary') for ON *mark*. It is curious that while the first element is uninflected in the Old Norse form of the name, in the Old English form it is either in the nominative plural *Dene* or in the genitive plural *Dena*.[18]

Finnas (Bately 1980, 14.3, 23, 29, 15.10, 14, 25). The Old English and Old Norse forms of the name were identical except for inflexion (*Finnas/Finnar*). The name of this people was well known to the Anglo-Saxons: it is also found in *Beowulf* (line 580) and *Widsith* (lines 20 and 76, with *Scridefinnas* line 79) (Klaeber 1950, 22; Krapp and Dobbie 1936, 150, 151, 152).[19]

Gotland (Bately 1980, 16.11, 18). This is a problematic name. Kemp Malone (1925; 1928) argued that the name derives from ON *Gautland*, with ON *au* represented in Old English as *o* (a not uncommon practice); most other commentators, however, take this as a form of the name for Jutland, and on geographical grounds this seems much more likely (see for example Gordon 1927b, 78; Chambers 1959, 333 n.3; Langenfelt 1961, 13; Bately 1980, 195). As Malone himself points out (1928, 337), the name is also marked with a length mark <Gótland> on one of its two occurrences in the Cotton MS; but this (if anything) points to Jutland rather than

---

[16]The name also occurs, in slightly different form, in the preceding geography (*Cwenland*: Bately 1980, 13.26).

[17]Indeed, this is probably the first occurrence of a form of the name *Denmark* in any language (Haugen 1976, 137 (§9.2.1)).

[18]*Dene* also occurs as the second element in the compound names *Norðdene* and *Suþdenum* in the preceding geography (Bately 1980, 13.14, 16, 19).

[19]The name *Scridefinnas* also occurs in the preceding geography (Bately 1980, 13.27).

Gautland. The Old Norse form for Jutland was *Jótland*; to this Malone objects that the first element of ON *Jótland* would still be a falling diphthong in the late ninth century (i.e. **Iot-*, which would feature in Old English as **Eot-, Iot-*), but this is unpersuasive as the Norse change from falling to rising diphthongs occurred earliest in word-initial position and can indeed be observed in Norse words and names in England (see Ross 1939–40, 2–4). There are two possible problems, however: (1) One would arguably expect an ON *Jótland* to be reproduced in Old English as *Geotland, with <e> as a diacritic vowel indicating the palatal nature of the preceding consonant. Whitelock overcomes this by suggesting that an <e> has been lost through scribal error (1967, 230), while Langenfelt simply asserts that in Old English orthography <g> could indeed represent /j/ before a back vowel (1961, 13; on this orthographic question see for example Hogg 1992a, 38, 41 (§§2.68, 2.76)). (2) The native Old English name-form for the Jutes, as is known from *Beowulf* and the *Finnsburh Fragment*, was *Ēotan*: why then didn't the scribe write *Ēotenaland? I would suggest that ON *Jótland* does indeed lie behind the Orosius form *Gotland*, but that what we have here is a precise reproduction of Ohthere's Norse form, rather than the substitution of the native form. Scribal error (that is, omission of diacritic <e>) is indeed plausible at this point, since Wulfstan later refers to a place *Gotland*, and this must indicate the island of Gotland (see below); thus, as Whitelock points out, a scribe (as opposed to an auditor) who did not realise that these were two different places could easily have confused or regularised the two forms.

Hālgoland (Bately 1980, 16.1). ON *Hálogaland*: the Old English form reproduces the Old Norse form accurately, with the exception of syncope of the unstressed second syllable. This may conceivably be on account of the unfamiliarity of such a trisyllabic vowel sequence in Old English, and therefore by analogy with long-stemmed disyllabic nouns and adjectives that show syncope in their medial syllable before a vocalic inflexion (for example, nom.sg. *engel* ('angel'), dat.pl. *englum*; nom.sg. *hālig* ('holy'), dat.pl. *hālgum*: see Campbell 1959, 227, 266 (§§574.4, 643.5); Mitchell and Robinson 1992, 25, 32 (§§42, 68)).

æt Hǣþum, to Hǣþum (Bately 1980, 16.13–14, 17). This is the town of Hedeby (see Roesdahl 1982, 70–76), which appears as *Haiþabu* in a runic inscription from Viking Age Denmark, and *Heiðabýr/Heiðabœr* in tenth- and eleventh-century skaldic verse — 'the settlement at the heaths'.[20] The Old English form of the name also occurs in Wulfstan's account, with a different preposition, as *of Hǣðum* (Bately 1980, 16.21); otherwise the only occurrence of the name in Anglo-Saxon sources is Æthelweard's *Haithaby*, a form that reproduces exactly the Old Norse form (see further p 119 below). Clearly the Old English form in the Orosius could either represent a native English name for the place or cognate lexical substitution of the first element of the Norse form; on account of its importance as a trading-centre in the

---

[20]For skaldic occurrences of the name see Finnur Jónsson 1912–15, IB, 149 (Hallfreðr vandræðaskáld, *Óláfsdrápa*), 333 (Þjóðólfr Arnórsson, *Magnúsflokkr*), 365 (Þórleikr fagri, *flokkr* on Sveinn Úlfsson), 396 (anonymous).

Viking Age (witness the Anglo-Saxon Wulfstan's journey there), one should probably follow the first alternative, though presumably *(æt) Hæðum* must have been derived from the first element of the Norse name at some earlier stage.

Iraland (Bately 1980, 16.6, 7). Excluding *Beormas*, this name has received more attention than any other in Ohthere's account, and there are two schools of thought: that which holds that Ohthere referred to Ireland and was correctly understood, and that which holds that he referred to Iceland and was misunderstood on account of the fame of that recently discovered country not yet having reached Alfred's court (pro-Ireland: Malone 1930a; 1930b; 1933; Stokoe 1957; Lund 1984, 12; Bately 1980, 193–94; pro-Iceland: Craigie 1917; Binns 1980, 40; Fell 1984, 63). The presence of medial -*a*- in the Orosius form is, though, just one of the objections to the theory that Ohthere really said *Ísland*. Janet Bately has elsewhere discussed the usual terms for Ireland in Anglo-Saxon texts, and she points out that the usual rendering of *Hibernia* in the Orosius translation is *Scotland* (1988, 114–18); but since Ohthere and Wulfstan's accounts are insertions from a different source this is not necessarily a clinching argument. It still seems to me, however, that Ohthere's *Iraland* is best understood as deriving from ON *Íraland*, even though the more usual form in Icelandic sagas is *Írland*. *Iraland* is also found in the *Anglo-Saxon Chronicle*, so the Old English and Old Norse forms would have been identical.

Norðmanna land, *Norðmen* (Bately 1980, 15.21, 34, 35, 37). Whenever the Anglo-Saxons differentiated between the various Scandinavian nationalities they did so by calling Norwegians *Norðmenn* (and Norway therefore *Norðmanna land*). This usage is found in the *Anglo-Saxon Chronicle*, most conspicuously in the poem *sub anno* 942 on Edmund's capture of the Five Boroughs (see further pp 140–41 below). The English and Norse forms at this time would have been identical; it is likely, though, that the Old English form was originally derived from the Norse, as one does not find the people name *Norðmenn* in pre-Viking Age texts (as I take *Beowulf* and *Widsith* to be).[21]

Norðweg (Bately 1980, 16.9). This is the only occurrence of this name in Old English; later citations (from the *Anglo-Saxon Chronicle* in the late eleventh century) usually give the form *Norweg(as)*, with loss of medial *ð*.[22] The English and Norse forms would have been identical at this time (VAN *Norð-vegr*, later *Norvegr*, *Nóregr*), so it is unclear whether Orosius gives the native form or a form derived from Ohthere's Old Norse; the name of the country must have been all too familiar to Alfred and his court, but (as with *Norðmenn*) there is no reason for doubting that the Old English name derived originally from the Old Norse.[23]

---

[21] The name also occurs in the preceding geography (*Norþmenn*: Bately 1980, 13.27–28, 29–30).

[22] The term *norðwegas* does however occur as a poetic *hapax legomenon* in the Old English *Exodus* (Krapp 1931, 93 (line 68)).

[23] As with *Denmark*, this too is probably the first occurrence of a form of the name *Norway* in any language (Haugen 1976, 137 (§9.2.1)).

Scīringesheal (Bately 1980, 16.3, 8, 9, 12, 15). This is a name which poses more problems than would appear at first. The place itself is usually identified with the excavated trading-centre later known as Kaupang, in Tjølling, Vestfold (see Blindheim 1975); toponymically, it is assumed that behind the Orosius form lies the Old Norse name *Skíringssalr* (which occurs once in the *Ynglingatal* of Þjóðólfr ór Hvini (Finnur Jónsson 1912–15, IB, 12; Snorri Sturluson 1941–51, I, 76)), with apparent phonemic substitution of cognate OE /ʃ/ for ON /sk/ in the initial consonant-cluster (see for example Whitelock 1967, 230). However, the second element is more problematic; as has been pointed out by Bately (1980, 193) and Fell (1984, 62–63), one would expect ON *Skíringssalr* to result in an Anglicisation as *Scīringessele (with cognate lexical substitution of OE *sele* ('hall') for ON *salr*). Furthermore, the indication of masculine gender in *þone Scīringesheal* (at the name's third occurrence) means that the *-heal* cannot derive from the semantically equivalent OE *heall* ('hall') (which was feminine), but must rather be the common place-name element *healh* ('nook') (which was masculine); and this is confirmed by a dative in *-heale* (Bately 1980, 16.8, 12, 15). There is thus some support for Alan Binns's view that OE *Scīringesheal* 'seems more likely to be the result of familiarity with the place than a one-off translation specially produced for Ohthere's account' (1980, 39). A distinctive Old English name for the place, with a second element differing from the Norse name, seems plausible, since *Scīringesheal* was clearly a key trading-centre in Viking Age Scandinavia; but, as with *(æt) Hǣðum*, it is also reasonable to assume that the first element of the English name was at least derived from the first element of the Norse name at some earlier stage.

Seaxum (Bately 1980, 16.14). The Old Norse form was *Saxar* ('Saxons') (dat.pl. *Saxum*), so Orosius shows substitution of the cognate Old English form.[24]

Sillende (Bately 1980, 16.11, 18). Ekblom (1939–40, 178–82) has provided a thorough elucidation of this name, which represents not modern Sjælland (Zealand), as many commentators have assumed, but rather the east coast of southern Jutland. The name is found in Old High German as *Sinlendi*; OHG *sin-* ('large, extensive') corresponds with OE *sin-*, ON *sí-*, thus giving a form in Ohthere's Old Norse as *Sílende. The Orosius form reproduces this closely; the double <ll> in the Old English form is probably without significance, although Ekblom suggests it may possibly represent an assimilation from *nl* (1939–40, 180 n.2).

Swēoland (Bately 1980, 15.33). Although this particular form of the name for Sweden is not found elsewhere, *Beowulf* contains *Swēo-rīce* (lines 2383 and 2495) and *Swēo-ðēod* (line 2922), as well as (four times) the people name *Swēon* (Klaeber 1950, 90, 93, 94, 110, 111 (X2), 113); *Swēon* is also found in *Widsith* (Krapp and Dobbie 1936, 150, 151 (lines 31 and 58)) and in Wulfstan's account. The name in Orosius, therefore, clearly represents the native and ancient Old English form, rather than being derived by contemporary contact from ON *Svíar, Svía-land*.[25]

---

[24]The name also occurs as the second element of *Ealdseaxna* in the preceding geography (Bately 1980, 13.18).

[25]The name also occurs in the preceding geography (*Swēon*: Bately 1980, 13.23, 24).

Terfinna land (Bately 1980, 14.25). Ross identifies the *Terfinnas* as Lapps of the Terskij Bereg and concludes that the Old Norse form of the name would be **Ter-finnar*, perhaps from an earlier **Teria-finnar* (1981, 24–28). The Orosius form is therefore a precise reproduction of the Old Norse, with Old English inflexion.

Westsǣ (Bately 1980, 14.1). This is another form that reveals the Norse narrative of Ohthere behind the Orosius's Old English account, as it must represent a translation of ON *Vestmarr*, with OE *sǣ* for ON *marr*, of identical meaning; the first elements would have been identical in Norse and English in the Viking Age. *Vestmarr* was an Old Norse name for the sea off the west coast of Norway, indicating a Scandinavia-centred (and, specifically, Norway-centred) nomenclature, and thus contrasting with the Anglocentric *North Sea* in Modern English (see Smyth 1977, 111).

Winedum (Bately 1980, 16.14). The Old Norse name for the Wends was *Vinðr*, *Vinðir*; the Orosius editor, however, has replaced Ohthere's Norse form with the native Old English form *Winedas*, which is also found in *Widsith* (line 60) (Krapp and Dobbie 1936, 151).[26]

(2) Norse names in Wulfstan's account[27]

Blecingaēg (Bately 1980, 16.27). The Old Norse name for this region was **Bleikinge*, later undergoing East Norse monophthongisation to *Blēkinge*. Since there is little or no evidence for Old East Norse *ei > ē* in stressed syllables in the Norse language in England (and certainly not in the ninth century),[28] and since phonemic substitution would give *Blāc-*, the medial *-e-* in Orosius is problematic and only explicable as a scribal error or as a failure of hearing on the part of either Wulfstan (in Scandinavia) or the scribe taking notes (at Alfred's court). That the latter explanation is the more likely one is suggested by the mistaken interpretation of the final syllable of the Norse form as a genitive plural, with the consequent addition of *ēg* ('island') as a necessary generic in the nominative.[29]

Burgenda land (Bately 1980, 16.25, 26–27). This name was ancient and well known to the Anglo-Saxons, as can be seen from its occurrence in *Widsith* and *Waldere* (Krapp and Dobbie 1936, 150, 151 (lines 19 and 65); Dobbie 1942, 6

---

[26]The name also occurs in the preceding geography (*Winedas*: Bately 1980, 13.22).

[27]Non-Norse names in Wulfstan's account (Prussian, Slavonic, etc.) are as follows (Bately 1980): *Estland* 16.34 [MS *eastland*], 17.1 [MS *eastland*], *Estmere* 16.32 (X2), 33, 34, *Estum* 16.31, 17.5, 6, 31, 34 [MS *eastum*]; *Ilfing* 16.33, 34, 35; *Truso* 16.21, 33; *Weonoðland* 16.23, *Weonodland* 16.29, 30, 31, *Winodland* 16.35; *Wisle* 16.30, 31, 35 (X2), *Wislemuðan* 16.29, 37; *Witland* 16.30, 31.

[28]See for example *SSNY* 237–38; *SSNEM* 269; *SSNNW* 323. Malone however claims that Wulfstan's form does shows this monophthongisation (1931, 576).

[29]Blekinge is not an island, but the addition may have been motivated by analogy with *Scōnēg* (see below).

(fragment 2, line 14)). The Old Norse form was *Borgundarholmr*; Wulfstan (and/or his scribe) was therefore using the native Old English form.³⁰

Denemearcan (Bately 1980, 16.25). See above.

Eowland (Bately 1980, 16.28). Malone (1931, 577–78) provides a lengthy and, in my view, satisfying discussion of this name. The Old Norse name for this island was *Eyland, Øyland* (modern Öland), but Wulfstan's *Eowland* can be explained neither as a phonetic reproduction of the Norse form (which would probably be something like *Oeland) nor as a phonemic or lexical substitution (which would probably be *Āland or **Ēgland/Īegland*). *Eowland* is explicable, though, as a native and ancient name deriving from a Germanic nom.sg. *awi ('island') rather than oblique case *aujō (whence ON *ey*, OE *ēg*, *īeg*). That this is not simply philological ingenuity is perhaps confirmed by the presence of the people name *Eowan* in *Widsith* (Krapp and Dobbie 1936, 150 (line 26)). In the Orosius we therefore have the native Old English form of the name, and not one derived from the Old Norse form which Wulfstan must have encountered in Scandinavia.³¹

Falster (Bately 1980, 16.24). The Old Norse form of this island's name was *Falst(e)r*, so Wulfstan reproduces this precisely.

Gotland (Bately 1980, 16.28). The Old Norse form of this island's name was *Gotland*, home of the *Gotar*. Wulfstan therefore reproduces the Norse form precisely.

of Hǣþum (Bately 1980, 16.21). See above.

Langaland (Bately 1980, 16.24). The Old Norse form of this island's name was *Langaland*, both elements of which were identical with their Old English cognates. The name has therefore been accurately transmitted.

Lǣland (Bately 1980, 16.24). The Old Norse form of this island's name was *Láland* (modern Låland). Malone believes that this is another old and native name 'which the English brought with them when they migrated to England' (1931, 575), but there is nothing in the form of the name which demands such an explanation; more likely is that this represents a straightforward case of phonemic substitution, with OE *ǣ* replacing cognate ON *á*. A possible objection to this, though, would be that if Wulfstan were an Anglian one would expect *Lēland rather than *Lǣland* (Gmc *ǣ* > WS *ǣ¹*, Anglian *ē*); perhaps one should therefore attribute the form to a West Saxon scribe at Alfred's court.

Meore (Bately 1980, 16.27). This spelling poses problems. The Old Norse name for this region was *Møre* (modern Möre, in eastern Sweden); an attempt to reproduce this phonetically in Old English would be spelt something like *Moere, so I would

---

³⁰The name also occurs in the preceding geography (*Burgendan*: Bately 1980, 13.22, 22–23).

³¹Malone writes (1931, 578): 'Everyone agrees that the *Eowan* were islanders, and *Eowland* by virtue of its name is obviously the proper island for them to live in. [. . .] *Eowland* is therefore as old as *Eowum* [dat.pl., *Widsith* line 26] in the English language, and the two names can only with violence be separated'.

suggest, albeit without great confidence, that the Orosius's *Meore* represents a transposition of vowels through scribal error — not unlikely in copying such an unusual spelling in late-ninth-century West Saxon (for what was possibly an unfamiliar name).[32]

Scōnēg (Bately 1980, 16.24). This undoubtedly represents a borrowing or reproduction of the contemporary Old Norse form *Skáney, Skáni* (modern Skåne), since the older English form was *Scedenig* (*Beowulf* line 1686; also *Scedeland* line 19: Klaeber 1950, 1, 63).[33] Æthelweard is the only other Anglo-Saxon writer to use the Norse-derived name, in the form *Scani* (see p 120 below). Æthelweard reproduces the Old Norse form exactly; Wulfstan's *Scōnēg*, however, shows lexical substitution of cognate OE *ēg* ('island') for ON *ey* in the second element, whilst the *ō* in the first element is somewhat problematic. Kock (1918, 74) suggests that *Scōnēg* shows phonemic substitution of OE *ō* before nasals (that is, by analogy with such pairs as OE *mōna*/ON *máni* ('moon'), OE *mōnaþ*/ON *mánuðr* ('month'), OE *spōn*/ON *spánn* ('chipping')), and this is followed by Whitelock (1967, 230–31); this seems a satisfactory explanation, and is certainly preferable to Malone's notion that *Scōnēg* is an intrusive eleventh-century spelling showing the rounding of OE *ā* to ME long open *ō* (1931, 575–76). Initial <sc> could indicate either reproduction of ON /sk/ or phonemic substitution of cognate OE /ʃ/.

Swēon (Bately 1980, 16.28). See above.

This completes the gazetteer of Norse-derived names in the Old English Orosius. Whether derived from Ohthere's Norse at the court of Alfred, or derived via Wulfstan from Norse speakers in Scandinavia, these names can therefore be classified into six types according to their treatment:[34]

(1) Names where a native Old English form was pre-existent which differed (phonologically and/or morphologically) from the Old Norse form, and has been substituted for it: *Burgenda land, Eowland, Seaxe, Swēoland, Winedas*. The occurrence of such substitution requires, of course, that the equivalence of the Norse and English names should be recognised, whether on account of similarity in form or the fact that both names evidently refer to the same place or people; that is, either signifier or signified (or both) could trigger the substitution. Although the usual practice where an older English form was pre-existent, the example of *Scōnēg* indicates that such substitution was not, however, invariable.

---

[32]This seems preferable to the explanation of Malone (1931, 576–77), who suggests that *Meore* represents an intrusive eleventh-century spelling following the monophthongisation of *eo* in English.

[33]The name is thought to be a compound of Gmc **skaþi(n)-* ('harm, damage') and **awi-* ('island'), and occurs in Pliny's *Natural History* as both (correctly) *Scadinavia* and (incorrectly) *Scandinavia* (Prokosch 1939, 26). See further Björkman 1918; Kock 1918.

[34]In all six types the names have been morphologically adapted where necessary to Old English inflexional systems.

(2) Names where a native Old English form was pre-existent, but was identical to the Old Norse form in the Viking Age: *Angel, Finnas, Íraland*.

(3) Names which are derived from Old Norse and were lexically transparent, but where the English and Norse forms of the constituent elements would be identical in the Viking Age: *Langaland, Norðmanna land, Norðweg*.

(4) Names which are derived from Old Norse and were lexically transparent, and hence have undergone lexical substitution of Old English cognates in their constituent elements: *Denemearce, Westsæ*. The form *(æt) Hæðum* represents lexical substitution in only one element of the name.

(5) Names which are derived from Old Norse, but were lexically meaningless to English speakers in at least one element (due to lack of an Old English lexical cognate), and have consequently undergone phonemic substitution of cognate Old English sounds in that element: *Læland, Scōnēg*. *Scīringesheal* probably represents phonemic substitution in the initial consonant-cluster of the first element, with non-cognate lexical substitution in the second element.[35]

(6) Names which are derived from Old Norse and in at least one element were lexically meaningless to English speakers (due to lack of an Old English lexical cognate), and hence have been phonetically reproduced as precisely as possible: *Beormas, Blecingaēg, Cwena land, Falster, Gotland* (Jutland), *Gotland* (Gotland), *Hālgoland, Meore, Sillende, Terfinna land*. Since some of these names must have been unfamiliar to Alfred's court, the accuracy of such reproductions indicates an impressive clarity of hearing.

Conclusion

To review this discussion of 'The Voyages of Ohthere and Wulfstan': (1) this text presents us with the record of a Scandinavian in England, and an Englishman in Scandinavia; (2) the evidence of Norse influence on the language of Ohthere's account suggests that Ohthere spoke to Alfred and the court in his native Norse; (3) Odenstedt's theory that for Ohthere an interpreter was required, and Wulfstan was that interpreter, is to be firmly rejected; and (4) the patterns of adoption and adaptation of Norse-derived names in these accounts show, for the most part, both the successful operation of a switching-code where cognates existed and an impressive clarity of hearing where they did not. Finally, it should again be stressed that the particular value of this text to a study of Anglo-Norse language contact lies in its earliness, dating indubitably from the reign of Alfred — that is, only twenty or so years after the initial Scandinavian settlements in England. As will be seen, the other two texts to be examined in this chapter date necessarily from almost a century later.

---

[35] I have not classified *Denemearce, (æt) Hæðum, Norðmenn, Norðweg*, and *Scīringesheal* under (1) or (2) on the grounds that, while these Old English names no doubt pre-dated the visits of Ohthere and Wulfstan to Alfred's court, I am doubtful whether they pre-dated the Viking Age; I suspect that rather they are names derived from contemporary Old Norse.

Æthelweard's Chronicle

The identification of the Æthelweard who was ealdorman of Wessex beyond Selwood with the Æthelweard who composed a Latin adaptation of the *Anglo-Saxon Chronicle* has been generally accepted (see Campbell 1962, xii–xvi). This important figure wrote his *Chronicle* sometime during the decade 978–988, and probably later rather than earlier within that period (see Campbell 1962, xiii n.2; on the work's dedicatee see van Houts 1992). Æthelweard's *Chronicle* is of great interest for a variety of reasons, not least for its author's Latin style (see Winterbottom 1967); Chambers, for instance, characterised his *Chronicle* as 'bombastic' (1959, 70), and Stenton complained of 'the cloud of his verbiage' (1925, 21). However, Audrey Meaney, while commenting on Æthelweard's 'obscure and peculiar Latin', does at least recognise 'his independence of mind and eagerness for knowledge' (1970, 105, 132). One of the most appealing aspects of Æthelweard's *Chronicle* is in fact its author's evident interest in questions of language and nomenclature. He is often ready to remark on the significance or etymology of names (especially place-names) or to pause for some other philological aside — for example, in his digressions on the etymologies of the place-name *Wippedesfleot*, of the tribal name *Escingas*, and of the personal name *Eadgar* (Campbell 1962, 10–11, 18, 56). An awareness of linguistic differences is often revealed, and perhaps also a somewhat pedantic pleasure in possessing the necessary linguistic competence to explicate them.[36] In keeping with this tendency, Æthelweard tends to reproduce foreign names — that is, names which are not Old English or Latin — with considerable care. Campbell devotes some space to a discussion of this in the introduction to his edition (1962, lviii–lx), and Æthelweard's form *Vurthgern* for Bede's *Vortigern* may be adduced as a good example: the phonological adaptations lead Campbell to assert that '[i]t would seem evident that Æthelweard had heard a Celt pronounce the word, and accordingly partly modified Bede's spelling' (1962, lx).[37]

By the time of composition England had seen a hundred years of Scandinavian settlement and almost two hundred years of contact through raids, and Æthelweard himself had recorded dealings with the next wave of attackers: his name, as an ealdorman of Wessex, is found as one of the three witnesses to the treaty known as II Æthelred, almost certainly made in 994 (see Lund 1987, 264–68; Keynes 1991, 103–07; Wormald 1999a, 320–21). In the light of such circumstances, and considering his philological interests, it is no surprise to find that, as Campbell observes,

---

[36] See, for instance, Æthelweard's repeated use of the term *uulgo*, evidently meaning 'in the vernacular' (rather than 'by the common people', as Campbell habitually translates): examples can be found in Campbell 1962, 9, 10 (X2), 13, 19, 21, 24, etc.

[37] Indeed, the precision with which Æthelweard generally reproduces Celtic names has led to the suggestion that he may have employed a Celtic secretary in the composition of his *Chronicle*; but as Campbell points out, 'Æthelweard's interest in the forms of Norse names suggests a Germanic speaker' (1962, xxxvii).

'Æthelweard had perhaps some interest in the language and beliefs of the Danish invaders' (1962, xxxv–xxxvi; however, on Æthelweard's scornful attitude to the Viking attackers of the ninth century see Page 1987, 3). Beyond Campbell's brief notice (1962, xxxvi, lix–lx), Æthelweard's Scandinavian interests have not been analysed either closely or systematically; nor has his witness been greatly adduced in the study of Anglo-Norse language contact.

One finds these interests suddenly cropping up again and again throughout his *Chronicle*, in both large and small details. So, for example, while Æthelweard, like Asser, translates as *consul* the *Anglo-Saxon Chronicle*'s *eorl* (< ON *jarl*, used as a term of rank), at one point in his account of 871 he pauses to spell out more explicitly the significance of this and to introduce a quotation from a foreign language (Campbell 1962, 40):

> Fueruntque in ter squalidissima eorum dominatione ab Anglis uidelicet certamina tria, exscepto supra memoratis bellis, quorum undecim consules ruunt, quos illi 'eorlas' solent nominare, et rex eorum unus.

> (And in their [i.e. the Vikings'] hateful period of ascendancy there were three times three battles [fought] by the English, not including those mentioned above, and eleven of their *consules* fell, whom they usually call earls, and one king.)

The *Anglo-Saxon Chronicle* here merely notes that nine *eorlas* and one *cyning* were killed; the comment on the usual term employed by the Scandinavians for their leaders is Æthelweard's. Of course, since he is writing in Latin, it is only by means of such circumlocutions and digressions that Æthelweard is able to include actual Norse words and so draw attention to them.[38]

Another example of Æthelweard's Scandinavian interests is his version of the *Anglo-Saxon Chronicle* entry for 877. In MS 'A' the Old English text records that a Viking fleet sailed from Wareham to Exeter, but a great storm arose 'ꝥ þær forwearþ .cxx. scipa æt Swanawic' (Bately 1986, 50) ('and there 120 ships perished at Swanage'). Æthelweard renders this as 'mergitur pars non minima, centum numero carinæ supremæ, iuxta rupem quæ Suuanauuic nuncupatur' ('a large part [of the fleet] was lost, in number *centum* tall ships, near the cliff known as Swanage') (Campbell 1962, 42). *Centum* for *cxx* seems an unlikely mistake, and it is more probable that Æthelweard has here been influenced by the Norse *hundrað* or 'long hundred' of 120.

These are only two minor examples. In what follows three larger topics will be discussed in detail: (1) Æthelweard's astute forms of Norse personal names; (2) his

---

[38] Among other Norse-derived lexical items, it is interesting that Æthelweard renders the *Anglo-Saxon Chronicle*'s *sumorlida* ('summer army') (< ON *sumarliði*) as *æstiuus exercitus* (Campbell 1962, 39). See also Frank 1994b, 89 n.8, who suggests that Æthelweard's use of *turbo* ('storm') as a term for 'battle' (Campbell 1962, 53) may be due to the influence of skaldic poetry; on the possible influence of Old English poetry on Æthelweard see Lutz 2000.

unusual interest in Norse place-names; and (3) his surprising introduction of Norse elements into the Anglo-Saxon royal genealogies.

Norse Personal Names

Campbell remarks that 'Æthelweard so changes (and generally improves) the forms of the names of Norse leaders seen in *OEC* [i.e. the *Anglo-Saxon Chronicle*], that it seems likely that he took some interest in the language of the invaders' (1962, lix). Seventeen different names occur. Considering the relatively large number of names featuring in this one relatively short text, and in particular the especial attention which Æthelweard seems to have given to his name-forms, it is surprising that this minor corpus of names has not been analysed in any of the studies of Norse personal names in England. Erik Björkman (1910) cited a number of Æthelweard's forms as additional examples in his pioneering study of Norse anthroponymy in England, but he did not draw on Æthelweard for base material; and Lehiste's helpful supplement to Björkman is confined to names in the Old English versions of the *Anglo-Saxon Chronicle* (1958; Fellows-Jensen 1968 and Insley 1994 are both regional in basis). Hence a full listing and analysis follows of the Norse personal names found in Æthelweard's *Chronicle*, arranged alphabetically and with brief identifications.

Anlaf (Campbell 1962, 54 (*sub anno* 948, *recte* 944)): Óláfr cuaran of Dublin, recorded in Old English as *Anlaf Sihtrices sunu Cwaran*. Æthelweard mentions him as being expelled with *Ragnald* from York by *Vulfstan episcopus duxque Myrciorum* ('Bishop Wulfstan and the ealdorman of the Mercians') (on the confusion in Æthelweard's account of this event see Campbell 1938, 51 n.6; Smyth 1987, II, 123 n.30). *Anlaf* is the usual form of ON *Óláfr* in Old English sources, and so Æthelweard provides no new information (see Björkman 1910, 4–5; Lehiste 1958, 7–8, 21–22; Fellows-Jensen 1968, 204; Insley 1994, 309–11).

Annuth (Campbell 1962, 41 (*sub anno* 875)): one of three Scandinavian *reges*, together with *Oscytel* and *Guðrum*, who are mentioned as moving camp from Repton to Cambridge. The form of this name in the *Anglo-Saxon Chronicle* is *Anwynd*, *Anwend*, and is usually held to represent OWN *Ǫnundr*, OEN *Anund(er)*, whose second element (*vǫndr* ('wand')) still shows a retained /w/ (see Björkman 1910, 5–6; Lehiste 1958, 8; Insley 1994, 15–17). Æthelweard thus gives a less archaic form (suggesting loss of medial /w/ in the course of the ninth century?), though his alteration *nd > th* seems hard to explain.

Berse (Campbell 1962, 37 (*sub anno* 871)): a Scandinavian *rex* killed at the battle of Ashdown. *Bachsecg cyng* is the first Scandinavian to be named in the *Anglo-Saxon Chronicle*, but the name has proved to be entirely opaque (other forms are *Bagsecg*, *Bagsceg*, *Bægsæc*) (see Björkman 1910, ix; Lehiste 1958, 8–9). Campbell declares *Bachsecg* to be 'obviously distorted' (1962, lix), and this is clearly right; Æthelweard, recognising this, abandons the name altogether and substitutes *Berse*. As Campbell comments, this is 'sound but certainly not equivalent'. The name is not found in the *Anglo-Saxon Chronicle*, though related forms occur in the Durham

Liber Vitae (see Björkman 1910, 27); it is a phonologically precise representation of ON *Bersi*, a name which Insley notes is 'rare in England' (1994, 94; see also Lind 1905–15, 132–33; Fellows-Jensen 1968, 53), and not, as Campbell claims, *Bersir* (a name not to be found in Norse sources). It is also to be noted that Æthelweard reproduces ON final *-i* as *-e*: this is a more precise representation than the usual OE *-a* (see, for instance, *Frœna* below).

Eyuuysl (Campbell 1962, 53 (*sub anno* 909, *recte* 910)): one of the three Scandinavian kings (together with *Healfdene* and *Iguuar*) said to have been killed at the battle of Wednesfield or Tettenhall (see Smyth 1987, I, 75–76). The forms in the *Anglo-Saxon Chronicle* are *Ecwils*, *Eowils*, *Eowilisc* (see Lehiste 1958, 10), but this is another name which Björkman considered inexplicable (1910, ix; among other scholars Collingwood proffered *Jógísl (1908, 126), implying the substitution of OE *eoh* for cognate ON *jór* ('horse') (see *Haruc* below), and Smyth makes the throwaway suggestion of *Audgísl* (1987, I, 101)). The form as it stands in both Æthelweard and the *Anglo-Saxon Chronicle* is baffling; Æthelweard's re-metathesis to *-sl* seems an improvement, but his alteration of the initial diphthong to *ey* is less easy to understand. The question must be left open.

Frœna (Campbell 1962, 37 (*sub anno* 871)): a Scandinavian *consul* killed at the battle of Ashdown. The *Anglo-Saxon Chronicle* forms are *Frœna*, *Frena* (see Björkman 1910, 42–43; Lehiste 1958, 10), and the Old Norse name is *Frœni, *Fráni*, derived from the weak form of the adjective *fránn* ('glittering, shining') (see Fellows-Jensen 1968, 85–86).[39] Clearly, Æthelweard adds no new information, and he takes over from his source the custom of representing ON final *-i* as OE *-a* (see Fellows-Jensen 1968, c (§147(i))).

Guðrum (Campbell 1962, 41, 47 (*sub annis* 875, 890)): first Scandinavian king of East Anglia. The usual form of the name in the *Anglo-Saxon Chronicle* is *Godrum*, with occasional variants *Guþram*, *Goðrum*, *Guðrum* (see Lehiste 1958, 10–11). The underlying Old Norse name is *Guðþormr*; the first element of *Godrum* therefore shows the substitution of cognate OE *god* for ON *guð* ('god'). But rather than preserving this Anglicisation, Æthelweard again attempts to reproduce more precisely the original Norse form and restores *guð*. The second element of the name consistently shows metathesis in both Æthelweard and the *Anglo-Saxon Chronicle*, perhaps on account of bearing low stress (see further Lind 1905–15, 395–400; Björkman 1910, 48–49; Fellows-Jensen 1968, 112; Insley 1994, 157–58; also Campbell 1959, 185 (§459.4)).

Guthfrid (Campbell 1962, 51 (*sub anno* 895)): described by Æthelweard as *rex Northhymbriorum*, he is said to have died in 895 and been buried in York Minster.[40]

---

[39] The name also occurs in the Lincolnshire place-names Franethorp, Framland, and Frampton (see *SSNEM* 126, 154, 191).

[40] It should be noted that Æthelweard sometimes appears to use *Northhymbrii* to mean 'the Scandinavians in Northumbria'. For details of Guthfrid's reign see Stenton 1971, 262–63; Smyth 1987, I, 43–46.

This king is not mentioned in the *Anglo-Saxon Chronicle*, although other Scandinavians of the same name are, and for these the prevalent forms are *Guðfrið*, *Guðferð* (see Lehiste 1958, 11).⁴¹ The underlying Old Norse name is **GuðfreðuR*, later OWN *Guð(f)røðr*, Old Danish *Guthfrith* (see Björkman 1910, 53–54; Lind 1905–15, 372, 391–93; Fellows-Jensen 1968, 110; Insley 1994, 150–52); in Æthelweard's form final OE *-d* has been substituted for cognate ON *-ð*.⁴²

Harald (Campbell 1962, 37 (*sub anno* 871)): a Scandinavian *consul* (that is, *jarl*) killed in the battle of Ashdown. This very common name usually occurs in the *Anglo-Saxon Chronicle* in the form *Harold*, though *Harald* and *Hareld* are also found (see Lehiste 1958, 12). The Old Norse name is *Haraldr*, and so Æthelweard's *Harald* is an exact reproduction (see further Björkman 1910, 63–64; Fellows-Jensen 1968, 132–34; Insley 1994, 195–97).

Haruc (Campbell 1962, 52 (*sub anno* 902)): the *rex barbarum* killed in the battle at the Holme, and presumably one of Guthrum's successors as king of East Anglia. In the *Anglo-Saxon Chronicle* MS 'D' the name of this king is given as *Eohric*, *Eoric* (see Björkman 1910, 36–37; Lehiste 1958, 10). *Eohrīc* represents an element-for-element Anglicisation of ON *Jórekr* (< **Iórīkr*) (see Insley 1994, 234–36), with OE *eoh* substituted for cognate ON *jór* ('horse') and OE *-rīc* for cognate ON *-ríkr*, although there may also be evidence for *Eohrīc* as a native Old English personal name.⁴³ However, *Haruc*, as Campbell points out (1962, lix), is an incorrect equation on Æthelweard's part, since it represents ON *Hárekr* and not *Jórekr*. *Hárekr* was certainly a common Norse name (see Lind 1905–15, 488–91), but curiously it occurs in none of the English sources surveyed by Björkman, Fellows-Jensen, and Insley.⁴⁴ Its presence in Æthelweard is therefore a valuable addition, and it is to be noted that he closely reproduces the Norse form; cognate substitution would have given **Hēahrīc*.

Healfdene (Campbell 1962, 41, 43, 53 (*sub annis* 875, 878, 909 *recte* 910)): (1) the *dux barbarorum* who established his rule in Northumbria and was held to be the brother of *Iguuar* (see below) and son of Ragnarr loðbrók; (2) one of the three *reges* killed at Tettenhall (see Smyth 1987, I, 75–76, 101). The *Anglo-Saxon Chronicle* forms modulate fairly evenly between *Healfdene* and *Halfdene* (see Lehiste 1958, 12), though not surprisingly the latter occurs more frequently in other sources (see Björkman 1910, 61–62; Fellows-Jensen 1968, 126–29; Insley 1994, 186–92). The Old Norse form was *Halfdan* 'half-Dane' (see Lind 1905–15, 451–52), and thus

---

⁴¹The name also features in the Nottinghamshire place-name Goverton (see *PNNt* 155; *SSNEM* 192; *DEPN* 201).

⁴²Fellows-Jensen suggests however that forms of Norse names in *-frid* 'are probably due to Frankish influence' (1968, lxxiv (§21)).

⁴³It appears to occur as the first element of the Wiltshire place-name Urchfont (see *PNW* 315; *DEPN* 488; Gelling 1988, 86).

⁴⁴It does, however, occur in one of the manuscripts of Roger of Wendover, in the form *Hœricus* (where other manuscripts show *Henricus*, clearly a mistake), as the name of one of the companions of Eiríkr blóðøx at his death on Stainmore (see Binns 1965, 188).

Healfdene shows cognate substitution in both elements, *Halfdene* only in the second.[45] Æthelweard gives *Healfdene* on all four occasions.[46]

Hæsten (Campbell 1962, 49, 50 (*sub annis* 892, 893)): a Scandinavian leader, briefly active in England in the early 890s. This is a notoriously difficult name: the *Anglo-Saxon Chronicle* gives *Hæsten*, with one exceptional *Hæsting* (see Lehiste 1958, 12–13), although in other sources one also finds *Hastin, Hasten, Æstan* (see Björkman 1910, 65). The most likely candidate is ON *Hásteinn* (see Lind 1905–15, 491; Fellows-Jensen 1968, 135). Æthelweard simply reproduces the form in his source and has no new insight to offer.

Iuuar, Iguuar, genitive *Iguuares* (Campbell 1962, 35, 36, 43, 53 (*sub annis* 865, 869, 878, 909 *recte* 910)): (1) the *rex* and *tyrannus* held to be the son of Ragnarr loðbrók; (2) one of the three *reges* killed at Tettenhall. There are two instances of the genitive *Iweres* in the *Anglo-Saxon Chronicle*; otherwise all forms contain a nasal: *Ingware, Inwæres, Ingwæres, Inweres* (see Lehiste 1958, 13–14; for other variations in English sources see Björkman 1910, 72–73; Fellows-Jensen 1968, 153; Insley 1994, 236–42; for the vexed question of the same name in Old Irish sources see Smyth 1977, 280). John Insley reads the forms of the name in English sources as follows (1994, 241):

> [*Ívarr*] appears in two forms, an earlier form in which the original nasalization of the original *Í-* is still apparent and a later form which shows no trace of this original nasalization. The evidence suggests that the nasalized variant was introduced into England with the Scand[inavian] settlements of the l[ate] 9th century while the form without nasalization must have been introduced subsequently at a time when all traces of the original nasalization had disappeared in the Scand[inavian] languages. [. . .] The variant without nasalization must have been introduced into England at some time in the 10th century or perhaps even as late as the reign of Cnut.

All later Norse sources do indeed preserve the name of the Scandinavian invader of England as *Ívarr*, and this form is recorded as early as *c*. 1027 in Sigvatr Þórðarson's *Knútsdrápa* (Finnur Jónsson, 1912–15, IB, 232; for the poem's probable date see Townend 2001, 153–56). Campbell points out that since in late-tenth-century Old English orthography <ig> can represent *i*, Æthelweard's form *Iguuar* (instead of *Ingware, Inwær*) reproduces the later Norse form very well (1962, lix).[47] Æthelweard's

---

[45] Alternatively, *Halfdene* may represent an Anglian form, with retraction of *æ* > *a* rather than breaking to *ea* before *l* + consonant.

[46] Tolkien suggested that the frequency with which *Halfdan* appears in Anglicised form as *Healfdene* in Anglo-Saxon sources 'cannot be solely due to the perspicuousness of the two elements; it must be in part due to English recognition of the name, although there is no evidence of their use of it for any other person than *Healfdene gamol* the Scylding, to whose fame in their traditions doubtless this recognition is largely due' (1982, 39 n.14).

[47] Insley, in fact, rejects this interpretation, and suggests that Æthelweard's spelling in <ig> arises from a continental spelling <igg> for *Ing-*, and therefore that Æthelweard's form still

work is within fifty years of Sigvatr's, and so it is likely that, since his written sources probably contained *Ingware* and its variants, his knowledge of the later native form *Ívarr* must have come from contemporary spoken contact.

Osbearn (Campbell 1962, 37 (*sub anno* 871)): a Scandinavian *consul* (that is, *jarl*) killed at the battle of Ashdown. The *Anglo-Saxon Chronicle* form is also *Osbearn* throughout, with a single *Esbeorn* (see Lehiste 1958, 15–16). The Old Norse name is *Ásbjǫrn* (VAN **Ásbiarn*) (see Björkman 1910, 10; Fellows-Jensen 1968, 18–19; Insley 1994, 24–33); Æthelweard has here simply followed his source.

Oscytel (Campbell 1962, 41 (*sub anno* 875)): one of the three *reges* who are reported as moving camp from Repton to Cambridge. The predominant *Anglo-Saxon Chronicle* form is also *Oscytel*, with occasional *Oskytel* and *Oskitel* (see Lehiste 1958, 16), and thus Æthelweard gives no new information. The underlying Old Norse name is *Ásketill*, later *Áskell* (see Lind 1905–15, 73–75; Björkman 1910, 16–20; Fellows-Jensen 1968, 25–32; Insley 1994, 48–60).

Ragnald (Campbell 1962, 54 (*sub anno* 948, *recte* 944)): son of Guðferð and king of York 943–44 (on Æthelweard's confused account of his expulsion, see above, under *Anlaf*; on his reign see Smyth 1987, II, 110–14). The dominant *Anglo-Saxon Chronicle* form is *Regnold*, other variants including *Regnald*, *Rægenald*, *Rægnold* (see Lehiste 1958, 17; for forms in other sources see Björkman 1910, 112; Fellows-Jensen 1968, 213; Insley 1994, 320). The Old Norse name is *Rǫgnvaldr*, earlier **Ragnvaldr* (see Lind 1905–15, 861–64). The first element is ON *rǫgn* ('powers, gods'), for which cognate OE *regn* has been substituted in the *Anglo-Saxon Chronicle* forms. As in other instances, however, Æthelweard endeavours to reproduce more closely the Norse form, and hence restores the vowel *a* in the first element as well as giving *a* in the second.

Sigeferð (Campbell 1962, 50 (*sub anno* 893)): an obscure figure who is described by Æthelweard as a *piraticus* coming from Northumbria (Stenton considered his ravages to have been in the region of Kesteven (1909, 81–83); Smyth rather sees them as constituting an attempt on Dublin (1987, I, 33–37)). The name does not occur in the *Anglo-Saxon Chronicle*, and Æthelweard is here following a now-lost independent source. However, the name represents ON *Sig(f)røðr* and occurs in other English sources as *Sigeferð*, *Sigferð*, *Siferð* (see Lind 1905–15, 877; Björkman 1910, 117–18; Fellows-Jensen 1968, 231; Insley 1994, 327–28). The first element, ON *sigr* ('victory'), was cognate with OE *sige*, and so it is not clear whether Æthelweard's form shows cognate substitution or reproduces the Norse form; the two are hardly to be distinguished. In the second element the metathesised *-ferð* is a common Anglicisation of ON *-friðr*, *-freðr* (see von Feilitzen 1937, 126 (§150)).[48]

---

preserves a nasalised first element (1994, 239). However, this leaves Insley having to derive the alternative form <Iuuar> from a misread <Inuar>, and unable to account for the *Anglo-Saxon Chronicle*'s <Iwer>.

[48] The name *Sigeferð* also occurs in the *Finnsburh Fragment* (Dobbie 1942, 3 (lines 15 and 24)), and so it is conceivable that the whole form may have been influenced by association with this hero's name.

Sihtrix (Campbell 1962, 37 (*sub anno* 871)): the name of two Scandinavians killed in the battle of Ashdown, described respectively as *ueteranus Sihtrix consul* and *iunior* [. . .] *Sihtrix* (*Anglo-Saxon Chronicle* MS 'A': 'Sidroc eorl [. . .] se alda ꝼ Sidroc 'eorl' se gioncga' (Bately 1986, 48)). The *Anglo-Saxon Chronicle* forms are dominated by *Sidroc, Sidrac*, but *Sihtric* occurs in some versions (see Lehiste 1958, 17; Björkman 1910, 120). Since the version of the *Anglo-Saxon Chronicle* used by Æthelweard appears to have been close to MS 'A', one may assume that *Sidroc* (the MS 'A' form) was the form occurring in his source, and hence the alteration (and improvement) to *Sihtrix* may be due to personal knowledge. The underlying Old Norse name is OWN *Sigtryggr* (see Lind 1905–15, 888; Fellows-Jensen 1968, 235). The Old Norse devoicing of *g* was in process during the Viking Age itself, and Æthelweard is thus a witness to the operation of this sound-change (represented as <h> in Old English). The change of final *-c* to Latin nominative *-x* may perhaps be an affected flourish on the part of Æthelweard.[49]

Norse Place-Names

Æthelweard's philological interests extend not only to anthroponymy but to all aspects of languages and names, and one finds Norse place-names featuring also in his *Chronicle*. Æthelweard was writing some hundred years or so after the first Scandinavian settlements in England, at a time when speakers of the Norse language had clearly been present for a sufficiently long time and in sufficient numbers for places in England to become known by Norse names by the English-speaking population. To find Norse place-names for places in England in Æthelweard, or the *Anglo-Saxon Chronicle*, or charters, does not surprise us as much as it perhaps should, for we know by the outcome how many such names established themselves permanently. But it *is* surprising, since for Norse place-names to occur in English sources, the names must have been current and familiar to the English-speaking population as well as the Norse. So when we come upon English writers using Norse place-names at a time when Norse was still a living vernacular in England, we are catching a glimpse of the point of contact between speakers of the two languages (see further pp 185–89 below).

Æthelweard's 871 account of the burial of the ealdorman Æthelwulf illustrates this very well (Campbell 1962, 37):[50]

---

[49] *-rix* for *-ric* is sometimes also found in personal names in Domesday Book (see von Feilitzen 1937, 111 (§123)).

[50] It may be noted here that *Danaam* is one of the curiosities of Æthelweard's vocabulary: elsewhere he uses it in the phrase *Danaa suda* 'the *Danaa* rampart' (Campbell 1962, 50). Campbell regards *Danaa, Danaam* as genitive forms which 'can only be regarded as due to fanciful form-making on Æthelweard's part' (1962, lvi), but this seems unlikely, since elsewhere Æthelweard uses the normal genitive plural *Danorum*. Rather, their grammatical concord in each instance with the following noun suggests that, although possibly of Æthelweard's own devising, they may be intended as adjectival forms.

Corpus quippe supra dicti ducis abstrahitur furtim, adduciturque in Merciorum prouinciam in loco qui Northuuorthige nuncupatur, iuxta autem Danaam linguam Deoraby.

(The body of the ealdorman mentioned above was carried away secretly, and was taken into Mercia, to the place called *Northworthig*, but in the Danish language Derby.)

As noted in the previous chapter, Derby is one of the few recorded examples of the replacement of an Old English place-name by an unrelated Norse one. For how long can we imagine the coexistence of the two forms? *Deoraby* occurs for the first time in the *Anglo-Saxon Chronicle sub anno* 917 and on some coins of Athelstan; *Norðweorðig* [sic] occurs for the last time c. 1020 (see *PNDb* 446; *SSNEM* 43; *DEPN* 142). Both forms were obviously known to Æthelweard: the place of burial of Ealdorman Æthelwulf is not recorded in any extant version of the *Anglo-Saxon Chronicle*, and while one must assume that it was in Æthelweard's source there is no reason to doubt that the linguistic digression is his own.

There are two other Norse place-names in England mentioned by Æthelweard. The first is in his account of 894, in which he refers to 'condensa syluæ, quæ uulgo Ceostefne nuncupatur' ('the thickets of the wood called Kesteven by the common people') (Campbell 1962, 51).[51] The second element of the name is ON *stefna* ('a meeting'), while the first is 'probably an old district name derived from Brit[ish] *ceto*-, Welsh *coed* "wood"' (*DEPN* 273); Æthelweard therefore reproduces the Norse second element precisely. The second place-name is found in his account of 902, where he writes that 'bella parantur Holme in loco contra orientalem' ('hostilities soon developed at the Holme against the eastern enemy [i.e. the Danes of East Anglia]') (Campbell 1962, 52). The details of this battle are given in the *Anglo-Saxon Chronicle* MSS 'AD' *sub anno* 905, but not the name of the site. However, MSS 'BC', here drawing on the so-called Mercian Register, declare *sub anno* 902 that the battle was fought *æt þam Holme* (Taylor 1983, 49); this evidently represents ON *holmr* ('island, elevated ground'), a common place-name element in Scandinavian parts of England (see Smith 1956, I, 258–59, 268). As for the precise location of the battle, Campbell lists *Holme* in his index as an 'unidentified place in Kent' (1962, 52), and in doing so he has presumably been guided by the reference in Eadgifu's will of c. 961 to 'þā tīd þæt mann beōnn ealle Cantware tō wīgge, tō Holme' (Whitelock 1967, 55) ('the time when all the men of Kent were summoned to battle at *Holme*'). However, the *Anglo-Saxon Chronicle* accounts make it clear that the battle took place somewhere further north, near the fen country; and consequently Cyril Hart argues persuasively for locating it at Holme in Huntingdonshire (1992, 511–15, esp. 515).

The preceding are all the Norse place-names in England mentioned by Æthelweard, but he also makes mention of a small number in the Scandinavian homelands,

---

[51] As Stenton notes rather grandly (1909, 82), this is 'the first appearance in history of the name Kesteven'.

and the forms in which these occur leave no doubt that Æthelweard is drawing his linguistic information from contemporary Norse contact, rather than traditional English sources. Thus in place of Bede's famous statement that the Angles' continental home had remained deserted since their migration to Britain, Æthelweard makes the following observation (Campbell 1962, 9):

> Porro Anglia uetus sita est inter Saxones et Giotos, habens oppidum capitale, quod sermone Saxonico Slesuuic nuncupatur, secundum uero Dano, Haithaby.
>
> (The old land of the Angles lies between the Saxons and Jutes, and has as its capital the town known in the Saxon language as Schleswig, but by the Danes as Hedeby.)

Here one finds again the interest in linguistic differences and in places with more than one name. The names *Slesuuic* and *Haithaby* occur nowhere else in Anglo-Saxon writings; as has been seen, the only other reference to the town *Haithaby* in Anglo-Saxon sources is in the Old English Orosius, where the name is given in the form *(æt) Hæðum* (see pp 103–04 above).[52] Æthelweard however reproduces the Norse form exactly, and there is no doubt as to the correctness of his statement that such is the name of the place *secundum* [...] *Dano*. The claim that *Slesuuic* is the name of the place *sermone Saxonico* is intriguing: it is possible that by this phrase Æthelweard means the Old English language, but it is more likely that the Germanic language(s) of the continent are intended, as the site features in early Frankish sources as *Sliesthorp* and *Sliaswich* — if exactly the same place is being referred to, as in time, of course, the towns of Hedeby and Schleswig were to be distinguished from one another (see Roesdahl 1982, 73).

A more doubtful example of an Old Norse name is the form by which Æthelweard refers to the Danish homeland, when he writes that in the early fifth century the Saxons were active in piracy 'in tota maritima a Rheno fluuio usque in Doniam urbem, quæ nunc uulgo Danmarc nuncupatur' ('in the whole coastal stretch from the river Rhine to Donia, which is now called Denmark by the common people') (Campbell 1962, 6–7).[53] Elsewhere in Anglo-Saxon writings the name only occurs in the Orosius and the *Anglo-Saxon Chronicle*, where it is *Denemearce, Denemarce*; in Old Norse it is *Danmǫrk*, earlier *Danmark* (see p 102 above). Æthelweard's *Danmarc* may possibly be a reproduction of the Norse form, but the normal Latin name for the people is *Dani* (OE *Dene*, ON *Danir*), and so *Danmarc* may simply be a Latin-influenced form.

---

[52] It is interesting to note, however, that a lost settlement in Lincolnshire bore the same name as the Danish town, perhaps indicating a transferred name: *Hedebi* DB, *Heidebi* c. 1128, *Heytheby* 1246 (*PNL* 6.65–66; *SSNEM* 53).

[53] As Campbell points out (1962, xxxv n.3), Æthelweard must have known that Denmark was not an *urbs*, and so perhaps one should here regard *urbem* as 'an unhappy scribal addition'. On the other hand, Æthelweard twice describes Lindsey as an *urbs*, and so 'perhaps his use of the word is lax'.

In his (ultimately Bede-derived) account of the Anglo-Saxon migration, Æthelweard concludes (Campbell 1962, 8),

> Ergo illa aduectio ex tribus prouinciis, quæ tum eminentiores habebantur Germaniæ, uenisse leguntur, hoc est de Saxonia, Anglia, atque Giota. Cantuarii de Giotis traxerunt originem, Vuhtii quoque, qui a Vuihta insula adhærente Brittaniæ nomen sortiti sunt.

> (And that immigration is said to have come from the three provinces of Germany then held in the highest repute, that is to say from the lands of the Saxons, Angles and Jutes. The men of Kent derived their origin from the Jutes, and so did the men of Wight, who got their name from the island of Wight, which is close to Britain.)

As Chadwick remarked long ago (1907, 98), Æthelweard's rather curious form *Giotis* (nominative **Gioti*) 'seems to be an attempt to represent the Scandinavian form *Iótar*'; and *Giota* for Jutland is obviously a related form (see pp 102–03 above).

There can similarly be no doubt about the final Norse place-name given by Æthelweard, which is found in his well-known version of the Sceaf legend and comes at the end of King Æthelwulf's genealogy (Campbell 1962, 33):

> septimus decimus Beo, octauus decimus Scyld, nonus decimus Scef. Ipse Scef cum uno dromone aduectus est in insula oceani que dicitur Scani, armis circundatus, eratque ualde recens puer, et ab incolis illius terræ ignotus. Attamen ab eis suscipitur, et ut familiarem diligenti animo eum custodierunt, et post in regem eligunt; de cuius prosapia ordinem trahit Aðulf rex.

> (his seventeenth [father] Beow, his eighteenth Scyld, his nineteenth Sceaf. And this Sceaf arrived with one light ship in the island of the ocean which is called Skaney, with arms all round him. He was a very young boy, and unknown to the people of that land, but he was received by them, and they guarded him with diligent attention as one who belonged to them, and elected him king. From his family King Æthelwulf derived his descent.)

Scani here represents a precise reproduction of ON *Skáni, Skáney*, in contrast to the somewhat Anglicised form found in the Old English Orosius and the traditional English form found in *Beowulf* (see p 108 above); again Æthelweard seems to be concerned with accurately preserving the contemporary form.

Æthelweard's form must derive from contemporary contact with speakers of Norse, and it is therefore worth briefly considering how much of the Sceaf legend Æthelweard may also have derived from contact with contemporary Scandinavian tradition. The issue is a complicated one, and has often been discussed, but it is generally agreed that there was in Scandinavia no living tradition of the mysterious arrival by boat of a boy called Sceaf; that no such legend attached to Skjǫldr either, and that he was merely the eponymous ancestor of the house of the Skjǫldungar; and that the application of the boat-legend to Scyld, and the collocation *Scyld Scēfing*, are likely to be the invention of the *Beowulf*-poet (the best guide to these issues remains Chambers 1959, 68–86; see also Chadwick 1907, 256–77; Newton 1993, 71–76; North 1997, 182–94; while Murray 1981 takes a different view). The first point is the most important here. When the West Saxon royal genealogy came to be copied into Icelandic manuscripts there appears to have been no recognition of the name *Sce(a)f*, and a curious misunderstanding arose: when the genealogy reached *Scef* and the statement that *Se Scef wæs Noés sunu* ('This Sceaf was the son of Noah'), the copyist interpreted *Se Scef* as being a single name rather than demonstrative + name, and hence a new figure, *Sescef*, was created in the Icelandic genealogies (see further Faulkes 1977, 179–80); and *Sescef* thus appears in the Prologue to Snorri's *Edda* (Snorri Sturluson 1982, 5). This misunderstanding would seem to confirm that Sceaf was not a familiar figure in Scandinavian legend — there are no other references to him except in his manifestation as Sescef — and hence it appears unlikely that Æthelweard should have drawn the legend of Sceaf as well as the name of *Scani* from contemporary contact; rather the ealdorman can be seen to be co-ordinating inherited English traditions with contemporary Norse information and restructuring them in that light.

Norse Elements in Æthelweard's Genealogies

The genealogy of King Æthelwulf of Wessex has just been mentioned, containing as it does the names of Scyld and Sceaf, and of course Æthelwulf's genealogy, although the longest and most elaborate, is only one of a number to be found in the *Anglo-Saxon Chronicle*.[54] Since this was Æthelweard's most important source, his Latin *Chronicle* also contains a number of genealogies, namely those of the royal houses of Wessex, Mercia, and Kent. Beside other, minor changes (which will not be noted here), Æthelweard alters these genealogies by introducing specifically Norse elements at three different points.[55]

Kenneth Sisam (1953b) demonstrated that the extant Anglo-Saxon royal genealogies are, on the whole, written constructs of the Christian period, although importantly, as Hermann Moisl (1981) has shown, they are ultimately derived at least in part from older oral traditions. Naturally, in pre-Christian times the pedigrees cannot have gone back beyond Woden: it was only when the pagan gods were given a euhemeristic interpretation by Christian writers and so were regarded as great kings

---

[54] A number of other manuscripts also bear witness to the importance attached to royal genealogies in the Anglo-Saxon period, and the various records have been extensively studied (see especially Sisam 1953b; Dumville 1976; 1977).

[55] By 'Norse elements' I mean names or relationships that have clearly been introduced under the influence of the contemporary Scandinavian presence in Viking Age England. In their (genealogically) earliest and most legendary stages (especially pre-Woden), the royal genealogies already contained figures who cannot have been regarded as natively Anglo-Saxon (for instance, Noah); and some of these have strong connections with parts of Scandinavia (for instance, Heremod). See further Chambers 1959, 73–74.

or heroes, that the way became clear to add further generations beyond Woden. Æthelweard is himself a proponent of such euhemerism (see further Johnson 1995), and describes Woden/Óðinn as (Campbell 1962, 9)[56]

> rex multitudinis barbarorum. In tanta etenim seductione oppressi aquilonales increduli ut deum colunt usque in hodiernam diem, viz. Dani, Northmanni quoque, et Sueui.
>
> ([a] king of a multitude of the barbarians. The heathen northern peoples are overwhelmed in so great a seduction that they worship [him] as a god to the present day, that is to say the Danes, Norwegians and also the Suebi.)

As a Christian, and also as a writer whose sources contained genealogies going back as far as Noah, Æthelweard regarded Woden as merely a human king of the legendary past; but he was also aware of the pagan beliefs of the Scandinavians, and that they worshipped this same figure as a god *in hodiernam diem* ('to the present day'). How then to refer to this key figure?

The native Old English form of the name was of course *Wōden*, the Old Norse form *Óðinn* (see further p 140 below). Æthelweard is writing of a figure who is at the same time both an ancestor of the Anglo-Saxon royal house and a current Scandinavian god, and hence he elects to use a form that is a compromise between the English and the Norse, namely *Vuothen*: initial OE *w* is preserved, but medial ON *ð* introduced in place of OE *d*. This form occurs seven times in Æthelweard (Campbell 1962, 9, 12, 13, 18 (X2), 25, and 33), while by comparison the purely Old English form *Vuoddan* occurs only once, at the first appearance of the name (Campbell 1962, 7); perhaps Æthelweard hit on the idea of a compromise form only in the course of composition.[57] The Old English form of the name does, however, outnumber the compromise form by two to one as an element in English place-names in Æthelweard (Campbell 1962, 14, 21, 53), but this is perhaps not surprising (*Wodnesbyrg* and *Vuodnesfelda*, in contrast to *Vuothnesbeorhge*, the same place as *Wodnesbyrg*).

If Æthelweard's first Norse element in the genealogies is a compromise form arising from the coexistence of competing English and Norse forms of the same name, his second seems to be a simple case of borrowing from Scandinavian myth; it appears in the Kentish genealogy of Hengest and Horsa. Æthelweard's innovation occurs in the section of the pedigree between Woden and Hengest, and so it is necessary first to give that section as it exists in other sources:[58]

---

[56]As Campbell notes (1962, 9 n.1), in this passage Æthelweard seems to be confusing Suebi and Swedes.

[57]Curiously, the compromise form <woðen> also occurs (once only) in London, BL, MS Cotton Tiberius A.xiv, a mid-eighth-century manuscript of Bede's *Historia Ecclesiastica* (see Sweet 1885, 133; Ström 1939, xxxi).

[58]Sources are as follows: OE Bede from Miller 1890–91, I, 52; *Anglo-Saxon Chronicle* MS 'E' (*sub anno* 449) from Plummer and Earle 1892–99, I, 13; and London, BL, MS Cotton Vespasian B.vi, CCCC 183, and London, BL, MS Cotton Tiberius B.v from Dumville 1976.

Anglo-Norse Contact in Anglo-Saxon Sources

Bede	*ASC* MS 'E'	Vesp. B.vi	CCCC 183	Tib. B.v
Woden	Woden	Uoden	Woden	Woden
Wihta	Wecta	Uegdaeg	Wægdæg	Wægdæg
Witta	Witta	Uihtgils	Wihtgisl	Wihtgils
Wihtgyls	Wihtgils	Uitta	Witta	Witta
Hengest	Hengest	Hengest	Hengest	Hengest

The differences among these versions are clear enough: fluctuations between the forms of *Wecta/Wægdæg* and between the order of *Witta* and *Wihtgils* (see further Sisam 1953b, 323–25). Drawing his information from Bede (probably in the Old English translation), Æthelweard gives the ancestry of Hengest twice, once while telling of the first coming of the Anglo-Saxons to Britain and once while expatiating on the origins of the *Escingas* (Campbell 1962, 9, 18):

Præfati enim duces eorum inde uenerunt Britanniam primi: hoc est Hengest et Horsa filii Vuyhtelsi, auus eorum Vuicta, et proauus eorum Vuithar, atauus quidem eorum Vuothen, qui et rex multitudinis barbarorum.

(Now the above-named leaders of those people were the first to come to Britain from the lands we have been discussing, that is to say Hengest and Horsa, the sons of Wihtels; their grandfather was Wihta, their great-grandfather Withar, and their great-great-grandfather Woden, who was king of a multitude of the barbarians.)

Ese quippe pater fuit Hengest, qui primus consul et dux de Germania fuerat gentis Anglorum. Cuius pater fuit Wihtgels, auus Wicta, proauus Wither, atauus Wothen, qui et rex multarum gentium, quem pagani nunc ut deum colunt aliqui.

(Esc's father was Hengest, who was the first earl of the English people and their leader out of Germany. His father was Wihtgils, his grandfather Wihta, his great-grandfather Wither, and his great-great-grandfather Woden, who was king of many nations, and whom some pagans now worship as a god.)

Thus according to Æthelweard the line of descent to Hengest runs as follows:

Vuothen/Wothen
Vuithar/Wither
Vuicta/Wicta
Vuyhtelsi/Wihtgels
Hengest/Hengest

Æthelweard is following Bede, so it is to be expected that he cites *Vuyhtelsi/Wihtgels* as the father of *Hengest*, rather than *Witta* as in the Anglian collection of genealogies. However, the major change is *Vuithar-Vuicta* for *Wihta-Witta* (Bede) or *Wægdæg-Wihtgils* (Anglian collection). Æthelweard's *Vuicta* is evidently Bede's

Wihta, and so the real surprise is that the two generations below *Vuothen* have been reversed in order and Bede's *Witta* has been replaced by *Vuithar/Wither* — that is, by the name of the Norse god *Víðarr*. This is the only occurrence of the god's name in extant Anglo-Saxon writings, and, since ON /w/ > /v/ is a post-Viking Age development, Æthelweard's *Vuithar* characteristically reproduces the Norse form exactly.

Before concentrating on Víðarr, it is necessary briefly to consider Wihta and Witta — if they are indeed in origin separate names, and separate figures, and not simply variants of the same name. Nothing is known of Wihta in Old English writings beyond the name, and this occurs only in versions of the Kentish genealogy. The name *Witta* is found in one other place, namely line 22 of *Widsith* which states that *Witta weold Swæfum* ('Witta ruled the *Swæfe*') (Krapp and Dobbie 1936, 150; see further Alan Bliss in Tolkien 1982, 172–73). It was noted above that Æthelweard shows ignorance or uncertainty concerning the *Swæfe* (Latin *Suebi*) and confuses them with the Swedes, and so it would seem unlikely that he knew any living traditions or stories concerning Witta beyond his name in the Kentish genealogies.

In extant Norse texts Víðarr is the son of Óðinn, and the only major stories known about him concern his role in the events at the end of the old world and the beginning of the new. At *ragnarøkr* he will avenge his father by killing Fenrisúlfr, setting his foot (clad in a special shoe) on the wolf's lower jaw and his hand on the upper, and so tearing his maw apart. He will survive *ragnarøkr*, and afterwards inhabit Iðavellir with the other remaining gods (for the standard prose account see Snorri Sturluson 1982, 50–54; of the Eddic poems it is *Vafþrúðnismál* (stanzas 51 and 53) that has most to say about Víðarr, and its most recent editor tentatively ascribes the poem to the tenth century on linguistic grounds (Machan 1988, 11)). There is no sign of any corresponding figure in the much more meagre records of Anglo-Saxon paganism.

Clearly the name of Víðarr had become familiar to Æthelweard in late-tenth-century England through the contemporary Scandinavian presence. He was presumably struck by the similarity of the names *Witta* and *Víðarr*, and replaced the former by the latter in his version of the Kentish genealogy.[59] However, not only the name of Víðarr was known to Æthelweard, but also some traditions concerning him: for, as has been seen, he reverses the order of the two generations below *Vuothen* and so makes *Vuithar* the son of *Vuothen* rather than *Vuyhtelsi*. Evidently there was a living tradition known to Æthelweard (through Scandinavian contact) that Víðarr was the son of Óðinn; as has been seen, there seems to have been little or no tradition known about either Witta or Wihtgils, and so Æthelweard has followed the living tradition and reversed the order, so making the Kentish genealogy accord with the Scandinavian stories.

---

[59] The two names are not, it seems, etymologically related: the first element in *Víðarr* is related to ON *víðr* ('wide, extensive'), and so in Old English one would be looking for a name in *wīd* (see Sturtevant 1952, 1161–62; de Vries 1961, 659).

As noted above, Æthelweard's *Vuithar/Wither* (son of *Vuothen*) represents the only occurrence of the name of the Norse god in extant Anglo-Saxon writings, although a personal name *Wiðer* does appear in some late Old English documents (see Searle 1897, 503). However there exists another well-known witness to the presence of myths about Víðarr among the Scandinavian settlers in England, namely the Gosforth Cross in Cumbria, thought to have been carved in the mid- or late tenth century and thus broadly contemporary with Æthelweard's reference (for depiction and discussion see Collingwood 1927, 155–57; Bailey 1980, 125–31; Bailey and Cramp 1988, 100–04, Illustrations 288–308). On its east side is portrayed a warrior-figure confronting a wolf-like monster, with one foot on the monster's lower jaw and one hand on its upper, and the identification of the scene as Víðarr slaying Fenrisúlfr at *ragnarøkr* seems certain. The Gosforth Cross therefore gives contemporary confirmation of the circulation of myths concerning Víðarr in tenth-century England.

Thirdly and lastly, Æthelweard makes an alteration to the West Saxon genealogy of King Æthelwulf, found in the *Anglo-Saxon Chronicle sub anno* 855. In MS 'A' the four generations up to and including Woden are given as 'Friþogar Bronding, Brond Beldæging, Beldæg Wodening, Woden Friþowalding' (Bately 1986, 45–46). In Æthelweard, these ancestors of Æthelwulf become 'sextus pater eius Frithogar, septimus Brond, octauus Balder, nonus Vuothen' ('his sixth father Frithogar, his seventh Brond, his eighth Balder, his ninth Woden') (Campbell 1962, 33). Æthelweard has thus replaced the name *Beldæg* with *Balder* — that is, with the name of the Norse god Baldr. As with Víðarr this is the only occurrence of the name in extant Anglo-Saxon writings, and again Æthelweard reproduces the Norse form with impressive accuracy.

Beldæg represents another figure unknown outside of the royal genealogies, whereas Baldr, of course, is a central figure in Norse mythological texts. According to Snorri, he is the son of Óðinn and Frigg, the *beztr* ('best') of the gods and *hann lofa allir* ('everyone loves him'); he is the most *fagr álitum* ('beautiful in appearance') and also the 'vitrastr Ásanna ok fegrst talaðr ok líknsamastr' ('the wisest of the Æsir, the fairest-spoken and most gracious') (Snorri Sturluson 1982, 23; all translations from Snorri my own). He is unwittingly killed by Hǫðr through the deceit of Loki, and it is (probably) only Loki who prevents Baldr from being wept back out of Hel (Snorri Sturluson 1982, 45–48). Nevertheless he will return when the new earth rises after *ragnarøkr* (Snorri Sturluson 1982, 53).

There are no native Anglo-Saxon traditions known concerning a figure corresponding to Baldr; nor (as has been said) is Baldr himself noticed in England beyond this reference in Æthelweard. Evidently, as with Víðarr, the name of the Norse god had become known to Æthelweard, and also (almost certainly) some traditions concerning him. For it is easy to understand why Æthelweard should have changed *Beldæg* to *Balder*: as with Víðarr, the two were identified on the basis of the similarity of names and similarity of relationships (both being the son of Wōden/Óðinn), and Æthelweard has again preferred the name to which living tradition attached rather than that which was (seemingly) lost in obscurity. It is most unlikely, however, that

Beldæg-Baldr represents anything more than a substitution based on the similarity of name and relationship.

Interestingly, though, the identical substitution is found also in thirteenth-century Iceland. It is well known that a manuscript containing many of the Anglo-Saxon royal genealogies, and related very closely to Cotton Tiberius B.v, was copied into Icelandic in perhaps the twelfth century (see further Chambers 1959, 313; Faulkes 1977); and the creation of *Sescef* has already been mentioned. Eventually, and most famously, certain of these genealogies made their way into the Prologue to Snorri's *Edda*. In Snorri's source, seemingly a descendant of the original Icelandic manuscript and very similar to the extant AM 1 e β II fol, it appears that after the name *Voden* in the first list an explanatory note was appended in terms similar to that found in the Arnamagnæan manuscript: 'Þat kollum ver Oðinn fra honum eru comnar flestar kononga ettir i norðr halfu heimsins' (Faulkes 1977, 182–83) ('We call him Óðinn from whom most families of kings are descended in the northern half of the world'). As Anthony Faulkes points out (1977, 183), the first four words of this comment are found in the Prologue to Snorri's *Edda*:

[B]ut the prologue also includes a number of other alternative names that claim to be the Norse equivalents of the English forms in the genealogies, and none of these others were in Resen's manuscript [i.e. AM 1 e β II fol]. These associations were presumably made by the compiler of the prologue (perhaps inspired by the note in the genealogical list he was using), who in most cases was probably only indicating what he thought was the corresponding Norse pronunciation of the Old English names, and may not always have intended to imply identity between the persons in these lists and persons in Norse tradition who were known by the corresponding Norse names.

Thus, for example, one finds in Snorri's Prologue identifications such as 'Svebdegg, er vér kǫllum Svipdag' ('*Svebdegg*, whom we call *Svipdag*') and 'Gevis, er vér kǫllum Gavi' ('*Gevis*, whom we call *Gavi*'); accordingly one also finds the statement, 'Annarr son Óðins hét Beldegg, er vér kǫllum Baldr' ('Another son of Óðinn was called *Beldegg*, whom we call *Baldr*') (Snorri Sturluson 1982, 5).[60] The question is, of course, whether this represents a true correspondence and identification, or is merely provoked by the similarity of name. Faulkes considers that 'the compiler may well have thought that the names Beldegg and Balldr [sic] did represent the same person' (1977, 183), but this only seems likely if Faulkes means that it must have seemed improbable to the compiler that two such similar names should not refer to the same person. If it is not due to chance, a genuine identification can have been made only through knowledge, and what can a thirteenth-century Icelander have known when Anglo-Saxon sources themselves are so silent? Furthermore, the names Beldæg and Baldr do not in fact correspond etymologically. De Vries states of *Baldr* that '[d]as Wort ist bis jetzt unerklärt' (1961, 24) ('the word is so far unexplained'),

---

[60]It is to be noted however that the name *Vitta* provokes no identification with *Víðarr*.

but its Old English cognate is *bealdor*, and this is usually translated as 'prince, lord'.[61] The etymology of *Beldæg*, on the other hand, is usually taken to be simply *bǣl* ('fire') and *dæg* ('day').

The fact that both Æthelweard and the Prologue to Snorri's *Edda* equate the two names is certainly striking, but it is perhaps less surprising when one considers that both writers, as has been seen, are positively striving to make such equations; and the phonetic similarity (though not the etymological) cannot be denied. The fact that both are sons of Wōden/Óðinn can only have helped such an equation. Further than this, however, one cannot go. The importance of Æthelweard's *Balder* is that it shows us an Anglo-Saxon revealing an awareness of and interest in Norse mythology and names; it does not necessarily mean that he regarded Beldæg as the native equivalent of the Norse god Baldr, and still less that one can begin to reconstruct Anglo-Saxon paganism using the equation 'Beldæg = Baldr'.

Conclusion

In ealdorman Æthelweard, then, we encounter an Anglo-Saxon with linguistic interests, and moreover an Anglo-Saxon who is a layman and statesman rather than a cleric. The presence of Scandinavian settlers and raiders in tenth-century England means that Æthelweard's general inclinations are revealed especially in an interest in the language and beliefs of these Scandinavians, and this interest is manifested in various ways: in a particular concern with the forms of Norse personal names and the existence of Norse place-names; in an awareness of Norse as a second vernacular current in Anglo-Saxon England; and in the introduction of Norse elements into the Anglo-Saxon royal genealogies. What distinguishes Æthelweard's Scandinavian interests above all is his desire (and ability) to reproduce Norse forms as accurately as possible, rather than employing Anglicised forms — that is, he shows a preference for forms derived from contemporary spoken contact rather than inherited book-forms, and one might argue that much the same principle informs his re-ordering of the royal genealogies. Audrey Meaney, in the course of her survey of evidence for Norse paganism in England, and especially in Northumbria, considers the possible channels of Anglo-Norse contact through which Æthelweard may have gained his information. She concludes (1970, 131–32),

> We do not have to assume [...] that Æthelweard derived all his Scandinavian knowledge from one informant. The improvement of the Danish names in the Chronicle need not have been due to the same person who told him about Othin, Baldr and Vithar. It is surely not beyond the bounds of possibility that a relative of King Alfred

---

[61]*Bealdor* occurs some ten times in Old English poetic texts, with the curious syntactic trait of always being preceded by a genitive plural noun (for example, *sinca baldor* ('lord of treasures') and *winia bealdor* ('lord of friends') in *Beowulf* (Klaeber 1950, 91, 96 (lines 2428 and 2567))).

[...] should have sufficient intellectual curiosity to interview and get snippets of information from anyone who came his way.

In all of these ways Æthelweard reveals an impressive sensitivity and knowledge, and his *Chronicle* thus gives us an invaluable impression of how the presence of the Norse language in England struck one philologically minded observer.

Ælfric and Wulfstan: De Falsis Diis

We turn finally to the third Anglo-Saxon source chosen for analysis. Ælfric and Wulfstan are, of course, the two most important Old English prose writers from the period of renewed Viking attack in the late tenth and early eleventh centuries (for literary and biographical introductions see Bethurum 1957; 1966; Clemoes 1966; Gatch 1977; Whitelock 1981; Wilcox 1994, 1–65). The majority of Ælfric's works were written in the 990s; the final version of Wulfstan's most famous piece, the *Sermo Lupi ad Anglos*, was delivered in 1014. Between them their writing lives span the ill-fated reign of Æthelred, and one might therefore expect their works to have considerable relevance for the question of Anglo-Norse contact. This is especially true of Wulfstan, who not only was Archbishop of York, and therefore at the Northumbrian centre of the northern Danelaw, but also was conspicuous for his activities as a statesman and lawmaker, under Cnut as well as Æthelred.

The Norse elements in Wulfstan's language have in fact received some attention, in particular from Dietrich Hofmann (1955, 188–93 (§§274–86); see also Whitelock 1976, 44–45; Townend 2000a, 92–93). Ælfric, writing in the south-west, was understandably less exposed to Norse linguistic influence than Wulfstan, but a few loanwords are to be found in his language, the most important of which is *lagu* ('law'): this gradually comes to replace OE *ǣ* in his writing, and its increasing use may be due at least in part to the influence of Wulfstan (see Godden 1980, 214–17; Fischer 1989a). This body of Norse loans in the language of Ælfric and Wulfstan will therefore not be discussed here.

In the text by Ælfric most obviously concerned with the Viking attacks, namely his *Life of St Edmund* (Skeat 1881–1900, IV, 314–35), only two Norse names feature — *Hinguar* and *Hubba* (ON *Ívarr* and *Ubbi*), in slightly varying forms — and these appear to have been derived scribally from Ælfric's source, Abbo's *Passio Sancti Eadmundi*, with the tell-tale presence of initial *H*-. The bookish origin of Ælfric's *Hinguar* can thus be contrasted with Æthelweard's *Iguuar*, which appears to derive from contemporary spoken contact (see pp 115–16 above). As far as I am aware, the only other Norse name to be found in Ælfric's works is a single reference, in the Epilogue to his translation of the Book of Judges, to Óláfr Guðfriðsson of York and Dublin, defeated by Athelstan at the battle of Brunanburh. In this Epilogue Ælfric is concerned to trace the victories of Christian kings beyond biblical times, via such figures as Constantine, into his own country and period. Three Anglo-Saxon kings who were *sigefæste þurh God* ('victorious through God') are therefore selected for praise, namely Alfred, Athelstan, and Edgar: Athelstan, Ælfric says, 'wið Anlaf gefeaht ⁊ his firde ofsloh ⁊ aflimde hine sylfne, ⁊ he on sibbe wunude siþþan mid his leode' (Crawford 1922, 416) ('fought against *Anlaf* and slaughtered his army and put him to flight, and afterwards lived in peace amongst his people'). But *Anlaf* is the usual form of the Old Norse name in Old English sources, and so Ælfric's witness supplies no new information (see p 112 above).

The text to be primarily considered here from the point of view of Anglo-Norse contact is therefore *De Falsis Diis*, a homily by Ælfric of which Wulfstan subsequently made his own adaptation. Ælfric's homily has long been famous on account of the equations he makes in it between certain of the classical gods and corresponding Norse gods, as this would seem to indicate some knowledge of the pagan beliefs of the Scandinavians in England. The section in which these equations are made comes early in the homily and is derived in its classical particulars from Martin of Braga's sixth-century sermon *De Correctione Rusticorum* (see Pope 1967–68, II, 671–73). The key passage is as follows (Pope 1967–68, II, 683–85 (lines 122–49)):[62]

> Þes Iouis is arwurðust ealra þæra goda
> þe þa hæþenan hæfdon on heora gedwylde;
> and he hatte Þór betwux sumum þeodum,
> þone þa Deniscan leoda lufiað swiðost.
> His sunu hatte Mars, se macede æfre saca,
> and wrohte and wáwan he wolde æfre styria[n].
> Þisne wurðodan þa hæðenan for healicne god,
> and swa oft swa hi fyrdadon, oððe to gefeohte woldan,
> þonne offrodon hi heora lac on ær þisum god[e].
> Hi gelyfdon þæt he mihte micclum him [f]ultumian
> on þam gefeohte, for þam þe he gefeoht lufode.
> Sum man wæs gehaten Mercurius on life,
> se wæs swiðe facenfull and swicol on dædum,
> and lufode eac stala and leasbregdnyssa.
> Þone macodan þa hæþenan him to mæran gode,
> and æt wega gelætum him lac offrodan,
> and to heagum beorgum him brohtan onsæg[ed]nysse.
> Ðes god wæs [a]rwyrðe betwyx eallum hæþenum,
> and he is Óðon geháten oðrum naman on Denisc.
> Nu secgað þa Deniscan on heora gedwylde
> þæt se Iouis wære, þe hi Þór hátað,
> Mercuries sunu, þe hi Oðon hatað;
> ac hi nabbað na riht, for þam þe we rædað on bocum,
> ge on hæþenum ge on Cristenum, þæt se hetola Iouis
> to soðan wære Saturnes sunu,

---

[62]Since some manuscripts lack lines 141–49, Pope argues that these possibly represent a slightly later insertion, but one certainly made by Ælfric himself (1967–68, II, 673).

and þa béc ne magon beon awægede
þe þa ealdan hæðenan be him awriton þuss;
and eac on martira þrowungum we gemetað swa awriten.

(This Jove is the most venerable of all the gods which the heathens, in their error, possessed, and amongst certain nations he is called Þórr, whom the Danish people love most of all. His son was called Mars, who always caused strife, and he desired always to stir up contention and misery. The heathens honoured this man as an exalted god, and whenever they went to war, or desired battle, they made their sacrifice beforehand to this god. They believed that he could help them greatly in battle, because he loved battle. There was a certain man who was called Mercury when alive, who was very deceitful and treacherous in his deeds, and he also loved theft and deceptions. The heathens made him into a great god for themselves, and made sacrifice to him at crossroads, and brought him offerings on high mountains. This god was honoured amongst all heathens, and by another name he is called Óðinn in Danish. Now in their error the Danes say that this Jove, whom they call Þórr, was the son of Mercury, whom they call Óðinn; but they do not maintain the truth, for we read in both heathen and Christian books that this cruel Jove was without doubt the son of Saturn, and the books cannot be rejected in which the ancient heathens wrote about him thus; and we also find this recorded in the passions of the martyrs.)

The early section of Ælfric's *De Falsis Diis* was reworked by Wulfstan to form his own shorter homily; Wulfstan's selection of only this part suggests perhaps that it was the issue of the Norse gods that moved him to make his adaptation. Pope believes that Wulfstan probably received a copy of the homily directly from Ælfric (1967–68, II, 675), and in general Wulfstan follows Ælfric very closely, usually adapting or interpolating only for characteristic rhythmical purposes. The relevant passage in Wulfstan's *De Falsis Diis* is therefore as follows (Bethurum 1957, 223 (lines 54–76); see 336–39 for very full notes on this passage):

[Iouis] is geteald eac arwurðost ealra þæra goda þe þa hæðenan on ðam dagum for godas hæfdon on heora gedwylde. And he hatte Þor oðrum naman betwux sumum þeodum; ðone Denisca leoda lufiað swyðost ⁊ on heora gedwylde weorðiaþ geornost. His sunu hatte Mars, se macode æfre gewinn ⁊ wrohte, ⁊ saca ⁊ wraca he styrede gelome. Ðysne yrming æfter his forðsiðe wurðodon þa hæðenan eac for healicne god, ⁊ swa oft swa hy fyrdedon oððe to gefeohte woldon, þonne offrodon hy heora lac on ær to weorðunge þissum gedwolgode; ⁊ hy gelyfdon þæt he miclum mihte heom fultumian on gefeohte forðan þe he gefeoht ⁊ gewinn lufude on life. Sum man eac wæs gehaten Mercurius on life, se wæs swyðe facenfull ⁊ ðeah full snotorwyrde swicol on dædum ⁊ on leasbregdum. Ðone macedon þa hæðenan be heora getæle eac heom to mæran gode, ⁊ æt wega gelætum him lac offrodon oft ⁊ gelome þurh deofles lare, ⁊ to heagum beorgum him brohton oft mistlice loflac. Ðes gedwolgod wæs arwurðe eac betwux eallum hæðenum on þam dagum, ⁊ he is Oðon gehaten oðrum naman on Denisce wisan. Nu secgað sume þa Denisce men on heora gedwylde þæt se Iouis wære þe hy Þor hatað, Mercuries sunu, þe hi Oðon namiað, ac hi nabbað na riht, forðan þe we rædað on bocum, ge on hæþenum ge on Cristenum, þæt se hetula Iouis to soðan is Saturnes sunu.

([Jove] is also reckoned the most venerable of all the gods which the heathens, in their error, took for gods in those days. And by another name he is called Þórr amongst certain nations; and the Danish people love him most of all and honour him most eagerly. His son was called Mars, who always caused conflict and contention, and often stirred up strife and misery. After his death the heathens also honoured this wretch as an exalted god, and whenever they went to war or desired battle, they made their sacrifice beforehand in honour of this idol; and they believed that he could help them greatly in battle because he loved battle and conflict when alive. There was also a certain man called Mercury when alive, who was very deceitful and moreover very wise of speech and treacherous in deeds and in deceptions. The heathens, by their reckoning, also made him into a great god for themselves, and very frequently, through the teaching of the devil, made sacrifice to him at crossroads, and often brought him various offerings on high mountains. This idol was also honoured amongst all the heathens in those days, and by another name he is called Óðinn in the Danish idiom. Now in their error certain Danish men say that this Jove, whom they call Þórr, was the son of Mercury, whom they call Óðinn; but they do not maintain the truth, for we read in both heathen and Christian books that this cruel Jove is without doubt the son of Saturn.)

As well as the passage on Jove and Mercury, Ælfric also explains in his *De Falsis Diis* the origins of the names of the days of the week. The pagan explanations for the etymologies of Tuesday, Wednesday, and Thursday are conspicuous by their absence, and the usual explanation given for this silence is that Ælfric does not want to complicate the issue by introducing the topic of former English paganism, but rather confines himself to contemporary Scandinavian practices (see Pope 1967–68, II, 716; but also Meaney 1984, 127–28).[63] However, Ælfric does say about Friday that (Pope 1967–68, II, 686 (lines 176–77))

> Ðone sixtan dæg hi gesetton þære sceamleasan gydenan
> Uen[us] gehaten, and Fric[g] on Denisc.

(They appointed the sixth day to the shameless goddess called Venus, and Frigg in Danish.)

Therefore in *De Falsis Diis* Ælfric makes three equations between classical gods and Scandinavian ones: Jove and Þórr, Mercury and Óðinn, and Venus and Frigg; and Wulfstan, in his adaptation of Ælfric's work, repeats the first two of these. Elsewhere Ælfric makes the same three equations in his *Life of St Martin* (No. 31 of the *Lives of the Saints*), when describing the various forms the Devil assumed in his attempts to deceive the saint (Skeat 1881–1900, IV, 264 (lines 710–18)):

---

[63]Johnson (1995, 52–62) suggests Ælfric may also have been motivated by political tact towards aristocratic West Saxon patrons who counted Woden as an ancestor. Later marginal glosses to Wulfstan's text in Oxford, Bodleian Library MS Hatton 113 do make explicit the connection with the names of the week, but falsely derive these names from the Norse gods in the homily: *Þor unde Þornes dæg* and *Oþon unde Wodones deg* (Bethurum 1957, 223, glosses to lines 56 and 72).

> Mid þusend searo-cræftum wolde se swicola deofol
> þone halgan wer on sume wisan beswican .
> and hine ge-sewen-licne on manegum scin-hiwum
> þam halgan æteowde . on þæra hæþenra goda hiwe .
> hwilon on ioues hiwe . þe is ge-haten þór .
> hwilon on mercuries . þe men hatað oþon .
> hwilon on ueneris þære fulan gyden .
> þe men hatað fricg . and on manegum oþrum hiwum
> hine bræd se deofol on þæs bisceopes gesihþe .

(The treacherous devil desired to deceive the holy man in some way with a thousand cunning skills, and he visibly showed himself to the saint in many phantasmal shapes, in the form of the gods of the heathens: sometimes in the form of Jove, who is called Þórr, and sometimes in the form of Mercury, whom men call Óðinn, and sometimes in the form of the foul goddess Venus, whom men call Frigg; and the devil changed himself into many other forms in the sight of the bishop.)

These equations in Ælfric and Wulfstan have often been discussed before in the context of reconstructing Norse paganism; in the present investigation three somewhat different issues will be explored, namely the very fact of Ælfric's knowledge, his emphasis on linguistic difference, and the forms of the names.

Knowledge of the Norse Gods

Precisely what knowledge does Ælfric reveal of the Scandinavian gods, and from where is he likely to have derived it? It should be remembered that the homilist is primarily discussing the classical gods; but of course in order to make the equations he does, Ælfric must have known that certain of the characteristic features of the classical deities were paralleled in the beliefs concerning the Scandinavian ones. He may also have been guided by the equivalences enshrined in the names of the days of the week and so drawn on native knowledge (Wōden-Óðinn, Þunor-Þórr, Frīg-Frigg); this however raises the question of how much was remembered of the characteristics of the ancient English gods by the time of Ælfric, and one suspects that it can have been very little indeed.

The Jove-Þórr equation was no doubt provoked by the name of the fifth day of the week (*dies Jovis - Þunresdæg*), as well as by the obvious connection with thunder. But Ælfric's statement that it is Þórr 'þone þa Deniscan leoda lufiað swiðost' ('whom the Danish people love most of all') is intriguing, if this does indeed mean that Þórr is the god the Danes love most, rather than that the Danes are the people who most love Þórr. In the later Icelandic written sources it is Óðinn who holds the pre-eminent position in the Norse pantheon occupied by Jove in the Roman, and so it is possible that Ælfric has here been led astray by his equation and erroneously transferred Jove's eminence onto Þórr. However, other evidence suggests that Ælfric may well be making an important and accurate observation on this point. Personal names with *Þór(r)-* as their first element seem to have enjoyed very considerable popularity in Norse nomenclature in England (see Björkman 1910, 146–64; Fellows-Jensen 1968, 295–318; Insley 1994, 390–432; also Insley 1979, 52–53), and Turville-Petre (1972) argued that it was Þórr and not Óðinn who was (in the words of a phrase from *Úlfljótslǫg*, quoted in *Landnámabók*) *hinn almáttki áss* ('the all-powerful god'), the most important deity worshipped by the settlers in Iceland; it is therefore plausible that this was a colonial phenomenon found in England as well, perhaps due to the agricultural lifestyle of the settlers (for a brief summary of evidence for the worship of Þórr in England see further Turville-Petre 1964, 94–95).

Ælfric's equation of Mercury with Óðinn is very persuasive, and it is of course also found in the correspondence in the days of the week between *dies Mercurii* and *Wōdnesdæg*. In Norse mythological texts Óðinn is notoriously fickle and untrustworthy, corresponding well with Ælfric's description of the god as 'swiðe facenfull and swicol on dædum' ('very deceitful and treacherous in his deeds'), with a great love of *stala and leasbregdnyssa* ('theft and deceptions'). The claim that he was worshipped with sacrifices on *heagum beorgum* ('high mountains'), which was not, as far as is known, a feature of the worship of Mercury, has led some commentators to believe that Ælfric was governed here by closer knowledge of Scandinavian practices or remembrance of the English cult of Wōden, especially in the light of place-names linking that god's name with hills and mountains (see Bethurum 1957, 338–39; Pope 1967–68, II, 715–16). Wulfstan adds the further information that the god was *full snotorwyrde* ('very wise of speech'), and the knowledge and control of language is a prominent feature of Óðinn's character in Icelandic sources.

The equation of Venus and Frigg is the only one which Ælfric acknowledges as being enshrined in the days of the week (*dies Veneris - Frīgedæg*). In Norse mythological writings Frigg is the wife of Óðinn and the goddess of matrimony, but by no means is she the sexually licentious figure associated with the Roman goddess. Indeed, it is the fertility goddess Freyja who corresponds more closely in character with Venus; and furthermore Venus was the wife of Vulcan, not Mercury, although the latter was the father of Cupid, her child. Richard North therefore argues that no such figure as Freyja was known in Viking Age England, and that her sexual role in later Icelandic mythography has been transferred from Frigg, who bore the role up to that point (1997, 256–57).

So much for the correspondences made by Ælfric and, significantly, endorsed by the Northumbrian Wulfstan. It is therefore convenient to pause at this point and to note that, as is well known, an Icelandic translation of Ælfric's *De Falsis Diis* is found in the early-fourteenth-century *Hauksbók*, under the rubric *Um þat hvaðan otru hofst* (Eiríkur Jónsson and Finnur Jónsson 1892–96, 156–64) ('Concerning whence unbelief arose'). Arnold Taylor's discussion of the text of this *Hauksbók* translation remains the fundamental one (1969): he concludes that the translation, which follows Ælfric's text very closely for the most part, was originally made in the twelfth or thirteenth century, and that there are signs of a Norwegian scribe at some point in the transmission. The Scandinavian translator preserves the main equations of Jove/Jupiter-Þórr and Mercury-Óðinn (Eiríkur Jónsson and Finnur Jónsson 1892–96, 158–59):

> En sa Íupíter var þeira alra rikastr hinna heiðnu manna. er sumír menn kalla Þor. en sa var allr einn en hann blotaðo menn a danska tungu allra mest. [. . .] En var einn maðr sa er Merkuríus het [. . .] en hann het Oðenn a donsku.
>
> (And this Jupiter, whom some men call Þórr, was the most powerful of all those heathen men. And he was pre-eminent, and men of the Norse language worshipped him most of all. [. . .] And there was a certain man who was called Mercury [. . .] but he was called Óðinn in Norse.)

The equation between Venus and Frigg is similarly preserved in the passage on the days of the week, where it is preceded by a unique 1st person addition that reiterates the Mercury-Óðinn correspondence: 'hinn fiorða dag gafo þeír Mercurio. þann er ver kollum Oðenn. En hinn .vi. dag gafo þeír hinni orgu Venu. er heítír Frígg a donsko' (Eiríkur Jónsson and Finnur Jónsson 1892–96, 159) ('they gave the fourth day to Mercury, whom we call Óðinn. And they gave the sixth day to the infamous Venus, who is called Frigg in Norse'). The omission of any mention of the fifth day of the week is presumably due to an error in copying at some stage.

Furthermore, the equations Jove-Þórr and Mercury-Óðinn are made elsewhere in Old Norse writings: for example, in the passage in *Páls saga postola* describing the adventures of Paul and Barnabas in Lystra. The Old Norse narrative here follows very closely the wording of Acts 14, and after Paul's healing of the man crippled in his feet the saga records (Unger 1874, 220),

> En er lyþrinn sa þat, er Paulus hafði gert, þa melte alþyða: 'Guþ com til var i manna li[ciom]' oc cølluþo þeir Paulum Oþin en Barnabas Þor.
>
> (And when the people saw what Paul had done, then they all said: 'The gods have come to us in the forms of men.' And they called Paul Óðinn and Barnabas Þórr.)

The sentence in the Vulgate from which this is ultimately derived (Acts 14. 11) reads, 'vocabant Barnaban Jovem, Paulum vero Mercurium' (Weber 1975, II, 1722).

Returning, then, to *De Falsis Diis*: how much of the above information must Ælfric have derived from contemporary contact with Scandinavians in England? The equation of Mercury and Wōden/Óðinn is of considerable antiquity: among classical writers it is made by both Caesar and Tacitus, although neither gives the god his Germanic name (see North 1997, 79), and it is also recorded in a number of Anglo-Saxon glossaries (see below). This so-called *interpretatio germanica* led to the evolution of the Germanic names for the days of the week, and it is thought that this was completed by or during the fourth century (Simek 1993, 243; see further Green 1998, 236–53); but at the very least Ælfric must have learned of the names of the corresponding Norse gods through contemporary contact, and presumably also a sufficient quantity of detail concerning the Norse gods to know that the equations he was making were valid ones. This is suggested by the specification that Óðinn was worshipped on high mountains, and probably by the claim that Þórr was the most popular god among the Scandinavians in England, as well as by Wulfstan's additional remark concerning Óðinn's facility with language. But certain confirmation that Ælfric is drawing on considerable contemporary knowledge is provided by his denial that Þórr is the son of Óðinn, as *þa Deniscan* ('the Danes') insist. In the records of Norse mythology this is of course the case, but in Roman myth Jove is not the son of Mercury — in fact it is the other way round — but rather of Saturn.[64] Clearly Ælfric was aware of the familial relationships between certain of the Norse gods, just as Æthelweard was in his recognition that Víðarr and Baldr were both sons of Óðinn (see pp 122–27 above). But whereas Æthelweard, with his strong Scandinavian interests, prefers the contemporary tradition and thus restructures the Kentish genealogy so that the line reads Óðinn-Víðarr, Ælfric places his trust rather in the testimony of classical and Christian writers; that is, in what *we rædað on bocum* ('we read in books'). One might perhaps suggest that Ælfric and Æthelweard's differing attitudes to the relationships between the Norse gods are indicative of the differences between the book-based orthodoxy of a churchman and the somewhat haphazard inquisitiveness of a layman.[65] For Ælfric, the claim that Þórr was the son of Óðinn is simply yet another example of the *gedwyld* ('error') of the heathen Scandinavians. But the very fact that he is both able and feels obliged to reject this belief indicates the vitality of the traditions with which Anglo-Saxon churchmen like Ælfric were coming into contact. *De Falsis Diis* is not the lesson in ancient history that some commentators have implied, but is rather, at least in part, an urgent tract to counter the perennial threat of idolatry.

One must therefore ask through precisely what channels of contact this information might have reached Ælfric. Inevitably this is a difficult question, and in some ways what is important is the simple fact that it evidently did. We do, however, have the testimony of Ælfric's Latin Preface to his Second Series of *Catholic Homilies*, in which he explains that his work on the homilies was seriously hindered by the *multis iniuriis infestium piratarum* (Godden 1979, 1) ('many injuries of hostile Vikings'). Ælfric wrote these at Cerne Abbas in Dorset, and therefore it seems likely that the reference is to one or other of the heavy Viking raids on the south coast recorded in the *Anglo-Saxon Chronicle sub annis* 991 and 994 (and probably to the latter: see Sisam 1953a, 157–60; Godden 1979, xci–xcii; 2000, xxxii–xxxvi). Furthermore, at a number of points in his writings (other than *De Falsis Diis*) Ælfric alludes to the Scandinavians in England, almost invariably in emphatic, Wulfstan-like terms,

---

[64]It is interesting that the *Hauksbók* text omits entirely Ælfric's denial that Jove/Þórr was the son of Mercury/Óðinn: which genealogy was an Icelandic writer to follow?

[65]Both Ælfric and Æthelweard, however, provide euhemeristic explanations for the rise of the worship of the Norse gods (see Johnson 1995).

presenting them as a serious heathen threat to a Christian people.[66] So, for example, in a passage on persecution in *The Forty Soldiers* (No. 11 of the *Lives of the Saints*) Ælfric speaks generally of heathens, but in present-tense language obviously referring to the Vikings (Skeat 1881–1900, II, 258–60 (lines 353–54)):

> Ac þa hæðenan hynað and hergiað þa cristenan
> and mid wælhreowum dædum urne drihten gremiað.

(But the heathens humiliate and ravage the Christians, and anger our Lord with cruel deeds.)

In concluding his *Life of St Swithun* (No. 21 of the *Lives of the Saints*) Ælfric looks back reverently to the reign of Edgar, and takes the absence of Viking raiders as one of its distinguishing merits (Skeat 1881–1900, II, 468 (lines 443–49)):

> We habbað nu gesæd be swiðune us sceortlice .
> and we secgað to soðan *þæt* se tima wæs gesælig
> and wynsum on angel-cynne . þaða eadgar cynincg
> þone cristen-dom ge-fyrðrode . and fela munuclifa arærde .
> and his cynerice wæs wunigende on sibbe .
> swa *þæt* man ne gehyrde gif ænig scyp-here wære
> buton agenre leode þe ðis land heoldon .

(We have now briefly spoken about Swithun, and we declare truthfully that the time was happy and joyful among the English people, when King Edgar promoted Christianity and built many monasteries; and his kingdom remained in peace, so that no fleet was ever heard of, unless it was that of the people who occupied this land.)

Similarly, in the lengthy account of *The Maccabees* (No. 25 of the *Lives of the Saints*) Ælfric articulates the notion of the just war in urgent and immediate terms (Skeat 1881–1900, III, 114 (lines 708–09)):

> *Iustum bellum* . is rihtlic gefeoht wið ða reðan flot-menn .
> oþþe wið oðre þeoda þe eard willað fordón .

(*Justum bellum* is a just war against the cruel Vikings, or against other peoples who wish to destroy our country.)

Naturally the *Life of St Edmund* (No. 32 of the *Lives of the Saints*) has a good deal to say about Norse depredations; for example, the Viking presence is introduced as still

---

[66]Many of the following references are taken from Godden 1985, 95–96. On Ælfric's various attempts to interpret the moral and theological significance of the Viking attacks, see Godden 1994, 131–42.

a current threat a hundred years after the martyrdom of Edmund (Skeat 1881–1900, IV, 316 (lines 26–28)):[67]

> Hit ge-lamp ða æt nextan þæt þa deniscan leode
> ferdon mid scip-here hergiende and sleande
> wide geond land swa swa heora gewuna is .

(Finally it happened then that the Danish people went with their fleet far and wide throughout the land, plundering and killing, as their custom is.)

And lastly, in the homily edited by Pope as *Dominica VI Post Pentecosten* Ælfric equates the defection of Anglo-Saxons to the Scandinavian cause as equivalent to apostasy and submission to the devil (Pope 1967–68, II, 521 (lines 128–35)):[68]

> Swa fela manna gebugað mid ðam gecorenum
> to Cristes geleafan on his Gelaðunge,
> þæt hy sume yfele eft ut abrecað,
> and hy on gedwyldum adreogað heora líf,
> swa swa þa Engliscan men doð þe to ðam Deniscum gebugað,
> and mearciað hy deofle to his mannrædene,
> and his weorc wyrcað, hym sylfum to forwyrde,
> and heora agene leode be(læwað) to deaðe.

(So many men turn with the disciples to Christ's faith, in his Church, that some of them afterwards break out evilly, and they spend their life in errors, just as the Englishmen do who turn to the Danes, and they sign themselves to the devil for his service, and carry out his work to their own destruction, and betray their own people into death.)

All of these passages show Ælfric pressingly concerned with the presence of Scandinavians in England who are both heathen and destructive, a concern that to some degree is likely to have been motivated and informed by personal contact and observation.

In more general terms Audrey Meaney has, as noted earlier, surveyed some of the possible means by which knowledge of Scandinavian paganism in Northumbria might have reached southern England, such as trade, hostages, and ecclesiastical contacts, in addition to the Scandinavian armies in the 990s (1970, 125–32). As an

---

[67] The phrase *swa heora gewuna is* is also used of Viking depredations in the *Anglo-Saxon Chronicle* MS 'D' *sub annis* 1009 and 1016 (Cubbin 1996, 55, 62); MS 'E' however changes both of these to the retrospective *swa heora gewuna wæs* (Plummer and Earle 1892–99, I, 139, 150). On Ælfric's *Life of St Edmund* see further pp 161 and 171 below.

[68] In this passage Ælfric is expounding the spiritual meaning (*gastlice andgit*) of the disciples' catch of fish that was so great that it split the net (Luke 5. 6).

ealdorman Æthelweard was deeply involved in conflicts and negotiations during that decade, and Æthelweard was of course one of the most important of Ælfric's secular patrons.[69] Similarly, contact between Ælfric and Wulfstan is well recorded (see Clemoes 1960, 281–83), and as Archbishop of York it is possible that Wulfstan observed Norse heathenism at close quarters (see Meaney 1970, 120–21). There must also have been many men in Wessex of Scandinavian blood (either recently arrived in England, or second-generation or later) to confirm Ælfric's facts, including churchmen;[70] and similarly one might speculate that he had access to the testimony of English clergy returned from missionary enterprises in Scandinavia (on the English church and English priests in medieval Scandinavia see for example Birkeli 1971; McDougall 1987–88, 189–91; Abrams 1995). But one need hardly regard it as remarkable, or requiring particular explanation, that a Christian writer in the 990s should make himself well informed about a resurgent paganism threatening his country; Ælfric was after all moved to compose *De Falsis Diis* and to make his other allusions to the contemporary danger. In short, the English church at the time of Ælfric can hardly have been too conscious of the heathenism of the Scandinavian invaders.

The Norse Language in England

It will be recalled that Æthelweard's 871 account of the burial of ealdorman Æthelwulf at *Norðworðig/Deoraby* gives a brief but valuable sense of Norse and English as two Germanic vernaculars coexisting in late Anglo-Saxon England (see pp 117–18 above); this same sense is to be gained also from the passages from *De Falsis Diis* under discussion. For Ælfric not only states that the classical gods are called by other names by the Danish people ('he hatte Þór betwux sumum þeodum, þone þa Denisca leoda lufiað swiðost [. . .] þe hi Þór hátað [. . .] þe hi Oðon hatað' ('amongst certain nations he is called Þórr, whom the Danish people love most of all [. . .] whom they call Þórr [. . .] whom they call Óðinn')), but he also says explicitly that they are called by other names *in Danish* ('he is Óðon geháten oðrum naman on Denisc [. . .] Uen[us] gehaten, and Fric[g] on Denisc' ('by another name he is called Óðinn in Danish [. . .] called Venus, and Frigg in Danish')). This is an important distinction, as it indicates a consciousness among at least certain Anglo-Saxons of Old Norse as a different language from their own. In his adaptation of *De Falsis Diis* Wulfstan expands this to a characteristic two-stress phrase, and in so doing alters

---

[69]Ælfric's *Lives of the Saints* are prefaced by a dedicatory epistle to Æthelweard, as is his translation of the Book of Genesis, and the monastery at Eynsham, of which Ælfric became the first abbot, was founded in 1005 by Æthelmær, Æthelweard's son (see further Wilcox 1994, 9–14).

[70]Most famously (in an earlier generation) Oda, a priest of Danish ancestry who rose to become Archbishop of Canterbury 941–58; other members of his family became Archbishops of York (Oscytel 956–71, Oswald 971–92). On Oda and his kin see Brooks 1984, 222–37; Wareham 1996; Barrow 2000, 161–63.

Denisc from a noun to an adjective, stating that 'he is Oðon gehaten oðrum naman on Denisce wisan' ('by another name he is called Óðinn in the Danish idiom').

References to the Old Norse language in England are scarce, and therefore worth dwelling upon (see further pp 185–86 below). It is also worth asking whether Æthelweard's *Danaa lingua*, Ælfric's *Denisc*, and Wulfstan's *Denisc wise* might not be Old English translations of the Old Norse phrase *dǫnsk tunga*. Among Norse speakers this was the usual term for the language spoken in Scandinavia throughout the Middle Ages, and its implication was that the language at that time was a unitary one, with only minor dialectal variations (see Skautrup 1956–78; Karker 1977). Is it possible that Anglo-Saxon writers learned this native term from the Scandinavians, and consequently employed it themselves? The main reason to reject such a conclusion would be the use in Old English writings of *Dene* and *Denisc* as blanket terms for Scandinavians of whatever origin, and Ælfric's usage seems no different from the prevailing habit. Two points, though, might deter one from an unequivocal rejection of the possibility. The first is that this use of *Dene/Denisc* as blanket terms in Anglo-Saxon texts, although common, is not invariable: Æthelweard, for example, sometimes employs *Norþmenn* as an alternative term restricted to Norwegians, and the 942 Anglo-Saxon Chronicle poem *The Capture of the Five Boroughs* draws a deliberate distinction between *Dene* and *Norþmenn* (see Mawer 1923). The second point is the formal precision with which Æthelweard's *Danaa lingua* corresponds to ON *dǫnsk tunga*, though coincidence rather than borrowing might still be the explanation.[71]

The Forms of Norse Names[72]

For both occurrences, *Þór* is the form found in all the manuscripts collated by Pope; bearing in mind the care Ælfric is known to have taken in the copying and dissemination of his works, it seems reasonable to regard this as an authorial form. Ælfric's *Þór* represents a precise reproduction of the Old Norse form of the name: Gmc **Þunraz* became *Þunor* in Old English by loss of the final inflexional syllable and addition of non-organic *o* for ease of articulation, whereas in Old Norse assimilation of the medial nasal to the following *r*, with compensatory lengthening of the vowel, gave *Þúrr* (de Vries 1961, 618). Björkman implies that *Þórr* is an Old West Norse form of the name, *Þúrr* an Old East Norse (1900–02, 180; see also Noreen 1923, 101–02 (§112.1), 220 (§299.3)); if so, this would indicate that Ælfric's form is derived from the Norwegians in England. Ekwall discusses the variants *Þórr*

---

[71]Although of no evidential value, it is interesting to note the form taken by Ælfric's phrases in the *Hauksbók* translation. The two occurences of *on Denisc* remain as *a donsku*, and the earlier reference to *þa Deniscan leoda* becomes *menn a danska tungu*.

[72]In all instances, the forms in Wulfstan follow those in Ælfric, and one can therefore regard them as a Northumbrian vote of confidence in Ælfric's accuracy. Exactly the same forms are also found in the passage from Ælfric's *Life of St Martin* quoted earlier.

and *Þúrr* (*PNLa* 245), but while upholding the view that the former is usually West Norse and the latter East Norse, he concludes, 'Whatever may be the relations between *Þōr* and *Þūr*, both were possible developments in East and West Scandinavian, and the practically regular W.Scand. *Þōr* is due to generalization' (on the alternation and dialectal significance of *Þór-/Þúr-* in Norse personal names in England, see von Feilitzen 1937, 390; Fellows-Jensen 1968, lxxv (§28); Insley 1994, 398). The (usually) East Norse form is found, however, together with the native English form, in a gloss in London, BL, MS Cotton Cleopatra A.iii, which reads *Joppiter, þunor oððe ður* (Wright and Wülcker 1884, I, 425 (line 36)). A later gloss in the same manuscript reads simply *Ioppiter, þunor*, but one also finds the intriguing *Latona, þures modor* (Wright and Wülcker 1884, I, 526 (line 20), 437 (line 16); see also Sievers 1891, 328–29). Ker dates Cleopatra A.iii to the mid-tenth century (1957, 180–82 (No. 143)); elsewhere such a gloss is found only in the eighth-century, pre-Viking Age Corpus Glossary (MS CCCC 144): *Iovem, ðuner* (Lindsay 1921, 101 (gloss 479); Ker 1957, 49–50 (No. 36)).

Óðon/Oðon can likewise be regarded as an authorial form on both occurrences.[73] The god's name is derived from Gmc *Wōðinaz or *Wōðanaz: in Old English this became *Wōden* by loss of the final inflexional syllable and the unconditioned change *ð > d*. In Old Norse medial Gmc *ð* was preserved, but initial *w* lost before a rounded vowel (see p 40 above). According to de Vries (1961, 416), *Oðon* is a characteristic Old West Norse form, with Old East Norse tending to show *Oþin, Oþan*, or *Oþun*. However, it is not clear how certain this rule is, as of course later Icelandic texts consistently give *Óðinn*; but if true, Ælfric's form is therefore a precise reproduction of the West Norse form.

If one accepts the suggestions that one can distinguish between Old West Norse and Old East Norse forms of the names of the two gods, then it is interesting that Ælfric's forms *Þór* and *Oðon* should suggest that the names of the Scandinavian deities were known in late Anglo-Saxon England in distinctively Old West Norse — that is, Norwegian — form. The poem in the *Anglo-Saxon Chronicle sub anno* 942, celebrating Edmund's capture of the Five Boroughs, implies strongly that the Danes in that area had been Christianised, but subsequently subjected to pagan rule by the Norwegian dynasty of York and Dublin (Dobbie 1942, 21 (lines 8–13)):

> Dæne wæran æror
> under Norðmannum   nyde gebegde
> on hæþenra   hæfteclommum
> lange þrage,   oþ hie alysde eft
> for his weorþscipe   wiggendra hleo,
> afera Eadweardes,   Eadmund cyning.

---

[73] In the manuscripts collated by Pope this is the universal form, save once in Paris, Bibliothèque nationale, lat. 7585, where *oðen* is found on the first occurrence.

(The Danes had previously been forcibly oppressed for a long time under the Norwegians, in the bonds of the heathens, until King Edmund, the son of Edward, the protector of warriors, afterwards released them through his excellence.)

There is a dual opposition in these lines between Norwegians and Danes, and between heathens and Christians (though the last of these is unstated, it must be understood for *hæþenra* to make sense). The persistent, and conspicuous, paganism of the York-Dublin Norwegians is one of the points argued most forcibly by Alfred Smyth (1987), and forms of the names similar to those in Ælfric are also found in the tenth-century *Historia de Sancto Cuthberto* (Arnold 1882–85, I, 196–214), in a story concerning a militantly pagan Scandinavian from the York-Dublin aristocracy. This witness is worth attending to, as the anonymous author of the *Historia* clearly had some knowledge of the names and beliefs of the contemporary Scandinavians, since, for example, he refers to the York-Dublin dynasty as *Scaldingi* no fewer than three times (see further Binns 1965, 184); that Scandinavian conquerors of England wished to present themselves as descending from this dynasty has recently been demonstrated by Roberta Frank, who points out that the poetry of Cnut's skalds boasts frequent reference to the *Skjǫldungar* (1994a, 111–12). The *Historia* tells the story of one Óláfr *ball* (from ON *ballr* ('stubborn')?), a thane rewarded by Ragnall after the first battle of Corbridge (see Smyth 1987, I, 97–103). The relevant episode is worth quoting in full:

> Quibus fugatis et tota terra superata, [Ragnall] divisit villas sancti Cuthberti, et alteram partem versus austrum dedit cuidam potenti militi suo qui vocabatur Scula, a villa quæ vocatur Iodene, usque ad Billingham. Alteram vero partem dedit cuidam qui vocabatur Onalafball, a Iodene, usque ad fluvium Weorram. Et hic filius diaboli inimicus fuit, quibuscunque modis potuit, Deo et sancto Cuthberto. Quadam itaque die, cum plenus immundo spiritu cum furore intrasset ecclesiam sancti confessoris, adstante episcopo Cutheardo, et tota congregatione, 'Quid,' inquit, 'in me potest homo iste mortuus Cuthbertus, cujus minæ quotidie opponuntur? Juro per meos potentes deos, Thor et Othan, quod ab hac hora inimicissimus ero omnibus vobis.' Cumque episcopus et tota congregatio genua flecterent ante Deum et sanctum Cuthbertum, et harum minarum vindictam, sicut scriptum est, 'Mihi vindictam, et ego retribuam,' ab eis expeterent, conversus ille filius diaboli cum magna superbia et indignatione voluit egredi. Sed cum alteram pedem posuisset jam extra limen, sensit quasi ferrum in altero pede sibi altius infixum. Quo dolore diabolicum ejus cor transfigente, corruit, suamque peccatricem animam diabolus in infernum trusit. Sanctus vero Cuthbertus, sicut justum erat, terram suam recepit. (Arnold 1882–85, I, 209)

(When they had been put to flight and the whole land conquered, he [i.e. Ragnall] divided the estates of St Cuthbert, and he gave the one part, towards the south, from the estate which is called Eden as far as Billingham to a certain powerful thegn of his who was called Scula; and the other part, from Eden as far as the river Wear, to one called Olaf Ball. And this son of the devil was hostile in every way he could to God and St Cuthbert. And thus a certain day, when full of the unclean spirit he entered raging into the church of the holy confessor, he said in the presence of Bishop Cuthheard and the whole community: 'What can this dead man do against me, when his threats are daily disregarded? I swear by my mighty gods, Thor and Othin, that from this hour I will be a great enemy to all of you.' And when the bishop and the whole congregation knelt before God and St Cuthbert, and besought them for vengeance for these threats, as it is written: 'Vengeance is mine, and I will repay', this son of the devil turned away with great pride and indignation, wishing to depart. But when he had put one foot outside the threshold, he felt as if iron were deeply fixed in the other foot. With the pain piercing his diabolical heart, he fell, and the devil thrust his sinful soul into hell. And St Cuthbert, as was right, received his land.) (Whitelock 1979, 288 (No. 6))

As can be seen, the forms given are *Thor* and *Othan*, and they are therefore, except for the unstressed vowel in the latter name, identical to Ælfric's forms; it seems noteworthy that the accuracy and trustworthiness of Ælfric's witness is thus confirmed by the testimony of the well-informed *Historia*.[74]

The name of the goddess commemorated in the day of the week Friday was in Old English *Frīg*, with palatal /j/ in inflected syllables (thus, genitive singular *Frīge* as in *Frīgedæg*). By the change known as Sharpening or Holtzmann's Law Gmc *jj* became *ggj* in Old Norse (*gg* when word-final), but remained a palatal in Old English with lengthening or diphthongisation of the preceding vowel (see above p 40; see also Noreen 1923, 165–66 (§227.1); Campbell 1959, 45 (§120(1))). Ælfric's *Fricg* is therefore a precise reproduction of the Old Norse form *Frigg*. It is true that in Old English orthography <cg> usually indicates the affricate /dʒ/, but it is also sometimes used to indicate the velar stop /g/, especially in word-final position (though normally after a nasal). One might complain of the ambiguity of a spelling in <cg>, but in fact there was no unambiguous option available to Ælfric. To use the customary graph for /g/, namely <g>, would be disastrous, since the resultant spelling <Frig> would represent the Old English name for the goddess; and, as has been seen, Ælfric is eager not to mention the English names of any of the deities under discussion. Consonant-doubling was not necessarily a valid option either: in Old English this was normally used to indicate geminates, although by the time of Ælfric this had become another function of <cg> as well (e.g. *frogga, frocga* ('frog')) (see Campbell 1959, 27 (§64)). The omission of the final <g> in Pope's

---

[74] According to de Vries, however, *Othan* would be an Old East Norse form. Elsewhere in Old English, these two gods are mentioned in the pseudo-Wulfstan homily Napier XLII *De temporibus Anticristi* (Napier 1883, 191–205, at 197; on Napier XLII see Wilcox 1991, 11–16), in a catalogue of false gods that will be worshipped in the time of Antichrist: *þōr eac and Owðen, þe hæðene men herjað swiðe* ('also Þórr and Óðinn, whom heathen men worship greatly'). (I am grateful to Philip Shaw for this reference.) The form *Owðen*, in MS CCCC 419 and 421 (Ker 1957, 115–17 (No. 68)), is curious and hard to explain; in the other manuscript in which this homily occurs, Oxford, Bodleian Library, MS Hatton 113 and 114 (Ker 1957, 391–99 (No. 331)), the names are given as *þōrr* and *Oþen*.

base manuscript (CCCC 178) may perhaps indicate scribal confusion on this issue, since it was an uncommon word that was being written. In the other manuscripts collated by Pope (and where capitalisation is of course editorial), *fricg* is found twice, *frycg* once, and (oddly) *fricge* also once.

Therefore for all three names — *Þór*, *Óðon*, and *Fricg* — Ælfric gives a form which reproduces exactly the Old Norse form, and for the first two names (especially the first) it is arguable that he gives a specifically Old West Norse form. This is clearly a deliberate and significant strategy on Ælfric's part. This reproduction (sometimes termed adoption) is the opposite approach to cognate substitution, whether Anglicisation or Scandinavianisation. Substitutions, like calques or loan-translations, transpose words or names from one language into another; in this situation, were cognate substitutions to be employed, *Óðinn* would become *Wōden* and *Frigg* would become *Frīg*, while ON *Þórr* and OE *Þunor* had perhaps diverged too incongruently for cognate substitutions to be readily made. Ælfric, on the other hand, is determined to preserve the 'Norseness' of these names as fully and accurately as possible, and the reason for this is obvious: the homilist has no desire to remind his audience of English paganism, and every desire to portray the pagan Scandinavians, with their different language, as a discrete and dissimilar people. Ælfric's linguistic strategy in rendering the names of the Norse gods as accurately as possible in their Norse forms is therefore an essential part of his wider homiletic strategy.

CHAPTER 5

Literary Accounts and Anecdotal Evidence

Old Norse: The Witness of the Sagas

In Chapter 1 a number of opinions were surveyed concerning Anglo-Norse intelligibility, and it was noted that the main item of evidence to have been repeatedly adduced in support of these is a statement from *Gunnlaugs saga ormstungu*. The Icelandic sagas are, however, a much more fertile source on this issue than the repetition of this single statement would suggest, and indeed the witness of the sagas is a fruitful one more generally on the subject of linguistic relations between speakers of Norse and English. Hence although they derive from a significantly later date, the sources in Old Norse will in this chapter be considered before those in Old English and Anglo-Latin, as they present a richer and more directly relevant testimony. The problem, of course, is in knowing how far one can claim the witness of the sagas as valid and historical evidence. The consensus surveyed in Chapter 1 was initially established in the early twentieth century, at a time when the sagas were generally held to be faithful records of historical events. But the mid-century work of Sigurður Nordal and the so-called Icelandic school demonstrated that this confidence was misplaced, and the new orthodoxy that emerged held that the sagas should be regarded primarily as historical fictions, with relatively little value as historical documents except insofar as they illuminate the beliefs and sensibilities of the age of saga-writing (for a summary of the views of Nordal and the Icelandic school see Andersson 1964, 82–119; for a review and summary of trends in saga-scholarship see Clover 1985, esp. 241–45; Vésteinn Ólason 1993).

These issues remain far from resolved. There is no doubt that Nordal was right when he demonstrated the unhistorical basis of certain sagas; but this has too often been elevated to a general principle, and therefore used as a pretext to reject the sagas as potential evidence altogether. It has in turn become clear that, in general terms, such an all-embracing scepticism towards the sagas as historical sources can be at least as great a scholarly hindrance as an all-embracing confidence, and in recent years there has been something of a reaction against this methodological impasse. As Alfred Smyth fearlessly remarks (1987, I, 11),

> A modern trend which treats the Icelandic sagas strictly as literature while occasionally allowing for some added anthropological interest, fails to do justice to the historical sense of the saga compilers and indeed fails to understand the basic nature of the saga form. The detailed information which occurs in Icelandic literature on events in the British Isles in the Viking Age has not found its way there by chance. It is a reflection of the great interest shown by medieval Icelanders in those of their ancestors who emigrated to Iceland from Britain and Ireland.

Thus while recognising that there are no objective tests that can be infallibly applied, I would argue that the testimony of the sagas does constitute important evidence which it would be foolish to ignore, and that what struck medieval Icelandic authors as noteworthy is indeed likely to be worthy of note — quite apart from the (strong) probability that Icelandic sources may preserve genuine traditions and material. This is not to say, however, that one should not distinguish between different types of text; as will be seen, the relevant sources range from the carefully naturalistic to the avowedly fantastic, and their reliability must be tested against other forms of evidence, in this case of a more purely linguistic kind (as presented in Chapters 2, 3, and 4, and co-ordinated in Chapter 6).

Foreign Languages in the Sagas

By way of perspective, then, one may first ask how saga-authors view foreign languages in general — whether differences in language are in any way an issue to them, or indeed are even recognised, and what literary conventions appear to be operative when speakers of different languages communicate in the sagas.

In her 1983 study of the role of foreign languages in medieval Icelandic romances, Marianne Kalinke compares the awareness of these which is found in Norse *riddarasögur* ('sagas of knights') with that found in continental romances, and with regard to the latter she remarks that '[a]uthors of medieval romance appear to be blissfully ignorant of linguistic borders — and their heroes immune to linguistic unintelligibility' (1983, 850). In contrast, Kalinke shows, Norse romances reveal an awareness of the basic fact that the people one meets in different countries speak different languages from one's own, and the authors of *riddarasögur* often make a point of explaining how it is that their heroes are able to communicate with the natives when on adventure in faraway places. This is often achieved by an emphasis on the hero's education, in which instruction in foreign languages is prominent; and this prominence is found as much in the *fornaldarsögur* ('sagas of old times' or heroic sagas) as in the *riddarasögur*. For example, *Vǫlsunga saga* tells us about Sigurðr's education (Finch 1965, 23):

> Reginn hét fóstri Sigurðar ok var Hreiðmars sonr. Hann kenndi honum íþróttir, tafl ok rúnar ok tungur margar at mæla sem þá var títt konungasonum, ok marga hluti aðra.

> (The foster-father of Sigurðr was called Reginn and was the son of Hreiðmarr. He taught him various skills — chess, and runes, and how to speak many languages (as was then customary for the sons of kings), and many other things.)

In similar fashion *Yngvars saga víðfǫrla* reports of its eponymous hero's formative years in Russia that 'Þar uar Ynguar iij uetur ok nam þar margar tungur at tala' (Olson 1912, 12) ('Yngvarr was there for three years, and he learnt to speak many languages') (for further examples of the hero's instruction in foreign languages see McDougall 1987–88, 210–11). However, as Kalinke demonstrates, this polyglot ability seems never to dwindle into mere cliché, and the narrative crux of at least one saga, *Konráðs saga keisarasonar*, turns on the hero's ability to speak an exotic tongue; rather, the saga-authors seem to show a genuine awareness of language difficulties and want to show how these are overcome by practical measures. As Kalinke says (1983, 861), '[t]he fictional heroes reflect a traditional Icelandic reverence for learning and the pragmatism of an insular people with an uncommon language and devoted to travel'. It is true, of course, that in one respect the saga-authors are merely replacing one sort of implausibility with another, for such resources of language tuition were hardly, one assumes, to be found in Norway or Iceland. But what appears to be significant is that it was felt necessary to provide such an explanation in the first place.

As a final example from a *fornaldarsaga*, one may head north-east towards the White Sea and the land of the Bjarmians — that is, the *Beormas* whom Ohthere told King Alfred about (on descriptions of Bjarmaland in Scandinavian literature see Ross 1981, 29–41). At one point in *Ǫrvar-Odds saga*, a saga greatly concerned with adventures in Bjarmaland, the hero Oddr and his companion Ásmundr are standing outside a great hall, inside which there is much revelry (Boer 1888, 28 (M-version)):

> 'Skilr þú hér nǫkkut mál manna?' segir Oddr. 'Eigi heldr en fugla klið,' segir Ásmundr, 'eða þykkiz þú nǫkkut of skilja?' segir Ásmundr. 'Eigi er þat síðr,' segir Oddr. 'Þat muntu sjá,' segir hann, 'at einn maðr skenkir hér á báða bekki, en þat gefr mér grun um, at hann muni kunna at tala á norrœna tungu.'

> ('Can you understand anything of the language of the people here?' asked Oddr. 'No more than the noise of birds,' said Ásmundr. 'Can you understand anything?' 'No more than you,' said Oddr. 'But you can see that man there serving drink to both the benches — well, I suspect that he may well know how to speak Norse.')

No suggestion is given as to how Oddr knows that the man is a Norse speaker (Bjarmian with a Norwegian accent?), and in literary terms the man's sole *raison d'être* is that, since it turns out that he is indeed a Scandinavian and hence able to talk with Oddr, he is able to inform the acquisitive hero of details of potential Bjarmian plunder of which he would otherwise have remained ignorant. Thus the episode seems to confirm a surprising naturalistic rationale behind the literary treatment of foreign languages, since it was clearly deemed necessary to introduce this improbable figure for the sole purpose of explaining how it is that Oddr is able to learn of the Bjarmian hoard.

If such pragmatism, even pseudo-realism, is evidenced by *riddarasögur* and *fornaldarsögur*, one would not expect it to be lacking in the more local and un-fabulous sagas of kings and Icelanders; and this is indeed the case. To begin with a king's saga in the Baltic, one learns from an episode in Oddr Snorrason's life of Óláfr Tryggvason that Wendish is another language regarded as being unintelligible to monolingual Norse speakers (for other references to Wendish in the sagas see McDougall 1987–88, 217–18). Óláfr and his men are aboard his famous ship, *Ormr inn langi* ('The Long Serpent'), when a much smaller, sixteen-oared vessel approaches (Oddr Snorrason 1932, 209):

> geck maðr or stafninum oc talaði við Olaf konung. með ukunnre tungu. Oc sua mælti oc konungr imoti. at Norðmenn skilðu eigi. [...] Oc er þeir varu ibrottu spurðu menn konungs huerir þeir menn veri. er við hann hafðu talat. Hann sagþi at þeir veri ukunir menn oc komnir af Vinðlandi.

> (A man came from the prow and spoke with King Óláfr in a strange language. And he and the king spoke in a way that the Norwegians couldn't understand. [...] And when they had gone, the king was asked who those men were who had spoken to him. He said that they were strange men who came from Wendland.)

It is part of Óláfr's kingly excellence that he has acquired proficiency in Wendish; to the rest of the Norwegians the language remains *ukunnre* ('unknown'), and indeed in other sagas interpreters are often recorded as being necessary for communicating with the Wends.[1]

To move westwards to the British Isles and a region where the Vikings engaged in both raiding and settlement over a considerable period, it can be seen that Irish too is portrayed as an unintelligible language in the sagas, and one for which explanation is required if a saga-character is able to communicate in that language (again, for a survey of Irish in the sagas see McDougall 1987–88, 180–85). The case of Óláfr pái in *Laxdœla saga* may be taken as representative. Óláfr is the son of the Icelander Hǫskuldr Dala-Kollsson and the Irish princess Melkorka, and in due course he

---

[1] Indeed, the Old Norse word for 'interpreter', *túlkr*, is a loanword derived from Old Slavonic (Fischer 1909, 45).

leaves Iceland to visit Ireland since he has been told that his grandfather Myrkjartan is king there. On arrival he and his crew are hailed by two guards in a boat, and the saga-author records that 'Óláfr mælti ok svarar á írsku, sem þeir mæltu til' (Einar Ól. Sveinsson 1934, 54) ('Óláfr answered in Irish, just as they had spoken to him'). The Irish guards seem to be some sort of customs officials and claim that the visitors must forfeit their property; but Óláfr knows his rights, and retorts that that is only the law 'ef engi væri túlkr með kaupmǫnnum' (Einar Ól. Sveinsson 1934, 55) ('if no interpreter were with the traders'), a statement which suggests that interpreters were normally required for Norse-Irish communication. Óláfr is brought before the king, and Myrkjartan's verdict is that '"Auðsætt er þat á Óláfi þessum, at hann er stórættaðr maðr, hvárt sem hann er várr frændi eða eigi, ok svá þat, at hann mælir allra manna bezt írsku"' (Einar Ól. Sveinsson 1934, 57) ('"It's clear that, whether or not he's our kinsman, this Óláfr is a high-born man, and also that he speaks, of all people, the best Irish"'). But how is it, one may ask, that Óláfr is able to speak *bezt írsku* ('the best Irish') in the first place? It seems not unlikely that such a question would occur to the original saga-audience, for the author of *Laxdæla saga* has in fact been careful to prepare the way for Óláfr's success in Ireland. When he is about to depart on his travels, his mother Melkorka says good-bye to him with the reassurance that '"Heiman hefi ek þik búit, svá sem ek kann bezt, ok kennt þér írsku at mæla, svá at þik mun þat eigi skipta, hvar þik berr at Írlandi"' (Einar Ól. Sveinsson 1934, 51) ('"I have prepared you for leaving home as best as I could, and have taught you to speak Irish, so that it won't make any difference to you in which part of Ireland you land"') — an emphasis on prior linguistic instruction that is strongly reminiscent of the 'hero's education' motif in the more fantastic saga-genres.[2]

Bjarmian, Wendish, and Irish may satisfactorily be regarded as representative of the great number of languages which the sagas portray as being unintelligible to Norse speakers, but with continental Germanic languages we move much closer to Old English. Yet even here, in the depiction of Saxon and Frankish missionaries preaching in Scandinavia, the sagas as often as not make mention of the need for interpreters; Ian McDougall (1987–88, 186–88) has listed a good number of such references. Thus, for example, in *Kristni saga* the Frankish missionary Friðrekr is said to have employed the Icelander Þorvaldr Koðránsson, whom he met in Saxony (see Kahle 1905, 5–6). And although in the sagas there appear to be no communication problems between Scandinavians and Frisians (witness, for example, the *frískr maðr* ('Frisian man') Túta in *Sneglu-Halla þáttr* (see Jónas Kristjánsson 1956, 269, 274)), yet the Germanic language spoken in more southerly regions of the continent — called in Old Norse *þýzka* — is regularly regarded as unintelligible to a monolingual Norse speaker. That this was seen as a real difference in language is suggested by the mid-twelfth-century *Leiðarvísir* of Abbot Nikulás of Munkaþverá: this is a guidebook for Icelandic pilgrims to the Holy Land, and Nikulás notes that when one

---

[2]The implication of the last clause in Melkorka's speech would seem to be that in those parts of Ireland where Norse was spoken no language difficulties would arise.

crosses into Saxony on the way south *nú skiptazt tungur* (Kålund 1908–18, I, 13) ('now the languages change') (for secondary literature on Nikulás's *Leiðarvísir* see Hill 1993, 433–34). So, for instance, one may consider the following episode in *Grœnlendinga saga*, concerning Tyrkir, who is described as a *suðrmaðr* (a southern German) and is the foster-father of Leifr inn heppni (Einar Ól. Sveinsson and Matthías Þórðarson 1935, 252):

> Hann talaði þá fyrst lengi á þýzku ok skaut marga vega augunum ok gretti sik, en þeir skilðu eigi, hvat er hann sagði. Hann mælti þá á norrœnu, er stund leið.

> (He first spoke for a long time in German, and rolled his eyes in all directions and frowned, and they couldn't understand what he was saying. Then after a while he spoke in Norse.)

Tyrkir has just discovered grapes on the American mainland, and so while he does, understandably, appear to be somewhat drunk, nevertheless the natural unintelligibility of his native language is clear.

Norse and English in the Sagas

What, then, of England and the English? The obvious place to begin is with the influential observation in Chapter 7 of *Gunnlaugs saga ormstungu* (quoted above p 16; for a survey of other scholars' opinions on this passage see Fjalldal 1993, 602–03). The Icelandic poet Gunnlaugr finds himself in England, and at the court of Æthelred, and the saga-author remarks of the country at that time (Nordal and Guðni Jónsson 1938, 70),[3]

> Ein var þá tunga á Englandi sem í Nóregi ok í Danmǫrku. En þá skiptusk tungur í Englandi, er Vilhjálmr bastarðr vann England; gekk þaðan af í Englandi valska, er hann var þaðan ættaðr.

> (The language in England then was the same as in Norway and Denmark. But the languages changed in England when William the bastard conquered it; from then on French became current in England, because he was from France.)

Of this *ein tunga* ('one language' or 'the same language') Alan Boucher comments in his translation of the saga that '[t]his probably refers to the Scandinavian language still spoken in large areas of eastern England (the Danelaw) at this time' (1983, 76), but this explanation cannot be correct. The narrative point of the digression is to explain how it is that Gunnlaugr is able to communicate without difficulty at the court of Æthelred, in much the same way as an explanation (albeit a different one)

---

[3]It is worth noting that the same construction is used here as in Nikulás' *Leiðarvísir*: *skiptask tungur*.

was required to account for Óláfr pái's ability to communicate in Ireland. For what difference would William's *valska* or French make to the speech of the Danelaw? Gunnlaugr's English adventures occur in London and at the court, and the point is that *valska* was the speech of the court at the time of the thirteenth-century author, but not at the time of his Viking Age hero.

The basic claim, then, of the author of *Gunnlaugs saga* is that the English and Norse languages were the same — *ein tunga* — in about the year 1000. In the light of this one would expect to find the sagas silent on the question of language difficulties experienced in England, for the simple reason (it is claimed) that there weren't any difficulties. It is therefore worthwhile to briefly survey a number of sagas where this does indeed appear to be the case.

Most sagas are lamentably jejune about the visits of their characters to England. Thus, for instance, *Bjarnar saga Hítdælakappa* simply tells us of Bjǫrn Arngeirsson that 'Um sumarit eptir fór Bjǫrn vestr til Englands ok fekk þar góða virðing ok var þar tvá vetr með Knúti inum ríka' (Nordal and Guðni Jónsson 1938, 124) ('The following summer Bjǫrn went westwards to England, and received great honour there, and was with Cnut the Great for two years'). And *Fóstbrœðra saga* relates of Þorgeirr Hávarsson and his companions (Björn K. Þórólfsson and Guðni Jónsson 1943, 159),

> Þeir fóru þaðan til Englands ok váru þar um hríð, ok hefir Þormóðr svá um ort, at Þorgeirr þægi þar góðar gjafar at hǫfðingjum. Eptir þat fór hann til Danmerkr.

(From there they went to England, and spent some time there, and Þormóðr has told in his poetry that Þorgeirr received splendid gifts from the chieftains there. After that he went to Denmark.)

However, there are some sagas in which further details are given and conversations between Norse and English speakers are quoted. The story told in *Haralds saga ins hárfagra* (in *Heimskringla* and elsewhere) of the fostering of Hákon Haraldsson is a good example of a brief scene or episode progressing without reference to questions of language. King Athelstan sends a deputation to King Haraldr, and the chief *sendimaðr* or messenger tricks Haraldr into accepting a sword, thereby symbolising Haraldr's submission to Athelstan. Two speeches are quoted and there appear to be no problems of communication. As a response Haraldr sends his retainer Haukr hábrók over to Athelstan's court in London, and this time the messenger tricks the English king into accepting a baby on his knee, namely the young Hákon, later known as *Aðalsteinsfóstri* ('Athelstan's foster-son'). Once more two speeches are quoted. The humour may be fairly ponderous, but for present purposes the significance of the episode is the assumption that communication between Englishmen and Norwegians was able to occur without difficulty. Admittedly, the story is one of ambassadors, and so one might argue that different conventions are operative, but in view of the conscientiousness with which, as has been seen, saga-authors usually refer to interpreters or bilingualism, the episode's diplomatic context need not, I think, make any real difference (for the *Heimskringla* version of this episode see Snorri Sturluson 1941–51, I, 143–46; for a discussion of this and other versions of the Athelstan-Hákon tradition see Page 1981, 113–16; Williams 2001, 113–14).

The saga that deals most fully with an Icelander's stay in England is of course *Egils saga*, with its eponymous hero's two extended visits: the first at the time of Vínheiðr, and the second at the time of the composition of *Hǫfuðlausn*. Within these passages in the saga a good number of Norse-English conversations are either quoted or reported (Nordal 1933, 127–47, 177–96): for example, before the battle of Vínheiðr Egill and his brother Þórólfr meet Athelstan and are placed in charge of certain divisions in the king's army, and after the battle Athelstan pays Egill compensation for his brother's death in the form of portable treasures and the offer of land in England. Egill spends the winter with Athelstan and in the spring discusses with him the matter of Þórólfr's widow and inheritance; once again the king offers Egill a permanent place with him, and indeed many of his followers do choose to remain with Athelstan. Finally, at the end of Egill's first visit, 'skilðusk þeir Aðalsteinn konungr með mikilli vináttu; bað hann Egil koma aptr sem skjótast; Egill kvað svá vera skyldu' (Nordal 1933, 147) ('Egill and King Athelstan parted with great friendship; Athelstan invited Egill to return as soon as possible, and Egill said that he would do so'). The substance of Egill's adventures on his second visit to England occur in Northumbria and at York, and these will be discussed later. On leaving York, though, Egill and his friend Arinbjǫrn journey south and are well received by Athelstan; and for the third and final time the king offers to the Icelander land and authority. These he declines, preferring to pursue inheritance-claims in Norway; but the two part with very great *vinátta* (Nordal 1933, 196) ('friendship').

All of these conversations are related in *Egils saga* without any indication of the slightest difficulty in communication, and what I am therefore advocating in this case is the significance of silence: since Kalinke's so-called 'foreign language requirement' in Norse sagas meant that certain practical or naturalistic expectations needed satisfying in the depiction of the linguistic aspects of overseas travel, one appears to be justified in concluding that, if no language difficulties are mentioned or recognised, then it is likely that none would be felt to exist by the saga-author and his audience. The treatment of Irish, Wendish, and Bjarmian indicates that, in the world of saga-literature, linguistic matters are an issue; yet of the considerable number of sagas that detail Anglo-Norse contact, as far as I am aware not a single one mentions or even hints at any difficulties of communication.[4] I would therefore conclude that taking silence to be significant in this instance is not a case of reading too much into the evidence, but is rather, in Sherlockian terms, a genuine example of a dog doing nothing in the night-time.

---

[4] Moulton (1988, 17–18) also adduces an episode from Saxo's *Gesta Danorum* which tacitly assumes Anglo-Norse intelligibility in *c.* 1170.

Literary Accounts and Anecdotal Evidence 153

The evidence becomes more equivocal, however, when one turns to the recitation of skaldic verse. For *Egils saga* also makes the implicit claim that not only was Norse speech intelligible to an English hearer and vice versa, but Norse poetry was also.[5] Clearly there is a very great difference between being able to understand conversation, with its social rules and pragmatic non-verbal aids, and being able to understand skaldic verse as it is recited. Nowadays we may find it hard to believe that anyone, let alone a non-Scandinavian, might understand such poetry at a single hearing, and the family sagas do indeed contain examples of characters mulling over skaldic strophes, recognising their meaning only long after the first hearing (for a review of the evidence see Gade 1995, 21–27). Nonetheless the author of *Egils saga* quotes five verses which claim to have been composed for, or at least in the presence of, Athelstan (namely verses 19–22 and 35 in Nordal's Íslenzk Fornrit edition), and two of which are understood as coming from a longer, and now-lost, *Aðalsteinsdrápa* (Nordal 1933, 146–47; see Jesch 2001, 315–16):

Þá orti Egill drápu um Aðalstein konung, ok er í því kvæði þetta [. . .] [verse 21]. [. . .]
En þetta er stefit í drápunni [. . .] [verse 22].

(Then Egill composed a poem about King Athelstan, and the following is in the poem [. . .] [verse 21]. [. . .] And the following is the poem's refrain [. . .] [verse 22].)

The witness of *Egils saga* is supported in this respect by that of *Gunnlaugs saga*, in that verse 5 is a *lausavísa* supposedly spoken by Gunnlaugr in response to a question of Æthelred's, and earlier verse 3 is spoken at the first meeting between the two (Nordal and Guðni Jónsson 1938, 71):

Konungr spyrr, hvaðan af lǫndum hann væri. Gunnlaugr segir sem var, — 'en því hefi ek sótt á yðvarn fund, herra, at ek hefi kvæði ort um yðr, ok vilda ek, at þér hlýddið kvæðinu.' Konungr kvað svá vera skyldu. Gunnlaugr flutti fram kvæðit vel ok skǫruliga; en þetta er stefit í:
   Herr sésk allr enn ǫrva
   Englands sem goð þengil;
   ætt lýtr grams ok gumna
   gunnbráðs Aðalráði.
Konungr þakkaði honum kvæðit ok gaf honum at bragarlaunum skarlatsskikkju [. . .] ok gerði hann hirðmann sinn.

(The king asked what country he was from. Gunnlaugr told him, 'and I have sought an audience with you, my lord, because I have composed a poem about you, and I would

---

[5]It is important to stress that in what follows I am discussing the literary depiction of the intelligibility of skaldic verse to English audiences, not whether or not such verse really was intelligible to such audiences (or indeed, whether it actually needed to be intelligible to fulfil its social function). For some preliminary discussion of the latter question see Townend 2000b, 361.

like you to listen to it.' The king said that so it would be. Gunnlaugr recited his poem boldly and well; and this is the refrain: 'All the host fears the generous king of England as they do God. The kin of the battle-brave king, and of the people, bow down to Æthelred.' The king thanked him for the poem and gave him a scarlet cloak as a reward for his poetry [. . .] and he made him his retainer.)

As in *Egils saga*, the familiar skaldic pattern of composition, (apparent) intelligibility, and reward is claimed by the saga-author, although it should be noted that in *Gunnlaugs saga* this pattern subsequently becomes something of a convention, as Gunnlaugr journeys successively to the courts of the Norse kings of Ireland, Orkney, and Gautland, and to each king the diplomatic Gunnlaugr declares, with little variation, ' "kvæði hefi ek ort um yðr, ok vilda ek hljóð fá" ' (Nordal and Guðni Jónsson 1938, 75) (' "I have composed a poem about you, and would like to gain a hearing" ').

Another good example of a relationship between an English patron and an Icelandic poet is to be found in what the kings' sagas have to say about Earl Waltheof (in Old Norse, *Valþjófr jarl*) and Þorkell Skallason. Details of their relationship are to be found in the various versions of *Haralds saga Sigurðarsonar*; in *Fagrskinna* the post-Conquest martyrdom and miracles of Waltheof are related at some length, and the author remarks (Bjarni Einarsson 1985, 294),

Frá þessum tíðendum segir inniliga Þorkell sonr Þórðar skalla. Hann var hirðmaðr Valþjófs jarls, ok orti hann kvæði eptir fall jarlsins.

(Þorkell, the son of Þórðr skalli, relates these events in detail. He was a retainer of Earl Waltheof, and composed a poem after the death of the Earl.)

Two stanzas of Þorkell's elegy for Waltheof, *Valþjófsflokkr*, have survived, and these record the Earl's part in the rebellion against William the Conqueror and William's subsequent murder of the Earl (see Finnur Jónsson 1912–15, IB, 383–84; Scott 1953–57 also gives an edition of these two stanzas). Their importance here is that they again show an Icelandic poet composing for an English (or Anglo-Scandinavian) patron (see Jesch 2001, 321–23); *Valþjófsflokkr* was, by definition, composed after the Earl's death in 1075, but, as has been seen, *Fagrskinna* tells us that Þorkell was his *hirðmaðr* ('retainer') when the Earl was alive.

More ambiguous evidence about the comprehension of skaldic verse is found in a comic incident in *Sneglu-Halla þáttr* which seems to turn on a linguistic issue. The *þáttr* is found embedded in *Morkinskinna*, and, in a fuller form and as an independent work, in *Flateyjarbók* (both versions are printed in Jónas Kristjánsson 1956, 263–95). Halli is something of a low poet, crude, forthright, and an inveterate trickster; and on one occasion his wanderings bring him to the court of the English king, said in *Flateyjarbók* to be Harold Godwineson. Halli, like Gunnlaugr, declares that he has composed a poem for the king, and is given a hearing (Jónas Kristjánsson 1956, 290 (*Flateyjarbók* version)):

Sezk Halli fyrir kné konungi ok flutti fram kvæðit; ok er lokit var kvæðinu, spurði konungr skáld sitt, er var með honum, hvern veg væri kvæðit. Hann kvezk ætla, at gott væri. Konungr bauð Halla með sér at vera, en Halli kvezk búinn vera til Nóregs áðr. Konungr kvað þá þann veg fara mundu af hendi um kvæðislaun – 'við þik sem vér njótum kvæðisins, því at engi hróðr verðr oss at því kvæði, er engi kann.'

(Halli settled before the knee of the king and recited his poem; and when it was finished, the king asked his poet, who was with him, what the poem was like. He said that he thought it was good. The king invited Halli to stay with him, but Halli said that he had already prepared to go to Norway. Then the king said that he would pay a reward for the poem in the same way 'towards you, as we can benefit from the poem, because no honour accrues to us from the poem that nobody knows.')

A laborious joke follows in which Halli manages to retain the gold which is literally showered upon him by previously using tar as shampoo, and then without more ado 'vildi gjarna í brott, því at hann hafði ekki kvæði ort um konung annat en kvæðit endilausu, ok mátti hann því ekki kenna þat' (Jónas Kristjánsson 1956, 291 (*Flateyjarbók* version)) ('he wished eagerly to be away, because he had only composed an endless poem for the king, and thus he couldn't teach that').

It may well be asked wherein the linguistic joke lies. At first it appears as if the point is that the English king is unable to understand skaldic poetry and has to ask his court poet for advice; as will be seen, this is indeed a more probable explanation than that Harold is simply deferring to his poet's taste in the matter of judgement. But why, then, should Harold have a *skáld* in his retinue if such a poet's work is unintelligible to him? Alternatively, it may be suggested that the poet is an English one (*skáld* being used as a general term), that he too cannot understand skaldic poetry but only pretends to do so for the sake of his position, and that Halli is having the laugh on both of them. For Halli freely confesses afterwards that his poem was in fact meaningless: it was *endilauss* ('endless'), and while I am unaware of any evidence for *endilauss* as a technical skaldic term, the emptiness it implies is clear from Halli's unwillingness to teach the poem to the English court and his glee at having successfully tricked them. According to such a reading, the reason why nobody knows Halli's praise-poem is not because no-one at the English court understands it (although that is true) but because no-one has the opportunity to learn it (for only a poem that is actually in circulation can bring praise to a king). Humorously, then, there is something of a central redundancy: Halli's poem, it appears, is unintelligible to the English court (this is a joke), but the poem is in fact *endilauss* (this is a second joke). Halli can only pass off an inadequate composition because of the English court's inability to understand skaldic verse, but in terms of comic effect the second joke would appear to some degree to cancel out the first, and the only consistent butt of humour remains the English *skáld* who, by any reading, pretends to understand Halli's poem (see further Faulkes 1993, 17–18, who discusses Sneglu-Halli as a type of the insubservient skald). That this reading is correct appears to be confirmed by the stanza which Halli speaks on his return to the Norwegian court (Jónas Kristjánsson 1956, 292–93 (only in *Flateyjarbók*)):

> Ortak eina
> of jarl þulu,
> verðrat drápa
> með Dǫnum verri.
> Fǫll eru fjórtán
> ok fǫng tíu;
> opit es ok ǫndvert,
> ǫfugt stígandi;
> svá skal yrkja,
> sás illa kann.

(I made a poem about an earl. A *drápa* could not be worse amongst the Danes: there are fourteen falls and ten catches; and it is open and reversed, rising harshly. So shall he who is incompetent compose.)

This stanza therefore represents Halli looking back on the earlier incident at the English court, gleefully cataloguing the many failings and metrical faults in the poem that he had been able to effortlessly pass off before such an undiscriminating audience (see further Gade 1991).[6]

Sneglu-Halla þáttr, then, provides an important caveat to the usual saga-claims for the apparent intelligibility of skaldic verse to English audiences; and from here we can return to the central assertion of *Gunnlaugs saga*, which is tacitly supported by other relevant sagas, namely that in the Viking Age there were normally no problems of communication between speakers of Norse and speakers of English. The next question to ask, therefore, is whether Old Norse sources offer any explanation for this intelligibility, or draw any finer distinctions between Norse and English.

As has been seen, *Gunnlaugs saga* explains such intelligibility by claiming that Norse and English were quite simply *ein tunga* ('the same language') at the time of Æthelred, and a remarkably similar explanation is to be found in the linguistically acute *First Grammatical Treatise*, written in Iceland in the mid-twelfth century. Having considered how the English adapted the Roman alphabet in order to meet particular requirements in writing English, the First Grammarian goes on to explain, 'Nú eptir þeira dœmum, alls vér erum einnar tungu, þó at gǫrzk hafi mjǫk ǫnnur tveggja eða nǫkkut báðar, [. . .] þá hefi ek ok ritit oss íslendingum stafróf' (Haugen 1972, 12) ('Now following their example, since we are of the same tongue, although there has been much change in one of them or some in both, [. . .] I have also written an alphabet for us Icelanders'). The same two points are made as in *Gunnlaugs saga*: Scandinavians (in this case Icelanders) and English share *ein tunga*, but at the time

---

[6] If genuine, this stanza must date from the 1060s (Frank 1978, 102). A curious feature that might incline one to accept its genuineness is the statement in the second line that Halli had composed his poem for an earl, not a king; the only Anglo-Saxon king who was previously an earl was Harold Godwineson, the name attached to the ruler in the *Flateyjarbók* version of the *þáttr*.

of writing this identity of language has been obscured by linguistic changes. But whereas in *Gunnlaugs saga* these changes are conceived of in terms of the importation of *valska* or French, in the *First Grammatical Treatise* the reference seems to be to phonological and morphological changes that have led to linguistic divergence between Norse and English (for other scholars' opinions on this passage see Fjalldal 1993, 603–04).

For a medieval Scandinavian this *ein tunga* was of course *dǫnsk tunga* ('the Danish tongue'), sometimes later known to Icelanders as *norrœnu tunga* ('the Norse tongue') (see above p 139); thus it might seem that in *Gunnlaugs saga* and the *First Grammatical Treatise* English is being linked with this common Scandinavian tongue. Furthermore, the fragment edited as *Upphaf allra frásagna* (after its opening words), offers a legendary origin for this common tongue (Bjarni Guðnason 1982, 39):

> Upphaf allra frásagna í norrœni tungu, þeira er sannindi fylgja, hófsk, þá er Tyrkir ok Ásíámenn byggðu norðrit. Því er þat með sǫnnu at segja, at tungan kom með þeim norðr higat, er vér kǫllum norrœnu, ok gekk sú tunga um Saxland, Danmǫrk ok Svíþjóð, Nóreg ok um nokkurn hluta Englands.

> (The beginnings of all those stories in the Norse language which tell the truth began when the Turks and men of Asia settled in the north. For it's true to say that the language which we call Norse came northwards with them to here, and that language went through Saxony, Denmark, and Sweden, and through Norway and a certain part of England.)

It is noteworthy that this language was spread only *um nokkurn hluta* ('through a certain part') of England. One might think that this refers to the Danelaw as opposed to the rest of Anglo-Saxon England, but as will be seen the more recent historical reasons why the Norse language was to be found in Danelaw regions were perfectly well remembered and not confused with any legendary origins of the *Ásíámenn*. Rather, I would argue, *um nokkurn hluta* refers to the Germanic- as opposed to the Celtic-speaking regions. This would explain the reference to Saxony, and that this is the more likely explanation is confirmed and clarified by one of Snorri's observations in the Prologue to his *Edda*. Snorri is thought to be adapting a source related to the *Upphaf allra frásagna* fragment when he writes as follows (Snorri Sturluson 1982, 6):

> þeir Æsir hafa haft tunguna norðr hingat í heim, í Nóreg ok í Svíþjóð, í Danmǫrk ok í Saxland; ok í Englandi eru forn lands heiti eða staða heiti þau er skilja má at af annari tungu eru gefin en þessi.

> (The Æsir brought the language northwards in the world to here, into Norway and Sweden, Denmark and Saxony; and in England there are ancient names of regions and places which one can tell have been given in a different language from this one.)

The assertion here seems to be that certain place-names in England are not in the common Germanic language imported by the Æsir, as they demonstrably represent an earlier linguistic stratum, for the qualifying adjective *forn* ('ancient, old') is meaningless — as indeed is the whole digression — unless it indicates that all the other place-names in England were recognised by Snorri and his audience as being in the same *tunga* as names in the other lands mentioned. If such an interpretation is correct, then Snorri not only corroborates *Gunnlaugs saga* and the *First Grammatical Treatise*, but also gives a reasonably accurate account of linguistic history.

The assumption of these texts, and the internally consistent picture they present, is that Norse and English were originally part of the same *tunga*, and hence in the Viking Age their speakers were mutually intelligible to one another; and certain legends are given in an attempt to explain this connection. But as has been seen, both *Gunnlaugs saga* and the *First Grammatical Treatise* remark on how linguistic divergence has since obscured this relationship. Hence one finds that in the thirteenth century, the golden age of saga-literature, Norse writers do not usually go so far as to identify English with, or to label it as, *dǫnsk tunga*. Thus, for example, Snorri himself remarks in *Skáldskaparmál* of the influential men who are appointed to govern districts that 'heita þeir hersar eða lendir menn í Danskri tungu, en greifar í Saxlandi, en barúnar í Englandi' (Snorri Sturluson 1998, I, 80) ('they are called *hersar* or landed men in the Danish tongue, but *greifar* in Saxony, and *barúnar* in England'). The important point is not so much that *barún* is a French word being used in England, but the implication that *dǫnsk tunga* is not, at Snorri's time of writing, what is spoken in England, and nor for that matter in Saxony.[7] The languages have moved on and moved apart since the time of Gunnlaugr (and before that of the Æsir). Similarly, Ian McDougall (1987–88, 190) has drawn attention to a passage in the medieval Icelandic law-code *Grágás* which states that

> if men who speak a language other than the *dǫnsk tunga* die in Iceland — Englishmen or those still 'more foreign' (*úkunnari*) — then only a father or a son may claim an inheritance after them. The implication is clearly that, of those races whose language made them 'strange' to Icelanders, the English were, at least, the *least* foreign.

The last issue to consider is what the sagas have to say about Scandinavian settlement in England and the language of the Danelaw, and it will be seen that this draws together a number of the topics already discussed. To begin with, two passages may be quoted which show awareness of the historical and linguistic background in *Norðimbraland* or Northumbria, a name which in Norse sources appears to be used

---

[7] ON *greifi* is in fact a loan from OE *gerēfa* 'reeve', found first in Sigvatr Þórðarson's *Víkingarvísur* 8.8 in the compound *portgreifi* (Finnur Jónsson 1912–15, IB, 215; see Hofmann 1955, 82 (§78); Fell 1981a, 117); interestingly, the word later re-enters English in its Norse phonological form (e.g. *greyues* in *Havelok* lines 266, 1750, 1772 (Smithers 1987, 9, 47, 48)).

to refer to the whole area of Scandinavian settlement in England. Firstly, the author of *Egils saga* writes as follows (Nordal 1933, 129):[8]

> Norðimbraland er kallat fimmtungr Englands, ok er þat norðast, næst Skotlandi fyrir austan; þat hǫfðu haft at fornu Danakonungar; Jórvík er þar hǫfuðstaðr. Þat ríki átti Aðalsteinn ok hafði sett yfir jarla tvá; hét annarr Álfgeirr, en annarr Goðrekr; þeir sátu þar til landvarnar, bæði fyrir ágangi Skota ok Dana eða Norðmanna, er mjǫk herjuðu á landit ok þóttusk eiga tilkall mikit þar til lands, því at á Norðimbralandi váru þeir einir menn, ef nǫkkut var til, at danska ætt átti at faðerni eða móðerni, en margir hvárirtveggju.

(Northumbria is reckoned a fifth part of England, and it is the most northerly, closest to Scotland on the east side. Danish kings held it in the past, and York is its capital. Athelstan ruled that kingdom, and he had set two earls over it: one was called Álfgeirr [OE *Ælfgār*?] and the other Goðrekr [OE *Godrīc*?]. They were there to guard the land against the attacks of both the Scots and the Danes or Norwegians, who greatly harried the country there and thought that they had a great claim on the country, because in Northumbria the only people who were of any importance were of Danish ancestry on their father's side, or on their mother's side, and many on both.)

And secondly, Snorri records in a related passage in *Hákonar saga góða* (in *Heimskringla*) (Snorri Sturluson 1941–51, I, 152–53),

> Norðimbraland er kallat fimmtungr Englands. Hann [i.e. Eiríkr blóðøx] hafði atsetu í Jórvík, þar sem menn segja, at fyrr hafi setit Loðbrókarsynir. Norðimbraland var mest byggt Norðmǫnnum, síðan er Loðbrókarsynir unnu landit. Herjuðu Danir ok Norðmenn optliga þangat, síðan er vald landsins hafði undan þeim gengit. Mǫrg heiti landsins eru þar gefin á norrœnu tungu, Grímsbœr ok Hauksfljót ok mǫrg ǫnnur.

(Northumbria is reckoned a fifth part of England. Eiríkr had taken residence in York, where, men say, the sons of Loðbrók had previously resided. After the sons of Loðbrók conquered the land, Northumbria was mostly settled by Norwegians. And after control of the land had been taken away from them, Danes and Norwegians often harried there. Many place-names there are in the Norse language, such as *Grímsbœr* [Grimsby] and *Hauksfljót* [?] and many others.)

Both passages show a clear historical grasp of the settlement of the Danelaw, and Snorri also seems to allude to its (re)conquest by the West Saxon kings. The second passage is also significant in that it shows that Icelandic writers could and did distinguish between Norse and English as two different languages in England in the Anglo-Saxon period: Snorri is perfectly clear as to which place-names are *á norrœnu tungu* ('in the Norse language') and which are not.

---

[8]Evans 1997, 355–56, suggests that in this passage the last phrase *en margir hvárirtveggju* means in fact 'and each of these two groups was numerous'.

Yet there are, naturally, no more difficulties of communication in Northumbria than elsewhere in England. When Egill and his men are shipwrecked on their second visit to England *við Humru mynni* ('at the mouth of the Humber'), they are able to learn the latest news from some locals: 'Ok er þeir hittu menn at máli, spurðu þeir þau tiðendi' (Nordal 1933, 177) ('And when they met people to talk to, they asked the news'). Likewise Egill is able to ask and receive directions in the city of York: 'Egill spurði, hvar garðr sá væri í borginni, er Arinbjǫrn átti; honum var þat sagt' (Nordal 1933, 178) ('Egill asked, whereabouts in the town was the house which Arinbjǫrn owned; and he was told') (on the saga-episode of Egill in York see for example Jones 1952; Vésteinn Ólason 1990; Hines 1995b). Similarly *Haralds saga Sigurðarsonar* (in *Heimskringla* and elsewhere) records a number of conversations between that king and the inhabitants of Northumbria, especially of York, during the campaign leading up to the battle of Stamford Bridge; in none of them is there any hint of anything other than perfectly adequate intelligibility.

But there is one celebrated episode in *Haralds saga Sigurðarsonar*, involving not the king himself but one of his marshals, which is very remarkable, and this is the account of the escape of Styrkárr stallari after the defeat of the Norwegian army (this passage has often been noted: see for example Fellows-Jensen 1975a, 8; Fjalldal 1993, 605–06). The story is found in *Morkinskinna*, *Fagrskinna*, and *Heimskringla*, but differences are only minor ones of wording, and so Snorri's version will be quoted here. Styrkárr escapes from Stamford Bridge on a horse, but when the evening comes a cool breeze arises, and since Styrkárr is only lightly clad and the effects of battle have worn off, he begins to feel the cold (Snorri Sturluson 1941–51, III, 192):

Þá kom í móti honum vagnkarl einn ok var í kǫsungi fóðruðum. Þá mælti Styrkárr: 'Viltu selja kǫsunginn, bóndi?' 'Eigi þérna,' segir hann. 'Þú munt vera Norðmaðr, kenni ek mál þitt.' Þá mælti Styrkárr: 'Ef ek em Norðmaðr, hvat viltu þá?' Bóndi svarar: 'Ek vilda drepa þik, en nú er svá illa, at ek hefi ekki vápn, þatt er nytt sé.'

(Then a wagoner came towards him who was dressed in a fur-lined jacket. Styrkárr said, 'Will you part with your jacket, farmer?' 'Not to you,' he said. 'You're a Norwegian — I recognise your speech.' Then Styrkárr said, 'If I'm a Norwegian, what do you want to do about it?' The farmer answered, 'I'd like to kill you, but it's unfortunate that I haven't got a suitable weapon at the moment.')

Such bellicosity is, however, unwise on the part of the wagoner, because although he may not have a suitable weapon Styrkárr certainly does; and he promptly strikes off the wagoner's head, takes the jacket, and rides away to the ships. As has been seen, the sagas record Northumbria as being an area of both Danish and Norwegian settlement, and so the point here is that, to the wagoner, Styrkárr's speech is recognisable as Norse as spoken in Scandinavia (or, more specifically, in Norway), as distinct from English or Norse as spoken in Northumbria. According to this episode in

Haralds saga, then, the languages are mutually intelligible; but clearly they are not likely to be mistaken for one another.

Old English and Anglo-Latin: Interpreters in Anglo-Saxon England

The Icelandic sagas, therefore, are a fruitful source for commentary on Anglo-Norse language contact in the Viking Age, and present a surprisingly coherent and (where testable) accurate account of the history of Old Norse in England; but such a wealth of narrative texts does not exist in Old English, and so the issue cannot be examined in the same manner from the Anglo-Saxon side. Many Old English and Anglo-Latin texts record contact between Norse speakers and English speakers (see pp 3–8 above), but very few go so far in their narrative dimension as to record dialogue; the two obvious texts which do are *The Battle of Maldon* (Dobbie 1942, 7–16) and Ælfric's *Life of St Edmund* (Skeat 1881–1900, IV, 314–35), and in neither is there any hint of bilingualism or the use of interpreters, nor indeed any other indication as to how members of the one speech community are able to understand members of the other. In *Maldon* the *wicinga ar* ('messenger of the Vikings') shouts a threatening demand for Danegeld at Byrhtnoth and his men, and the ealdorman shouts back a scornful response (lines 29–41 and 45–61; a second speech of Byrhtnoth's to the Viking army is quoted at lines 93–95); this exchange is presented as no simple mouthing of basic sentences, and Byrhtnoth's speech in particular is rhetorically heightened, even witty (see for example Shippey 1985, 228–30).[9] In Ælfric's *Life of St Edmund*, the speeches of a similar exchange are quoted, between Hingwar's messenger and the East Anglian king (lines 48–55 and 85–93). With such a paucity of narrative material, then, is one justified in applying the same approach as to saga-literature, by believing that since the Anglo-Saxon writers make no mention of interpreters or bilingualism, such methods for cross-language communication were unnecessary? For as was seen in the examples given in Chapter 1, none of the less literary texts, such as the procedures for settling Anglo-Norse disputes or the *Chronicle*'s accounts of Anglo-Norse diplomacy, make reference to language difficulties either.

Certainly William Moulton feels justified in making such an argument from silence in his brief but suggestive discussion of intelligibility between Germanic dialects. He evaluates *The Battle of Maldon* as follows (1988, 16):

> The two sides constantly shout demands and threats at each other. Not a word is said about dialect, language, or mutual intelligibility. But that, I believe, is just the point. It seems unlikely that these sturdy and probably untutored warriors used the language of the other side in their shouting, so that the English shouted in Norwegian and the Norwegians in English. It is more likely that the English shouted in English and the

---

[9] For the debatable notion that the speech of the Viking messenger shows deliberate traces of Norse dialect, see Robinson 1976, 26–27; see also Griffith 1998.

Norwegians in Norwegian. Furthermore, the fact that the author of the poem says nothing about language implies that any sensible hearer of the poem would of course already know that the Englishmen and the Norwegians could understand each other. My conclusion is that this is excellent proof of mutual intelligibility, precisely because nothing is said about it.

But before one follows Moulton in his conclusion, or adduces the *Life of St Edmund* as further evidence, it is reasonable to ask for some sort of proof of a saga-like naturalism in the Anglo-Saxon literary presentation of language contact.

This can, I think, be provided in a somewhat roundabout way by an analysis of the treatment of foreign languages in another sort of narrative text from the Anglo-Saxon period — namely, saints' lives, and other Christian writings influenced by them — and especially if one concentrates on the literary presentation of interpreters. Inevitably a number of these texts are in Latin, at least at first; but whether in Anglo-Latin or Old English, they suggest an Anglo-Saxon awareness of language differences, and of the need to explain how cross-language communication is able to occur in a narrative.

As an introductory example, Felix's eighth-century *Life of St Guthlac* (Chapter 34) provides a good exemplification of just such an awareness, when his hagiographer explains how it is that the saint is able to understand the voices of the demons who assail him in his fenland retreat (Colgrave 1956, 110–11):

> arrectis auribus adstans, verba loquentis vulgi Brittanicaque agmina tectis succedere agnoscit; nam ille aliorum temporum praeteritis voluminibus inter illos exulabat, quoadusque eorum strimulentas loquelas intelligere valuit.

> (standing, with ears alert he recognized the words that the crowd were saying, and realized that British hosts were approaching his dwelling: for in years gone by he had been in exile among them, so that he was able to understand their sibilant speech.)

This is not dissimilar to the 'hero's education' motif in the Icelandic sagas, found in the family sagas as well as the *fornaldarsögur* (for example, Óláfr pái's ability to understand Irish in *Laxdœla saga*); Felix is giving a comparable explanation for his subject's command (in this case, passive command) of a foreign language which is normally unintelligible.

As said above, though, it is in the literary presentation of interpreters that an Anglo-Saxon awareness of language differences can best be demonstrated, and the rest of this section will accordingly be devoted to this: a wide range of examples will be assembled before proceeding to an analysis and summary at the end. To begin with, then, a couple of good instances of passing reference to interpreters can be cited from Adomnán's *Life of Columba*, a text which is admittedly not Anglo-Saxon, but can of course be viewed within the wider orbit of Anglo-Irish Christianity in the seventh and eighth centuries. The first of these examples (in Book I Chapter 33) concerns the conversion of an aged pagan named Artbranán who arrives on the isle of Skye, and who is said to have believed and been baptized 'statim uerbo dei a sancto per interpraetem recepto' ('as soon as he had, through an interpreter, received the word of God from the saint') (Anderson and Anderson 1991, 62–63). Columba spoke Irish, but Artbranán's own language is not clear: although his name is possibly Irish, David Dumville (1978) has suggested, partly on account of the reference to an interpreter and partly on account of his title (*Geonae primarius cohortis* ('the leader of the cohort of Geon (?)')), that he was most probably a Pict.

The second example is found in Book II Chapter 32 and is a clear instance of Irish-Pictish communication (Anderson and Anderson 1991, 138–39):

> Illo in tempore quo sanctus Columba in Pictorum prouincia per aliquot demorabatur dies, quidam cum tota plebeus familia uerbum uitae per interpretatorum sancto predicante uiro audiens credidit, credensque babtizatus est maritus cum marita liberísque et familiaribus.

> (At the time when Saint Columba passed some days in the province of the Picts, a certain layman with his whole household heard and believed the word of life, through an interpreter, at the preaching of the holy man; and believing, was baptized, the husband, with his wife and children, and his servants.)

As Anderson and Anderson note (1991, 139 n.168), Adomnán's reference to an *interpretator* must imply 'that the Irish language was not understood by the people living east of the Spine [of Britain]'.[10]

Bede's *Historia Ecclesiastica*, written a little later than Adomnán's *Life of Columba*, provides a number of interesting allusions to the use of interpreters (for an exploration of some references to linguistic differences in Bede's work see Derolez 1992, 285–88). The first and most famous of these comes early in the work, as the Roman mission arrives in England in 597. How Augustine and his companions intended to overcome the linguistic barrier is the first thing we are told when they reach land at Thanet (Book I Chapter 25): 'Acceperant autem, praecipiente beato papa Gregorio, de gente Francorum interpretes' ('They had acquired interpreters from the Frankish race according to the command of Pope St Gregory') (Colgrave and Mynors 1969, 72–73); and Wallace-Hadrill (1988, 33) observes appositely that, 'Considering the Frankish presence at Æthelberht's court, it is unnecessary to suppose that the court did not understand Frankish'. The later story of King Cenwealh and Bishop Agilbert (Book III Chapter 7) tells us that while West Saxon and Frankish were

---

[10] A. P. Smyth (1984, 106) is mistaken in stating that Adomnán records Columba as having employed an interpreter when preaching at Urquhart in Book III Chapter 14; the two episodes quoted above, on Skye and in the Great Glen, are the only ones for which Adomnán mentions such a practice. However, one might perhaps have expected such a reference, as Urquhart is said to be *ultra Brittaniae dorsum* ('on the other side of the Spine of Britain') (Anderson and Anderson 1991, 200–01). On the importance of interpreters and language learning in early medieval missionary enterprises more generally see Fletcher 1997, 263.

adequately intelligible in the seventh century, communication between the two was not without effort and strain (Colgrave and Mynors 1969, 234–35):

> [Agilbert] multis annis eidem genti sacerdotali iure praefuit. Tandem rex, qui Saxonum tantum linguam nouerat, pertaesus barbarae loquellae, subintroduxit in prouinciam alium suae linguae episcopum, uocabulo Uini, et ipsum in Gallia ordinatum.

> ([Agilbert] presided over the nation [i.e. Wessex] as bishop for a number of years. But at last the king, who knew only the Saxon language, grew tired of his barbarous speech and foisted upon the kingdom a bishop named Wine who had been consecrated in Gaul but who spoke the king's own tongue.)

Later in Bede's *Historia* one of the key figures at the Synod of Whitby (Book III Chapter 25) is 'uenerabilis episcopus Cedd, iamdudum ordinatus a Scottis [...] qui et interpres in eo concilio uigilantissimus utriusque partis extitit' ('the venerable Bishop Cedd, who [...] had been consecrated long before by the Irish and who acted as a most careful interpreter for both parties at the council') (Colgrave and Mynors 1969, 298–99).[11]

In the late-ninth- or early-tenth-century Old English translation of Bede the first reference to Augustine's use of interpreters is rendered as 'Nóman hi eac swylce him wealhstodas of Franclande mid, swa him Scs Gregorius bebead' (Miller 1890–91, I, 58) ('They also brought interpreters with them from France, just as St Gregory had commanded them'). As this quotation indicates, the Old English word for 'interpreter' is *w(e)alhstod*. The second element of the compound is obscure; its first element, though, is plainly *wealh* (Anglian *walh*), the most common Old English word for 'Briton, Celt', with also a later meaning 'slave' (Faull 1975 provides a thorough investigation into the word's evolution; this is complemented by Cameron 1979–80). Although cognates of OE *wealh* are found in several Germanic languages (for example, ON *val-* in several compounds), the word *wealhstod* is unique to Old English, and so it appears that the term arose in Britain, after the Anglo-Saxon migration. The word therefore carries its own history: as Tolkien puts it (1963, 24), it seems to have been coined by the newly migrated Anglo-Saxons to refer to 'an intermediary between those who spoke English and those who spoke a *wælisc* [British] tongue, however he had acquired a knowledge of both languages'. There is no evidence to suggest that the word was originally applied only to a native British speaker, though Margaret Faull (1975) believes this to be likely; although Faull does not give her reasons for this, one assumes that she is following Kenneth Jackson's view that it was the Britons, and not the Anglo-Saxons, who became bilingual in the situations of language contact existing from the fifth century onwards (see Jackson 1953, 241–42). Subsequently the word's reference was generalised in Old English,

---

[11]Further examples derived from Bede's *Historia* are given below in the discussion of Ælfric.

so that it is used to refer to an interpreter between any two languages, not just between English and British.

The Latin term, then, is *interpres*, and the corresponding Old English is *wealhstod*; and a number of Anglo-Saxon glossaries do indeed give the equation *Interpres, wealhstod*.[12] These are Ælfric's *Glossary* (Zupitza 1880, 230 (lines 12–13)), both the main and the miscellaneous glosses in the eleventh-century London, BL, MS Cotton Cleopatra A.iii, and the mid-twelfth-century Worcester glosses (Wright and Wülcker 1884, I, 337 (line 24), 425 (line 5), 510 (line 2), 553 (line 13)). A number of the glossed manuscripts of Aldhelm's *De Laudibus Virginitatis* also contain the gloss on the genitive plural, in varying spellings: Oxford, Bodleian Library, MS Digby 146 has *interpretum, wealcstoda*; London, BL, MS Royal 6.A.vi has *interpretum, wealhstoda*; and London, BL, MS Royal 5.E.xi has *interpretum, walcstoda* (Napier 1900, 65 (gloss 2422), 159 (gloss 149), 166 (gloss 120)). The equation is also to be found in Ælfric's *Grammar*, in the section on noun inflexions (Zupitza 1880, 51 (line 14)); and the miscellaneous Cleopatra A.iii glosses additionally contain the definition *Interpres, qui linquam transfert* (Wright and Wülcker 1884, I, 477 (line 32)).

The word *wealhstod* is also found in Old English as a personal name. Names such as *Walh*, *Welisc*, and *Cumbre* (or *Cumbra*) all occur as personal names in the Anglo-Saxon period, and in Margaret Gelling's view (1992, 62) such names were most probably 'acquired as nicknames by men who were known to have Welsh connections'.[13] *Wealhstod* (Anglian *Walhstod*) would therefore seem to be another such name, and in extant sources it is recorded as having been borne by at least four different individuals (see Searle 1897, 481). One of these was a monk of Lindisfarne mentioned by Bede in Chapter 38 of his *Vita Cuthberti* (*Walchstod* in the Latin); this unfortunate monk suffered from chronic diarrhoea until he was healed by Cuthbert at the very end of the saint's life (see Colgrave 1940, 276–83). Another bearer of the name was a bishop in the West Midlands in the early eighth century, of whom the Old English Bede records that 'þæm folcum þa þe eardiað be westan Sæferne is Wealhstod bisceop' (Miller 1890–91, II, 478) ('Wealhstod is bishop for the peoples who live west of the Severn') (for the Latin original see Colgrave and Mynors 1969, 558–59). As Gelling comments (1992, 100), 'It is clear that the bishop of the Magonsætan see in Bede's day needed to be bilingual'.

In Old English texts, the word *wealhstod* is first found in continuous prose (three times) in the works of King Alfred, twice in his translation of Gregory's *Cura Pastoralis*. The first occurrence is in the famous prefatory letter, as Alfred considers the translation of Christian books (and in particular the Scriptures) into the vernacular by other nations (Sweet 1871, I, 5–6):

---

[12]OE *wealhstod* failed to survive into the Middle English period, which is when French *interpreteur* entered the language, so giving MnE *interpreter*.

[13]Cameron goes further in asserting (1979–80, 6), '[P]ersonally, I have little doubt that *w(e)alh* was used originally in personal names to denote people of British stock or of mixed parentage'.

Ða gemunde ic hu sio æ wæs ærest ærest [sic] on Ebreisc geðiode funden, & eft, þa þa hie Crecas geleornodon, þa wendon hi hie on hiora ægen geðiode ealle, & eac ealle oðre bec. And eft Lædenware swa same, siððan hi hie geleornodon, hi hie wendon ealla ðurh wise wealhstodas on hiora agen geðeode.

(Then I remembered how the Law was first of all found in the Hebrew language, and later, when the Greeks learned it, they translated it all into their own language, and also all the other books. And later the Romans similarly, after they had learned them, they translated them all into their own language by means of wise translators.)

The *wise wealhstodas* here are translating from Greek to Latin; of these, Jerome must have been the foremost (as will be seen from one of Ælfric's examples below). As Faull therefore notes (1975, 26), 'Certainly by Alfred's time it [i.e. the word *wealhstod*] was no longer restricted specifically to one knowledgeable in the Celtic languages and its meaning had been extended to include that of "literary interpreter" or "translator"'. Indeed, the second occurrence in the *Cura Pastoralis* demonstrates an extended, more metaphorical meaning, when in Chapter 3 cautions are made concerning the burden of teaching (Sweet 1871, I, 32):

Swiðe medomlice Iacobus se apostol his stirde, þa he cwæð: Broður ne beo eower to fela lareowa. Forðæm se wealhstod self Godes & monna, ðæt is Crist, fleah eorðrice [eorþlic rice] to underfónne.

(Very reasonably the apostle James restricted this when he said, 'Brothers, may there not be too many teachers among you.' For this reason the *wealhstod* between God and men, that is Christ himself, fled from undertaking earthly rule.)

To describe Christ as 'se wealhstod [. . .] Godes & monna' is of course to continue to draw on the concepts and terminology of language, with Christ as God's *Logos*, the Word made flesh to men; but it is a usage of *wealhstod* well beyond the usual range of meaning.

This is therefore a suitable point at which to mention the word's only occurrence in the extant poetic corpus, namely in the famous call to interpretation in *Exodus*, as here too it is being used in a more generalised sense (Krapp 1931, 105–06 (lines 523–26, my punctuation)):

Gif onlucan wile   lifes wealhstod,
beorht in breostum,   banhuses weard,
ginfæsten god   Gastes cægon,
run bið gerecenod,   ræd forð gæð.

(If the interpreter of life, bright in the breast, the guardian of the body, will unlock great benefits with the keys of the Spirit, the mystery will be explained, and counsel will come forth.)

The most recent editor of *Exodus* takes the *lifes wealhstod* to be the intellect and offers the following note to line 523 (Lucas 1994, 142–43):

> *Wealhstod* usually means 'translator' or 'mediator' and the word clearly implies elucidation of the correspondence between two sets of information, in this context the correspondence between literal and allegorical and the typological connection between historically separate events or personages. The perception of those correspondences is a source of life (cf. 2 Cor. 3.6).

This single poetic citation is the only example where the meaning of *wealhstod* has no linguistic reference, but only indicates the interpretation of events. *Exodus*, like virtually all Old English poems, is impossible to date with any certainty, so we cannot plot this meaning chronologically into the word's semantic development during the Anglo-Saxon period.[14] This non-linguistic sense may have been a common meaning of the word, or it may have been restricted to verse,[15] or (perhaps most probably) it may be regarded as another example of the verbal athleticism of the *Exodus*-poet, driving words into new contexts and new meanings.

To return to Alfred, the third and final occurrence of *wealhstod* in his works is in the Proem to his translation of Boethius's *De Consolatione Philosophiae*, in which he declares in his first sentence (Sedgefield 1899, 1),

> ÆLFRED KUNING wæs wealhstod ðisse bec, ⁊ hie of boclædene on englisc wende, swa hio nu is gedon. Hwilum he sette word be worde, hwilum andgit of andgite.
>
> (King Alfred was the translator of this book, and turned it from Latin into English, as has now been done. Sometimes he translated word for word, sometimes sense for sense.)

Wealhstod is here being used, therefore, to refer to someone translating from Latin to English, confirming that by the late ninth century the word could be used to refer to communication between any two languages.

A century after Alfred, and at the height of the second wave of Viking attacks, the works of Ælfric furnish a number of examples of cross-language communication using *wealhstodas*. The earliest of these is in his sermon *Assumptio Sanctae Mariae Virginis* (No. 30 of the First Series of *Catholic Homilies*), in which he begins by explaining that Jerome wrote an epistle 'be forðsiðe þære eadigan marian' (Clemoes 1997, 429) ('on the death of the blessed Mary'):

---

[14] *Exodus* is, however, usually regarded as being one of the older Old English poems (see Lucas 1994, 69–72, including a review of earlier opinions; see also Fulk 1992, 391–92 (§421)).

[15] This seems unlikely, since (as far as we can judge) Old English words tend to have a distinctive meaning in verse as opposed to prose when they are patently ancient or archaic words, deriving from the old Germanic wordhoard, whereas *wealhstod* (as has been seen) is a coinage from the Anglo-Saxon period itself.

ðes hieronimus wæs halig sacerd ⁊ getogen on hebreiscum gereorde. ⁊ on greciscum. ⁊ on ledenum fulfremedlice ⁊ he awende ure bibliothecan of hebreiscum bocum to ledenspræce; He is se fyrmesta wealgstod betwux hebreiscum. ⁊ grecum. ⁊ ledenwarum.

(This Jerome was a holy priest, and perfectly learned in the Hebrew, Greek, and Latin tongues; and he translated our library from Hebrew books into Latin. He is the first interpreter between the Hebrews, and Greeks, and Romans.)

This passage, with its trio of Hebrews, Greeks, and Romans, is reminiscent of Alfred's Preface to the *Cura Pastoralis*, and here Jerome does indeed receive his merited distinction as *se fyrmesta wealgstod* ('the first interpreter'). In his later sermon *Sancti Gregorii Pape* (No. 9 of the Second Series of *Catholic Homilies*), Ælfric draws on Bede's account when he demonstrates Pope Gregory's foresight in equipping Augustine's mission with the required linguistic tools (Godden 1979, 78):

On ðam dagum rixode Æþelbyrht cyning on cantwarebyrig ríclice. and his rice wæs astreht fram ðære micclan éa humbre. oð suðsæ; Augustinus hæfde genumen wealhstodas of francena rice. swa swa Gregorius him bebead. and hé ðurh ðæra wealhstoda muð þam cyninge. and his leode godes word bodade. hu se mildheorta hælend mid his agenre ðrowunge þysne scyldigan middaneard alysde. and geleaffullum mannum heofenan rices infær geopenode.

(In those days King Æthelberht ruled powerfully in Canterbury, and his kingdom stretched from the mighty River Humber to the English Channel. Augustine had brought interpreters from the kingdom of the Franks, just as Gregory had commanded him, and through the mouths of the interpreters he preached the word of God to the king and his people, telling how the merciful saviour redeemed this sinful world by his own passion, and opened the entry to the heavenly kingdom for men of faith.)

Also deriving from Bede are three accounts of Aidan of Iona at Oswald's Northumbrian court, with its situation of Irish-English language contact: Bede's own account in the *Historia Ecclesiastica* (Book III Chapter 3), and then in turn the Old English Bede and Ælfric's *Life of St Oswald*. Bede's Latin version is as follows (Colgrave and Mynors 1969, 220–21):

Vbi pulcherrimo saepe spectaculo contigit, ut euangelizante antistite, qui Anglorum linguam perfecte non nouerat, ipse rex suis ducibus ac ministris interpres uerbi existeret caelestis, quia nimirum tam longo exilii sui tempore linguam Scottorum iam plene didicerat.

(It was indeed a beautiful sight when the bishop was preaching the gospel, to see the king acting as interpreter of the heavenly word for his ealdormen and thegns, for the bishop was not completely at home in the English tongue, while the king had gained a perfect knowledge of Irish during the long period of his exile.)

Literary Accounts and Anecdotal Evidence

In the Old English Bede this becomes (Miller 1890–91, I, 158),

⁊ oft fægre wæfersyne gelomp, þa se biscop codcunde lare lærde se ðe Englisc fullice ne cuðe, þæt he se cyning seolfa, se ðe Scyttisc fullice geleornad hæfde, his aldormonnum ⁊ his þegnum þære heofenlecan lare wæs walhstod geworden.

(And a fair spectacle was often to be seen, when the bishop, who did not know English fully, was teaching holy doctrine — namely that the king himself, who had learned Irish fully, acted as interpreter of the heavenly teaching to his noblemen and thanes.)

Finally, a century later Ælfric uses Bede's *Historia* as his source for his *Life of St Oswald* (No. 26 of his *Lives of the Saints*), where this passage is refashioned into characteristic rhythmical prose (Skeat 1881–1900, III, 128–30 (lines 64–69)):

Hit gelamp þa swa þæt se geleaffulla cyning
gerehte his witan on heora agenum gereorde
þæs bisceopes bodunge mid bliþum mode .
and wæs his wealhstod for-þan þe he wel cuþe scyttysc .
and se bisceop aidan ne mihte gebigan his spræce
to norðhymbriscum gereorde swa hraþe þa git .

(It happened then that the faithful king, with a cheerful mind, explained to his counsellors in their own language the preaching of the bishop and was his interpreter, because he knew Irish well and bishop Aidan could not yet turn his speech into the Northumbrian language as quickly.)

This therefore constitutes thrice-asserted confirmation of the etymological significance of *wealhstod* — namely that Irish-English communication required the use of an interpreter, unless one of the parties was bilingual (as Aidan, like Oswald, subsequently became). Bede feels it necessary to explain Aidan's ability to preach in Northumbria, and Ælfric (in the Viking Age) chooses to retain this explanation amidst some fairly radical editing of Bede's narrative (on Ælfric's use of Bede in his *Life of St Oswald* see Cross 1965, 94–98).

Ælfric's *Life of St Basilius* (No. 3 of his *Lives of the Saints*) presents St Ephrem of Syria as needing to employ an interpreter in his dealings with the Greek-speaking Basil (Skeat 1881–1900, I, 80 (lines 522–26)). The two saints therefore pray that God might miraculously grant to Ephrem a knowledge of Greek, so that he can discourse freely with Basil:

Hi cneowdon þa æft . and æffrem þa spræc
mid greciscum gereorde . god herigende .
and se halga biscop hine hadode to messe-preoste .
and his wealh-stód to diacone . and hí wendon eft on-gean
to þam wid-gyllan westene . wuldrigende gód.

(Then they knelt again, and Ephrem then spoke in the Greek language, praising God, and the holy Bishop ordained him as mass-priest, and his interpreter as deacon; and they went back again to the vast desert, glorifying God.)

Ælfric does not tell us Ephrem's own language (and perhaps, for the purposes of the miracle, it does not matter), but since Ephrem's origins were in Mesopotamia (Farmer 1997, 163), it is likely to have been Aramaic; therefore *wealhstod* is here employed for perhaps Greek-Aramaic communication.

Byrhtferth's early-eleventh-century *Enchiridion* is the final Old English text in which the word *wealhstod* features, in Byrhtferth's discussion of the duration of the Second Age of the World (Baker and Lapidge 1995, 234):

Seo oðer yld þises middaneardes wæs standende æfter þære Ebreiscan þeode twa hund wintra and twa and hundnigontig wintra, and æfter þæra hundseofontigra wealhstoda gesetnyssa se tima stod on þusend wintrum and on twa and hundseofontigum wintrum.

(The second age of this world, according to the Hebrew people, lasted for two hundred and ninety-two years; and according to the account of the seventy translators, the period lasted for one thousand and seventy-two years.)

The 'seventy translators' are those who produced the Greek Septuagint; therefore we have here another allusion to literary translators from Hebrew to Greek, to set alongside those of Alfred and Ælfric.

This laborious trek through the extant occurrences, while undoubtedly somewhat tedious, has however supplied the context we require by demonstrating that references to the use of interpreters are by no means infrequent in Anglo-Saxon texts. *Wealhstodas* or *interpretes* are recorded as being necessary for communication between speakers of the following languages: Irish and Pictish (Adomnán on Columba), Irish and English (Bede's account of Cedd at Whitby and of Aidan in Northumbria, the latter of which is confirmed by Ælfric as well as by the Old English Bede), Vulgar Latin and English (Bede's account of Augustine's mission, confirmed by Ælfric and the Old English Bede), and perhaps Greek and Aramaic (Ælfric on Basil), in addition to the literary translation recorded between Hebrew and Greek (Byrhtferth on the Septuagint), Greek and Latin (Alfred and Ælfric on Jerome), and Latin and English (Alfred on his own translation of Boethius). I would argue therefore that this constitutes a sufficient number and range of references to indicate that not only were the Anglo-Saxons amply conscious of linguistic differences, but also that they often made a point in their texts of explaining how it was that speakers of different languages were able to communicate. In other words, a similar, broadly naturalistic, rationale is operating behind the depiction of language contact in Anglo-Saxon texts as was found to be operating in the Icelandic sagas. This would seem to give us the framework we need in order to follow Moulton in claiming a significance in silence: no mention is made in *The Battle of Maldon* of linguistic difficulties, and thus, presumably, none were felt to exist.

One might still argue that *Maldon*'s poetic evidence is insufficiently documentary; in that case, it must be Ælfric's witness that decides the issue. Ælfric gives us two separate accounts of the use of interpreters in his *Lives of the Saints* (Aidan and Basil), as well as a third in his hagiographic homily on Pope Gregory (Augustine's mission). Thus whether one takes these references as generic convention, or naturalistic accuracy, or both, it remains significant that no mention is made of interpreters in the Norse-English communication in the *Life of St Edmund*. As has been seen (see above p 139), Ælfric was well aware of the *dǫnsk tunga* in England, giving us our only references to *Denisc* in Old English, and he was able to reproduce the Norse names of the Scandinavian deities with impressive accuracy; his silence in *St Edmund* concerning interpreters or communication problems can therefore be taken as significant, and arguably conclusive.

To summarize, then, the findings of this chapter so far: there are a good many references in Anglo-Saxon texts to the use of interpreters as the means of overcoming the barrier of unintelligibility existing between speakers of two languages, and a good range of languages are specified in such a context. But on no occasion, either in *Maldon* or in Ælfric's *Life of St Edmund* or in the many *Chronicle* entries recording Anglo-Norse contact, is there a single reference to the use of interpreters in the context of Anglo-Norse communication. This was true of the references to interpreters in Icelandic saga-literature, and it is equally true of the references in Anglo-Saxon texts. It therefore seems reasonable to conclude that interpreters were not normally required for Anglo-Norse communication.

The Old English Carta Dominica *Homilies*

As was seen in the first part of this chapter, later Icelandic sources have a good deal to say about Anglo-Norse contact and the Old Norse language in England. But of course these sources derive from some two or three centuries after the contact situation in Viking Age England, and genuinely contemporary witnesses are much harder to come by. Indeed, as far as I am aware, only one strictly contemporary observation on Anglo-Norse intelligibility has ever been adduced; and this was done by Otto Jespersen in his classic book *Growth and Structure of the English Language* — first published in 1909, but subsequently running through ten editions and still in print in the 1980s. In his discussion of Anglo-Norse contact and the Norse element in English Jespersen suggests that the evidence for Anglo-Norse intelligibility is equivocal, and he remarks as follows (where the 'positive evidence' referred to is plainly *Gunnlaugs saga* and other Icelandic texts) (1956, 60):

> An Englishman would have no great difficulty in understanding a viking — nay, we have positive evidence that Norse people looked upon the English language as one with their own. On the other hand, Wulfstan speaks of the invaders as 'people who do not know your language'.

Jespersen's discussion of Anglo-Norse language contact may be old, but it is still widely influential; for example, the passage just quoted clearly lies behind Baugh and Cable's treatment in their standard *History of the English Language*, staple reading for many an undergraduate course. Baugh and Cable write (1978, 95 (§71)),

> The Anglian dialect resembled the language of the Northmen in a number of particulars in which West Saxon showed divergence. The two may even have been mutually intelligible to a limited extent. Contemporary statements on the subject are conflicting, and it is difficult to arrive at a conviction.

This observation by Jespersen has been briefly discussed by Ian McDougall (1987–88, 223 n.5), and the first thing to note is Jespersen's mistranslation of the relevant clause, as well as the misattribution of the text itself. To take the latter point first: the statement comes not in a proven work by Wulfstan himself but in an Old English homily based on the apocryphal text known as the *Carta Dominica* (or *Sunday Letter* or *Letter from Heaven*). In Clare Lees's characterisation (1990, 39), this letter, which commands all men to observe the Sabbath or else incur divine wrath, 'purports to be from Christ, and to be written variously in his own blood, with a golden rod, or dictated to an angel, and to have fallen on one of the principal altars of Christendom — often Rome, Jerusalem, or Bethlehem'. The *Carta* is first attested in the sixth century, and, as can be deduced from the various modes of composition and places of appearance listed by Lees, it exists in a number of Latin recensions and variant versions from the early medieval period (see Priebsch 1936; Deletant 1977; Lees 1985; 1990). Perhaps surprisingly, no Latin versions are extant in manuscripts from Anglo-Saxon England, but in the vernacular it is drawn on by at least six late Old English homilies, with varying degrees of closeness (see Priebsch 1899; Napier 1901, 355–57; Jost 1950, 221–36); the text Jespersen is alluding to is that surviving in the eleventh-century London, Lambeth Palace Library, MS 489 and edited by Napier as Homily LVII under the title *Sermo ad populum dominicis diebus* (1883, 291–99; on MS Lambeth 489 see Ker 1957, 344–46 (No. 283)). In this text one of the threatened punishments for forsaking the Sabbath is as follows (Napier 1883, 295–96):

> and ic sênde ofer eow þa þeode eow to hergjanne and eower land to awestenne, þe ge heora spræca ne cunnan, forþan þe ge ne healdað sunnandæges freols, and forþan þe ge me forseoð and mine beboda noldon healdan.
>
> (and I will send against you a people to harry you and lay waste your land, whose language you do not understand, because you do not observe the festival of Sunday, and because you scorn me and have not wanted to obey my commands.)

The threat, which closely follows one of captivity into heathen hands, is therefore of a people 'whose language you do not [or 'will not be able to'] understand', and not of a people 'who do not understand your language' (as Jespersen translates). The question that needs addressing, therefore, is whether this statement can confidently be taken at face value, as apparently the only contemporary and explicit assessment of Anglo-Norse intelligibility to be found in Anglo-Saxon sources, and therefore of prime importance in the study of Anglo-Norse language contact.

McDougall is doubtful that it can, as he points out that the threat of heathen invasion is by no means unique to the Old English versions of the *Carta*: it is also in an eighth-century Irish version of the letter, as well as in early Latin versions,[16] and he therefore concludes that '[g]iven the evidence available, it is impossible to prove (and it is implausible) that an eleventh-century English audience would have associated a reference to foreign-speaking invaders in this context specifically with Norsemen or any other contemporary foreign enemies' (1987–88, 223 n.5). The fact that the threat is of a future invasion, and not of a past or present one, would also be in support of this view.

However, there is more to be said, and before looking more closely at these Anglo-Saxon texts influenced by the *Carta Dominica*, it is necessary to bring into consideration the widespread Anglo-Saxon view of the Vikings as a purposefully heathen people, and also the occasional Anglo-Saxon conception of themselves as, by contrast, a covenant-people under God's special protection — a self-image derived, of course, from the experience of Israel in the Old Testament and given expression in prophets such as Jeremiah. A brief examination of these larger issues will enable the statement in the Old English *Carta Dominica* to be appreciated in context.

As has been seen, Ælfric and other late Anglo-Saxon writers are profoundly worried by paganism because the pagans they are confronting — the Vikings — are perceived as violent, destructive, and determinedly anti-Christian, as can be seen, for example, from the Anglo-Saxons' use of Old English *hæþen* and Latin *paganus* as their standard terms for the Vikings — a usage notable both for the speed with which it is established and the subsequent frequency with which it is employed. From all types of evidence — documentary, chronicle, and poetic — it is clear that right throughout the period of Anglo-Norse contact the Anglo-Saxons habitually used *hæþen*/*paganus* as a defining term for the Vikings (see for example the quotations on pp 4, 5, 92, and 140–41) and conceived of a system in which 'English' was conceptually and semantically equated with 'Christian', and 'Scandinavian' with 'heathen'; and the two pairs were frequently set in binary opposition.[17] Indeed, there

---

[16]The Irish version, in the tract known as *Cáin Domnaig*, talks of sword-wielding foreigners who will carry Sabbath-breakers off in bondage *i tíre geinte* ('into pagan lands') (Hull 1966, 170–71 (line 97)). J. G. O'Keeffe was therefore led into dating the tract to the ninth century or later on the grounds that *ge[i]nti* = 'Perhaps "Northmen"' (1905, 213); see however Hull 1966, 156–58, who argues that the extant text can be no later than the first half of the eighth century. See further Ní Mhaonaigh 1998, 387–90; and for knowledge of the *Carta* in Ireland see also McNamara 1975, 60–63.

[17]This is not, of course, a perception of the Vikings unique to the Anglo-Saxons; Frankish writers articulate much the same views, at times even more strongly (see Wallace-Hadrill 1975; Coupland 1991; Foot 1991).

seems at times to have been a genuine fear that Christianity in England as a whole might be wiped out. The repetition in a number of Old English wills of this period that a bequest is made to a church or monastery 'ðā hwīle þe fulwiht sīo on Angelcynnes ēalonde' (Whitelock 1967, 203 (lines 47–48)) ('for as long as baptism may endure in the island of the English people') indicates how precarious some Anglo-Saxons felt their Christian faith and heritage to be in the face of Norse paganism (for similar phrases see Whitelock 1967, 201 (line 9), 203 (lines 37–38, 41–42), 205 (lines 12–13, 16–17); the idiom is noted in Ashdown 1928–29, 92 n.52; Brooks 1979, 13 n.52).[18]

Into this picture one may add the recurrent Anglo-Saxon image of themselves as a covenant-people under God, an image founded upon the model of Israel in the Old Testament. There is no need to rehearse this in detail here, as it is a well-known view that has been vigorously advocated by, for example, Patrick Wormald, Nicholas Howe, and Sarah Foot (see Howe 1989; Wormald 1992, 23–26; 1994, 14–18; 1999a, 416–29, 449–65; 1999b, 244–46; Foot 1996);[19] and Wormald has argued that for the Anglo-Saxons this self-image was given its defining expression in Bede's *Historia Ecclesiastica*, the closing moral of which he reads as follows (1992, 24):

> If the English sin as the Britons had, they face the same fate. The *Gens Anglorum* is a people with a Covenant, like Israel. Its future depends on keeping its side of a bargain with a God who is in every sense its maker.

Subsequently, three of the best-known and most articulate exponents of this theme are Alcuin, Alfred, and Wulfstan, as can be seen, for example, in (respectively) the Letter to Ethelhard, the Preface to the Old English *Cura Pastoralis*, and the *Sermo Lupi* (see Dümmler 1895, 45–49; Sweet 1871, I, 2–9; Bethurum 1957, 255–75). As these references make clear, the Anglo-Saxon image of themselves as a second Israel was conclusively cemented by their view of the Vikings as a heathen scourge sent to chastise them for their backsliding, just as God had earlier sent the Assyrians and Babylonians to chastise the Israelites (on Wulfstan's presentation of divine anger in the *Sermo Lupi*, see Godden 1994, 152–56). To quote Wormald again (1992, 26), 'Any medieval *gens* could see its mirror image in the Old Testament. Some did. But English identification with Israel arose from direct experience.'

Let us return, then, to the *Carta*-dependent homily found in Lambeth 489 and edited as Napier LVII, and to the apparent statement of linguistic unintelligibility which Jespersen set such store by. One important fact that neither Jespersen nor

---

[18]For discussion as to how virulent and destructive Scandinavian paganism in England actually was, see for example Wormald 1982, 137–41; Foot 1991; Smyth 1995, 77–84; Hadley 1996; Barrow 2000, 157–58; Abrams 2000; 2001a, 136–38; 2001b.

[19]Howe wishes in particular to emphasize the role of the Anglo-Saxon migration in this self-identification, as he believes it correlates with the Israelite Exodus.

Literary Accounts and Anecdotal Evidence 175

McDougall note is that there is a similar statement in another Old English version of the *Carta* found as the fourth homily in the early-eleventh-century MS CCCC 162 (see Ker 1957, 51–56 (No. 38)). This homily was edited separately by Napier, who compared it with that in Lambeth 489 and concluded that '[a]lthough they differ entirely in their wording, their contents are to a large degree identical, and they are evidently independently derived from one and the same Latin original' (1901, 356); this conclusion was also reached by Dorothy Whitelock (1982, 55), though it should be noted that the nearest extant Latin version (that in Munich, Bayerische Staatsbibliothek clm 9550, an eleventh-century manuscript edited by Delehaye (1899, 179–81)) is in many ways not very close at all: in particular, it contains nothing about languages or linguistic unintelligibility. In the Old English version in CCCC 162 the corresponding passage reads as follows (Napier 1901, 359):

⁊ ic eow gelæde to hergienne on þa ðeode þe ge heora gereord ne cunnon, ⁊ hi gegripað ongean eow scyldas ⁊ flana; ⁊ þære þeode stefen angryslice fram norðdæle ofer eow swegð, ⁊ heora hlisa eow gebregð ærðanðe he to eow cume, ⁊ geswenceð mid sare ⁊ gegripeð eow swa þ eacnigende wíf, forþiðe gé ne healdað þone halgan sunnandæg, ⁊ forðanðe ge onscuniað me ⁊ ge nellað mine word gehyran.

(and I will bring forth to harry you a people whose language you cannot understand, and they will grasp shields and missiles against you; and the voice of that people will sound terribly over you from the north, and the rumour of them will terrify you before it reaches you and will oppress you with sorrow and afflict you like a woman in childbirth, because you do not observe the holy Sabbath, and because you reject me and will not hear my words.)

The added detail found in this version is that these foreign ravagers, whose language the Sabbath-breakers will not understand, will come from the north, and this might, on face value, appear to make an identification with the Vikings more certain. But what it does in fact is to give a clear signal as to the textual source for some of the *Carta*'s ideas — namely, that it is beyond doubt that the specification of the north is not, as one might hope, a detail drawn from life by observation of the Vikings in England, but is rather a book-based motif deriving ultimately from the Old Testament, and in particular from the Book of Jeremiah. For throughout the Book of Jeremiah many of the threats of an invading people specifically warn that that people will come from the north, since in the time of Jeremiah, who prophesied in the southern kingdom of Judah, the northern kingdom of Samaria was occupied by the Assyrians (see for example Jeremiah 1. 13–16, 4. 6, 6. 1, 6. 22–23, 10. 22, 13. 20, 25. 9). Accordingly, and as is well known, this firm association of the north with heathen invasion became a familiar idea in Christian interpretation in the patristic period and beyond (on Alcuin's use of the motif, for example, see Page 1981, 118); and one of the fullest articulations of this notion in the Anglo-Saxon period is by Abbo of Fleury, who states in his *Passio Sancti Eadmundi*,

> Denique constat iuxta prophetae uaticinium quod ab aquilone uenit omne malum, sicut plus aequo didicere, perperam passi aduersos iactus cadentis tesserae, qui aquilonalium gentium experti sunt seuitiam. (Winterbottom 1972, 71–72 (§5))

> (In fine it is proverbial, according to the prediction of the prophet, that from the north comes all that is evil, as those have had too good cause to know, who through the spite of fortune and the fall of the die have experienced the barbarity of the races of the north.) (Hervey 1907, 19)

It is therefore easy to see how the moral significance of the north would gain a new poignancy for those Christian nations attacked by the Vikings; indeed, in Abbo's *Passio* the above passage serves as an introduction to the Vikings who are shortly to martyr St Edmund.

The Anglo-Saxons, then, conceived of themselves as a covenant-people and of the Vikings as a heathen nation sent to try them, and the experience of Israel in the Old Testament supplied them with the necessary means of interpretation for making sense of their own situation. It therefore seems reasonable to take the specification in CCCC 162 that heathen invasion will come from the *norðdæl* as a motif which is not primarily drawn from life in the Viking period, but rather derives from a recurrent theme in the Old Testament (and in particular from Jeremiah) which was elevated to familiar status in the patristic period, and which Anglo-Saxon writers felt able to apply to their own contemporary experience. In apparent confirmation of this, it is furthermore to be noted that the term *norðdæl* is nowhere used in Old English as a designation for Scandinavia (see Venezky and Healey 1980; Roberts and Kay 1995, I, 569 (§12.06.01.03)): its habitual meaning is simply as a point of the compass, often translating Latin *aquilo*.[20]

We can therefore turn again to the specific issue of linguistic unintelligibility as stated in the *Carta Dominica*. It will be recalled that the threat in Napier LVII is of 'þa þeode eow to hergjanne and eower land to awestenne, þe ge heora spræca ne cunnan' (Napier 1883, 295–96) ('a people to harry you and lay waste your land whose language you do not understand'), and in fact this threat and this phrase are also of Old Testament origin. Referring to the captivity in Egypt, Psalm 81. 4–5 declares (Vulgate, Psalm 80. 5–6, here quoted *iuxta LXX*),

> quia praeceptum Israhel est et iudicium Dei Iacob testimonium in Ioseph posuit illud cum exiret de terra Aegypti linguam quam non noverat audivit. (Weber 1975, I, 872)

> (Duty demands it of Israel; it was a decree the God of Jacob made, bidding Joseph remember the day when he escaped from Egypt. He had (till then) been hearing a language he did not know.) (Knox 1949, II, 855 and n.4)

---

[20] The only ambiguous occurrence is in the *Anglo-Saxon Chronicle* MS 'D' *sub anno* 1016 (quoted above p 7), where *norðdæl* signifies the portion of the country received by Cnut in his division with Edmund Ironside, and is set in opposition to *Westsexe*; conceivably one might take this to indicate 'Scandinavian England', but this seems exceptional.

Literary Accounts and Anecdotal Evidence

And even more pertinently for the *Carta* homilies, Jeremiah 5. 15 says,

> ecce ego adducam super vos gentem de longinquo domus Israhel ait Dominus gentem robustam gentem antiquam gentem cuius ignorabis linguam nec intelleges quid loquatur. (Weber 1975, II, 1173)

> (A nation from far away I am summoning, even now, to the attack; a warlike nation, of ancient lineage, whose very tongue shall be strange to thee, no word of it well understood.) (Knox 1949, II, 1170)

Returning to the Anglo-Saxon period, one finds Bede employing the same image at least twice. The first occurrence is in his *Historia Abbatum*, detailing the foreign burial of Abbot Ceolfrith in Langres, Burgundy: 'partim ad tumbam defuncti inter eos, quorum nec linguam nouerant, pro inextinguibili patris affectu *residere*' (Plummer 1896, I, 386) ('and the rest [of his party of pilgrims], in their undying love for him, remained to keep watch by his tomb in the midst of a people whose language they could not understand': Webb and Farmer 1983, 207). Since the language spoken in eighth-century Burgundy will probably have been Frankish — speakers of which Augustine collected en route to England to act as interpreters with the Anglo-Saxons — Bede cannot be intending this as a purely literal statement of linguistic history, but rather as a pointer to the devotion of Ceolfrith's followers. The second occurrence is in the *Historia Ecclesiastica* (Book I Chapter 23), where Augustine and his companions are seized with terror only a short way into their journey: 'redire domum potius quam barbaram feram incredulamque gentem, cuius ne linguam quidem nossent, adire cogitabant' ('They began to contemplate returning home rather than going to a barbarous, fierce, and unbelieving nation whose language they did not even understand') (Colgrave and Mynors 1969, 68–69).

Clearly, then, this is something of a standard motif for either isolated Christian fortitude in unfavourable (pagan) circumstances (Psalm 81, Bede), or retributory conquest by a hostile nation (Jeremiah, *Carta* homilies). Nicholas Howe, discussing only Bede's use of the motif in the instance from the *Historia Ecclesiastica*, suggests that 'this emphasis on linguistic difference reveals the characteristic, even involuntary, response of a Christian writer confronted by paganism' (1989, 112).[21] The Anglo-Saxon use of the motif derives from the circumstances of Israel in the Old Testament, and in particular, it appears, from the Jeremiah citation. If one returns to CCCC 162 and the question of an invading nation coming from the *norðdæl*, this use of Jeremiah as a source seems without doubt to be the solution. For the two Old

---

[21] Howe misinterprets Anglo-Norse contact in this regard, though, and argues that 'The Anglo-Saxons could not distinguish themselves as a þeod [i.e. people] on linguistic grounds because the Scandinavians on the island spoke a closely related language' (1989, 12); on the contrary, this is exactly what the Old English *Carta* homilies do, linguistic similarity notwithstanding.

English versions of the *Carta Dominica* under scrutiny (that is, Priebsch's so-called 'third group' of homilies (see Napier 1901, 356)) are marked by the conspicuous influence of Jeremiah, and many of their details evidently derive from the first part of that prophet's book. This is clear, for example, from the citation of the four judgements that will be sent on the backsliding people. Jeremiah 15. 2 threatens death, the sword, starvation, and captivity (Vulgate *mortem, gladium, famem,* and *captivitatem* (Weber 1975, II, 1187)):[22] in Napier LVII one finds 'hunger and sweordes ecge, cwyld and hæftnunge' (Napier 1883, 295) ('hunger and the sword's edge, death and captivity') and in CCCC 162 'hungor ꝛ hæftned ꝛ gefeoht ꝛ cwelm' (Napier 1901, 359) ('hunger and captivity and battle and death').

Jespersen was thus mistaken in regarding the motif in Napier LVII as an anecdotal statement on Anglo-Norse intelligibility drawn from contemporary observation of Anglo-Norse contact. But of course, simply to note that a detail or declaration is in fact a recurrent book-based motif, and not a specific observation drawn from life, does not in itself explain why an author should choose to employ a particular motif at a particular moment; in other words, source study does not demonstrate how far a motif is an apt one, and selected for use precisely on account of its perceived aptness and ability to supply the ideal language of expression. Some literate Anglo-Saxons perceived the Vikings as conspicuously heathen, and themselves perhaps as a new Israel; such beliefs would permit the appropriation of biblical history and motifs, making it possible, for example, to correlate the Vikings with the Assyrians — the heathen enemies of God's people, pouring forth from the north. Once one grants that it was felt to be acceptable therefore to appropriate biblical patterns in this way, it becomes difficult to judge how far motifs are being reapplied in Anglo-Saxon texts on the stringent grounds on perceived suitability and eloquence, and how far on the simple and less illuminating grounds that they happen to be found in the Old Testament being applied to God's people there.

So, for instance, it will be recalled that McDougall's conclusion (1987–88, 223 n.5) was that the references in Napier LVII and elsewhere are not specifically to the Vikings in England, but are rather to a deliberately unspecified nation of heathen ravagers lurking just around the corner for all Sabbath-breakers. On the other hand, one might reasonably feel that Anglo-Saxon writers would only reapply to themselves those Old Testament motifs which were in fact readily applicable, such as the north being the compass point from which heathen ravagers habitually issue. Furthermore, and crucially, the incorporation of the theme of unintelligibility does seem, as far as source study can tell, to be something distinctive to these two Old English homilies, as it does not appear to be found in any of the extant versions of the Latin *Carta*. However, since these two homilies are thought to be independently drawing on the same (now-lost) Latin version of the *Carta*, it may well be that such a theme was indeed to be found in that source.

---

[22] It is important to stress that (as throughout) Jeremiah represents the ultimate source, not necessarily the immediately antecedent one.

Perhaps most likely is that, whether or not they believed the Old Norse language to be genuinely unintelligible to English speakers, the Old English adaptors of the *Carta Dominica* certainly believed that it *should* be unintelligible. As Hans Wolff (1959) observed, social attitudes are a crucial factor in determining intelligibility; in cross-dialectal communication a good deal depends on how much one *wants* to understand (see also Milroy 1997, 318–19). It is clear that an Anglo-Saxon self-identification as a new Israel acted as a stimulus to appropriate biblical images of a Christian nation plagued by surrounding heathens, and Anglo-Saxon sources (especially ecclesiastical ones) were eager to stress the otherness of the Scandinavian invaders on account of their repellent paganism. One way to express both of these convictions was therefore to deploy the biblical motif of linguistic difference, and in particular the motif of unintelligibility, as such unintelligibility would then seem to act as a confirmation that in Viking Age England Christians and heathens could and should have no common ground.

CHAPTER 6

Old Norse in England: Towards a Linguistic History

Review: Evidence for Intelligibility

It was noted in Chapter 1 that contemporary methods of intelligibility testing are essentially fourfold, of which three are linguistic and one extralinguistic: (1) Linguistic comparison; (2) Test-the-informant; (3) Ask-the-informant; and (4) Analysis of social relations. This final chapter will begin by reviewing how far the three linguistic methods were found to be applicable to the historical situation of Anglo-Norse contact, and then go on to consider various implications arising from the central conclusion.

(1) Linguistic comparison. In Chapter 2 the phonological systems of Viking Age Norse and English were compared, and it was seen that the two languages (or dialects of Germanic) were remarkably similar at the time of contact, with their major divergences being largely congruent and predictable; this similarity was understandable in the light of the evidence for a North-West Germanic language-group and the continental divergence between Norse and English occurring as late as the fifth century — that is, when the Anglo-Saxon tribes migrated to Britain.

(2) Test-the-informant. Through the use of Recorded Text Tests, this is the main empirical method used in modern intelligibility testing, and in the light of discussions by Hockett (1987) and by Milliken and Milliken (1993), it was argued that the same principle of phonemic substitution involved in dialect intelligibility is observable in the Scandinavianisation of English names by Norse speakers, and the Anglicisation of Norse names by English speakers. Chapter 3 considered the Scandinavianisation of Old English place-names as recorded in medieval documents, and it was found that phonemic substitution was successfully performed with impressive

consistency, and that all the major phonological divergences between Viking Age English and Norse were negotiated. The empirical conclusion was thus that cognate English words and names were readily intelligible to Norse speakers in Viking Age England. Chapter 4 considered the evidence for the intelligibility of Norse words and names to English speakers in three Anglo-Saxon sources, namely 'The Voyages of Ohthere and Wulfstan' in the Old English Orosius, Æthelweard's *Chronicle*, and Ælfric's *De Falsis Diis*; although pursued less systematically than Chapter 3 (on account of the degree to which much of this and other Anglo-Saxon evidence has already been analysed), for the most part the same results were observed, and the central conclusion reached was that both Anglo-Saxons and Scandinavians, in the terms of Hockett, appear to have operated a switching-code which enabled them to understand much of the language of the other speech community.

(3) Ask-the-informant. In addition to some of the cultural contact considered in Chapter 4, the anecdotal evidence of literary sources surveyed in Chapter 5 spoke in favour of Anglo-Norse intelligibility in the Viking Age. Although from a significantly later date, the Icelandic sagas demonstrate a naturalistic rationale in the depiction of foreign languages, in which Norse and English are two languages causing no difficulties of intelligibility between speakers, although other languages do cause such difficulties. The evidence from the English side is more oblique, but it was seen that while references to the use of interpreters are common in Anglo-Saxon texts, no such reference is ever found in the context of Anglo-Norse contact. However, a statement in Old English homilies derived from the *Carta Dominica*, if not to be seen simply as a traditional motif duplicated unthinkingly from its source, may indicate an Anglo-Saxon awareness that Old Norse could be regarded as less than fully intelligible to English speakers. In this context it was found salutary to recall Wolff's 1959 emphasis on the importance of social relations in intelligibility, and in particular on the role of social attitudes between speech communities in situations of non-reciprocal intelligibility: whether one finds the speech of another group intelligible turns at least partly on whether one wants to find it so and is therefore willing to make the effort required to understand.

From these three complementary approaches (with Test-the-informant carrying the greatest weight on account of its empirical basis) I would therefore conclude that the available evidence points fairly unequivocally to a situation of adequate mutual intelligibility between speakers of Norse and English in the Viking Age. This intelligibility was adequate in the sense that it would seem to have been sufficient to preclude the need for interpreters or widespread bilingualism; this is not to argue that it was either perfect or instantaneous, and indeed it is important that 'adequate intelligibility' is under no circumstances equated with perfect intelligibility. Many features of Anglo-Norse language contact (like many features of spoken language from all periods) are entirely irrecoverable, and a key point to stress again here is that, strictly speaking, the empirical, non-anecdotal evidence of the Scandinavianisation of English place-names (and vice versa) demonstrates only lexical intelligibility; but, as was argued in Chapter 3, lexical intelligibility is based on the ability to make phonemic correspondences with regularity, and also certain morphological correspondences (see further below). Thus, it can be argued that the evidence of Chapters 3 and 4 does certainly seem to demonstrate 'adequate intelligibility' — a phenomenon to be defined in pragmatic terms on the grounds of simple face-to-face communication (and indeed, 'pragmatic intelligibility' would be an acceptable alternative term).

This definition is crucial, as some commentators on Anglo-Norse contact seem to suggest that a contact situation only qualifies as an example of 'mutual intelligibility' when complex sentences are spoken and understood in all their lexical variety and syntactic fullness. This is most clearly expressed by Helmut Gneuss (1993, 130):

> By mutual intelligibility I do not mean the ability to understand individual words whose utterance, moreover, may have been accompanied by gestures or even by pointing to the denoted object. I am thinking of whether a speaker of Old English or Old Norse would have been in a position to follow coherent sentences in the foreign language. When one considers the marked differences between English and Norse that must have obtained very early, when one thinks of differences in vocabulary, of various sound changes, and especially of the inflexional endings, the pronominal system and the suffixed article in Norse, then it must seem difficult to believe that an Anglo-Saxon could have carried on a conversation with a Scandinavian speaker.

However, by adequate or pragmatic intelligibility I do precisely mean, amongst other things, the ability to understand individual words, if this ability was sufficiently widespread and sufficiently successful to permit face-to-face and day-to-day transactions, and so to preclude the need for one or both of the speech communities in the Danelaw to become bilingual, or for interpreters to be habitually used for the purposes of Anglo-Norse communication. If the Norse and English speech communities did communicate with one another without the use of interpreters or widespread bilingualism (as the evidence surveyed in this book suggests), then there are no valid grounds to disqualify this as a situation of 'mutual intelligibility'. Indeed, one suspects that a good deal of modern English conversation would fail to qualify if, like Gneuss, one insisted on setting the pass-mark so high;[1] and one can hardly imagine many day-to-day transactions between Anglo-Saxons and Scandinavians (such as bartering) to have required any great degree of syntactic complexity. If frequent and repeated communication takes place habitually without recourse to bilingualism or interpreters, then two speech communities are adequately intelligible.

Let us now turn, then, to the concerns of this final chapter, and to the larger linguistic history of Old Norse in England. It is, I think, not yet possible to attempt a

---

[1] *Contra* Gneuss, it should however be noted that there is no evidence for the suffixed article in Old Norse in England, and indeed this is a development which is not recorded in any source before the eleventh century (Noreen 1923, 316–18 (§472); Barnes 1993c, 376). The only evidence offered for suffixation in England is a solitary place-name form cited by Ekwall (1930, 29), namely *Stanraysinum* in the thirteenth-century Lancaster Cartulary (and see Parsons 2001, 304).

full history of the Old Norse language in England, as so many aspects are unknown and so much work remains to be done (for a helpful review article see Fellows-Jensen 1994b; Kisbye 1982 is a useful digest of material, while a more popular account is Geipel 1971). For assessing the nature of the Old Norse language in England the corpus of material must primarily be loanwords and place-names, as the runic evidence is so slight (see Page 1971; Barnes 1993b; Holman 1996, 14–85); personal names also enter the picture (see Björkman 1910; Fellows-Jensen 1968; Insley 1994), as do (arguably) Old Norse poems which seem to have been composed in England (on Old Norse skaldic poetry from England see Campbell 1971; Poole 1987; Frank 1994a; Townend 1998; 2000b; 2001; Jesch 2000; 2001; on the question of whether any of the extant Eddic poetry was composed in England see McKinnell 2001). The study of Norse place-names is of course well advanced, especially in the form of the county volumes of the English Place-Name Society and the three great regional studies by Gillian Fellows-Jensen (*SSNY*; *SSNEM*; *SSNNW*; for Norse place-names in England, East Anglia remains the region in need of systematic attention: see Fellows-Jensen 1999). On the other side, however, we need a much fuller survey of the Old Norse loanwords that enter English and are found in English texts, especially Middle English ones; McIntosh's 1978 appeal for work towards a dictionary of Norse loans is still unanswered. Old English is well served by the studies of Hofmann (1955, 149–252 (§§201–395)) and Peters (1981; see also Wollmann 1996), but for Middle English Björkman's pioneering work continues to dominate the field (1900–02), though other landmarks are the investigations of Rynell (1948) and Hug (1987) into the diachronic and diatopic distribution of particular Norse items in Middle English, and their rivalry with English-derived lexemes in the same semantic field (for accounts in more general histories of English see especially Serjeantson 1935, 61–103; Jespersen 1956, 55–77; Baugh and Cable 1978, 90–104 (§§67–80)). Above all, though, more studies are needed on a textual or regional basis, in particular along the lines of Richard Dance's painstaking analysis of the Norse-derived lexical element in early Middle English texts from the South-West Midlands (forthcoming).[2]

When more such studies have been undertaken, we may begin to reliably assess the nature of the Old Norse language in England in terms of its phonology and morphology, as well as its geographical distribution. How archaic or how progressive was Old Norse in England? In what ways, if at all, did it diverge from Old Norse as spoken in the Scandinavian homelands? As it is broadly thought that the Norse dialects in Scandinavia began to diverge into their permanent subdivisions in perhaps the tenth century, and as it seems to be the nature of colonial languages both to fail to share in developments back home and to undergo influence from native

---

[2]For a review of some methodological questions see also Dance 1999; 2000. For an impressive example of a survey of the Norse loans in one particular Middle English text one may go back to Brate 1884. On the Norse elements in Modern English dialects see for example Wall 1898; Thorson 1936; Wakelin 1977, 130–38.

languages, this is a line of investigation that demands attention. Some attempts to assess the state of phonological and morphological development in the Old Norse language in England have of course been made (for example, the studies of particular sound-changes by Eduard Kolb (1962; 1969) and Kristian Hald (1978)), and Gillian Fellows-Jensen's digests of the toponymic evidence on a regional basis are invaluable (*SSNY* 237–41; *SSNEM* 269–76; *SSNNW* 323–28); but it is symptomatic that the only attempt in English to combine all strands into a general picture is both very old and very brief — namely that of E. V. Gordon (1927a, 304–07).

This final chapter, then, will in no way attempt a full history of the Old Norse language in England, but rather will seek to explore a few of the linguistic issues that are related to, or arise from, the central conclusion offered here that speakers of Norse and English appear to have been 'adequately intelligible' in the Viking Age. The following topics will therefore be discussed, as provisional contributions towards an account of Old Norse in England: (1) the coexistence of Norse and English at the spoken level; (2) their contrastive distribution at the written level; (3) the consequences of spoken coexistence in terms of inflexional loss in both languages; and finally (4) the practical means by which Norse-derived words may subsequently have entered English. As throughout this book, my approach is informed by the sociolinguistic principle articulated by Angus McIntosh (1994, 137) and quoted in Chapter 1: 'Fundamentally, what we mean by "languages in contact" is "users of language in contact" and to insist upon this is much more than a mere terminological quibble and has far from trivial consequences.'

Societal Bilingualism in Viking Age England

Although the prime objective of the preceding chapters was to address the question of possible intelligibility, it was also hoped that, as one of a number of incidental matters, some sort of sense would be gained of the coexistence of Norse and English as the two vernaculars in Viking Age England. In other words, Viking Age England was a bilingual society, but not a society comprised of bilingual individuals — it showed societal but not individual bilingualism (see Appel and Muysken 1987, 1). This impression of the coexistence of Norse and English is perhaps gained most readily from Æthelweard's explanation that the place of Ealdorman Æthelwulf's burial was known as *Northuuorthige* to the English, but *Deoraby* to the Vikings. To be precise, what Æthelweard says is that the place was known as *Deoraby iuxta* [. . .] *Danaam linguam* ('in the Danish language') (Campbell 1962, 37); this reference can thus go with Ælfric's two citations of names of heathen gods *on Denisc* (Pope 1967–68, II, 683–86) ('in Danish') as the limit of our allusions in Anglo-Saxon sources to the Norse language in England. It is thus interesting to note that Ælfric mentions the Norse language in the context of personal names, and Æthelweard in the context of a place-name, as if the linguistic difference between Norse and English was, to the Anglo-Saxons, most apparent in the onomastic sphere; this is also implied in a 1044 charter that introduces a Scandinavian recipient with an unfamiliar name as follows: 'qui juxta suę proprię gentis consuetudinem ab infantili ętate nomen accepit Orc' (Kemble 1839–48, IV, 84 (No. 772; S1004)) ('who according to the custom of his own people from infancy has borne the name Orc') (see further Harmer 1952, 576; Fellows-Jensen 1995a, 8–9). It is perhaps surprising that we can point to only three specific references (in two texts) to the Norse language in England; but it may well indicate that, to the Anglo-Saxons, Norse and English were not invariably thought of as discrete languages. Later-eleventh-century sources appear to confirm this, as those which refer specifically to the Norse language in England tend to do so in the context of a name or distinctive term for which there is no English equivalent, or to explain a situation of apparent intelligibility. As a first example, one may note that Osbern of Canterbury's late-eleventh-century *Translatio Sancti Ælfegi* seems to be linguistically well-informed (Rumble 1994a, 302–03; on this passage see also Frankis 2000, 17):

> mandans omnibus familiæ suæ militibus quos lingua Danorum huscarles uocant. ut eorum alij per extremas ciuitatis portas seditiones concitent. alij pontem & ripas fluminis armati obsidant.
>
> (He [i.e. Cnut] told all the soldiers of his household, who are called 'housecarls' in the language of the Danes, that some of them should incite strife at the outer gates of the city, and others, fully armed, should take possession of the bridge and the banks of the river.)

As a second example, one may take Book I of the *Vita Ædwardi Regis*, which dates most probably from 1065–66 and so is (just) pre-Conquest (see Barlow 1992, xxx–xxxi). The anonymous author's statement concerning the 1051 assembly at Gloucester is noteworthy (Barlow 1992, 34–35):

> Conuenerant siquidem eo Siwardus, dux Northumbrorum, Dan<ic>a lingua 'Digara,' hoc est fortis, nuncupatus; Leofricus quoque dux, uir scilicet eximius, ut plurimum deo deuotus; Alfgarus etiam eiusdem ducis Leofrici filius.
>
> (Gathered there were Siward, earl of the Northumbrians, called in the Danish tongue 'Digri', that is 'The Strong', Earl Leofric, an excellent man, very devoted to God, and Ælfgar, Earl Leofric's son.)

Thus these two later-eleventh-century texts give us one reference to the *lingua Danorum* and one to the *Danica lingua*,[3] and in doing so they usefully complement the remarks of Ælfric and Æthelweard in indicating, from an Anglo-Saxon perspective, an occasional awareness of the distinctiveness of the language spoken by Scandinavians in England.

---

[3] A fulsome passage in Richard of Cirencester, derived from the *Vita Ædwardi*, also ascribes to Queen Edith knowledge of the *lingua Danorum* (see Barlow 1992, 22).

Place-names can also give us a sense of the coexistence of Norse and English as the two vernaculars spoken in Viking Age England. The famous case of *Streoneshalh*/*Hvítabý* in the North Riding has been mentioned earlier (see above p 49); Birklands in Nottinghamshire may therefore be cited here as another good example (see *PNNt* 77; *DEPN* 45). This is recorded as *Birchwude* in 1188 (OE *birce* + *wudu*) but *Birkelund* in 1250 (ON *birki* + *lundr*). In discussing the name Margaret Gelling covers her options by noting that the Old Norse form 'has been substituted for (or perhaps coexisted with)' the Old English (1984, 207–08; repeated in Gelling and Cole 2000, 242), but since ON *viðr* is the usual substitution for OE *wudu* I would see this as almost certainly an example of the coexistence of two names, especially as both forms are current so late and are recorded relatively close together in time. The fact that this is a descriptive topographical name might also make it more likely that the Old Norse name was given independently of the Old English.

I have stated earlier my disagreement with the notion that the Scandinavian settlers sometimes 'left the English names unchanged' (*SSNY* 251) (see above pp 48–49). This would of course be the case if English and Norse cognates were identical, but otherwise this study has argued that the settlers adapted names to their own speech habits, just as they did loanwords (for example, OE /ʃ/ > ON /sk/, OE /tʃ/ > ON /k/, etc.). The continued existence of unaltered English forms in areas of Scandinavian settlement can therefore be more plausibly explained by the continued survival of sufficient English speakers to pass on the English form; the evidence of an English and a Scandinavianised form existing concurrently for the same place, like the evidence of independent English and Norse forms existing concurrently (for example, *Norðworðig*/*Deoraby*), is thus widespread evidence for societal bilingualism, and for the coexistence of Old English and Old Norse in the late Anglo-Saxon period. This remains true even when the forms are preserved only in the Middle English period (for example, *Birchwude*/*Birkelund*), at a time when Old Norse must have already died out as a spoken language, for the two forms must at least have *arisen* in such a bilingual community.[4]

It is also important to remember that literacy was the preserve of the English speaking community (see further below), and that therefore there was arguably little likelihood of the Norse names being preserved (whether Scandinavianisations or original coinages) unless they passed into general currency, or at least were not known solely to the Norse-speaking community. This would explain why so few Norse names are recorded in areas which came under Scandinavian rule for a brief time but did not undergo intensive settlement. Gillian Fellows-Jensen, for example, writes as follows when discussing the absence of Norse names from the *Historia de Sancto Cuthberto* (1994a, 132; see also Fellows-Jensen 1995a, 21):

---

[4]This is similar, I would suggest, to the most plausible explanation for the coexistence of Norse- and English-derived variants in certain Middle English texts such as the *Ormulum* (see below).

> There are [. . .] areas, however, from which Scandinavian names are absent, even though there is documentary evidence for a Danish presence there. It can only be assumed that the Danes, though resident in these areas, for some reason did not coin place-names. [. . .] In the north-east, for example, there is evidence that a number of vills in the eastern part of the county of Durham were purchased from the Danish king Guthred at some time before his death in 894 or 895. In spite of a period of Danish ownership, none of these vills has a Danish name.

But I would suggest that there is no real mystery here, for it is a question not of the coinage of names but of their preservation (see further Townend 2000a, 99–100). Where the pre-existing English names were not identical with their Norse cognates Guthred and his followers must, in referring to these places amongst themselves, have 'coined' place-names, whether new ones of their own or (much more likely) Scandinavianisations of the English names; but there is no reason at all why the monks of St Cuthbert, and specifically the author of the *Historia*, should have used these Scandinavianised forms when referring to the estates of their saint. What Guthred and his men called them was irrelevant to the English, unless perhaps they were new coinages for new settlements. To attempt a modern analogy, during the Second World War monolingual Germans must have 'Germanicised' French place-names in the course of their occupation whenever they spoke such names, but one would hardly expect therefore to find the Germanicised forms employed by French writers.[5]

Indeed, as noted earlier, there are relatively few Old Norse place-names from England recorded in pre-Conquest English documents (see *SSNY* 236–37; *SSNEM* 292–94; *SSNNW* 336). The usual explanation for this is one often cited also to account for the paucity of Norse loanwords in Old English, namely the great scarcity of pre-Conquest documents from areas of heavy Scandinavian settlement (Stenton's 'essential Danelaw') — that is to say, it would be documents from exactly such areas that one would expect to show greatest Norse influence, if they existed. No doubt this explanation is fundamentally correct, but one might also suggest that the paucity of Norse place-names in Anglo-Saxon sources is to be partly explained by the discreteness of the two languages, and the two speech communities, in the pre-Conquest period. Similarly, in lexical terms, Eric Stanley (1988, 322) concludes from the surprisingly small number of Norse loanwords in Aldred's late-tenth-century Northumbrian gloss to the Lindisfarne Gospels that '[t]he overall impression is that either the Scandinavians were linguistically still very much apart from the English, or were at least sufficiently apart linguistically for English speakers to be able to recognize Scandinavian words and to keep them out when they did not want them in'. In other words, for as long as Old Norse was a living language in Viking Age England, one might perhaps expect the Old Norse speech community to be

---

[5] Or from the First World War one would not expect English adaptations such as *Eatapples* and *Wipers* to occur in French or Belgian sources, let alone to have any lasting effect on the nomenclature of those countries.

reasonably discrete, and therefore Old Norse place-names may have not yet made the cross-over into the habitual use of the English-speaking population; it is instances such as Æthelweard's citation of *Deoraby* which are exceptional.

Naturally, this raises the imponderable question as to exactly how long Old Norse *was* a living language in England. There is no need to discuss this in detail here, as the classic papers of Ekwall (1930) and Page (1971) give the issue a thorough airing, and the subject has recently been revisited by David Parsons (2001). Leaving aside the possible insights which might be forthcoming from the corpus of place-names and loanwords, one may briefly note that the evidence for the continued vitality of Old Norse in England into at least the mid- to late eleventh century, and quite possibly beyond, is essentially of three types:[6] (1) the allusions to the Old Norse language by Æthelweard, Ælfric, and later writers, which seem to be phrased so as to imply that *Denisc*, or the *lingua Danorum*, is a language still spoken by most, if not all, of those in England who are discernibly Scandinavian; (2) the vibrancy of Old Norse vernacular culture at the court of Cnut, as testified by the extant skaldic poetry from that milieu (see further below);[7] and (3) the few dateable runic inscriptions in Old Norse, such as those from Carlisle and Pennington, which seem to indicate the continuance of Old Norse in more remote areas as late as the twelfth century (again, see further below).

Late Anglo-Saxon England was thus a bilingual society in which both Old English and Old Norse were spoken. We have a number of references to the Norse language in England, and place-name evidence can also help to give us a dramatic sense of the two languages coexisting at the spoken level; the question therefore arises as to the possible ways in which Viking Age England was also a bilingual society at the written level.

Old Norse Literacy in England

The Norse inscriptions in England have primarily been analysed with a view to establishing their date, in order in turn to establish how long the Old Norse language survived in England. As noted above, Ekwall's remains the standard discussion of the question (1930), and Page's 1971 piece reviews in detail Ekwall's epigraphical evidence. For dating the survival, this written evidence is of course crucial, but I would suggest that a correct interpretation has not necessarily been put on the epigraphical material, or at least that one important point has been insufficiently stressed. Both Ekwall and Page assume that since the inscriptions at the Yorkshire

---

[6] It is arguable that Ekwall pays insufficient attention to the first of these, and he does not mention the second at all.

[7] Parsons (2001, 307) and Jesch (2001, 321–23) also draw attention to the importance in this regard of Þorkell Skallason's post-Conquest *Valþjófsflokkr*.

churches of Aldbrough, Kirkdale, and St Mary Castlegate, York, were erected by patrons with Old Norse personal names, but are composed in the Old English language using the Roman alphabet, this must mean that Old Norse had been given up in those areas as the language of the settlers (this assumption is followed by, inter alia, McKinnell 1990, 12; Richards 2000, 14). I would suggest, though, that this is a mistaken interpretation, and would instead submit that in Viking Age England Old English was the natural language for writing, whatever language the patrons of these monuments may have spoken: there is no evidence for Old Norse literacy in England, except in runes, and nor indeed would one expect any such evidence.

For, leaving aside the runic question, the Scandinavians who participated in Viking Age colonisation were illiterate, and this of course is because they were pagan — since literacy came to all the northern barbarians with Christianity. The Scandinavian settlers in England thus encountered a literate society, and more specifically a society in which literacy and the Church were united. In other words, there was a pre-existing tradition and technique of literacy in Old English but not in Old Norse; in Viking Age England, and leaving aside runes, the vernacular language of writing was English.

One might suggest an analogy here. Kenneth Jackson argued that one should not be surprised that the written monuments from Roman Britain are in Latin rather than in British, as British had not yet become a language in which there was any tradition of literacy (1953, 100):

> [I]t would not occur to anyone to write in British, nor would they know how to do so. One tends to forget that to write down in an alphabet the sounds of a speech (even though it is one's own) which one has never been taught to write is a very considerable intellectual feat. [. . .] It is quite possible for one and the same man to speak a language which he cannot write and (when he has to) write a language which he cannot easily, or does not habitually, speak.

Though the linguistic analogy between Roman Britain and Viking Age England is far from perfect, I would suggest that this is likely to be the reason underlying the absence of non-runic writings in Old Norse in England. It would follow from this therefore that no light on the question of the survival of Old Norse in England can be gained from the fact that Old English is both the language of monumental inscriptions and the language of administrative documents issuing, for example, from the Anglo-Norse court of Cnut. Both of these will be examined in more detail.

First, then, let us review the status of Old English as the language of inscriptions in Viking Age England. It is in particular the Aldbrough and Kirkdale inscriptions which have received most attention in this context, and it is worth stating that they are both written in perfectly acceptable late Old English, rather than in any sort of Anglo-Norse *Mischsprache* or 'mixed language'. The Aldbrough text reads as follows: VLF [HE]T ARŒRAN CYRICE FOR H[A]NUM ꝫ FOR GVN[ÞARA] SAVLA ('Úlfr ordered the church to be erected for himself and for Gunnwaru's soul') (Okasha 1971, 47 (No. 1)). The Kirkdale inscription is more substantial, surrounding an impressive-looking sundial and comprising three texts: (1) ORM : GAMAL : SVNA : BOHTE : SCS GREGORIVS : MINSTER : ÐONNE HIT : ÞES ÆL : TOBROCAN : ꝫ TOFALAN : ꝫ HE HIT LET [:] MACAN [:] NEÞAN : FROM GRVNDE XPE : ꝫ SCS GREGORIVS : IN : EADÞARD : DAGVM : CNG ꝫ N TOSTI [:] DAGVM : EORL ('Orm Gamall's son bought St Gregory's church when it was completely ruined and collapsed, and he had it built anew from the ground to Christ and St Gregory, in the days of King Edward, and in the days of Earl Tostig'); (2) ÞIS [:] IS [:] DÆGES : SOLMERCA ÆT ILCVM [:] TIDE ('This is the day's sun-marker at every hour'); (3) ꝫ HAÞARÐ [:] ME ÞROHTE : ꝫ BRAND PRS ('And Hávarðr made me and Brandr the priest') (Okasha 1971, 88 (No. 64); for discussion of the physical form and function of the inscription, see Gameson 1995, 74–76).

Both of these inscriptions contain loanwords from Old Norse, but this does not instantly turn their language into a *Mischsprache*. Kirkdale's SOLMERCA is best explained as a loan from ON *sólmerki* (usually 'sign of the zodiac', but here evidently 'sun-dial') rather than as a unique Old English formation from two rare elements (*sōl* 'sun' + *mearca* 'space marked out') (see Okasha 1992, 334; Watts and others 1997, 86). Aldbrough's HANUM has sometimes been cited as evidence for an early Anglo-Norse mixed language, but a more reasonable interpretation is simply to see it as a loan which was made in eleventh-century Yorkshire dialect, but failed to become generalised through the language (see also Howe 1996, 154–55). Old English lacked a distinctive reflexive form, employing rather the personal pronoun; as the preposition *for* could take either the accusative or dative, one might have expected *hine* or *him* in the Aldbrough text. But in late Old English and early Middle English the personal pronoun system was undergoing great change on account of its efficiency having been weakened through centralisation and apocope, and in particular there was atrophy and loss in the accusative forms of the pronoun, with their function being taken over by the dative forms. It seems plausible therefore that in the Aldbrough text we have a local, alternative strategy to express an accusative reflexive at a time when the pronoun system was undergoing necessary renovation — a strategy which failed to survive on account of the subsequent generalisation of the new system which favoured the dative form.[8] ON *honum* was dative rather than accusative, but since the nominative and accusative were identical in the ON 3rd person masculine singular (namely, *hann*) it is conceivable that English speakers regarded *honum* simply as a marked form indicating an oblique case. Furthermore, as Page rightly points out (1971, 178), Old Norse would use the reflexive *sér* in the Aldbrough construction. This would seem to confirm that we have a straightforward case of pronoun-for-pronoun borrowing; that is, the English only borrowed from a grammatical category they themselves already possessed.[9]

---

[8]The parallel, of course, would be with the adoption of the 3rd person plural forms *they*, *them*, *their*.

[9]Eric Stanley (1995, 11–13) has recently resurrected an old and not unattractive theory that HANUM is not an Old Norse loan at all, but rather a late Old English dative singular form of

Another Yorkshire inscription is sometimes brought into this discussion, namely that forming part of the fragmentary sun-dial at the church of All Saints, Skelton-in-Cleveland. In fact two inscriptions are involved, one in Roman letters on the panel below the dial, the other in Norse runes in the border to the right. The extant runic text, seemingly incomplete at beginning and end, reads (meaninglessly) ...**iebel.ok**. (Barnes 1993b, 33; see also Holman 1996, 80). The extant Roman text, also seemingly incomplete at beginning and end, reads (equally meaninglessly): -[.]S : [.E]T : [...]NA : G[.]ERA [... O]C : HÞA [...]A : COMA : (Okasha 1971, 114 (No. 110); see also Holman 1996, 79–80). Okasha suggests, albeit tentatively, that the final word (the only one that seems to be complete) might be ON *koma* ('to come'). I would, however, note the following points: (1) the use of the graph wynn in the Roman inscription indicates Anglo-Saxon allegiances in its epigraphy, and thus Norse and Anglo-Saxon epigraphical traditions coexist on the Skelton sun-dial; (2) one might therefore reasonably expect the inscription in runes to be in Old Norse, and the inscription in Roman letters to be a complementary one in Old English; (3) since the runic inscription indicates that in the Skelton area there was continuing Norse vitality of some sort (whether linguistic or purely orthographic), it is possible that COMA might be a local loan from Old Norse or a form of the Old English infinitive influenced by Norse (final *-n* in verb infinitives had been lost in late Northumbrian, so the local cognate would be *cuma* < *cuman*); and (4) in general I think it would require the evidence of more than one word in a fragmentary and otherwise meaningless text to prove that a tradition of Old Norse literacy in the Roman alphabet existed in England (as a parallel, one might imagine, for example, if HANUM were the only legible word on the Aldbrough inscription: one would be mistaken in therefore concluding that the Aldbrough text was in Old Norse).

As noted above, Old English is also the language of administrative documents issuing from (or associated with) Cnut's court. These are of three sorts: (1) laws and letters, (2) writs, and (3) charters. The relevant texts are as follows:

(1) Cnut's law-codes testify in various ways to the authorship of Archbishop Wulfstan, and culminate in the mighty II Cnut (see Liebermann 1898–1916, I, 278–371; Kennedy 1983; Lawson 1993, 56–63; 1994; Wormald 1999a, 345–66); there are also two general letters to his subjects, dated 1019–20 and 1027 (see Liebermann 1898–1916, I, 273–77; Lawson 1993, 63–64).

(2) Cnut's Old English writs are as follows (numbers and probable dates are those given in Harmer's standard edition (1952)):[10]

    26 Christ Church, Canterbury (1017–20)
    28 Christ Church, Canterbury (1020)
    29 Christ Church, Canterbury (1035)

---

the personal name (byname?) *Hana* ('cock'). For occurrences of the personal name *Hana* see Searle 1897, 279; it may also be found in certain place-names (see Smith 1956, I, 233).

[10]There are also three Latin writs (Harmer 1952, Nos 36, 37, 48).

30 Christ Church, Canterbury (1035)
53 St Paul's, London (1033-35)

(3) Cnut's extant charters are approximately forty in number, and in the present context some of these are particularly interesting in being Dane-to-Dane grants (e.g. S955 Cnut to Agemund, or S961 Cnut to Orc) (for a full list of Cnut's charters and writs see Lawson 1993, 233-35).

In all this range of material, there is no more evidence for the use of Old Norse as a written language than in, say, the documents of Æthelred. Again, this is simply what one would expect; literacy means literacy in English and Latin, whether one believes that the king's scribes were clerical or a secular chancery. Like other Viking Age documents, some of the texts from Cnut's court do of course show Norse influence in terms of loanwords, but this does not alter the fact that they are written in standard late West Saxon (and many of these loans are also found as standard terminology in other late Old English legal texts (see Peters 1981, 89-93)). Elsewhere, the very few scraps of Old Norse which are found in Anglo-Saxon manuscripts are written in runes, and not the Roman alphabet (for a full discussion of the most curious text, the so-called 'Canterbury Runic Charm' (from the 1070s), see Frankis 2000). So, for example, MS CCCC 57, an eleventh-century Abingdon codex (see Ker 1957, 46–47 (No. 34)), contains the marginal dry-point incision]auarþ in Norse long-branch runes — that is, the Old Norse personal name *Hávarðr* (see Page 1993, 19; Graham 1996). Abingdon is a monastery for which pronounced Scandinavian connections have been demonstrated (see Abrams 1995, 223–24; Graham 1996), but even in such a place there are no Old Norse texts in Roman.

From the absence of written Norse in the documents of Cnut, however, one must not draw the conclusion that spoken Norse at Cnut's court enjoyed low prestige or was in disuse; on the contrary, the witness of Norse skaldic poetry demonstrates that Cnut's court was one in which the Norse language was spoken and celebrated and Norse literary traditions highly prized — for example, the three *Knútsdrápur*, or 'Poems in Praise of Cnut', by Sigvatr Þórðarson, Óttarr svarti, and Hallvarðr háreksblesi (on Cnut's skalds see Frank 1994a; Townend 2001). Juxtaposing this Norse poetry with Cnut's administrative documents it becomes clear that the distinction between spoken Norse and written English is one that runs right through Viking Age England: the circumstances of Cnut's court prove that the two could and did coexist at the highest level.

Concerning this question of literacy in Old Norse, however, there are two further aspects or exceptions which demand consideration. First, in addition to the argument that literacy in this period means literacy in English or Latin, the usual interpretation given for the scarcity of runic inscriptions from Viking Age England is that the Old Norse language in England was soon in a moribund state (or worse). On the contrary, however, I would suggest that certain examples of runic literacy demonstrate rather the vitality of Old Norse in England than its moribund state. In particular I would adduce the tympanum at Pennington in Furness, a twelfth-century inscription in Norse runes. The standard reading combines the versions of Bruce Dickins and

Eilert Ekwall: Dickins interpreted the text as KML : SETE : ThES : KIRK : HUBIRT : MASUN : UAN : M.... ('Gamel built this church. Hubert the mason carved. [...]') (Fell 1929, 217–19), while Ekwall (1930, 24) refined this by plausibly taking the sixth word to be *Másson* ('son of Már') rather than 'mason'. More recently, however, Michael Barnes, offering no translation, reads the inscription as **kml:*et*:þe**:kirk: hub*rt:-m sun:u*n:m...** (1993b, 33), while R. I. Page's latest version is **]kml:le*ta*:þena:kirk:*ub*rt:masu*n* :***:* +** (1999, 210; for an earlier reading see Page 1971, 171–72). Katherine Holman offers rather **kml:let:i:þe-a:kirk:hub-rt:m-sun:u[or þ]-(n):...** (1996, 73–77). Page's sceptical conclusion is that, on the basis of this inscription, he 'would hesitate to argue what language the people of the area spoke in the twelfth century' (1971, 172), but in fact the language seems to be perfectly acceptable Old Norse, albeit with weakened inflexions: a normalised reading (assuming the fourth rune to be **s** not **l**) would be *Gamall setti þessa kirkju. Hubert Másson vann* [...] ('Gamall built this church. Hubert son of Már made [...]').[11] The Pennington tympanum thus gives us a Norse runic inscription in an ecclesiastical context (indeed, in a very prominent position, above the entrance to the church), and I would argue that for this to have occurred — for the usual Latin or English text in Roman script to have been displaced — would require a very strong and vital tradition of Old Norse in the area (for one possible trace of Scandinavian influence on the area see Townend 1997, 34–35); and indeed there is other evidence for the continued vitality of the Norse language in Cumbria well into the post-Conquest period, most importantly the runic graffito in Carlisle Cathedral (*Dólfinn vreit þessi rúnar á þessi stein* (Barnes 1993b, 33; see also Holman 1996, 69–71) ('Dólfinn wrote these runes on this stone')).[12] Furthermore, as Holman points out (1996, 83), it is interesting that not only Pennington and Carlisle, but in fact all five inscriptions in Norse runes known from the north-west 'were found in ecclesiastical contexts', thus indicating their mainstream association with the establishment (the other three are Bridekirk, Conishead, and Dearham). In the ousting of Roman script, and of the English and Latin languages, it is therefore the use of Norse for the Pennington church inscription which is noteworthy, and not its absence from the Aldbrough and Kirkdale inscriptions.

---

[11]One of Page's principles is that the use of Norse runes need not indicate a Norse inscription (1971, 171), a principle which he derives from the Bridekirk font, whose Norse runes articulate a rhyming couplet in early Middle English: *Ricarþ he me iwrocte and to þis merð... me brocte* (Barnes 1993b, 33; see also Holman 1996, 66–69) ('Richard made me and brought me to this splendour [...]'). But there are no grounds for setting Bridekirk up as a rule (and indeed Page does not offer any) — it might just as well be an exception, and the presence among the runes of the non-runic letters eth, yogh, and wynn, as well as Tironian *et*, would strongly incline me to regard it as such. It should be noted, however, that by 1983 Page had come to regard the Pennington inscription as being written in 'bastard Norse', showing 'loss of inflexion and confusion of grammatical gender' (1983, 143; see also Page 1999, 210).

[12]Interestingly, both the Pennington and Carlisle inscriptions show the unusual word-order of article + noun, suggesting perhaps a local pattern (Page 1971, 172–73).

The second, very interesting point of qualification regarding Old Norse literacy is that there is in fact an exception to my earlier assertion that there are no non-runic texts in Old Norse from England; for there are. Some of the silver pennies struck in the name of Óláfr Guðfriðsson, king of Dublin and York 934–41, bear instead of the usual Latin title REX, the Norse equivalent CUNUNC (or CVNVNC: normalised ON *konungr*); examples include coins struck by the Derby moneyer Sigar and the York moneyer Æthelferth, both of which Michael Dolley dates to *c.* 940 (1965, 25, Plate IX Coin 32, Plate X Coin 33; 1978, 28–29).[13] This use of CUNUNC is, as far as I am aware, the only certain instance in Viking Age England of Old Norse being written other than in runes, and it is thus very remarkable and somewhat difficult to interpret. The last two years of the reign of Óláfr Guðfriðsson, after the death of Athelstan in 939, were a time of Scandinavian reconquest and (apparently) pagan defiance of the Christian West Saxons by the York-Dublin dynasty, and thus the coin-legend (dating from that period) is probably best seen as a linguistic articulation of political identity. As Eric John has pointed out (1996, 63), coinage was perhaps the only 'mass medium' available in Anglo-Saxon England, and so its legends and iconography supplied a communicative potential not to be neglected. The whole concept and practice of coinage was one that the Vikings encountered for the first time in England (whence it later reached the Scandinavian homelands); therefore the use of CUNUNC on Óláfr's coins can perhaps be seen as a reclamation of 'Norseness', in reaction to the Anglicisation otherwise involved in the issuing and idiom of coinage (on the earliest Danelaw coins see Dolley 1965, 16–17; on the 'Englishness' of later York coinage see Smyth 1987, II, 159–60). In decorative terms, other York coinage bears such conspicuously Viking emblems as a sword and Þórr's hammer, and Óláfr's shows also a raven, which Alfred Smyth reads symbolically:

> The bird of battle on Óláfr's coins [. . .] is an aggressively heathen symbol connected with the Óðinn cult, and the entire issue can be seen as a victory-coinage celebrating the return to power of Ívarr's descendants at York.

In similar terms, Richard Hall characterises Óláfr's York issue as 'propaganda coinage' (1994, 20, Illustration 5(b)), and the impetus behind the legend is thus, I think, intelligible; but less so the question of literacy. One word does not indicate the capability to write Old Norse in the Roman alphabet, and it is not difficult to imagine Óláfr's moneyers (presumably literate in English and Latin) simply receiving orders to replace *rex* with *konungr*. As Fran Colman points out, though, there is unfortunately no firm evidence from Anglo-Saxon England for the nature of the transmission to the die-cutters of the names and words which they engraved on the coin-dies (1992, 12, 18; see also Page 1999, 119). The question of possible readers is perhaps most intriguing: who could or was supposed to read this? For of course this

---

[13] In a Hiberno-Norse context, the title CVNVNC is also found on some rare post-997 coinage of Sigtryggr silkiskegg of Dublin (Dolley 1965, 27, Plate XIII Coin 43).

linguistic assertion of identity will only have been meaningful to the literate — in other words, to churchmen and other literate Anglo-Saxons, to whom it may have announced itself as a worrying declaration of Viking loyalties. These, though, are only tentative ideas, and the use of CUNUNC on some of Óláfr's coinage does not, I think, alter the essential point that, with the exception of runic inscriptions, the Old Norse language in England was a non-literate one.

Inflexional Loss in Old English and Old Norse

As the emphasis of the discussion shifts at this point from language contact to language change, it is valuable to begin by quoting at length Peter Trudgill's conclusions from his contemporary study of mutually intelligible 'dialects in contact' (1986, 126):[14]

> In a dialect mixture situation, large numbers of variants will abound, and, through the process of *accommodation* in face-to-face interaction, *interdialect* phenomena will begin to occur. As time passes and *focusing* begins to take place, particularly as the new town, colony, or whatever begins to acquire an independent identity, the variants present in the mixture begin to be subject to *reduction*. Again this presumably occurs via accommodation, especially of salient forms. This does not take place in a haphazard manner, however. In determining who accommodates to whom, and which forms are therefore lost, demographic factors involving proportions of different dialect speakers present will clearly be vital. More importantly, though, more purely linguistic factors are also at work. The reduction of variants that accompanies focusing, in the course of *new-dialect formation*, takes place via the process of *koinéization*. This comprises the process of *levelling*, which involves the loss of marked and/or minority variants; and the process of simplification, by means of which even minority forms may be the ones to survive if they are linguistically simpler, in the technical sense, and through which even forms and distinctions present in all the contributory dialects may be lost. Even after *koinéization*, however, some variants left over from the original mixture may survive. Where this occurs, *reallocation* may occur, such that variants originally from different regional dialects may in the new dialect become *social-class dialect variants*, *stylistic variants*, *areal variants*, or, in the case of phonology, *allophonic variants*.

It will be seen that a good number of these phenomena can indeed be observed to have occurred as a result of dialect contact between speakers of Norse and speakers of English; as James Milroy states more bluntly (1997, 311), 'Linguistic change is initiated by speakers, not by languages'. This present section will briefly consider morphological features, while the next will attend to lexical and phonological features.

---

[14]It should be noted that by 'dialect mixture' Trudgill means the total repertoire of variants to be found in the contact community, and not the repertoire of variants to be found in the usage of each individual speaker (which will of course fluctuate greatly).

A number of writers on Anglo-Norse contact have suggested that inflexions were largely non-functional in communication between speakers of the two languages, and that consequences of this for English were the atrophy and loss of inflexions and the concomitant development of fixed word-order, readily observable in later Middle English. Henry Bradley's discussion of the issue is old and informal, but still seems to me to be highly lucid and full of good sense (1904, 26–28; for details of levelling and convergence in dialect contact see Trudgill 1986):

> Let it be imagined that an island inhabited by people speaking a highly inflected language receives a large accession of foreigners to its population. [. . .] In our imaginary island the foreigners will soon pick up a stock of words; if the island language is like the Germanic ones, in which the main stress is never on the inflexional syllables, their task will be much easier. The grammatical endings will be learnt more slowly, and only the most striking will be learnt at all. The natives will soon manage to understand the broken jargon of the new comers, and to adopt it in conversation with them, avoiding the use of those inflexions which they discover to be puzzling to their hearers. But if they acquire the habit of using a simplified grammar in their dealings with foreigners, they will not entirely escape using it in their intercourse with each other. If there is intermarriage and absorption of the strangers in the native population, the language of the island must in a few generations be deprived of a considerable number of its inflexional forms.
>
> Let us now consider a somewhat different case. Suppose that the two peoples who live together and blend into one, instead of speaking widely distinct languages, speak dialects not too far apart to allow of a good deal of mutual understanding from the first, or at any rate as soon as the ear has been accustomed to the constant differences of pronunciation. The two dialects, let us suppose, have a large common vocabulary, with marked differences in inflexion — a very frequent case, because phonetic change is apt to cause greater divergences in the unstressed endings than in the stressed stems of words. The result will be much the same as when peoples speaking distinct languages are mingled; indeed there are reasons for thinking that the change will be even more rapid and decisive. For one thing, the blending of the two peoples is likely to take place more quickly. Then, as the speakers of neither dialect will be disposed to take the other as their model of correct speech, two different sets of inflexional forms will for a time be current in the same district, and there will arise a hesitation and uncertainty about the grammatical endings that will tend to render them indistinct in pronunciation, and hence not worth preserving.

Although apparently speaking in general terms, Bradley is of course thinking of the linguistic consequences of the Scandinavian settlements; as he writes later, 'since we know for a fact that those districts in which the Danes had settled are precisely those in which English grammar became simplified most rapidly, there can be no doubt that the Scandinavian admixture in the population was *one* of the causes that contributed to bring about the disuse of the Old English inflexions' (1904, 32; Jespersen 1956, 75–76, echoes much the same beliefs). In support of this view, Tom

Shippey gives an anecdotal recreation of an imagined example of Anglo-Norse contact (McCrum, Cran, and MacNeil 1992, 69):[15]

> Consider what happens when somebody who speaks, shall we say, good Old English from the south of the country runs into somebody from the north-east who speaks good Old Norse. They can no doubt communicate with each other, but the complications in both languages are going to get lost. So if the Anglo-Saxon from the South wants to say (in good Old English) 'I'll sell you the horse that pulls my cart,' he says: 'Ic selle the that hors the draegeth minne waegn.'
> Now the old Norseman — if he had to say this — would say: 'Ek mun selja ther hrossit er dregr vagn mine.'
> So, roughly speaking, they understand each other. One says 'waegn' and the other says 'vagn'. One says 'hors' and 'draegeth'; the other says 'hros' and 'dregr', but broadly they are communicating. They understand the main words. What they don't understand are the grammatical parts of the sentence. For instance, the man speaking good Old English says for one horse 'that hors' but for *two* horses he says 'tha hors'. Now the Old Norse speaker understands the word *horse* all right, but he's not sure if it means one or two because in Old English you say 'one horse', 'two horse'. There is no difference between the two words for horse. The difference is conveyed in the word for 'the' and the old Norseman might not understand this because his word for 'the' doesn't behave like that. So: are you trying to sell me one horse or are you trying to sell me two horses? If you get enough situations like that there is a strong drive towards simplifying the language.

More recently, it is this supposed phenomenon of simplification in grammar through contact — linked with a boom area in research — that has led some linguists to argue that early Middle English can be regarded as a creole arising from Anglo-Norse contact (see, for example, Domingue 1977; Fisiak 1977; Poussa 1982; J. Milroy 1984, 11–12; Ruiz Moneva 1997, 188–89; for a somewhat different (and more sophisticated) version of the idea see Hines 1991). There is no need to go into this question here, since Manfred Görlach has effectively put a stop to such speculations, and Bruce Mitchell supplies a useful guide to the controversy (Görlach 1986; Mitchell 1994, 163–70; see also Wallmannsberger 1988; Allen 1997; 1998). As Görlach concludes (1986, 355), 'unless simplification and language mixture are thought to be sufficient criteria for the definition of a creole or creoloid (and I do not think they are, since this would make most languages of the world creoles, and the term would consequently lose its distinctiveness), then Middle English does not appear to be a creole'. What should be noted, though, is that Görlach and Mitchell are believers in what Mitchell calls 'the traditional view' of the reasons behind English's change from being a synthetic language to being an analytic one (1994, 164; see also Allen 1997, 67–74):

---

[15]One might, however, query the form of a couple of Shippey's Old Norse words in this example, namely *vagn* and *hrossit*: in Viking Age Norse initial /w/ had not yet become /v/, and the definite article had not yet been suffixed.

[A] major factor was the Scandinavian invasions and the consequent establishment of bilingual communities of speakers of English and Scandinavian dialects — all Germanic in origin. As a result, the inflexional endings (which differed from dialect to dialect) were confused and reduced so that they were no longer distinctive. Such reduction was possible only because Old English was already moving towards the SVO order.

It should be pointed out, however, that few if any of the proponents of this view would argue that Norse contact acted as the trigger for these developments in English, but rather that it augmented or accelerated existing tendencies, themselves largely a consequence of the Germanic fixing of stress on the first syllable.

What contribution can the present investigation make to this question? It is primarily the intelligibility of English words to Norse speakers and vice versa that has been demonstrated by studying the processes of cognate substitution, resulting in the conclusion that speakers of Norse and English enjoyed adequate intelligibility in Viking Age England. In other words, neither speech community acquired widespread active competence in the language of the other, a process that would have required, as well as the intelligibility of lexemes, the learning of inflexions. There are some examples of cognate morphological substitution to be found in the Scandinavianisation of English names and words (and vice versa), but these tend to be confined to the genitive singular and the nominative/accusative plural. Morphological substitution of OE gen.sg. *-es* for cognate ON *-s* can be seen, for example, in the forms of the Yorkshire place-name Brandesburton ('Brandr's *burhtūn*': *Branzburtone, Brantisburtune* DB) (*PNYE* 74; *SSNY* 143; *DEPN* 77; see also *SSNEM* 273); the opposite of this, substitution of ON *-s* for OE *-es*, can be seen in other Yorkshire place-names, such as Lebberston ('Leodbeorht's *tūn*': *Ledbestun, Ledbeztun* DB) (*PNYN* 105; *SSNY* 116; *DEPN* 293) and Whixley ('Cwic's *lēah*': *Cucheslage* DB, *Quixle* 1206) (*PNYW* 5.9–10; *SSNY* 167; *DEPN* 515). In the Old English Orosius it was seen how Ohthere's plural *hreinar* 'reindeer' assumed the form *hrānas* in the Old English text, thus showing, in addition to phonemic substitution of OE *ā* for ON *ei*, cognate morphological substitution of OE nom./acc.pl. *-as* for ON *–ar*; these are, of course, the dominant types of plural formation in each language. But beyond the most common types of genitive singular and nominative/accusative plural, one may indeed doubt whether, in a situation of mutual intelligibility rather than bilingualism, many other inflexions would be readily intelligible between the two speech communities. Certainly by the Viking Age the Old Norse and Old English inflexional systems had begun to diverge, and in Anglo-Norse contact between monolinguals this must presumably have provoked alternative strategies for the expression of grammatical relationships. Equally certainly, the Germanic fixing of stress on the first syllable had led by the Viking Age to reduction and obscuration in inflexional syllables, especially in English; it is worth recalling here the finding in Chapter 3 that Norse speakers misunderstood the second element in Old English compound place-names far more frequently than they misunderstood the first element, presumably because the second element received much less stress and any vowels in the second element were more likely to be centralised to schwa (thus obscuring the correspondence with their Old Norse cognates) (see p 65 above). Thus in general terms the findings of this study are entirely compatible with (and indeed support) Mitchell's 'traditional view', though they add relatively little in the way of new evidence — beyond of course the central demonstration that one is right to be thinking in terms of a situation of mutual intelligibility rather than one of bilingualism.

It is worth considering, though, the relevance of the fossilized inflexions preserved on certain Norse loans in English. There are, admittedly, not a great number of these, and they have been frequently noticed: *(a)thwart*, *bask*, *busk*, *scant*, and *want*. Additionally, there are others which are recorded in Middle English but have not survived into Modern English, such as *bi nither-tale* 'in the middle of the night' (< ON *á náttar-þeli*), found in *Havelok* and elsewhere (Smithers 1987, 56 (line 2026)); this example adds genitive singular *-ar* to *-t* and *-sk* as fossilized inflexions featuring in Norse loans. Since it would be reasonable to believe that language shift from Norse to English would involve, inter alia, the giving up of Norse inflexions, these inflected loans must derive from English borrowing rather than Norse imposition through shift (see below on the distinction between these two processes); and since the inflexions preserved are those which didn't exist in Old English (*-t*, *-sk*, *-ar*), this suggests that the English failed to recognise them as inflexions but rather mistook them for parts of the stem. If the English had learned Norse and were bilingual, they would have recognised *-t*, *-sk*, and *-ar* as inflexions; but they didn't, and this would therefore seem to indicate that they weren't. In other words, the inflected loans in English imply that the English did not as a rule learn the Norse inflexions, and this in turn implies that (1) as suggested throughout this study, each speech community spoke its own language, rather than one or both becoming bilingual, and (2) generally speaking, inflexions were non-functional in Anglo-Norse communication (or, at the very least, not all inflexions were functional).

The evidence of these inflected loans therefore supports the 'traditional view', as do the few examples of late Old Norse texts from England. For according to Bradley's scenario, inflexional loss would occur in both languages in situations of quotidian contact, and this does seem to be the case in the Old Norse inscription on the Pennington tympanum. It will be recalled that Michael Barnes (1993b, 33) read the Pennington inscription as **kml:*et*:þe**:kirk: hub*rt:-m sun:u*n:m...**, R. I. Page (1999, 210) as **]kml:leta:þena:kirk:*ub*rt:masun :***:* +**, and Bruce Dickins (Fell 1929, 217) as (in modern transcription) **kml:sete:þes:kirk:hubirt:masun:uan:m....**; assuming the fourth rune to be **s** not **l**, a normalised text and translation would be *Gamall setti þessa kirkju. Hubert Másson vann* [...] ('Gamall built this church. Hubert son of Már made [...]'). Therefore in comparing transcription with normalised text one sees that the inflexions of the former are greatly weakened: in the noun phrase 'this church' (feminine accusative singular) the noun *kirkju* appears as *kirk*, and (according to Dickins) the demonstrative *þessa* as *þes*. If one follows Page's reading, the demonstrative appears as *þena* (masculine accusative singular), and so there is confusion of grammatical gender between demonstrative and noun. Furthermore, if the second word is indeed *sete*, as maintained by Dickins (but denied by Page), then that too would seem to show centralisation in the verb inflexion (3rd person singular preterite indicative). In other words, whatever the disagreements between individual readings of the text, it is clear that the Old Norse inflexional system is here in some disarray. As has been seen, many historians of the English language have been eager to suggest that one of the key elements in the demise of English inflexions were the bilingual societies of Norse and English speakers in areas of Scandinavian settlement; and this book's findings would be in agreement with this. But evidence such as the Pennington inscription suggests that the same thing also happened to the Norse language in England, and therefore if one wishes to entertain the idea of linguistic convergence between Old English and Old Norse in England, as a number of commentators have suggested, it is to the morphological evidence that one should look.

My conclusion, then, is that, with a few exceptions such as the dominant forms of the genitive singular and nominative/accusative plural, inflexions were largely non-functional in Anglo-Norse communication, and that therefore Anglo-Norse contact was indeed an important factor in the atrophy and loss of inflexions not only in the English language but also in the Norse language in England. As will be seen below, however, loss of inflexions does not necessarily mean the loss of distinct phonologies, and therefore one may query how far it means the development of some sort of 'mixed language'.

Norse Loans in English and Old Norse Language Death

As a general rule, there is an important difference in the phonological form taken by Norse loans in Old English and Norse loans in Middle English: in Old English Norse loans tend often to assume an English form (having undergone cognate substitution), whereas in Middle English they retain their Norse form.[16] This is in particular true of Old Norse loans for which Old English cognates existed. Furthermore, somewhere in the transition period between these two conventionally demarcated states of the English language, the Old Norse language in England died — that is, it ceased to be spoken, and those who had been Norse speakers shifted to speaking English. I would suggest that, in general, the Norse loans in Old English are borrowings made by English speakers while Old Norse was still a living language, whereas the Norse loans in Middle English are the result of Old Norse language death, being words 'imposed' by Norse speakers in shifting to English.

---

[16]Einar Haugen, in his influential study of lexical transfer, terms these two processes 'substitution' and 'importation' (1950, 212–13; it should be noted however that Haugen's use of 'substitution' does not necessarily imply cognateness). For general discussion of lexical borrowing see Bynon 1977, 217–39; Hock 1991, 380–425.

The various elements in this model will be discussed below in more detail, but the terms 'borrowing' and 'imposition' will first be defined. Many discussions of lexical transfer assume that bilingual speakers must be the medium of transmission (for example, Haugen 1950; Weinreich 1953), but for the present study such approaches would seem to be of limited value. I have argued that to make sense of Anglo-Norse contact in Viking Age England it is better to postulate a model of mutual intelligibility than one of bilingualism, and corroboratively I believe such a model serves also to make most sense of the Norse loans in English. For a suitable terminology for the study of lexical transfer without a predication of bilingual individuals, I have therefore turned to the work of Frans van Coetsem, whose theoretical framework is as follows (1988, 3); and I would suggest it is a framework into which Anglo-Norse contact and the Norse loans in English fit very well, particularly when one adds the factor of Old Norse language death:[17]

> The role of the speaker is of crucial importance to our definitions of *borrowing* and *imposition*. From the viewpoint of a speaker who comes in active contact with another language, there is a *source language* and a *recipient language*. If the recipient language speaker is the agent, as in the case of an English speaker using French words while speaking English, the transfer of material (and this naturally includes structure) from the source language to the recipient language is *borrowing (recipient language agentivity)*. If, on the other hand, the source language speaker is the agent, as in the case of a French speaker using his French articulatory habits while speaking English, the transfer of material from the source language to the recipient language is *imposition (source language agentivity)*. Of direct relevance here is the fact that language has a constitutional property of *stability*; certain components or *domains* of language are more stable and more resistant to change (e.g., phonology), while other such domains are less stable and less resistant to change (e.g., vocabulary). Given the nature of this property of stability, a language in contact with another tends to maintain its more stable domains. Thus, if the recipient language speaker is the agent, his natural tendency will be to preserve the more stable domains of his language, e.g., his phonology, while accepting vocabulary items from the source language. If the source language speaker is the agent, his natural tendency will again be to preserve the more stable domains of his language, e.g., his phonology and specifically his articulatory habits, which means that he will impose them upon the recipient language. *In short, the transfer of material from the source language to the recipient language primarily concerns less stable domains, particularly vocabulary, in borrowing, and more stable domains, particularly phonological entities, in imposition.* Each transfer type thus has its own characteristic general effect on the recipient language.

Considering first the Norse loans in Old English, one can see that when the Norse word is without a cognate in Old English (either lexical or phonemic), or if its

---

[17]Thomason and Kaufman (1988, 37–45) independently present much the same model but employ different terminology, preferring 'shift-induced interference' to van Coetsem's 'imposition'.

constituent phonemes would be identical, it is adopted into English in its Norse form, and reproduced with considerable accuracy. Examples include the following (where VAN = Viking Age Norse):

Old Norse	Old English	
barð	barð	'ship'
félagi	feolaga	'fellow, comrade'
grið	grið	'truce'
knǫrr, VAN *knarr	cnear	'ship'
lǫg, VAN *lagu	lagu	'law'
níðingr	niðing	'villain'
skeið	scegð	'ship'

However, where Old English cognates exist (lexical or phonemic), or the corresponding phonemes show phonological divergence, one can observe the operation of a switching-code, as in the adaptation of place-names studied earlier; also as with place-names, this is most readily observable in one or both elements of a compound. Examples include the following:

Old Norse	Old English	
askr	æsc	'warship'
drekkulaun	drincelēan	'entertainment given by lord to tenants'
heimsókn	hāmsōcn	'attack on a man's house'
hǫfuðsmaðr, VAN *haufuðsmaðr	hēafdesmann	'captain'
ráða á	rǣdan on	'to attack'
saklauss	saclēas	'innocent'
stýrismaðr	stēoresmann	'steersman'
veðrfastr	wederfæst	'weatherbound'

I would suggest, then, that the forms taken in Old English by this second group of loans indicate that they are borrowings made by English speakers of words originally heard from the lips of Norse speakers; in the terms of van Coetsem, they are the result of recipient language agentivity, showing acceptance of vocabulary from the source language but preservation of the phonology of the recipient language.

Traditionally, it is a linguistic commonplace that, generally speaking, words are borrowed from one language to another on account of either need or prestige (see for example Hock 1991, 408–11). The Norse loans in English have posed problems to linguists, as it is not clear which of these two causations is operative, or whether there are diachronic and diatopic variations in causation. As can be seen from the examples above, the Norse loans in Old English tend to be need-based borrowings, denoting new objects (particularly nautical and legal terminology), whereas many of the Norse loans in Middle English can in no way be regarded as need-based borrowings as they constitute so-called core vocabulary. Normally, this would imply that Norse enjoyed greater prestige in the Middle English period than it did in the Old English, but this seems impossible, since it was in the Viking Age (if ever, and only in certain areas) that the Norse-speaking population was in authority over the English-speaking. To regard the Norse core vocabulary items appearing in Middle English as the result of imposition through shift rather than of borrowing would appear to remove this problem (again, see below). My suspicion is that Norse and English were roughly adstratal in Viking Age England — that is, they enjoyed more or less equal prestige. For if Old English were of much greater prestige one would expect the rapid death of Old Norse and few Norse loans in Old English; and if Old Norse were of much greater prestige one would expect many Norse loans in Old English of a non-need nature, and certainly not the death of Old Norse.

No doubt the demise of a sense of Scandinavian identity and the death of the Old Norse language in England are related, the latter probably being an event of the eleventh and twelfth centuries. As Milroy and Milroy declare (1997, 80), 'The key to understanding [linguistic] change lies ultimately in the shifting and changing affirmations of identity and solidarity by human beings in social groups'. My tentative model for the process of Old Norse language death would be that during this period political factors, Anglo-Scandinavian integration, and the continued practice of mixed marriage (which appears to have been an important element in the Viking Age itself) led to the gradual breakdown of a distinctive Scandinavian culture and identity.[18] Linguistically, these factors would lead to gradual accommodation to the dominant dialect (English) on the part of Norse speakers and, through dialect shift, a gradual increase in the number of English speakers in relation to Norse. Once such a momentum had begun, one would rapidly see a widespread shift from Norse to English (on the factors involved in language maintenance and shift see for example Appel and Muysken 1987, 33–45). Old Norse survived longest in those pockets of Scandinavian settlement most isolated from English language and culture, such as the Lake District, as the Pennington tympanum would seem to testify. Eventually even in these places the Old Norse language died — that is, the population shifted to speaking English rather than Norse (for other recent discussions or reconstructions of the death of Old Norse in England see Hansen 1984, 83–88; Thomason and Kaufman 1988, 275–304; Kastovsky 1992, 327–32).

It is through this language shift, I would suggest, that a great number of Norse lexical items entered English — through imposition (that is, in van Coetsem's terms,

---

[18]On the evidence for Anglo-Norse mixed marriages see (inter alia) Ashdown 1928–29, 82–84; Arngart 1947–48, 73–82; Clark 1979, 17–18. Clark's work is especially important in that it is non-anecdotal in approach, while Fellows-Jensen 1995a reconstructs certain Anglo-Norse family relationships.

source language agentivity). Very many of the Norse loans first recorded in Middle English rather than Old English retain their Norse phonology, and this is exactly what one would expect through imposition. These Norse items were then generalised through Middle English through social and geographical diffusion.

A difficult question is therefore whether one should regard the Norse pronouns in Middle English (*they*, *them*, *their*, and possibly *she*) as the result of borrowing or imposition. It is traditional to see them as need-based borrowings after the OE 3rd person masculine singular, feminine singular, and plural personal pronouns had all homophonously become merely *h*- plus schwa in late Old English/early Middle English (see Werner 1991; Howe 1996, 154–65; Smith 1996, 128–34). A recent argument has, however, presented them as the result of imposition, partly on the grounds that all other examples of pronoun-transfer among western European languages appear to have occurred through that process rather than borrowing (Buccini 1992, 20–21). I see no reason, though, why both processes might not have been involved, and I would suggest also that Anglo-Norse intelligibility may have played a part, and that the borrowing of Norse pronouns into English is explicable as an example of morphological accommodation on the part of English speakers. If two languages in persistent contact are adequately intelligible, but divergent and possibly unintelligible in an important paradigm (such as personal pronouns), it is possible that, through accommodation, the forms in one language would be lost, and the forms in the other generalised, in the interests of continued (indeed, enhanced) intelligibility (as suggested by Milroy 1997, 320–21); in other words, this transfer of Norse pronouns may have occurred not simply on account of Old English drawing on Old Norse as a resource to improve its own paradigm-efficiency, but also as a result of the two speech communities trying to communicate.

Imposition through shift — source language agentivity — is in particular the most plausible explanation for the presence in Middle English of common Norse words which had equally common English cognates (so that in Middle English one finds Norse- and English-derived lexical variants, differing only in phonology). Many of these represent core vocabulary, and so borrowing on account of need cannot be the explanation for the presence of these items in English; borrowing on account of prestige also seems unlikely, since as far as one can tell — and this is a major caveat — they enter English at the time of Old Norse language death. Examples are as follows, where column 1 gives the Norse-derived variant in Middle English, column 2 the classical Old Norse (Old West Norse) form, column 3 the English-derived variant in Middle English, and column 4 the classical Old English (West Saxon) form:[19]

---

[19]Inconsistently but necessarily, the Norse- and English-derived variants cited here are from various Middle English dialects and periods: see below, however, for a study of lexical variants in one specific text. Björkman 1900–02, 195–96, gives a list containing further examples.

(handwritten annotations: column 1 "Norse-derived variant", column 2 "ON", column 3 "English-derived variant", column 4 "OE")

	1	2	3	4	
a. ON *ei* — OE *ā*					
	bleik	*bleikr*	*bloke*	*blāc*	'white, pale'
	gayt	*geit*	*got*	*gāt*	'goat'
	heil	*heill*	*hol*	*hāl*	'healthy'[20]
	-leik	*-leikr*	*-lok*	*-lāc*	nominal suffix
	leiþ	*leiðr*	*loth*	*lāð*	'hateful'
	wei	*vei*	*wo*	*wā*	'sorrow'
	weik	*veikr*	*woke*	*wāc*	'weak'
b. ON *au* — OE *ēa*					
	gowke	*gaukr*	*yeke*	*gēac*	'cuckoo'
	coupe	*kaupa*	*chepe*	*cēapan*	'to buy'
	lone	*laun*	*len*	*lēan*	'reward'
	loupen	*hlaupa*	*lepe*	*hlēapan*	'to run'[21]
	rauþ	*rauðr*	*red*	*rēad*	'red'
c. ON /sk/ — OE /ʃ/					
	sker	*skirr*	*schire*	*scīr*	'bright, pure'
	skirte	*skyrta*	*shirte*	*scyrte*	'garment'[22]
	scour	*skúr*	*shur*	*scūr*	'shower'
	fisk	*fiskr*	*fish*	*fisc*	'fish'
d. ON /k/ — OE /tʃ/					
	ketel	*ketill*	*chetel*	*cytel*	'kettle'
	kirk	*kirkja*	*chirche*	*cyrice*	'church'
	dik	*diki*	*dich*	*dīc*	'ditch'
e. ON /g/ — OE /j/					
	giuen	*gefa*	*yive*	*gyfan*	'to give'
	egg	*egg*	*ey*	*ǣg*	'egg'

However, there are two ways of regarding these Norse variants in Middle English: either as the result of lexical imposition through shift or as English words showing Norse phonological substratum influence, and in some ways the latter seems more plausible, though the possibility of substratum influence has received little mention

---

[20]This is an example where both variants have persisted into Modern English, albeit with semantic divergence: *hail* and *whole*.

[21]These also survive in Modern English (with semantic divergence) as *lope* and *leap*.

[22]Again, the two variants have persisted into Modern English with semantic divergence: *skirt* and *shirt*.

in discussions of the Norse loans in Middle English. The suggestion, then, is simply that (for example) *bleik* represents ME *blok* pronounced with a Norse accent (that is, with Norse phonology imposed), initially by those who have shifted from Norse to English but subsequently (due to generalisation) by those whose first (and only) language is English. As Björkman remarked long ago (1900–02, 13 n.2), 'it is often very difficult to decide what is to be called a loan-word and what is only a native word influenced by Scandinavian'. Another important benefit of the substratum theory is that it would explain why Old Norse and Scandinavianised place-names were not (re-)Anglicised when Norse speakers shifted to English.

To restate van Coetsem's dichotomy (1988, 3):

[I]f the recipient language speaker is the agent, his natural tendency will be to preserve the more stable domains of his language, e.g., his phonology, while accepting vocabulary items from the source language. If the source language speaker is the agent, his natural tendency will again be to preserve the more stable domains of his language, e.g., his phonology and specifically his articulatory habits, which means that he will impose them upon the recipient language.

The model presented here for the two methods of transfer of Norse lexical items from Norse into English can therefore be summarised as follows, with the double transfer of the Old Norse word *hreinar* ('reindeer' (pl.)) serving as a useful illustration:

Period	Method of Transfer	Loan Phonology
tenth–eleventh century	Borrowing	Phonemic substitution e.g. *hrānas*
eleventh–twelfth century	Imposition through shift	Norse phonology preserved e.g. *reyne(dere)*

Of course to present the Norse lexical items in English as the result of two chronologically distinct phases — borrowing and then imposition through shift — is to be false in some degree to the complexity of Anglo-Norse contact, but as a general model I think it provides the best explanation. In some parts of the country, speakers of Norse must have shifted to English earlier than in other parts, and the genuine borrowings from Norse into English can no doubt be stratified more precisely. To quote Thomason and Kaufman (1988, 45):

In some cases [. . .] a language undergoes both types of interference at once. Target-language speakers may be borrowing words and possibly even structural features from a language whose speakers are in the process of shifting to the target language and incorporating their learners' errors into it.

The imposition of Norse items into Middle English through language shift, resulting in Norse- and English-derived variants of the same word, is thus a process having an important bearing on the pre- or non-standard Middle English lexicon, and, potentially, on the literary exploitation of variants by writers using that lexicon. The table given above presented a number of variants drawn from a range of sources; in conclusion one specific text will be considered here in further exemplification of this, namely the *Ormulum*.

Orm composed his *Ormulum* in the second half of the twelfth century, somewhere in Lincolnshire (for a plausible, though not conclusive, localisation see Parkes 1983); that is, in the region of the East Midlands which underwent the heaviest Scandinavian settlement (see *SSNEM*), and it is thus fair to assume that the coexistence of Norse- and English-derived lexical variants in his language arises from an earlier shift from Norse to English by the Norse-speaking population, and that therefore this coexistence reflects the contemporary language of the area of composition. Orm's name is a Norse one, perhaps suggesting some Scandinavian ancestry (hardly unlikely in such a region), and a number of features indicate heavy Norse influence on Orm's language: (1) there are over two hundred Norse loanwords to be found in the extant *Ormulum*, some of which are unparalleled elsewhere in Middle English, and many of which are there found in English for the first time (the standard study is still Brate 1884; see also Rynell 1948, 59–69); (2) the usual 3rd person plural pronouns are, even at this early stage, the Norse ones *þeȝȝ*, *þeȝȝm*, and *þeȝȝre* (though Old English *hem* and *here* survive as occasional variants) (see Johannesson 1995); (3) some of the Norse loans in the *Ormulum* are unique in showing late Norse sound-changes scarcely, if at all, paralleled in other loans in English, suggesting that they may be late adoptions (for example, denasalisation of the negative prefix from *un-* to *u-* in *usell* ('unhappy')) (see Olszewska 1962, 119 n.6); (4) some of the loans are found in alliterative pairs, a number of which are Norse in both parts and therefore seem to have entered English as units (see Olszewska 1962).

The *Ormulum* is a particularly good text to cite in exemplification in this context, since an obvious objection could be that the coexistence of Norse- and English-derived variants in the same text has only arisen through scribal interference in the process of copying (that is, a text from a Norse-influenced region has been copied by a scribe from a non-Norse-influenced region, or vice versa). The manuscript of the *Ormulum*, however, is universally regarded as an authorial autograph, and so the coexistence of Norse- and English-derived variants, rather than being the product of a scribal admixture of two or more dialects, must represent a feature of the dialect of Orm and his area of composition; and if this happened in Orm's area, there is no good reason for doubting its occurrence elsewhere.

Norse- and English-derived variants in the *Ormulum* are as follows. The list is not exhaustive, and the items have been presented here in alphabetical order of the Norse-derived variant rather than according to phonological divergence; this is because items which can only have arisen through lexical imposition rather than phonological substratum influence have also been included. As before, column 1 gives the Norse-derived variant, column 2 the classical Old Norse (Old West Norse) form, column 3 the English-derived variant, and column 4 the classical Old English (West Saxon) form:[23]

[Handwritten annotations: Column 1 "Norse derived variant"; Column 2 "ON"; Column 3 "English-derived variant"; Column 4 "OE"]

1	2	3	4	
aȝȝ	ei	a	ā	'always, forever'
aȝȝhe	agi	eȝȝe	ege	'awe, terror'
baðe	báðir	ba/beȝȝen	bā/bēgen	'both'
bennk	bekkr	bench	benc	'bench'
brennde	<brenna	bærnenn	bærnen	'to burn'
drinnk	drekka	drinnch	drinc	'drink'
epeþþ	<œpa	wepeþþ	<wēpan	'(he) cries'
fanngenn	fanga[24]	fon	fōn	'to acquire'
gett	<geta	ȝetenn	getan	'to obtain'
gifenn	gefa	ȝefenn	gyfan	'to give'
giferr	gifr	ȝiferr	gīfre	'covetous'
keȝȝsere	keisari	kaserr	cāser	'emperor'
make	maki	macche	(ge)maca	'wife, mate'
mennissk	menskr	mennissh	mennisc	'human' (adj.)
skir	skírr	shir	scīr	'bright, pure'
þeȝȝm	þeim	hem	heom	'them'
þeȝȝre	þeira	here	heora	'their'

Orm is a writer attempting to fashion his own form of a standard language for purposes of wide diffusion, and since one of the central principles in standardisation is the 'suppression of optional variability', Orm can be observed eliminating variants (orthographic, phonological, lexical) as systematically as possible (see Burchfield 1956, 69–79). Yet the Norse- and English-derived variants listed above do coexist in his work, and only a proportion can be explained on the grounds of metrical utility (baðe/ba/beȝȝen, fanngenn/fon, þeȝȝm/hem, and þeȝȝre/here). Therefore if the rest succeeded in slipping past his scrutiny, one might speculate that a great many others failed to do so.[25]

Taking the *Ormulum* as a representative text, there are three points to make about the coexistence of these lexical variants in the early Middle English period. Firstly, simply their quantity: the development of Norse-derived variants beside the native English ones, as a result of imposition through language shift, must have been an important and widespread feature of the spoken dialect in areas of heavy Scandinavian settlement.

---

[23] The flat-topped graph <g> is Orm's own invention for velar /g/; insular <ȝ> is his graph for palatal /j/.

[24] ON *fá* is of course much more common.

[25] In some cases, one of the pair of variants is eliminated in the course of revision (for example, ȝifenn is eliminated, gifenn persists).

Secondly, the co-occurrence of these Norse- and English-derived variants has an obvious relevance to the question of Anglo-Norse intelligibility. I have argued in this book that in the bilingual society of Viking Age England English words were intelligible to Norse speakers, and Norse words to English speakers; Orm's evidence must indicate the same. In view of Orm's ambition that his sermon-cycle should be declaimed from as many pulpits as possible, it is necessary to assume that the supposed audience of the *Ormulum* must have been able to understand both the Norse- and English-derived variants; and since the work seems to be intended for a general lay audience (that is, not restricted to the well-educated or linguistically talented), this would imply the intelligibility of both sets of variants to the whole speech community. And if these words posed no problems of intelligibility in the early Middle English period, there is no reason why they should have done so in the late Old English.

Thirdly and lastly, the utility of many of these variants to writers should be noted. Orm, of course, is concerned with standardisation and the elimination of variants, but even he retains a number of variants on account of their metrical utility, such as the various forms of 'both' which provide him with the option of none, one, or two syllables: *ba* (monosyllabic or able to be elided before a vowel or *h*), *baðe* (disyllabic or monosyllabic when elided), and *beʒʒen* (disyllabic). Similar practices can be observed in Middle English rhyming poets: for example, the *Havelok*-poet, also writing in Lincolnshire and perhaps a century or so after Orm, employs the English-derived variant *handes* ('hands') mid-line at line 95 since the metre requires a disyllable, but the Norse-derived mutation plural *hend* at line 505 to provide a rhyme with *fend* ('fiend') (Smithers 1987, 3, 17); and parallel techniques can still be observed two centuries later, for example in the York Plays. The literary utility of variants in a pre- or non-standard dialect has often been discussed, particularly with regard to the works of Chaucer (see for example Burnley 1989, 108–32), and thus the consequences of imposition through shift provided writers in the old Danelaw area with a fruitful source of variants in the early Middle English period.

Concluding Remarks

This book's main conclusions have been presented already, in the section of review at the start of this final chapter, and so only a few words are here needed to conclude. I have argued in this work that the model or hypothesis which best explains the fragmentary evidence and observable phenomena of Anglo-Norse language contact is that which predicates a situation of adequate mutual intelligibility between speakers of Norse and English, rather than one involving widespread bilingualism or the use of interpreters. This final chapter has accordingly explored some implications of this model as a way of making sense of the history of the Old Norse language in England, and has more generally re-affirmed the view that, for the last two centuries before the Conquest, we must be careful to think in terms of an England that was truly Anglo-Scandinavian.

Of course, like all models, the hypothesis presented in this book is no doubt too crude and over-generalised, insufficiently sensitive to the regional and chronological variations that must have obtained in Viking Age England; but this does not invalidate its position. Indeed, it is in the nature of early medieval studies that a constructive model must be attempted if one is not simply to scatter questions and point out the inadequacies of one's evidence. As an exercise in linguistic history, therefore, the interpretation of Anglo-Norse contact which has been put forward here is at least, I hope, substantially coherent in its composition and argument; but it is also in the nature of the discipline that all hypotheses must be made with the expectation of revision.

Bibliography

This bibliography is restricted to works to which reference is made in the text. Conventions are as follows: (1) Primary sources are listed by editor. (2) Icelandic authors with patronymics are listed under their first name. (3) Vowels with diacritics (other than acute accents) are placed at the end of the alphabet.

Abrams, L. 1995. 'The Anglo-Saxons and the Christianization of Scandinavia', *Anglo-Saxon England*, 24, 213–49
—— 2000. 'Conversion and Assimilation', in Hadley and Richards 2000, 135–53
—— 2001a. 'Edward the Elder's Danelaw', in Higham and Hill 2001, 128–43
—— 2001b. 'The Conversion of the Danelaw', in Graham-Campbell and others 2001, 31–44
Aitken, A. J., McIntosh, A., and Hermann Pálsson, eds, 1971. *Edinburgh Studies in English and Scots*, London: Longman
Allen, C. L. 1997. 'Middle English Case Loss and the "Creolization" Question', *English Language and Linguistics*, 1, 63–89
—— 1998. 'Genitives and the Creolization Question', *English Language and Linguistics*, 2, 129–35
Ambrosiani, B., and Clarke, H., eds, 1994. *Developments Around the Baltic and the North Sea in the Viking Age*, The Twelfth Viking Congress, Birka Studies, 3, Stockholm: Birka Project
Anderson, A. O., and Anderson, M. O., eds and trans, 1991. *Adomnán's Life of Columba*, rev. by M. O. Anderson, Oxford Medieval Texts, Oxford: Clarendon
Andersson, T., and Sandred, K. I., eds, 1978. *The Vikings: Proceedings of the Symposium of the Faculty of Arts of Uppsala University, June 6–9, 1977*, Acta Universitatis Upsaliensis, Symposia Universitatis Upsaliensis Annum Quingentesimum Celebrantis, 8, Uppsala: Almqvist & Wiksell
Andersson, T. M. 1964. *The Problem of Icelandic Saga Origins*, Yale Germanic Studies, 1, New Haven: Yale University Press
Antonsen, E. H. 1965. 'On Defining Stages in Prehistoric Germanic', *Language*, 41, 19–36
—— 1975. *A Concise Grammar of the Older Runic Inscriptions*, Tübingen: Niemeyer
Appel, R., and Muysken, P. 1987. *Language Contact and Bilingualism*, London: Arnold
Armstrong, A. M., Mawer, A., Stenton, F. M., and Dickins, B. 1950–52. *The Place-Names of Cumberland*, 3 vols, EPNS, 20–22, Cambridge: Cambridge University Press

Arndt, W. W. 1959. 'The Performance of Glottochronology in Germanic', *Language*, 35, 180–92

Arngart, O. 1947–48. 'Some Aspects of the Relation between the English and the Danish Element in the Danelaw', *Studia Neophilologica*, 20, 73–87

Arnold, T., ed., 1882–85. *Symeonis Monachi Opera Omnia*, 2 vols, Rolls Series, 75, London: Longman

Ashdown, M. 1928–29. 'The Attitude of the Anglo-Saxons to their Scandinavian Invaders', *Saga-Book of the Viking Society*, 10, 75–99

Bailey, R. N. 1980. *Viking Age Sculpture in Northern England*, London: Collins

Bailey, R. N., and Cramp, R. 1988. *The British Academy Corpus of Anglo-Saxon Stone Sculpture*, vol II: *Cumberland, Westmorland and Lancashire North-of-the-Sands*, Oxford: Oxford University Press

Baker, P. S., and Lapidge, M., eds, 1995. *Byrhtferth's Enchiridion*, EETS SS, 15, Oxford: EETS

Bakka, E. 1971. 'Scandinavian Trade Relations with the Continent and the British Isles in Pre-Viking Times', in *Early Medieval Studies*, vol. III, Antikvariskt Arkiv, 40, Stockholm: Almqvist & Wiksell, 37–51

Bammesberger, A. 1983. 'The Old English Adjective *Ambyre*', *English Studies*, 64, 97–101

——, ed., 1991. *Old English Runes and their Continental Background*, Anglistische Forschungen, 217, Heidelberg: Winter

—— 1992. 'The Place of English in Germanic and Indo-European', in Hogg 1992c, 26–66

Bammesberger, A., and Wollmann, A., eds, 1990. *Britain 400–600: Language and History*, Heidelberg: Winter

Barlow, F., ed., 1992. *The Life of King Edward who Rests at Westminster*, 2nd edn, Oxford Medieval Texts, Oxford: Clarendon

Barnes, M. 1977. Review of Johannes Brøndum-Nielsen, *Gammeldansk Grammatik i Sproghistorisk Fremstilling* VI–VIII, *Saga-Book of the Viking Society*, 19, 467–71

—— 1987. 'The Origins of the Younger *fuþark* — A Reappraisal', in *Runor och Runinskrifter*, Kungl. Vitterhets Historie och Antikvitets Akademien: Konferenser, 15, Stockholm: Almqvist & Wiksell, 29–45

—— 1993a. 'Norse in the British Isles', in Faulkes and Perkins 1993, 65–84

—— 1993b. 'Towards an Edition of the Scandinavian Runic Inscriptions of The British Isles — Some Thoughts', in *Twenty-Eight Papers Presented to Hans Bekker-Nielsen on the Occasion of his Sixtieth Birthday 28 April 1993*, Odense: Odense University Press, 21–36

—— 1993c. 'Language', in Pulsiano 1993, 376–78

—— 1997. 'How "Common" was Common Scandinavian?', *North-Western European Language Evolution*, 31/32, 29–42

Barrow, J. 2000. 'Survival and Mutation: Ecclesiastical Institutions in the Danelaw in the Ninth and Tenth Centuries', in Hadley and Richards 2000, 155–76

Bately, J. M., ed., 1980. *The Old English Orosius*, EETS SS, 6, London: EETS

——, ed., 1986. *The Anglo-Saxon Chronicle: A Collaborative Edition*, vol. III: *MS A*, Cambridge: Brewer

―――― 1988. 'Old English Prose before and during the Reign of Alfred', *Anglo-Saxon England*, 17, 93–138
Baugh, A. C., and Cable, T. 1978. *A History of the English Language*, 3rd edn, London: Routledge
Bekker-Nielsen, H., Foote, P., and Olsen, O., eds, 1981. *Proceedings of the Eighth Viking Congress, Mediaeval Scandinavia* Supplements, 2, Odense: Odense University Press
Bekker-Nielsen, H., Foote, P., Jørgensen, J. H., and Nyberg, T., eds, 1981. *Hagiography and Medieval Literature: A Symposium*, Odense: Odense University Press
Bethurum, D., ed., 1957. *The Homilies of Wulfstan*, Oxford: Clarendon
―――― 1966. 'Wulfstan', in Stanley 1966, 210–46
Bibire, P. 2001. 'North Sea Language Contacts in the Early Middle Ages: English and Norse', in Liszka and Walker 2001, 88–107
Biggs, F. M., Hill, T. D., and Szarmach, P. E., eds, 1990. *Sources of Anglo-Saxon Literary Culture: A Trial Version*, Medieval and Renaissance Texts and Studies, 74, Binghamton, NY: Center for Medieval and Early Renaissance Studies
Binns, A. L. 1961. 'Ohthere's Northern Voyage', *English and Germanic Studies*, 7, 43–52
―――― 1965. 'The York Viking Kingdom: Relations Between Old English and Old Norse Culture', in Small 1965, 179–89
―――― 1980. *Viking Voyagers*, London: Heinemann
Birch, W. de Gray, ed., 1885–93. *Cartularium Saxonicum: A Collection of Charters relating to Anglo-Saxon History*, 3 vols, London: Whiting [vols I–II], Clark [vol. III]
Birkeli, F. 1971. 'The Earliest Missionary Activities from England to Norway', *Nottingham Medieval Studies*, 15, 27–37
Bjarni Einarsson, ed., 1985. *Ágrip af Nóregskonunga Sǫgum. Fagrskinna-Nóregs Konunga Tal*, Íslenzk Fornrit, 29, Reykjavík: Íslenzka Fornritafélag
Bjarni Guðnason, ed., 1982. *Danakonunga Sǫgur*, Íslenzk Fornrit, 35, Reykjavík: Íslenzka Fornritafélag
Björkman, E. 1900–02. *Scandinavian Loan-Words in Middle English*, Studien zur englischen Philologie, 7, Halle: Niemeyer
―――― 1910. *Nordische Personennamen in England in alt- und frühmittelenglischer Zeit*, Studien zur englischen Philologie, 37, Halle: Niemeyer
―――― 1918. 'Fe. Scedeland, Scedenig', *Namn och Bygd*, 6, 162–68
Björn K. Þórólfsson and Guðni Jónsson, eds, 1943. *Vestfirðinga Sǫgur*, Íslenzk Fornrit, 6, Reykjavík: Íslenzka Fornritafélag
Blair, J. 1994. *Anglo-Saxon Oxfordshire*, Stroud: Sutton
Blair, P. H. 1985. 'Whitby as a Centre of Learning in the Seventh Century', in Lapidge and Gneuss 1985, 3–32
Blake, N. 1992a. 'Introduction', in Blake 1992b, 1–22
――――, ed., 1992b. *The Cambridge History of the English Language*, vol. II: *1066–1476*, Cambridge: Cambridge University Press
―――― 1996. *A History of the English Language*, London: Macmillan
Blindheim, C.. 1975. 'Kaupang in Skiringssal: A Norwegian Port of Trade from the Viking Age', in Jankuhn, Schlesinger, and Steuer 1975, II, 40–57

Boas, F. S., and Herford, C. H., eds, 1927. *The Year's Work in English Studies* 6 (for 1925), Oxford: Oxford University Press

Boer, R. C., ed., 1888. *Ǫrvar-Odds Saga*, Leiden: Brill

Boucher, A., trans., 1983. *The Saga of Gunnlaug*, Reykjavík: Iceland Review

Bradley, H. 1904. *The Making of English*, London: Macmillan

Brate, E. 1884. *Nordische Lehnwörter im Orrmulum*, Sonderabdruck aus den Beiträge zur geschichte der deutschen sprache und literatur, 10, Halle: Karras

Brooks, N. P. 1979. 'England in the Ninth Century: The Crucible of Defeat', *Transactions of the Royal Historical Society*, 5th Series, 29, 1–20

────── 1984. *The Early History of the Church of Canterbury*, Studies in the Early History of Britain, London: Leicester University Press

Brooks, N., and Cubitt, C., eds, 1996. *St Oswald of Worcester: Life and Influence*, Studies in the Early History of Britain, London: Leicester University Press

Brøndum-Nielsen, J. 1950. *Gammeldansk Grammatik i Sproghistorisk Fremstilling*, vol. I: *Inledning, Tekstkildernes, Vokalisme*, 2nd edn, Copenhagen: Schultz

────── 1957. *Gammeldansk Grammatik i Sproghistorisk Fremstilling*, vol. II: *Konsonantisme*, 2nd edn, Copenhagen: Schultz

Buccini, A. F. 1992. 'Southern Middle English *Hise* and the Question of Pronominal Transfer in Language Contact', in Lippi-Green 1992, 11–32

Burchfield, R. W. 1956. 'The Language and Orthography of the *Ormulum* MS', *Transactions of the Philological Society*, 56–87

Burnley, D. 1989. *The Language of Chaucer*, The Language of Literature series, London: Macmillan

Bynon, T. 1977. *Historical Linguistics*, Cambridge Textbooks in Linguistics, Cambridge: Cambridge University Press

Bøgholm, N., Brusendorff, A., and Bodelsen, C. A., eds, 1930. *A Grammatical Miscellany Offered to Otto Jespersen on His Seventieth Birthday*, Copenhagen: Munksgaard

Calder, D. G., and Christy, T. C., eds, 1988. *Germania: Comparative Studies in the Old Germanic Languages and Literatures*, Woodbridge: Brewer

Callister, S. 1977. 'Sociolinguistic Approaches to Dialect Surveying in Papua New Guinea', in Loving 1977, 187–216

Cameron, K. 1959. *The Place-Names of Derbyshire*, 3 vols, EPNS, 27–29, Cambridge: Cambridge University Press

────── 1973. 'Early Field-Names in an English-named Lincolnshire Village', in Sandgren 1973, 38–43

──────, ed., 1975. *Place-Name Evidence for the Anglo-Saxon Invasion and Scandinavian Settlements*, Nottingham: EPNS

────── 1979–80. 'The Meaning and Significance of Old English *walh* in English Place-Names', *Journal of the English Place-Name Society*, 12, 1–53

────── 1989– . *The Place-Names of Lincolnshire*, 6 vols so far, EPNS, 58, 64–66, 71, 73, 77, Nottingham: EPNS

────── 1996a. *English Place-Names*, new edn, London: Batsford

——— 1996b. 'The Scandinavian Element in Minor Names and Field-Names in North-East Lincolnshire', *Nomina*, 19, 5–27
Campbell, A., ed., 1938. *The Battle of Brunanburh*, London: Heinemann
——— 1959. *Old English Grammar*, Oxford: Clarendon
———, ed., 1962. *The Chronicle of Æthelweard*, Nelson's Medieval Texts, London: Nelson
——— 1971. *Skaldic Verse and Anglo-Saxon History*, Dorothea Coke Memorial Lecture, London: University College
Campbell, J., ed., 1982. *The Anglo-Saxons*, London: Phaedon
Carver, M. O. H. 1990. 'Pre-Viking Traffic in the North Sea', in McGrail 1990, 117–25
———, ed., 1992. *The Age of Sutton Hoo: The Seventh Century in North-Western Europe*, Woodbridge: Boydell
Casad, E. H. 1974. *Dialect Intelligibility Testing*, Dallas: SIL
Cassidy, F. G., and Ringler, R. N., eds, 1971. *Bright's Old English Grammar and Reader*, 3rd edn, New York: Holt, Rinehart, & Winston
Chadwick, H. M. 1907. *The Origin of the English Nation*, Cambridge Archaeological and Ethnological Series, Cambridge: Cambridge University Press
Chambers, R. W. 1912. *Widsith: A Study in Old English Heroic Legend*, Cambridge: Cambridge University Press
——— 1959. *Beowulf: An Introduction to the Study of the Poem*, 3rd edn, with a supplement by C. L. Wrenn, Cambridge: Cambridge University Press
Chapman, J., and Hamerow, H., eds, 1997. *Migrations and Invasions in Archaeological Explanation*, British Archaeological Reports International Series, 664, Oxford: Archaeopress
Chase, C., ed., 1981. *The Dating of Beowulf*, Toronto: Toronto University Press
Christophersen, P. 1992. 'The Spoken Word in International Contacts in Carolingian Europe', *North-Western European Language Evolution*, 20, 53–64
Clark, C. 1979. 'Clark's First Three Laws of Applied Anthroponymics', *Nomina*, 3, 13–19
——— 1995. *Words, Names and History: Selected Writings of Cecily Clark*, ed. by P. Jackson, Cambridge: Brewer
Clarke, H. B., Ní Mhaonaigh, M., and Ó Floinn, R., eds, 1998. *Ireland and Scandinavia in the Early Viking Age*, Dublin: Four Courts
Clemoes, P. 1960. 'The Old English Benedictine Office, Corpus Christi College, Cambridge, MS 190, and the Relations between Ælfric and Wulfstan: A Reconsideration', *Anglia*, 78, 265–83
——— 1966. 'Ælfric', in Stanley 1966, 176–209
———, ed., 1997. *Ælfric's Catholic Homilies. The First Series. Text*, EETS SS, 17, Oxford: EETS
Clemoes, P., and Hughes, K., eds, 1971. *England Before the Conquest: Studies in Primary Sources Presented to Dorothy Whitelock*, Cambridge: Cambridge University Press
Clover, C. J. 1985. 'Icelandic Family Sagas (*Íslendingasögur*)', in Clover and Lindow 1985, 239–315
Clover, C. J., and Lindow, J., eds, 1985. *Old Norse-Icelandic Literature: A Critical Guide*, Islandica, 45, Ithaca: Cornell University Press

Coates, R. 1980–81. 'The Slighting of Strensall', *Journal of the English Place-Name Society*, 13, 50–53
Colgrave, B., ed., 1940. *Two Lives of Saint Cuthbert*, Cambridge: Cambridge University Press
——, ed., 1956. *Felix's Life of Saint Guthlac*, Cambridge: Cambridge University Press
Colgrave, B., and Mynors, R. A. B., eds, 1969. *Bede's Ecclesiastical History of the English People*, Oxford Medieval Texts, Oxford: Clarendon
Collingwood, W. G. 1908. *Scandinavian Britain*, London: Society for Promoting Christian Knowledge
—— 1927. *Northumbrian Crosses of the Pre-Norman Age*, London: Faber
Colman, F. 1992. *Money Talks: Reconstructing Old English*, Trends in Linguistics Studies and Monographs, 56, Berlin: Mouton de Gruyter
Copeland, M. G. 1983. 'Copeland: A Lost Viking Treaty?', *Cumbria*, 33, 168–71
Coupland, S. 1991. 'The Rod of God's Wrath or the People of God's Wrath? The Carolingian Theology of the Viking Invasions', *Journal of Ecclesiastical History*, 42, 535–54
Craigie, W. A. 1917. ' "Iraland" in King Alfred's "Orosius" ', *Modern Language Review*, 12, 200–01
—— 1925. 'The Nationality of King Alfred's Wulfstan', *Journal of English and Germanic Philology*, 24, 396–97
Crawford, B. E., ed., 1995. *Scandinavian Settlement in Northern Britain: Thirteen Studies of Place-Names in their Historical Context*, Studies in the Early History of Britain, London: Leicester University Press
Crawford, S. J., ed., 1922. *The Old English Version of the Heptateuch*, EETS OS, 160, Oxford: EETS
Cross, J. E. 1965. 'Oswald and Byrhtnoth', *English Studies*, 46, 93–109
Crumlin-Pedersen, O. 1984. 'Ships, Navigation and Routes in the Reports of Ohthere and Wulfstan', in Lund 1984, 30–42
Cubbin, G. P., ed., 1996. *The Anglo-Saxon Chronicle: A Collaborative Edition*, vol. VI: *MS D*, Cambridge: Brewer
Cuesta, J. F., and Silva, I. S. 2000. 'Ohthere and Wulfstan: One or Two Voyagers at the Court of King Alfred?', *Studia Neophilologica*, 72, 18–23
Dallapiazza, M., Hansen, O., Sørensen, P. M., and Bonnetain, Y. S., eds, 2000. *International Scandinavian and Medieval Studies in Memory of Gerd Wolfgang Weber*, Trieste: Edizioni Parnaso
Dance, R. 1999. '*The Battle of Maldon* line 91 and the Origins of *Call*: A Reconsideration', *Neuphilologische Mitteilungen*, 100, 143–54
—— 2000. 'Is the Verb *Die* Derived from Old Norse? A Review of the Evidence', *English Studies*, 81, 368–83
—— forthcoming. *Words Derived from Old Norse in Early Middle English: Studies in the Vocabulary of the South-West Midland Texts*, Tempe: Medieval and Renaissance Texts and Studies
Davis, N., and Wrenn, C. L., eds, 1962. *English and Medieval Studies Presented to J. R. R. Tolkien on the Occasion of his Seventieth Birthday*, London: Allen & Unwin

Delehaye, H. 1899. 'Note sur la légende de la lettre du Christ tombée du ciel', *Bulletin de l'Académie Royale Belgique, Classe des Lettres*, 1, 171–213
Deletant, D. 1977. 'The Sunday Legend', *Révue des Études Sud-Est Européenes*, 15, 431–51
Derolez, R. 1971. 'The Orientation System in the Old English Orosius', in Clemoes and Hughes 1971, 253–68
―――― 1992. 'Language Problems in Anglo-Saxon England: *barbara loquella* and *barbarismus*', in Korhammer 1992, 285–92
de Vries, J. 1961. *Altnordisches Etymologisches Wörterbuch*, Leiden: Brill
Dobbie, E. V. K., ed., 1942. *The Anglo-Saxon Minor Poems*, Anglo-Saxon Poetic Records, 6, New York: Columbia University Press
Dodgson, J. McN. 1970–97. *The Place-Names of Cheshire*, 5 vols in 7, EPNS, 44–48, 54, 74, Cambridge: Cambridge University Press / Nottingham: EPNS
Dolley, M. 1965. *Viking Coins of the Danelaw and of Dublin*, London: British Museum
―――― 1978. 'The Anglo-Danish and Anglo-Norse Coinages of York', in Hall 1978, 26–31
Domingue, N. Z. 1977. 'Middle English — Another Creole?', *Journal of Creole Studies*, 1, 89–100
Dronke, U., Guðrún P. Helgadóttir, Weber, G. W., and Bekker-Nielsen, H., eds, 1981. *Speculum Norroenum: Norse Studies in Memory of Gabriel Turville-Petre*, Odense: Odense University Press
Dumville, D. N. 1976. 'The Anglian Collection of Royal Genealogies and Regnal Lists', *Anglo-Saxon England*, 5, 23–50
―――― 1977. 'Kingship, Genealogies and Regnal Lists', in Sawyer and Wood 1977, 72–104
―――― 1978. ' "Primarius cohortis" in Adomnán's Life of Columba', *Scottish Gaelic Studies*, 13, 130–31
Dümmler, E., ed., 1895. *Epistolae Karolini Aevi II*, Monumenta Germaniae Historica, Berlin: Weidmann
Düwel, K., ed., 1998. *Runeninschriften als Quellen interdisziplinärer Forschung: Abhandlungen des Vierten Internationalen Symposiums über Runen und Runeninschriften in Göttingen vom 4.9. August 1995*, Ergänzungsbände zum Reallexikon der Germanischen Altertumskunde, 15, Berlin: Walter de Gruyter
Eaton, R., Fischer, O., Koopman, W., and van der Leek, F., eds, 1985. *Papers from the 4th International Conference on English Historical Linguistics*, Current Issues in Linguistic Theory, 41, Amsterdam: Benjamins
Einar G. Pétursson and Jónas Kristjánsson, eds, 1977. *Sjötíu ritgerðir helgaðar Jakobi Benediktssyni 20 júlí 1977*, 2 vols, Reykjavík: Stofnun Árna Magnússonar
Einar Ól. Sveinsson, ed., 1934. *Laxdæla Saga*, Íslenzk Fornrit, 5, Reykjavík: Íslenzka Fornritafélag
Einar Ól. Sveinsson and Matthías Þórðarson, eds, 1935. *Eyrbyggja Saga*, Íslenzk Fornrit, 4, Reykjavík: Íslenzka Fornritafélag
Eiríkur Jónsson and Finnur Jónsson, eds, 1892–96. *Hauksbók*, Copenhagen: Thiele
Ekblom, R. 1939–40. 'Ohthere's Voyage from Skiringssal to Hedeby', *Studia Neophilologica*, 12, 177–90
―――― 1960. 'King Alfred, Ohthere and Wulfstan', *Studia Neophilologica*, 32, 3–13

Ekwall, E. 1922. *The Place-Names of Lancashire*, Manchester: Manchester University Press
—— 1930. 'How Long Did the Scandinavian Language Survive in England?', in Bøgholm, Brusendorff, and Bodelsen 1930, 17–30
—— 1943. 'Old English *ambyrne wind*', in *Mélanges de Philologie offerts à M. Johan Melander*, Uppsala: Lundequistska Bokhandeln, 275–84
—— 1960. *The Concise Oxford Dictionary of English Place-Names*, 4th edn, Oxford: Clarendon
—— 1964. *Old English Wīc in Place-Names*, Nomina Germanica, 13, Uppsala: Lundequistska Bokhandeln
Evans, D. A. H. 1997. 'Four Philological Notes', *Saga-Book of the Viking Society*, 24, 355–60
Faltings, V. F., Walker, A. G. H., and Wilts, O., eds, 1995. *Friesische Studien II*, NOWELE Supplement, 12, Odense: Odense University Press
Farmer, D. H. 1997. *The Oxford Dictionary of Saints*, 4th edn, Oxford: Oxford University Press
Farrell, R. T., ed., 1982. *The Vikings*, Chichester: Phillimore
Faulkes, A. 1977. 'The Genealogies and Regnal Lists in a Manuscript in Resen's Library', in Einar G. Pétursson and Jónas Kristjánsson 1977, I, 177–90
—— 1993. *What Was Viking Poetry For?*, Birmingham: University of Birmingham School of English
Faulkes, A., and Perkins, R., eds, 1993. *Viking Revaluations: Viking Society Centenary Symposium 14–15 May 1992*, London: Viking Society for Northern Research
Faull, M. L. 1975. 'The Semantic Development of Old English *Wealh*', *Leeds Studies in English*, n.s., 8, 20–44
Fell, A. 1929. *A Furness Manor: Pennington and Its Church*, Ulverston: Kitchin
Fell, C. 1981a. '*Vikingarvísur*', in Dronke and others 1981, 106–22
—— 1981b. 'Hild, Abbess of Streonæshalch', in Bekker-Nielsen and others 1981, 76–99
—— 1982–83. '*Unfrið*: An Approach to a Definition', *Saga-Book of the Viking Society*, 21, 85–100
—— 1984. 'Some Questions of Language', in Lund 1984, 56–63
Fell, C., Foote, P., Graham-Campbell, J., and Thomson, R., eds, 1983. *The Viking Age in the Isle of Man*, London: Viking Society for Northern Research
Fellows-Jensen, G. 1968. *Scandinavian Personal Names in Lincolnshire and Yorkshire*, Navnestudier udgivet af Institut for Navnesforskning, 7, Copenhagen: Akademisk forlag
—— 1969. 'The Scribe of the Lindsey Survey', *Namn och Bygd*, 57, 58–74
—— 1969–70. 'The Domesday Book Account of the Bruce Fief', *Journal of the English Place-Name Society*, 2, 8–17
—— 1972. *Scandinavian Settlement Names in Yorkshire*, Navnestudier udgivet af Institut for Navneforskning, 11, Copenhagen: Akademisk forlag
—— 1975a. 'The Attitude of the Vikings to English Place-Names in Yorkshire', *Selskab for Nordisk Filologi: Årsberetning for 1971–1973*, 5–12
—— 1975b. 'The Vikings in England: A Review', *Anglo-Saxon England*, 4, 181–206
—— 1978. *Scandinavian Settlement Names in the East Midlands*, Navnestudier udgivet af Institut for Navneforskning, 16, Copenhagen: Akademisk forlag

——— 1981. 'Scandinavian Settlement in the Danelaw in the Light of the Place-Names of Denmark', in Bekker-Nielsen, Foote, and Olsen 1981, 133–45

——— 1985. *Scandinavian Settlement Names in the North-West*, Navnestudier udgivet af Institut for Navneforskning, 25, Copenhagen: Reitzels

——— 1987a. 'The Vikings' Relationship with Christianity in the British Isles: The Evidence of Place-Names Containing the Element *kirkja*', in Knirk 1987, 295–307

——— 1987b. 'York', *Leeds Studies in English*, n.s., 18, 141–55

——— 1991. 'Scandinavian Influence on the Place-Names of England', in Ureland and Broderick 1991, 337–54

——— 1992. 'Scandinavian Place-Names in the Irish Sea Province', in Graham-Campbell 1992, 31–42

——— 1994a. 'Danish Place-Names and Personal Names in England: The Influence of Cnut?', in Rumble 1994b, 125–40

——— 1994b. 'From Scandinavia to the British Isles and Back Again: Linguistic Give-and-Take in the Viking Period', in Ambrosiani and Clarke 1994, 253–68

——— 1995a. *The Vikings and Their Victims: The Verdict of the Names*, Dorothea Coke Memorial Lecture, London: University College

——— 1995b. 'Scandinavian Settlement in Yorkshire — Through the Rear-View Mirror', in Crawford 1995, 170–86

——— 1999. 'Scandinavian Settlement Names in East Anglia: Some Problems', *Nomina*, 22, 45–60

Finch, R. G., ed., 1965. *Vǫlsunga Saga: The Saga of the Volsungs*, Nelson's Icelandic Texts, London: Nelson

Finnur Jónsson, ed., 1912–15. *Den Norsk-Islandske Skjaldedigtning*, 4 vols, Copenhagen: Gyldendal

Fischer, A. 1989a. 'Lexical Change in Late Old English: From *æ* to *lagu*', in Fischer 1989b, 103–14

———, ed., 1989b. *The History and the Dialects of English: Festschrift for Eduard Kolb*, Anglistische Forschungen, 203, Heidelberg: Winter

Fischer, F. 1909. *Die Lehnwörter des Altwestnordischen*, Palaestra, 85, Berlin: Mayer & Müller

Fisiak, J. 1977. 'Sociolinguistics and Middle English: Some Socially Motivated Changes in the History of English', *Kwartalnik Neofilologiczny*, 24, 247–59

———, ed., 1995. *Linguistic Change under Contact Conditions*, Trends in Linguistics Studies and Monographs, 81, Berlin: Mouton de Gruyter

Fjalldal, M. 1993. 'How Valid Is the Anglo-Scandinavian Language Passage in *Gunnlaug's Saga* as Historical Evidence?', *Neophilologus*, 77, 601–09

Fletcher, R. 1997. *The Conversion of Europe: From Paganism to Christianity 371–1386 AD*, London: HarperCollins

Foot, S. 1991. 'Violence Against Christians: The Vikings and the Church in Ninth-Century England', *Medieval History*, 1.3, 3–16

——— 1996. 'The Making of *Angelcynn*: English Identity before the Norman Conquest', *Transactions of the Royal Historical Society*, 6th Series, 6, 25–49

Frank, R. 1978. *Old Norse Court Poetry: The Dróttkvætt Stanza*, Islandica, 42, Ithaca: Cornell University Press

——— 1994a. 'King Cnut in the Verse of His Skalds', in Rumble 1994b, 106–24

——— 1994b. 'Poetic Words in Late Old English Prose', in Godden, Gray, and Hoad 1994, 87–107

Frankis, J. 2000. 'Sidelights on Post-Conquest Canterbury: Towards a Context for an Old Norse Runic Charm (DR 419)', *Nottingham Medieval Studies*, 44, 1–27

Frazer, W. O., and Tyrrell, A., eds, 2000. *Social Identity in Early Medieval Britain*, Studies in the Early History of Britain, London: Leicester University Press

Fulk, R. D. 1992. *A History of Old English Meter*, Philadelphia: University of Pennsylvania Press

Gade, K. E. 1991. '*Fang* and *fall*: Two Skaldic *termini technici*', *Journal of English and Germanic Philology*, 90, 361–74

——— 1995. *The Structure of Old Norse Dróttkvætt Poetry*, Islandica, 49, Ithaca: Cornell University Press

Gameson, R. 1995. *The Role of Art in the Late Anglo-Saxon Church*, Oxford: Clarendon

Garmonsway, G. N., trans., 1972. *The Anglo-Saxon Chronicle*, Everyman's Library, London: Dent

Gatch, M. McC. 1977. *Preaching and Theology in Anglo-Saxon England: Ælfric and Wulfstan*, Toronto: Toronto University Press

Geipel, J. 1971. *The Viking Legacy: The Scandinavian Influence on the English and Gaelic Languages*, Newton Abbot: David & Charles

Gelling, M. 1984. *Place-Names in the Landscape*, London: Dent

——— 1988. *Signposts to the Past*, 2nd edn, Chichester: Phillimore

——— 1992. *The West Midlands in the Early Middle Ages*, Studies in the Early History of Britain, Leicester: Leicester University Press

Gelling, M., and Cole, A. 2000. *The Landscape of Place-Names*, Stamford: Tyas

Giles, H., and Smith, P. M. 1979. 'Accommodation Theory: Optimal Levels of Convergence', in Giles and St. Clair 1979, 45–65

Giles, H., and St. Clair, R. N., eds, 1979. *Language and Social Psychology*, Oxford: Blackwell

Gimson, A. C. 1980. *An Introduction to the Pronunciation of English*, 3rd edn, London: Arnold

Gneuss, H. 1993. '*Anglicae linguae interpretatio*: Language Contact, Lexical Borrowing and Glossing in Anglo-Saxon England', Sir Israel Gollancz Memorial Lecture, *Proceedings of the British Academy*, 82, 107–48

Godden, M. R., ed., 1979. *Ælfric's Catholic Homilies. The Second Series. Text*, EETS SS, 5, Oxford: EETS

——— 1980. 'Ælfric's Changing Vocabulary', *English Studies*, 61, 206–23

——— 1985. 'Ælfric's Saints' Lives and the Problem of Miracles', *Leeds Studies in English*, n.s., 16, 83–100

——— 1994. 'Apocalypse and Invasion in Late Anglo-Saxon England', in Godden, Gray, and Hoad 1994, 130–62

―――― 2000. *Ælfric's Catholic Homilies: Introduction, Commentary and Glossary*, EETS SS, 18, Oxford: EETS

Godden, M., Gray, D., and Hoad, T., eds, 1994. *From Anglo-Saxon to Early Middle English: Studies Presented to E. G. Stanley*, Oxford: Clarendon

Gordon, E. V. 1927a. *An Introduction to Old Norse*, Oxford: Clarendon

―――― 1927b. 'Old English Studies', in Boas and Herford 1927, 67–82

Gover, J. E. B., Mawer, A., and Stenton, F. M. 1933. *The Place-Names of Northamptonshire*, EPNS, 10, Cambridge: Cambridge University Press

―――― 1939. *The Place-Names of Wiltshire*, EPNS, 16, Cambridge: Cambridge University Press

―――― 1940. *The Place-Names of Nottinghamshire*, EPNS, 17, Cambridge: Cambridge University Press

Gover, J. E. B., Mawer, A., Stenton, F. M., and Houghton, F. T. S. 1936. *The Place-Names of Warwickshire*, EPNS, 13, Cambridge: Cambridge University Press

Gradon, P. 1962. 'Studies in Late West-Saxon Labialization and Delabialization', in Davis and Wrenn 1962, 63–76

Graham, T. 1996. 'A Runic Entry in an Anglo-Saxon Manuscript from Abingdon and the Scandinavian Career of Abbot Rodulf (1051–2)', *Nottingham Medieval Studies*, 40, 16–24

Graham-Campbell, J., ed., 1992. *Viking Treasure from the North West: The Cuerdale Hoard in Its Context*, National Museums and Galleries on Merseyside Occasional Papers, Liverpool Museum, 5, Liverpool: National Museums and Galleries on Merseyside

Graham-Campbell, J., Hall, R., Jesch, J., and Parsons, D. N., eds, 2001. *Vikings and the Danelaw: Select Papers from the Proceedings of the Thirteenth Viking Congress, Nottingham and York, 21–30 August 1997*, Oxford: Oxbow

Green, D. H. 1998. *Language and History in the Early Germanic World*, Cambridge: Cambridge University Press

Greene, D. 1978. 'The Evidence of Language and Place-Names in Ireland', in Andersson and Sandred 1978, 119–23

Griffith, M. 1998. 'Dialect and Literary Dialect in *The Battle of Maldon*', *Notes and Queries*, n.s., 45, 272–73

Görlach, M. 1986. 'Middle English — a Creole?', in Kastovsky and Szwedek 1986, I, 329–44

Hadley, D. M. 1996. 'Conquest, Colonization and the Church: Ecclesiastical Organization in the Danelaw', *Historical Research*, 69, 109–28

―――― 1997. ' "And they proceeded to plough and to support themselves": The Scandinavian Settlement of England', *Anglo-Norman Studies*, 19, 69–96

―――― 2000a. *The Northern Danelaw: Its Social Structure c.800–1100*, Studies in the Early History of Britain, London: Leicester University Press

―――― 2000b. ' "Cockle amongst the Wheat": The Scandinavian Settlement of England', in Frazer and Tyrrell 2000, 111–35

―――― 2001. 'In Search of the Vikings: The Problems and the Possibilities of Interdisciplinary Approaches', in Graham-Campbell and others 2001, 13–30

Hadley, D. M., and Richards, J. D., eds, 2000. *Cultures in Contact: Scandinavian Settlement in England in the Ninth and Tenth Centuries*, Studies in the Early Middle Ages, 2, Turnhout: Brepols

Hald, K. 1978. '*A*-Mutation in Scandinavian Words in England', in Andersson and Sandred 1978, 99–106

Hall, R. A., ed., 1978. *Viking Age York and the North*, Council for British Archaeology Research Report, 27, London: Council for British Archaeology

—— 1989. 'The Five Boroughs of the Danelaw: A Review of Present Knowledge', *Anglo-Saxon England*, 18, 149–206

—— 1994. *Viking Age York*, English Heritage series, London: Batsford/English Heritage

Hansen, B. H. 1984. 'The Historical Implications of the Scandinavian Linguistic Element in English: A Theoretical Evaluation', *North-Western European Language Evolution*, 4, 53–95

Harmer, F. E. 1952. *Anglo-Saxon Writs*, Manchester: Manchester University Press

Hart, C. 1992. *The Danelaw*, London: Hambledon

Haugen, E. 1950. 'The Analysis of Linguistic Borrowing', *Language*, 26, 210–31

—— 1966. 'Semicommunication: The Language Gap in Scandinavia', *Sociological Inquiry*, 36, 280–97

——, ed., 1972. *First Grammatical Treatise: The Earliest Germanic Phonology*, The Classics of Linguistics series, London: Longman

—— 1976. *The Scandinavian Languages*, London: Faber

—— 1993. 'Dialects', in Pulsiano 1993, 130–34

Hervey, F., ed., 1907. *Carolla Sancti Eadmundi: The Garland of Saint Edmund King and Martyr*, London: Murray

Hicks, C., ed., 1992. *England in the Eleventh Century: Proceedings of the 1990 Harlaxton Symposium*, Harlaxton Medieval Studies, 2, Stamford: Watkins

Higham, N. J., and Hill, D. H., eds, 2001. *Edward the Elder 899–924*, London: Routledge

Hill, J. 1993. 'Pilgrimage and Prestige in the Icelandic Sagas', *Saga-Book of the Viking Society*, 23, 433–53

Hill, J. H., Mistry, P. J., and Campbell, L., eds, 1998. *The Life of Language: Papers in Linguistics in Honor of William Bright*, Trends in Linguistics Studies and Monographs, 108, Berlin: Mouton de Gruyter

Hills, C. 1991. 'The Archaeological Context of Runic Finds', in Bammesberger 1991, 41–59

Hines, J. 1984. *The Scandinavian Character of Anglian England in the Pre-Viking Period*, British Archaeological Reports British Series, 124, Oxford: British Archaeological Reports

—— 1990. 'Philology, Archaeology and the *adventus Saxonum vel Anglorum*', in Bammesberger and Wollmann 1990, 17–36

—— 1991. 'Scandinavian English: A Creole in Context', in Ureland and Broderick 1991, 403–27

—— 1992. 'The Scandinavian Character of Anglian England: An Update', in Carver 1992, 315–29

—— 1994. 'The Becoming of the English: Identity, Material Culture and Language in Early Anglo-Saxon England', *Anglo-Saxon Studies in Archaeology and History*, 7, 49–59

―――― 1995a. 'Focus and Boundary in Linguistic Varieties in the North-West Germanic Continuum', in Faltings, Walker, and Wilts 1995, 35–62

―――― 1995b. 'Egill's Hǫfuðlausn in Time and Place', *Saga-Book of the Viking Society*, 24, 83–104

Hines, J., and Odenstedt, B. 1987. 'The Undley Bracteate and Its Runic Inscription', *Studien zur Sachsenforschung*, 6, 73–94

Hock, H. H. 1991. *Principles of Historical Linguistics*, 2nd edn, Berlin: Mouton de Gruyter

Hockett, C. F. 1987. *Refurbishing Our Foundations*, Current Issues in Linguistic Theory, 56, Amsterdam: Benjamins

Hofmann, D. 1955. *Nordisch-Englische Lehnbeziehungen der Wikingerzeit*, Bibliotheca Arnamagnæana, 14, Copenhagen: Munksgaard

Hofstra, T., Houwen, L. A. J. R., and MacDonald, A. A., eds, 1995. *Pagans and Christians: The Interplay between Christian Latin and Traditional Germanic Cultures in Early Medieval Europe*, Mediaevalia Groningana, 16, Germania Latina, 2, Groningen: Forsten

Hogg, R. M. 1992a. *A Grammar of Old English*, vol. I: *Phonology*, Oxford: Blackwell

―――― 1992b. 'Introduction', in Hogg 1992c, 1–25

――――, ed., 1992c. *The Cambridge History of the English Language*, vol. I: *The Beginnings to 1066*, Cambridge: Cambridge University Press

Holman, K. 1996. *Scandinavian Runic Inscriptions in the British Isles: Their Historical Context*, Senter for Middelalderstudier Skrifter, 4, Trondheim: Tapir

Howe, N. 1989. *Migration and Mythmaking in Anglo-Saxon England*, New Haven: Yale University Press

Howe, S. 1996. *The Personal Pronouns in the Germanic Languages: A Study of Personal Pronoun Morphology and Change in the Germanic Languages from the First Records to the Present Day*, Studia Linguistica Germanica, 43, Berlin: Mouton de Gruyter

Hudson, R. A. 1996. *Sociolinguistics*, 2nd edn, Cambridge Textbooks in Linguistics, Cambridge: Cambridge University Press

Hug, S. 1987. *Scandinavian Loanwords and Their Equivalents in Middle English*, European University Studies, Series 21, Linguistics, 62, Bern: Lang

Hull, V. 1966. 'Cáin Domnaig', *Ériu*, 20, 151–77

Innes, M. 2000. 'Danelaw Identities: Ethnicity, Regionalism, and Political Allegiance', in Hadley and Richards 2000, 65–88

Insley, J. 1979. 'Regional Variation in Scandinavian Personal Nomenclature in England', *Nomina*, 3, 52–60

―――― 1986. 'Toponymy and Settlement in the North-West', *Nomina*, 10, 169–76

―――― 1994. *Scandinavian Personal Names in Norfolk: A Survey Based on Medieval Records and Place-Names*, Acta Academiae Regiae Gustavi Adolphi, 62, Uppsala: Almqvist & Wiksell

Jackson, K. 1953. *Language and History in Early Britain*, Edinburgh: Edinburgh University Press

Jankuhn, H., Schlesinger, W., and Steuer, H., eds, 1975. *Vor- und Frühformen der europäischen Stadt im Mittelalter*, 2 vols, Abhandlungen der Akademie der Wissenschaften in

Göttingen, Philologisch-Historische Klasse Dritte Folge, 84, Göttingen: Vandenhoeck & Ruprecht

Jesch, J. 2000. 'Knútr in Poetry and History', in Dallapiazza and others 2000, 243–56

——— 2001. 'Skaldic Verse in Scandinavian England', in Graham-Campbell and others 2001, 313–25

Jespersen, O. 1956. *Growth and Structure of the English Language*, 9th edn, Oxford: Blackwell

Johannesson, N.-L. 1995. 'Old English versus Old Norse Vocabulary in the *Ormulum*: The Choice of Third Person Plural Personal Pronouns', in Melchers and Warren 1995, 171–80

John, E. 1996. *Reassessing Anglo-Saxon England*, Manchester: Manchester University Press

Johnson, D. F. 1995. 'Euhemerisation versus Demonisation: The Pagan Gods and Ælfric's *De Falsis Diis*', in Hofstra, Houwen, and MacDonald 1995, 35–69

Jónas Kristjánsson, ed., 1956. *Eyfirðinga Sǫgur*, Íslenzk Fornrit, 9, Reykjavík: Íslenzka Fornritafélag

Jones, G. 1952. 'Egill Skallagrímsson in England', Sir Israel Gollancz Memorial Lecture, *Proceedings of the British Academy*, 38, 127–44

Jordan, R. 1906. *Eigentümlichkeiten des anglischen Wortschatzes*, Anglistische Forschungen, 17, Heidelberg: Winter

Jost, K. 1950. *Wulfstanstudien*, Swiss Studies in English, 23, Bern: Francke

Jørgensen, O. 1985. *Alfred den Store: Danmarks Geografi*, NOWELE Supplement, 1, Odense: Odense University Press

Kahle, B., ed., 1905. *Kristni saga*, Altnordische Saga-Bibliothek, 11, Halle: Niemeyer

Kalinke, M. E. 1983. 'The Foreign Language Requirement in Medieval Icelandic Romance', *Modern Language Review*, 78, 850–61

Karker, A. 1977. 'The Disintegration of the Danish Tongue', in Einar G. Pétursson and Jónas Kristjánsson 1977, II, 481–90

Kastovsky, D. 1992. 'Semantics and Vocabulary', in Hogg 1992c, 290–408

Kastovsky, D., and Bauer, G., eds, 1988. *Luick Revisited: Papers Read at the Luick-Symposium at Schloss Liechtenstein, 15.–18.9.1985*, Tübingen: Gunter Narr Verlag

Kastovsky, D., and Szwedek, A., eds, 1986. *Linguistics Across Historical and Geographical Boundaries in Honour of Jacek Fisiak on the Occasion of His Fiftieth Birthday*, 2 vols, Trends in Linguistics Studies and Monographs, 32, Berlin: Mouton de Gruyter

Keller, R. E. 1978. *The German Language*, London: Faber

Keller, W. 1925a. 'Skandinavischer Einfluss in der englischen Flexion', in Keller 1925b, 80–87

———, ed., 1925b. *Probleme der englischen Sprache und Kultur: Festschrift Johannes Hoops zum 60. Geburtstag überreicht von Freunden und Kollegen*, Germanische Bibliothek, Abteilung 2, Band 20, Heidelberg: Winter

Kemble, J. M. 1839–48. *Codex Diplomaticus Aevi Saxonici*, 6 vols, London: English Historical Society

Kennedy, A. G. 1983. 'Cnut's Law Code of 1018', *Anglo-Saxon England*, 11, 57–81

Ker, N. R. 1957. *Catalogue of Manuscripts Containing Anglo-Saxon*, Oxford: Clarendon

Ker, W. P., Napier, A. S., and Skeat, W. W., eds, 1901. *An English Miscellany Presented to Dr Furnivall in Honour of His Seventy-Fifth Birthday*, Oxford: Clarendon

Kershaw, P. 2000. 'The Alfred-Guthrum Treaty: Scripting Accommodation and Interaction in Viking Age England', in Hadley and Richards 2000, 43–64

Keynes, S. 1980. *The Diplomas of King Æthelred 'the Unready' 978–1016: A Study in Their Use as Historical Evidence*, Cambridge Studies in Medieval Life and Thought, 3rd Series, 13, Cambridge: Cambridge University Press

——— 1991. 'The Historical Context of the Battle of Maldon', in Scragg 1991, 81–113

——— 1997. 'The Vikings in England, c. 790–1016', in Sawyer 1997, 48–82

——— 2001. 'Edward, King of the Anglo-Saxons', in Higham and Hill 2001, 40–66

Keynes, S., and Lapidge, M., trans, 1983. *Alfred the Great*, Harmondsworth: Penguin

Kisbye, T. 1982. *Vikingerne i England — sproglige spor*, Copenhagen: Akademisk forlag

Klaeber, F., ed., 1950. *Beowulf and the Fight at Finnsburg*, 3rd edn, Lexington: Heath

Knirk, J. E., ed., 1987. *Proceedings of the Tenth Viking Congress: Larkollen, Norway, 1985*, Universitetets Oldsaksamlings Skrifter, Ny rekke, 9, Oslo: Universitetets Oldsaksamling

Knox, R. A., trans., 1949. *The Old Testament, Newly Translated from the Latin Vulgate*, 2 vols, London: Burns, Oates, & Washbourne

Kock, A. 1918. 'Är Skåne de gamles Scadinavia?', *Arkiv för Nordisk Filologi*, 34, 71–88

Kolb, E. 1962. 'English Light on the Scand. Assimilation of ht > tt', *English Studies*, 43, 307–10

——— 1969. 'The Scandinavian Loanwords in English and the Date of the West Norse Change MP>PP, NT>TT, NK>KK', *English Studies*, 50, 129–40

Korhammer, M., ed., 1992. *Words, Texts and Manuscripts: Studies in Anglo-Saxon Culture Presented to Helmut Gneuss on the Occasion of His Sixty-Fifth Birthday*, Cambridge: Brewer

Krapp, G. P., ed., 1931. *The Junius Manuscript*, Anglo-Saxon Poetic Records, 1, New York: Columbia University Press

Krapp, G. P., and Dobbie, E. V. K., eds, 1936. *The Exeter Book*, Anglo-Saxon Poetic Records, 3, New York: Columbia University Press

Kuhn, H. 1955. 'Zur Gliederung der germanischen Sprachen', *Zeitschrift für deutsches Altertum und deutsche Literatur*, 86, 1–47

Kålund, K., ed., 1908–18. *Alfræði Íslenzk*, 3 vols, STUAGNL, 37, 41, 45, Copenhagen: Møller

Labov, W. 1966. *The Social Stratification of English in New York City*, Washington, D.C.: Center for Applied Linguistics

——— 1972. *Sociolinguistic Patterns*, Oxford: Blackwell

Laing, M., and Williamson, K., eds., 1994. *Speaking In Our Tongues: Proceedings of a Colloquium on Medieval Dialectology and Related Disciplines*, Cambridge: Brewer

Langenfelt, G. 1961. 'Foreign Names in Old English, A Comparison between Alfred's "Orosius" and "Widsith"', *Neuphilologische Mitteilungen*, 62, 10–22

Lapidge, M., and Gneuss, H., eds, 1985. *Learning and Literature in Anglo-Saxon England: Studies Presented to Peter Clemoes on the Occasion of His Sixty-Fifth Birthday*, Cambridge: Cambridge University Press

Lawson, M. K. 1993. *Cnut: The Danes in England in the Early Eleventh Century*, London: Longman

——— 1994. 'Archbishop Wulfstan and the Homiletic Element in the Laws of Æthelred II and Cnut', in Rumble 1994b, 141–64

Lees, C. A. 1985. 'The "Sunday Letter" and the "Sunday Lists"', *Anglo-Saxon England*, 14, 129–51

───── 1990. 'Sunday Letter', in Biggs, Hill, and Szarmach 1990, 38–40

Lehiste, I. 1958. 'Names of Scandinavians in *The Anglo-Saxon Chronicle*', *Publications of the Modern Language Association*, 73, 6–22

Liebermann, F., ed., 1898–1916. *Die Gesetze der Angelsachsen*, 3 vols, Halle: Niemeyer

Liestøl, A. 1981. 'The Viking Runes: The Transition from the Older to the Younger *Fuþark*', *Saga-Book of the Viking Society*, 20, 247–66

Lind, E. H. 1905–15. *Norsk-Isländska Dopnamn ock Fingerade Namn från Medeltiden*, Uppsala: Lundequistska Bokhandeln

Lindsay, W. M., ed., 1921. *The Corpus Glossary*, Cambridge: Cambridge University Press

Lippi-Green, R., ed., 1992. *Recent Developments in Germanic Linguistics*, Current Issues in Linguistic Theory, 93, Amsterdam: Benjamins

Liszka, T. R., and Walker, L. E. M., eds, 2001. *The North Sea World in the Middle Ages: Studies in the Cultural History of North-Western Europe*, Dublin: Four Courts

Little, A. G., and Powicke, F. M., eds, 1925. *Essays in Medieval History Presented to Thomas Frederick Tout*, Manchester: Printed for the Subscribers

Loving, R., ed., 1977. *Language Variation and Survey Techniques*, Workpapers in Papua New Guinea Languages, 21, Ukarumpa: SIL

Loyn, H. 1976. *The Vikings in Wales*, Dorothea Coke Memorial Lecture, London: Viking Society for Northern Research

Lucas, P. J., ed., 1994. *Exodus*, rev. edn, Exeter Medieval English Texts and Studies, Exeter: University of Exeter Press

Luick, K. 1914–40. *Historische Grammatik der englischen Sprache*, 1 vol. in 2 parts [all published], Leipzig: Tauchnitz

Lund, N. 1984. *Two Voyagers at the Court of King Alfred*, trans. by C. E. Fell, York: Sessions

───── 1987. 'Peace and Non-Peace in the Viking Age — Ottar in Biarmaland, the Rus in Byzantium, and Danes and Norwegians in England', in Knirk 1987, 255–69

───── 1991. '"Denemearc", "Tanmarkar But" and "Tanmaurk Ala"', in Wood and Lund 1991, 161–70

Lutz, A. 2000. 'Æthelweard's *Chronicon* and Old English Poetry', *Anglo-Saxon England*, 29, 177–214

Machan, T. W., ed., 1988. *Vafþrúðnismál*, Durham Medieval Texts, 6, Durham: Durham Medieval Texts

Malone, K. 1925. 'King Alfred's "Geats"', *Modern Language Review*, 20, 1–11

───── 1928. 'King Alfred's "Gótland"', *Modern Language Review*, 23, 336–39

───── 1930a. 'The Date of Ohthere's Voyage to Hæthum', *Modern Language Review*, 25, 78–81

───── 1930b. 'King Alfred's North: A Study in Mediaeval Geography', *Speculum*, 5, 139–67

───── 1931. 'On Wulfstan's Scandinavia', *Studies in Philology*, 28, 574–79

───── 1933. 'On King Alfred's Geographical Treatise', *Speculum*, 8, 67–78

Markey, T. L. 1976. *Germanic Dialect Grouping and the Position of Ingvaeonic*, Innsbrucker Beiträge zur Sprachwissenschaft, 15, Innsbruck: Institut für Sprachwissenschaft der Universität Innsbruck

Markus, M., ed., 1988. *Historical English: On the Occasion of Karl Brunner's 100th Birthday*, Innsbrucker Beiträge zur Kulturwissenschaft Anglistische Reihe, 1, Innsbruck: Institut für Anglistik, Universität Innsbruck

Mawer, A. 1923. 'The Redemption of the Five Boroughs', *English Historical Review*, 38, 551–57

McCrum, R., Cran, W., and MacNeil, R. 1992. *The Story of English*, rev. edn, London: Faber

McDougall, I. 1987–88. 'Foreigners and Foreign Languages in Medieval Iceland', *Saga-Book of the Viking Society*, 22, 180–233

McGrail, S., ed., 1990. *Maritime Celts, Frisians and Saxons*, Council for British Archaeology Research Report, 71, London: Council for British Archaeology

McIntosh, A. 1978. 'Middle English Word-Geography: Its Potential Role in the Study of the Long-Term Impact of the Scandinavian Settlements upon English', in Andersson and Sandred 1978, 124–30

———— 1994. 'Codes and Cultures', in Laing and Williamson 1994, 135–37

McKinnell, J. 1990. 'The Context of *Vǫlundarkviða*', *Saga-Book of the Viking Society*, 23, 1–27

———— 2001. 'Eddic Poetry in Anglo-Scandinavian Northern England', in Graham-Campbell and others 2001, 327–44

McNamara, M. 1975. *The Apocrypha in the Irish Church*, Dublin: Dublin Institute for Advanced Studies

Meaney, A. L. 1970. 'Æthelweard, Ælfric, the Norse Gods and Northumbria', *Journal of Religious History*, 6, 105–32

———— 1984. 'Ælfric and Idolatry', *Journal of Religious History*, 13, 119–35

Melchers, G., and Warren, B., eds, 1995. *Studies in Anglistics*, Acta Universitatis Stockholmiensis, Stockholm Studies in English, 85, Stockholm: Almqvist & Wiksell

Miller, T., ed., 1890–91. *The Old English Version of Bede's Ecclesiastical History of the English People*, 2 vols, EETS OS, 95, 96, London: EETS

Milliken, M. E. 1988. 'Phonological Divergence and Intelligibility: A Case Study of English and Scots', unpublished doctoral dissertation, Cornell University

Milliken, M. E., and Milliken, S. R. 1993. 'System Relationships in Dialect Intelligibility', preprint, 1993 International Language Assessment Conference, Horsleys Green

Milroy, J. 1984. 'The History of English in the British Isles', in Trudgill 1984a, 5–31

———— 1992. *Linguistic Variation and Change. On the Historical Sociolinguistics of English*, Language in Society, 19, Oxford: Blackwell

———— 1997. 'Internal vs External Motivations for Linguistic Change', *Multilingua*, 16, 311–23

Milroy, J., and Milroy, L. 1997. 'Social Network and Patterns of Language Change', in Chapman and Hamerow 1997, 73–81

Milroy, L. 1984. 'Comprehension and Context: Successful Communication and Communicative Breakdown', in Trudgill 1984b, 7–31

Mitchell, B. 1994. 'The Englishness of Old English', in Godden, Gray, and Hoad 1994, 163–81

Mitchell, B., and Robinson, F. C. 1992. *A Guide to Old English*, 5th edn, Oxford: Blackwell

Moisl, H. 1981. 'Anglo-Saxon Royal Genealogies and Germanic Oral Tradition', *Journal of Medieval History*, 7, 215–48

Morris, C. D. 1981. 'Viking and Native in Northern England: A Case-Study', in Bekker-Nielsen, Foote, and Olsen 1981, 223–44

Moulton, W. G. 1988. 'Mutual Intelligibility among Speakers of Early Germanic Dialects', in Calder and Christy 1988, 9–28

Murray, A. C. 1981. '*Beowulf*, the Danish Invasions, and Royal Genealogy', in Chase 1981, 101–12

Myhre, B. 1993. 'The Beginning of the Viking Age — Some Current Archaeological Problems', in Faulkes and Perkins 1993, 182–204

Napier, A. S., ed., 1883. *Wulfstan: Sammlung der ihm zugeschriebenen Homilien nebst Untersuchnungen über ihre Echtheit*, Sammlung englischer Denkmäler in kritischen Ausgaben, 4, Berlin: Weidmannsche Buchhandlung

——, ed., 1900. *Old English Glosses*, Anecdota Oxoniensia, 11, Oxford: Clarendon

—— 1901. 'Contributions to Old English Literature. 1. An Old English Homily on the Observance of Sunday. 2. The Franks Casket', in Ker, Napier, and Skeat 1901, 355–81

Newton, S. 1993. *The Origins of* Beowulf *and the Pre-Viking Kingdom of East Anglia*, Cambridge: Brewer

Nicolaisen, W. F. H. 1975. 'Place-Names in Bilingual Communities', *Names*, 23, 167–74

—— 1976. 'Words as Names', *Onoma*, 20, 142–63

Nielsen, H. F. 1975. 'Morphological and Phonological Parallels between Old Norse and Old English', *Arkiv för Nordisk Filologi*, 90, 1–18

—— 1985. *Old English and the Continental Germanic Languages*, 2nd edn, Innsbrucker Beiträge zur Sprachwissenschaft, 33, Innsbruck: Institut für Sprachwissenschaft der Universität Innsbruck

—— 1989. *The Germanic Languages*, Tuscaloosa: Alabama University Press

—— 1998. 'The Linguistic Status of the Early Runic Inscriptions of Scandinavia', in Düwel 1998, 539–55

Nielsen, H. F., and Schøsler, L., eds, 1996. *The Origins and Development of Emigrant Languages*, NOWELE Supplement, 17, Odense: Odense University Press

Ní Mhaonaigh, M. 1998. 'Friend and Foe: Vikings in Ninth- and Tenth-Century Irish Literature', in Clarke, Ní Mhaonaigh, and Ó Floinn 1998, 381–402

Nordal, S., ed., 1933. *Egils Saga Skalla-Grímssonar*, Íslenzk Fornrit, 2, Reykjavík: Íslenzka Fornritafélag

Nordal, S., and Guðni Jónsson, eds, 1938. *Borgfirðinga Sǫgur*, Íslenzk Fornrit, 3, Reykjavík: Íslenzka Fornritafélag

Noreen, A. 1923. *Altnordische Grammatik*, vol. I: *Altisländische und Altnorwegische Grammatik*, 4th edn, Halle: Niemeyer

North, R. 1997. *Heathen Gods in Old English Literature*, Cambridge Studies in Anglo-Saxon England, 22, Cambridge: Cambridge University Press

Näsman, U. 1984. 'Vendel Period Glass from Eketorp-II, Öland, Sweden: On Glass and Trade from the Late 6th to the Late 8th Centuries AD', *Acta Archaeologica*, 55, 55–116

Oddr Snorrason. 1932. *Saga Óláfs Tryggvasonar*, ed. by Finnur Jónsson, Copenhagen: Gad

Odenstedt, B. 1994. 'Who Was Wulfstan? A New Theory of "Ohthere's and Wulfstan's Voyages"', *Studia Neophilologica*, 66, 147–57
———— 2000. 'The Runic Inscription on the Undley Bracteate', *Studia Neophilologica*, 72, 113–20
Okasha, E. 1971. *Hand-list of Anglo-Saxon Non-Runic Inscriptions*, Cambridge: Cambridge University Press
———— 1992. 'The English Language in the Eleventh Century: The Evidence from Inscriptions', in Hicks 1992, 333–45
O'Keeffe, J. G. 1905. 'Cáin Domnaig', *Ériu*, 2, 189–214
Olson, E., ed., 1912. *Yngvars saga víðfǫrla*, STUAGNL, 39, Copenhagen: Møller
Olszewska, E. S. 1962. 'Alliterative Phrases in the *Ormulum*: Some Norse Parallels', in Davis and Wrenn 1962, 112–27
Page, R. I. 1971. 'How Long Did the Scandinavian Language Survive in England? The Epigraphical Evidence', in Clemoes and Hughes 1971, 165–81
———— 1981. 'The Audience of *Beowulf* and the Vikings', in Chase 1981, 113–22
———— 1983. 'The Manx Rune-Stones', in Fell and others 1983, 133–46
———— 1987. *'A Most Vile People': Early English Historians on The Vikings*, Dorothea Coke Memorial Lecture, London: Viking Society for Northern Research
———— 1991. 'Anglo-Saxon Runic Studies: The Way Ahead?', in Bammesberger 1991, 15–39
———— 1993. 'Runes in Two Anglo-Saxon Manuscripts', *Nytt om Runer*, 8, 15–19
———— 1999. *An Introduction to English Runes*, 2nd edn, Woodbridge: Boydell
Parkes, M. B. 1983. 'On the Presumed Date of the Manuscript of the *Orrmulum*: Oxford, Bodleian Library, MS Junius 1', in Stanley and Gray 1983, 115–27
Parsons, D. N. 1996. 'The Language of the Anglo-Saxon Settlers', in Nielsen and Schøsler 1996, 141–56
———— 2001. 'How Long Did the Scandinavian Language Survive in England? Again', in Graham-Campbell and others 2001, 299–312
Parsons, D., and Styles, T. 1997. *The Vocabulary of English Place-Names (Á-Box)*, Nottingham: Centre for English Name Studies
Penzl, H. 1947. 'The Phonemic Split of Germanic *k* in Old English', *Language*, 23, 34–42
Peters, H. 1981. 'Zum scandinavischen Lehngut im Altenglischen', *Sprachwissenschaft*, 6, 85–124
Plummer, C., ed., 1896. *Venerabilis Baedae Opera Historica*, 2 vols, Oxford: Clarendon
Plummer, C., and Earle, J., eds, 1892–99. *Two of the Saxon Chronicles Parallel*, 2 vols, Oxford: Clarendon
Pons Sanz, S. M. 2000. *Analysis of the Scandinavian Loanwords in the Aldredian Glosses to the Lindisfarne Gospels*, Studies in English Language and Linguistics Monographs, 9, Valencia: Lengua Inglesa, Universitat de Valencia
Poole, R. 1987. 'Skaldic Verse and Anglo-Saxon History: Some Aspects of the Period 1009–16', *Speculum*, 62, 265–98
Pope, J. C., ed., 1967–68. *Homilies of Ælfric: A Supplementary Collection*, 2 vols, EETS OS, 259, 260, Oxford: EETS

Poussa, P. 1982. 'The Evolution of Early Standard English: The Creolization Hypothesis', *Studia Anglica Posnaniensia*, 14, 69–85

Priebsch, R. 1899. 'The Chief Sources of Some Anglo-Saxon Homilies', *Otia Merseiana*, 1, 129–47

────── 1936. *Letter from Heaven on the Observance of the Lord's Day*, ed. by W. E. Collinson and A. Closs, Oxford: Blackwell

Prokosch, E. 1939. *A Comparative Germanic Grammar*, Philadelphia: Linguistic Society of America

Pulsiano, P., ed., 1993. *Medieval Scandinavia: An Encyclopedia*, New York: Garland

Quirk, R., and Wrenn, C. L. 1955. *An Old English Grammar*, London: Methuen

Raine, J., ed., 1879–94. *The Historians of the Church of York and Its Archbishops*, 3 vols, Rolls Series, 71, London: Longman [vols I–II], Eyre & Spottiswoode [vol. III]

Reaney, P. H. 1960. *The Origin of English Place-Names*, London: Routledge & Kegan Paul

Richards, J. D. 2000. *Viking Age England*, rev. edn, Stroud: Tempus

Roberts, J., and Kay, C. 1995. *A Thesaurus of Old English*, 2 vols, King's College London Medieval Studies, 11, London: King's College

Robinson, F. C. 1976. 'Some Aspects of the *Maldon* Poet's Artistry', *Journal of English and Germanic Philology*, 75, 25–40

Robinson, O. W. 1992. *Old English and Its Closest Relatives: A Survey of the Earliest Germanic Languages*, London: Routledge

Roesdahl, E. 1982. *Viking Age Denmark*, trans. by S. Margeson and K. Williams, London: British Museum

Ross, A. S. C. 1939–40. 'Old Norse Diphthongs in English', *Acta Philologica Scandinavica*, 14, 1–10

────── 1940. 'Four Examples of Norse Influence in the Old English Gloss to the Lindisfarne Gospels', *Transactions of the Philological Society*, 39–52

────── 1954. 'Ohthere's Cwenas and Lakes', *Geographical Journal*, 120, 337–46

────── 1978. 'The Este', *Notes and Queries*, n.s., 25, 100–04

────── 1981. *The* Terfinnas *and* Beormas *of Ohthere*, rev. edn, London: Viking Society for Northern Research

Rowell, G., ed., 1992. *The English Religious Tradition and the Genius of Anglicanism*, Wantage: Ikon

Ruiz Moneva, M. A. 1997. 'A Relevance Theory Approach to the Scandinavian Influence upon the Development of the English Language', *Revista Alicantina de Estudios Ingleses*, 10, 183–91

Rumble, A. R. 1994a. 'Textual Appendix: *Translatio Sancti Ælfegi Cantuariensis archiepiscopi et martyris* (*BHL* 2519): Osbern's Account of the Translation of St Ælfheah's Relics from London to Canterbury, 8–11 June 1023', in Rumble 1994b, 283–315

────── , ed., 1994b. *The Reign of Cnut: King of England, Denmark and Norway*, Studies in the Early History of Britain, London: Leicester University Press

Rynell, A. 1948. *The Rivalry of Scandinavian and Native Synonyms in Middle English especially* taken *and* nimen, Lund Studies in English, 13, Lund: Gleerup

Salway, P. 1981. *Roman Britain*, Oxford History of England, 1A, Oxford: Clarendon

Samuels, M. L. 1971. 'Kent and the Low Countries: Some Linguistic Evidence', in Aitken, McIntosh, and Hermann Pálsson 1971, 3–19
—— 1985. 'The Great Scandinavian Belt', in Eaton and others 1985, 269–81
Sandahl, B. 1964. 'On Old Norse *jó, jú* in English', *Studia Neophilologica*, 36, 266–76
Sandgren, F., ed., 1973. *Otium et Negotium: Studies in Onomatology and Library Science Presented to Olof von Feilitzen*, Stockholm: Norstedt
Saussure, F. de. 1983. *Course in General Linguistics*, trans. by R. Harris, London: Duckworth
Sawyer, P. H. 1962. *The Age of the Vikings*, London: Arnold
—— 1968. *Anglo-Saxon Charters: An Annotated List and Bibliography*, London: Royal Historical Society
—— 1975. 'The Charters of Burton Abbey and the Unification of England', *Northern History*, 10, 28–39
——, ed., 1979. *Names, Words, and Graves: Early Medieval Settlement*, Leeds: School of History, University of Leeds
——, ed., 1997. *The Oxford Illustrated History of the Vikings*, Oxford: Oxford University Press
Sawyer, P. H., and Wood, I. N., eds, 1977. *Early Medieval Kingship*, Leeds: School of History, University of Leeds
Scott, F. S. 1953–57. 'Valþjófr jarl: An English Earl in Icelandic Sources', *Saga-Book of the Viking Society*, 14, 78–94
Scragg, D., ed., 1991. *The Battle of Maldon AD 991*, Oxford: Blackwell
Searle, W. G. 1897. *Onomasticon Anglo-Saxonicum*, Cambridge: Cambridge University Press
Sedgefield, W. J., ed., 1899. *King Alfred's Old English Version of Boethius*, Oxford: Clarendon
Seip, D. A. 1955. *Norsk Språkhistorie til omkring 1370*, 2nd edn, Oslo: Aschehoug
Serjeantson, M. S. 1935. *A History of Foreign Words in English*, London: Kegan Paul
Shippey, T. A. 1985. 'Boar and Badger: An Old English Heroic Antithesis?', *Leeds Studies in English*, n.s., 16, 220–39
Sievers, E. 1891. 'Zu den angelsächsischen glossen', *Anglia*, 13, 309–32
Simek, R. 1993. *Dictionary of Northern Mythology*, trans. by A. Hall, Cambridge: Brewer
Simons, G. F. 1977. 'Phonostatistic Methods', in Loving 1977, 155–85
—— 1979. *Language Variation and Limits to Communication*, Dallas: SIL
Sisam, K. 1953a. *Studies in the History of Old English Literature*, Oxford: Clarendon
—— 1953b. 'Anglo-Saxon Royal Genealogies', *Proceedings of the British Academy*, 39, 287–346
Skautrup, P. 1956–78. 'Dansk tunge', in *Kulturhistorisk Leksikon for Nordisk Middelalder*, 22 vols, Copenhagen: Rosenkilde & Bagger, II, 662–64
Skeat, W. W., ed., 1881–1900. *Ælfric's Lives of Saints*, 4 vols, EETS OS, 76, 82, 94, 114, Oxford: EETS
Small, A., ed., 1965. *The Fourth Viking Congress*, Edinburgh: Oliver & Boyd
Smith, A. H. 1928. *The Place-Names of the North Riding of Yorkshire*, EPNS, 5, Cambridge: Cambridge University Press

―――― 1937. *The Place-Names of the East Riding of Yorkshire*, EPNS, 14, Cambridge: Cambridge University Press
―――― 1956. *English Place-Name Elements*, 2 vols, EPNS, 25–26, Cambridge: Cambridge University Press
―――― 1961–63. *The Place-Names of the West Riding of Yorkshire*, 8 vols, EPNS, 30–37, Cambridge: Cambridge University Press
―――― 1967. *The Place-Names of Westmorland*, 2 vols, EPNS, 42–43, Cambridge: Cambridge University Press
Smith, J. 1996. *An Historical Study of English: Function, Form and Change*, London: Routledge
Smithers, G. V., ed., 1987. *Havelok*, Oxford: Clarendon
Smyth, A. P. 1977. *Scandinavian Kings in the British Isles 850–880*, Oxford: Oxford University Press
―――― 1984. *Warlords and Holy Men: Scotland AD 80–1000*, New History of Scotland, 1, London: Arnold
―――― 1987. *Scandinavian York and Dublin*, 2 vols in 1, Dublin: Irish Academic Press (reprint of 1975–79 edn)
―――― 1995. *King Alfred the Great*, Oxford: Oxford University Press
Snorri Sturluson. 1941–51. *Heimskringla*, ed. by Bjarni Aðalbjarnarson, 3 vols, Íslenzk Fornrit, 26–28, Reykjavík: Íslenzka Fornritafélag
―――― 1982. *Edda: Prologue and* Gylfaginning, ed. by A. Faulkes, Oxford: Clarendon
―――― 1998. *Edda: Skáldskaparmál*, ed. by A. Faulkes, 2 vols, London: Viking Society for Northern Research
Stanley, E. G., ed., 1966. *Continuations and Beginnings: Studies in Old English Literature*, London: Nelson
―――― 1977. 'How the Elbing Deprives the Vistula of Its Name and Converts It to the Elbing's Own Use in "Vistula-Mouth" ', *Notes and Queries*, n.s., 24, 2–11
―――― 1988. 'Karl Luick's "Man schrieb wie man sprach" and English Historical Philology', in Kastovsky and Bauer 1988, 311–34
―――― 1995. 'Owen Manning (1.) on Old English *æstel* and (2.) on the Aldbrough Inscription', *Notes and Queries*, n.s., 42, 10–13
Stanley, E. G., and Gray, D., eds, 1983. *Five Hundred Years of Words and Sounds: A Festschrift for Eric Dobson*, Cambridge: Brewer
Stenton, F. M. 1909. 'Æthelwerd's Account of the Last Years of King Alfred's Reign', *English Historical Review*, 24, 79–84
―――― 1910. *Types of Manorial Structure in the Northern Danelaw*, Oxford Studies in Social and Legal History, 2, Oxford: Clarendon
―――― 1925. 'The South-western Element in the Old English Chronicle', in Little and Powicke 1925, 15–24
―――― 1927. 'The Danes in England', Raleigh Lecture on History, *Proceedings of the British Academy*, 13, 203–46

——— 1936. 'Pre-Conquest Westmorland', in *Royal Commission on Historical Monuments, England: An Inventory of the Historical Monuments in Westmorland*, London: His Majesty's Stationery Office, xlviii–lv
——— 1971. *Anglo-Saxon England*, 3rd edn, Oxford History of England, 2, Oxford: Clarendon
Stevenson, W. H., ed., 1904. *Asser's Life of King Alfred*, Oxford: Clarendon
Stokoe, W. C. 1957. 'On Ohthere's *Steorbord*', *Speculum*, 32, 299–306
Strang, B. M. H. 1970. *A History of English*, London: Methuen
Ström, H. 1939. *Old English Personal Names in Bede's History*, Lund Studies in English, 8, Lund: Gleerup
Sturtevant, A. M. 1952. 'Etymological Comments upon Certain Old Norse Proper Names in the *Eddas*', *Publications of the Modern Language Association*, 67, 1145–62
Styles, T. 1998. 'Whitby Revisited: Bede's Explanation of *Streanaeshalch*', *Nomina*, 21, 133–48
——— 2001. 'Scandinavian Elements in English Place-Names: Some Semantic Problems', in Graham-Campbell and others 2001, 289–98
Sweet, H., ed., 1871. *King Alfred's West-Saxon Version of Gregory's Pastoral Care*, 2 vols, EETS OS, 45, 50, Oxford: EETS
———, ed., 1885. *The Oldest English Texts*, EETS OS, 83, London: EETS
Syrett, M. 1994. *The Unaccented Vowels of Proto-Norse*, NOWELE Supplement, 11, Odense: Odense University Press
Sørensen, J. K. 1979. 'Place-Names and Settlement History', in Sawyer 1979, 1–33
——— 1982. *Patronymics in Denmark and England*, Dorothea Coke Memorial Lecture, London: Viking Society for Northern Research
Taylor, A. 1969. 'Hauksbok and Ælfric's De Falsis Diis', *Leeds Studies in English*, n.s., 3, 101–09
Taylor, S., ed., 1983. *The Anglo-Saxon Chronicle: A Collaborative Edition*, vol. IV: *MS B*, Cambridge: Brewer
Thacker, A. 2001. 'Dynastic Monasteries and Family Cults: Edward the Elder's Sainted Kindred', in Higham and Hill 2001, 248–63
Thomason, S. G. 1998. 'On Reconstructing Past Contact Situations', in Hill, Mistry, and Campbell 1998, 153–68
Thomason, S. G., and Kaufman, T. 1988. *Language Contact, Creolization, and Genetic Linguistics*, Berkeley: University of California Press
Thorson, P. 1936. *Anglo-Norse Studies: An Inquiry into the Scandinavian Elements in the Modern English Dialects*, Part I [all published], Amsterdam: Swets & Zeitlinger
Tolkien, J. R. R. 1927. 'Philology: General Works', in Boas and Herford 1927, 32–66
——— 1963. 'English and Welsh', in *Angles and Britons: O'Donnell Lectures*, Cardiff: University of Wales Press, 1–41
——— 1982. *Finn and Hengest: The Fragment and the Episode*, ed. by A. Bliss, London: Allen & Unwin
Townend, M. 1997. '*Ella*: An Old English Name in Old Norse Poetry', *Nomina*, 20, 23–35
——— 1998. *English Place-Names in Skaldic Verse*, EPNS Extra Series, 1, Nottingham: EPNS

―――― 2000a. 'Viking Age England as a Bilingual Society', in Hadley and Richards 2000, 89–105

―――― 2000b. 'Pre-Cnut Praise-Poetry in Viking Age England', *The Review of English Studies*, 51, 349–70

―――― 2001. 'Contextualizing the *Knútsdrápur*: Skaldic Praise-Poetry at the Court of Cnut', *Anglo-Saxon England*, 30, 145–79

Trudgill, P. 1983. *On Dialect*, Oxford: Blackwell

――――, ed., 1984a. *Language in the British Isles*, Cambridge: Cambridge University Press

――――, ed., 1984b. *Applied Sociolinguistics*, Applied Language Studies, London: Academic Press

―――― 1986. *Dialects in Contact*, Language in Society, 10, Oxford: Blackwell

Turville-Petre, E. O. G. 1964. *Myth and Religion of the North*, London: Weidenfeld & Nicolson

―――― 1972. 'The Cult of Óðinn in Iceland', in his *Nine Norse Studies*, London: Viking Society for Northern Research, 1–19

Unger, C. R., ed., 1874. *Postola Sögur*, Christiania: Bentzen

Ureland, P. S., and Broderick, G., eds, 1991. *Language Contact in the British Isles*, Tübingen: Niemeyer

van Coetsem, F. 1988. *Loan Phonology and the Two Transfer Types in Language Contact*, Publications in Language Sciences, 27, Dordrecht: Foris

van Houts, E. 1992. 'Women and the Writing of History in the Early Middle Ages: The Case of Abbess Matilda of Essen', *Early Medieval Europe*, 1, 53–68

Venezky, R. L., and Healey, A. diP. 1980. *A Microfiche Concordance to Old English*, Toronto: Dictionary of Old English Project, Centre for Medieval Studies, University of Toronto

Vésteinn Ólason 1990. 'Jorvik Revisited — with Egil Skalla-Grimsson', *Northern Studies*, 27, 64–75

―――― 1993. 'The Sagas of Icelanders', in Faulkes and Perkins 1993, 26–42

Voegelin, C. F., and Harris, Z. S. 1951. 'Methods for Determining Intelligibility among Dialects of Natural Languages', *Proceedings of the American Philosophical Society*, 95, 322–29

von Feilitzen, O. 1937. *The Pre-Conquest Personal Names of Domesday Book*, Nomina Germanica, 3, Uppsala: Almqvist & Wiksells

Voss, M. 1995. 'Kent and the Low Countries Revisited', in Fisiak 1995, 327–63

Voyles, J. B. 1968. 'Gothic and Germanic', *Language*, 44, 720–46

Wainwright, F. T. 1975. *Scandinavian England*, ed. by H. P. R. Finberg, Chichester: Phillimore

Wakelin, M. F. 1977. *English Dialects: An Introduction*, rev. edn, London: Athlone

Wall, A. 1898. 'A Contribution towards the Study of the Scandinavian Element in the English Dialects', *Anglia*, 20, 45–135

Wallace-Hadrill, J. M. 1975. *The Vikings in Francia*, Stenton Lecture, Reading: University of Reading

―――― 1988. *Bede's Ecclesiastical History of the English People: A Historical Commentary*, Oxford Medieval Texts, Oxford: Clarendon

Wallmannsberger, J. 1988. 'The "Creole Hypothesis" in the History of English', in Markus 1988, 19–36

Wareham, A. 1996. 'St Oswald's Family and Kin', in Brooks and Cubitt 1996, 46–63

Watts, L., Rahtz, P., Okasha, E., Bradley, S. A. J., and Higgitt, J. 1997. 'Kirkdale — The Inscriptions', *Medieval Archaeology*, 41, 51–99

Watts, V. 1988–89. 'Scandinavian Settlement-Names in County Durham', *Nomina*, 12, 17–63

Webb, J. F., and Farmer, D. H., trans, 1983. *The Age of Bede*, Harmondsworth: Penguin

Weber, R., ed., 1975. *Biblia Sacra iuxta Vulgatam Versionem*, rev. edn, 2 vols, Stuttgart: Württembergische Bibelanstalt

Weinreich, U. 1953. *Languages in Contact: Findings and Problems*, Publications of the Linguistic Circle of New York, 1, New York: Linguistic Circle of New York

Werner, O. 1991. 'The Incorporation of Old Norse Pronouns into Middle English: Suppletion by Loan', in Ureland and Broderick 1991, 369–401

Whitelock, D. 1930. *Anglo-Saxon Wills*, Cambridge Studies in English Legal History, Cambridge: Cambridge University Press

——, ed., 1967. *Sweet's Anglo-Saxon Reader in Prose and Verse*, 15th edn, Oxford: Clarendon

——, ed., 1976. *Sermo Lupi ad Anglos*, rev. edn, Exeter Medieval English Texts, Exeter: University of Exeter Press

—— 1979. *English Historical Documents c.500–1042*, 2nd edn, English Historical Documents, 1, London: Eyre Methuen

—— 1981. *History, Law and Literature in 10th–11th Century England*, London: Variorum Reprints

—— 1982. 'Bishop Ecgred, Pehtred and Niall', in Whitelock, McKitterick, and Dumville 1982, 47–68

Whitelock, D., McKitterick, R., and Dumville, D., eds, 1982. *Ireland in Early Mediaeval Europe: Studies in Memory of Kathleen Hughes*, Cambridge: Cambridge University Press

Whiting, B. J. 1945. 'Óhthere (Óttar) and *Egils Saga*', *Philological Quarterly*, 24, 218–26

Wilcox, J. 1991. 'Napier's "Wulfstan" Homilies XL and XLII: Two Anonymous Works from Winchester?', *Journal of English and Germanic Philology*, 90, 1–19

——, ed., 1994. *Ælfric's Prefaces*, Durham Medieval Texts, 9, Durham: Durham Medieval Texts

Williams, G. 2001. 'Hákon *Aðalsteins fóstri*: Aspects of Anglo-Saxon Kingship in Tenth-Century Norway', in Liszka and Walker 2001, 108–26

Winterbottom, M. 1967. 'The Style of Æthelweard', *Medium Aevum*, 36, 109–18

——, ed., 1972. *Three Lives of English Saints*, Toronto Medieval Latin Texts, Toronto: Pontifical Institute of Mediaeval Studies

Wolff, H. 1959. 'Intelligibility and Inter-Ethnic Attitudes', *Anthropological Linguistics*, 1.3, 34–41

Wollmann, A. 1996. 'Scandinavian Loanwords in Old English', in Nielsen and Schøsler 1996, 215–42

Wood, I., and Lund, N., eds, 1991. *People and Places in Northern Europe 500–1600: Essays in Honour of Peter Hayes Sawyer*, Woodbridge: Boydell

Wormald, P. 1982. 'Viking Studies: Whence and Whither?', in Farrell 1982, 128–53
—— 1992. 'The Venerable Bede and the "Church of the English"', in Rowell 1992, 13–32
—— 1994. '*Engla Lond*: The Making of an Allegiance', *Journal of Historical Sociology*, 7, 1–24
—— 1999a. *The Making of English Law: King Alfred to the Twelfth Century*, vol. I: *Legislation and Its Limits*, Oxford: Blackwell
—— 1999b. 'Archbishop Wulfstan and the Holiness of Society', in his *Legal Culture in the Early Medieval West: Law as Text, Image and Experience*, London: Hambledon, 225–51
Wright, J. 1910. *Grammar of the Gothic Language*, Oxford: Clarendon
Wright, J., and Wright, E. M. 1925. *Old English Grammar*, 3rd edn, Oxford: Clarendon
Wright, T., and Wülcker, R. P. 1884. *Anglo-Saxon and Old English Vocabularies*, 2 vols, London: Tübner
Yamagiwa, J. K. 1967. 'Dialect Intelligibility in Japan', *Anthropological Linguistics*, 9, 1–17
Zachrisson, R. E. 1909. *A Contribution to the Study of Anglo-Norman Influence on English Place-Names*, Lunds Universitets Årsskrift Ny Fjöld, Första Afdelningen, IV, 3, Lund: Ohlsson
Zupitza, J., ed., 1880. *Ælfric's Grammatik und Glossar*, Sammlung englischer Denkmäler in kritischen Ausgaben, 1, Berlin: Weidmannsche Buchhandlung

Index

Abbo 128, 175–6
Abingdon monastery 193
accommodation theory 12, 196, 204–5
Achurch Nth 74
Ackton YW 70
Adomnán 162–3, 170
Agbrigg YW 72
Agemund 193
Agilbert 163–4
Aidan 168–71
Ainsty YW 71
Akefrith La 70
Alcuin 31, 174–5
Aldbrough inscription 190–2, 194
Aldhelm 165
Aldoth Cu 71
Aldred 90, 188
Alfred (king of Wessex) 4, 6, 11 n. 7, 90–5, 98–100, 104, 108–9, 127, 129, 165–8, 170, 174
Algarkirk L 74
Aller So 4
Allerston YN 82
Alney Gl 7
Amounderness La 5, 54
Ancoats La 71
Anderchurch Lei 74
Angeln 101, 109
Anglian dialect 26–9, 34, 39, 60 n. 5, 93, 99, 107, 115 n. 45, 172
Anglo-Norman orthography 69–70
Anglo-Saxon Chronicle 8, 102, 104, 110–19, 121, 135, 139–41, 161, 171
  MS A 1–2, 4, 31, 92, 111, 117–18, 125

MS B 92, 118
MS C 92, 118
MS D 5–7, 92, 114, 118, 137 n. 67, 176 n. 20
MS E 122–3, 137 n. 67
MS F 31
Annuth 112
Antrobus Ch 73
Aramaic 170
Artbranán 162–3
Ashdown, battle of 113–4, 116–7
Ashford Db 5, 70
Aske YN 70
Askham Nt 70
Aspatria Cu 70
Asser 92, 95
Assimilation (ON) 28, 36–7, 40, 92, 139
Athelney So 4
Athelstan 5–6, 118, 128–9, 151–3, 159, 195
Auburn YE 76
Aughton YE 70
Augustine of Canterbury 163–4, 168, 170–1, 177
a-umlaut (ON) 35, 63
Austwick YW 76
Ayntrepot Cu 71
Ayton (Great and Little) YN 76
Ælfgar 186
Ælfred (an ealdorman) 4
Ælfric 90, 96 n. 13, 128–43, 161, 165, 167–71, 182, 185–6, 189
Æthelberht (king of Kent) 163, 168
Æthelbryht (king of Wessex) 2

Æthelmær 138 n. 69
Æthelred (king of England) 6, 8, 16, 90, 128, 150, 153–4, 193
Æthe(l)red (king of Wessex) 2
Æthelric of Bocking 6
Æthelweard 90, 103, 108, 110–28, 135, 138–9, 182, 185–6, 189
Æthelwulf (an ealdorman) 117–18, 138, 185
Æthelwulf (king of Wessex) 120–1, 125

Bachsecg 112
Back Mutation (OE) 26, 28, 34, 36, 63, 93
Badby Nth 74
Bakestonedale Ch 75
Baldr 125–7, 135
Barnabas 134
Barnskew We 81
Barwick YW 85
Bashall YW 81
Basil 169–71
Battle of Maldon 161–2, 170–1
Beckwith YW 57 n. 3, 71, 85
Bede 25, 101 n. 15, 110, 119–20, 122 n. 57, 163–5, 168–70, 174, 177
  Old English translation of 122–3, 164–5, 168–70
Beighton Db 71
Beldæg 125–7
Bentham YW 78
Beorhtric 1
Beormas 91, 97, 101–2, 109, 147–8
Beow 120
Beowulf 29, 92, 102–5, 108, 115 n. 46, 120–1, 127 n. 61
Berse 112–13
Beston YW 82
Bible 165–6, 170; *see also* covenant theology
  Psalms 176–7
  Jeremiah 173, 175–8
  Luke 137 n. 68
  Acts 134
  2 Corinthians 167
  James 166
Billingham Du 141

Birkenhead Ch 72
Birkenshaw La 72
Birkin YW 72
Birklands Nt 187
Birkwood L 72
Biscathorpe L 86
Bispham La 78
Bispham with Norbreck La 78
Bjarnar saga Hítdœlakappa 151
Blekinge 106, 109
Boethius 167, 170
Bornholm 106–8
Bourne L 73
Bradley Cu 86
Bradley L 72
Bradleyfield We 72
Bradleys Both YW 72
Braithwell YW 72
Brandesburton YE 73, 199
Braybrooke Nth 72
Braystones Cu 72
Brayton YW 72
Breaking (OE) 33–4
Breaks We 87
Bridekirk inscription 194
Brigham Cu 72
Brigham YE 78
Brigsley L 73
Brindle La 73
Brisco Cu 57 n. 3, 72, 81
British *see* Celtic
Brond 125
Brunanburh, battle of 128–9
Bubwith YE 85
Burgenda land see Bornholm
Bustabeck Cu 86
Butterwick YE 85
Byrhtferth 170
Byrhtnoth 161

Caesar 134
Cáin Domnaig 173 n. 16
Caldy Ch 76
Cambridge Ca 112, 116
Canterbury K 4, 193
Capture of the Five Boroughs 104, 139–41
Carlisle inscription 189, 194

Carlton Curlieu Lei 74
Carlton hybrids *see* hybrid names
Carlton in Lindrick Nt 74
Carta Dominica 17, 171–9, 182
Casewick L 86–7
Cedd 164, 170
Celtic 49, 110, 157, 162, 164–6, 190; *see also* Gaelic; Irish
Cenwealh 163–4
Ceolfrith 177
Ceolwulf 2
Cerne Abbas Do 135
Chalgrave Bd 5
charters 5, 185–6, 193
Chaucer 210
Chippingdale La 75
Chronicle of the Archbishops of York 5
Cirencester Gl 2
Clapham YW 78
Cliburn We 73
Clotherholme YW 86
Cnut 7–8, 51, 115, 128, 141, 151, 176 n. 20, 184, 186, 189–90, 192–3
Cockerham La 78
coins 8, 118, 195–6
colonial languages 184–5
Columba 162–3, 170
compensatory lengthening 38
Conisbrough YW 57 n. 3, 73, 75
Conishead inscription 194
Constantine 128
Cookham Brk 6
Copeland Cu 5
Copeland Du 5 n. 2
Corbridge, battle of 141
Cotesbach Lei 71
Cottingwith YE 85
covenant theology 173–9
Coverham YN 78
creoles *see* pidgins and creoles
Cupid 133
Cuthbert 141–2
Cuthheard 141–2
Cwena land 102, 109

Dalbury Lees Db 74
days of the week 131–4, 142

Dearham inscription 194
Deerhurst Gl 7
definite article, suffixed (ON) 183 n. 1, 198 n. 15
denasalisation (ON) 96 n. 12, 115, 208
Denhall Ch 75
Denmark 102, 107, 109, 119
Derby Db 49, 54, 118, 138, 185, 187, 189
'dialect congruity' 33 n. 12, 41, 45–6, 60–3, 181–2
dialectology 20–1
dialects, Modern English 184 n. 2
dialects, Old English 26–8; *see also* Anglian dialect; Kentish dialect; Mercian dialect; Northumbrian dialect; West Saxon dialect
dialects, Old Norse 28, 139–40, 143, 184
Domesday Book 51–3, 56, 69–70, 89, 117 n. 49
Donia 119
Draughton Nth 75
Draughton YW 75
Drax YW 75
Dublin 112, 116, 128, 140–1, 195
Dundraw Cu 75
Dunkeswick YW 87
Durham *Liber Vitae* 112–13
dǫnsk tunga 139, 157–8, 171

Eadburg 1
Eadgifu 118
Eadgyth (sister of Athelstan) 6
Eagle L 70
Ealdred 5
Eamont We 76
Eastburn YE 57 n. 3, 73, 76
Eastburn YW 73
East Keswick YW 87
Ecgbryht 1
Eddic verse 32, 124, 184
Eden Du 141
Edgar 8, 110, 129, 136
Edington, battle of 4
Edith (wife of Edward the Confessor) 186 n. 3
Edmund (king of East Anglia) 128, 136–7, 161, 175–6

Edmund (king of England) 104
Edmund Ironside 7, 176 n. 20
Edward the Elder 5
Egils saga Skalla-Grímssonar 152–4, 159–60
Eiríkr blóðøx 114 n. 44
Elbing 106 n. 27
Ellerton YE 71
Ellerton on Swale YN 71
Elstronwick YE 82
Ephrem 169–70
Escingas 110, 123
Estland/Ests 93 n. 7, 106 n. 27
euhemerism 121–2, 131 n. 63, 135 n. 65
Exeter D 111
Exodus 104 n. 22, 166–7
Eynsham O 138 n. 69
Eyuuysl 113

Fagrskinna 154, 160
Falster 107, 109
Featherstone YW 82
Felix 162
Fenrisúlfr 124–5
field-names 47–8, 54
Figdale Ch 75
Finns 91, 97, 102, 109
Finnsburh Fragment 103, 116 n. 48
First Grammatical Treatise 156–8
Fishlake YW 76
Fiskerton L 76
Fiskerton Nt 76
Flateyjarbók 154–6
Fonaby L 86
Fosham YE 78
Fóstbrœðra saga 151
Fracture (ON) 26, 34, 36, 63
Framland L 113 n. 39
Frampton L 113 n. 39
Franethorp L 113 n. 39
Frankish 163–4, 168, 177
Freyja 133
Frīg *see* Frigg
Frigg 125, 131–4, 142–3
Friþogar 125
Friþowald 125
Frœna 113

Gaelic 50
Ganstead YE 84
Gargrave YW 77
Gateforth YW 77
Gavi *see* Gevis
Gayton le Wold L 77
Geddington Nth 77
Gemination 38
genealogies 121–7, 135
Germanic 11, 16, 20–6, 33, 35, 37, 39, 181, 199; *see also* North-West Germanic
'gestalt perception' 44, 60, 64–5
Gevis 126
Giggleswick YW 86
Gilling YN 86
glosses and glossaries 131 n. 63, 134, 140, 165; *see also* Lindisfarne Gospels, glosses to
Goodmanham YE 77
Gosberton L 74
Gothic 21–4
Gotland 107, 109
Goverton Nt 114 n. 41
Greasby Ch 74
Greek 166, 168–70
Gregory the Great 163–6, 168, 171
Gressingham La 78
Grimm's Law 20, 37
Grimsby L 159
Grimston hybrids *see* hybrid names
Grœnlendinga saga 150
Gumley Lei 77
Gunnlaugs saga ormstungu 16, 145, 150–1, 153–4, 156–8, 171
Guthfrid 113–14, 188
Guthlac 162
Guthred *see* Guthfrid
Guthrum 4, 113–14
Guðferð 116

Hákon Haraldsson *Aðalsteinsfóstri* 151–2
Hålgoland see Hålogaland
Harald (a Scandinavian *jarl*) 114
Haraldr hárfagri 151–2
Hardwick Nt 79
Harold Godwineson 154–6

Haruc 114
Haselbech Nth 77
Hatfield YW 77
Hauksbók 133–4, 135 n. 64, 139 n. 71
Hauksfljót 159
Havelok 158 n. 7, 200, 210
Hawkswick YW 79
Hawksworth Nt 79
Hazlebadge Db 78
Healfdene (brother of Ívarr) 2, 114–15
Healfdene (a Scandinavian king) 114
Healfdene (father of Hrothgar) 115 n. 45
Hebrew 166, 168, 170
Hedeby 91, 94, 99, 103–5, 107, 109, 119
Heimskringla 151–2, 159–61
Hengest 122–4
Heorot 29
Heremod 121 n. 55
Hessle YE 78
Hessle YW 78
Heversham We 78
Heysham La 78
Heytheby L 119 n. 52
High Melton YW 80
Historia de Sancto Cuthberto 90, 141–2, 187–8
Holbeach L 71
Holbeck Farm Nt 72
Holme, battle of the 114, 118
Holtham L 84
Holtzmann's Law 40, 142
Hope Db 5
Horsa 122
Hotham YE 86
Howbeck Ch 71
Howden YE 79
Humberston(e) L 82
hybrid names 54–7
Hæsten 115
Hålogaland 91, 97, 103, 109
Hǫðr 125

Iceland 104, 133
'Icelandic school' 145–6
i-mutation/*i*-umlaut 34–5, 62
inflexions, loss of 194, 196–201

inscriptions, non-runic 189–92, 194; *see also* runes and runic inscriptions
intelligibility testing 11–17, 51, 68, 181–3
intelligibility theory 32, 41, 43–6, 64–5, 68, 100, 179, 182–3
interpreters 3, 94–5, 98–101, 109, 148, 161–71, 177, 182–3
Ireland 49, 104, 109, 148–9, 173
Irish 148–9, 163, 168–70, 173
i-umlaut *see i*-mutation
Ívarr (son of Ragnarr loðbrók) 6, 115–16, 128, 161, 195
Ívarr (a Scandinavian king) 115–16

/j/, loss of (ON) 40
Jelling 102
Jerome 166–8, 170
Jove 129–32, 134–5, 140
Jupiter *see* Jove
Jutes/Jutland 22, 29, 102–3, 105, 109, 119–20

Kaupang 105
Kelfield L 87
Kelfield YE 87
Kelk (Great and Little) YE 87
Kellington YW 87
Kentish dialect 26–8, 30, 34, 36
Kesteven L 116, 118
Keswick Cu 87
Kilburn YN 73
Kilby Lei 87
Kildwick YW 87
Kilnwick YE 85
Kilpin YE 87
Kilsby Nth 87
Kilton YN 87
King's Meaburn We 73
Kir(k)by names 49
Kirkdale inscription 190–1, 194
Kirkham La 57 n. 3, 74, 78
Kirkham YE 75
Kirton in Lindsey L 75
Konráðs saga keisarasonar 147
Kristni saga 149

Labialisation and Delabialisation (OE) 34–5
Labial Umlaut (ON) 35–6
Landnámabók 133
Langdale (Orton) We 75
Langdales We 75
Langeland 107, 109
language death, Old Norse 187, 189–90, 200–1, 204–9
Latin 166–8, 170, 190, 194
law-codes 7–8, 158, 192
Laxdæla saga 148–9, 162
Leake L 79
Leake YN 79
Lebberston YN 199
Leek St 80
Legbourne L 80
Leiðarvísir 149–50
Leofric 186
Letter from Heaven see Carta Dominica
Levisham YN 78
lexicostatistics 14–15, 24
Leyburn YN 73
Lindisfarne 1
Lindisfarne Gospels, glosses to 90, 188
literacy 187–96
Littledale La 80
loanwords 6 n. 3, 7 n. 4, 7 n. 5, 10, 36, 47–8, 52, 89–90, 92, 95–9, 111, 128, 158 n. 7, 184, 187–9, 191–3, 199–210
Loki 125
Lothersdale YW 86
Louthesk L 71
Lund 93 n. 7
Lystra 134
Låland 107, 109

manuscripts
AM 1 e β II 126
CCCC 57 193
CCCC 144 140
CCCC 162 175–9
CCCC 178 143
CCCC 183 122–3
CCCC 201 7–8
CCCC 419 and 421 142 n. 74

London, BL, Cotton Cleopatra A.iii 140, 165
London, BL, Cotton Tiberius A.xiv 122 n. 57
London, BL, Cotton Tiberius B.i 93, 102
London, BL, Cotton Tiberius B.v 122–3, 126
London, BL, Cotton Vespasian B.vi 122–3
London, BL, Royal 5.E.xi 165
London, BL, Royal 6.A.vi 165
London, Lambeth Palace Library 489 172, 174–9
Munich, Bayerische Staatsbibliothek clm 9550 175
Oxford, Bodleian Library, Digby 146 165
Oxford, Bodleian Library, Hatton 113 131 n. 63, 142 n. 74
Paris, Bibliothèque nationale, lat. 7585 140 n. 73
Stockholm, Kungliga Biblioteket, A.135 4
marriages, mixed 6, 197, 204
Marrick YN 79
Mars 129–31
Martin of Braga 129
Maulds Meaburn We 73
Meathop We 80
Melbourne YE 80
Mercian dialect 78 n.7
Mercury 129–35
metathesis 39, 61, 73 n. 3, 113
Middleham YN 78, 80
Middleton YW 80
migrations, Anglo-Saxon 24–7, 29–30, 41, 123, 164, 174 n. 19, 181
Milton Db 80
Minskip YW 86
missionaries 138, 149, 163, 177
Modern Icelandic 32 n. 11, 96 n. 13
Monophthongisation (OEN) 28, 106
Morkinskinna 154, 160
Mortham YN 78
Mythop La 80
Möre 107–9

Napier XLII 142 n. 74
Napier LVII 172, 174–9
nasals, loss of 38; *see also* denasalisation (ON)
Naseby Nth 74
Newball L 74
Noah 121 n. 55, 122
Norman-French names 47, 52
North Stainley YW 83
Northumbrian dialect 40, 78 n. 7
North-West Germanic 22–5, 27 n. 8, 28, 33, 41, 181
Norway 29, 96–7, 106, 109

Oda 138 n. 70
Oddr Snorrason 148
Offa 1
Ohthere (a seafarer) 11 n. 7, 90–109, 182, 199
Ohthere (a Scandinavian *jarl* killed in 911) 91–2
Ohthere (a Scandinavian *jarl* active in 915) 91–2
Ohthere (son of Ongentheow) 92
Óláfr *ball* 141–2
Óláfr cuaran 112
Óláfr Guðfriðsson 128–9, 195–6
Óláfr Tryggvason 148
Ongentheow 92
Orc 186, 193
Ormulum 184 n. 2, 187 n. 4, 208–10
Orosius, Old English translation of 90–109, 119–20, 182, 199
Osbearn 116
Osbern of Canterbury 186
Oscytel (a Scandinavian king) 116
Oscytel (archbishop of York) 138 n. 70
Oswald (archbishop of York) 138 n. 70
Oswald (king of Northumbria) 168–9
Oxford O 7, 8 n. 6
Óðinn 121–7, 129–43, 195

paganism 92 n. 2, 173–9, 190, 195
Palatal Diphthongisation (OE) 28, 34, 60 n. 5
Palatalisation and Assibilation (OE) 39, 48, 54, 61

Páls saga postola 134
Paul 134
Peakirk Nth 75
Pennington inscription 189, 193–4, 200–1, 204
personal names 10, 17, 47, 79, 82 n. 11, 84 n. 12, 85–7, 89, 91–3, 110, 112–17, 125, 132–3, 165, 184–6, 190, 191 n. 9, 208
phonostatistics 15, 45–6
Pictish 163, 170
pidgins and creoles 11, 198–9
place-names 2, 10, 17, 47–87, 89, 101–10, 113 n. 39, 114 n. 41, 114 n. 43, 117–22, 157–9, 181–2, 184–5, 187–9, 191 n. 9, 199–200, 203
Pliny 108 n. 33
Plungar Lei 77
Prestwold Lei 84
pronouns, personal 191, 205, 208

Quenby Lei 74

Radstone Nth 83
Ragnald 116
Ragnall 141
Ragnarr loðbrók 2, 114–15, 159
Ravenstonedale We 83
Rawcliff Bank YN 80
reindeer 95, 97, 207
Repton Db 112, 116
Retraction (OE) 34, 115 n. 45
Rhine 119
Rhotacism 38
Ribston (Great and Little) YW 83
Richard of Cirencester 186
rising diphthongs 26, 36, 63
Riskenton L 86
R-mutation 38
Rockcliffe Cu 80
Roeburndale La 73
Roger of Wendover 114 n. 44
Romaldkirk YN 75
Roman alphabet 32, 156, 190, 192–5
Rudston YE 83
Rugby Wa 74

runes and runic inscriptions 21–2, 23 n. 2, 25 n. 6, 32, 38, 40 n. 17, 184, 189–90, 192–4, 200–1, 204
Ruskington L 86

Saltmarske YE 86
Saturn 129–31, 135
Saxo Grammaticus 152 n. 4
Saxons/Saxony 105, 108, 119–20, 150, 157–8
Scaldingi 141
Scaldwell Nth 86
Scalford Lei 86
Scamblesby L 86
Scarrington Nt 81
Sceaf legend 120–1, 126
Schleswig 119
Scīringesheal 91, 97, 105, 109
Scopwick L 86
Scorton YN 82
Scrayingham YE 87
Scredington L 87
Screveton Nt 87
Scridefinnas see Finns
Scriven YW 87
Scrooby Nt 87
Scula 141
Scyld 120–1
Second Fronting (OE) 78 n. 7
Severn, River 7, 165
Shaftesbury Do 8
Shallcross Manor Db 81
Sharpening (ON) 40, 142
Shelley YW 81
Sherbrook Lodge Db 72
Sherburn in Elmet YW 82
Shippen YW 87
ships and sailing 1, 6 n. 3, 91, 96–9, 111, 203–4
Shirley Db 87
Shitlington YW 87
Shoby Lei 74
Shrigley Park Ch 87
Sigeferð (a Scandinavian *piraticus*) 116
Sigeferð (of the Secgan) 116 n. 48
Sigtryggr caoch 5–6
Sigtryggr silkiskegg 195 n. 13

Sihtrix 'the older' 117
Sihtrix 'the younger' 117
Silecroft Cu 81
Sillende 105, 109
Siward digri 186
skaldic verse 32, 51, 103, 105, 111 n. 38, 115–16, 141, 153–6, 158 n. 7, 184, 189, 193
Skeffington Lei 81
Skelbrooke YW 81
Skellingthorpe L 81
Skelton Cu 81
Skelton YE 81
Skelton (Bulmer) YN 82
Skelton (Langbargh East) YN 82
Skelton (Skyrack) YW 82
Skelton-in-Cleveland inscription 192
Skendleby L 86
Sketteclyff Lei 86
Skibeden YW 86
Skidbrooke L 82
Skinburness Cu 86
Skiprigg Cu 86
Skipton YW 86
Skipton on Swale YN 86
Skipwith YE 85–6
Skirbeck L 82
Skirlaugh (North and South) YE 82
Skirlington YE 87
Skirwith Cu 87
Skjǫldungar 120–1, 141
Skyrack YW 70, 87
Skåne 108–9, 120
Smoothing (OE) 34
Sneglu-Halla þáttr 154–6
Snorri Sturluson 121, 124–7, 151–2, 157–9
sociolinguistics 11–13, 20, 64–5, 185, 196
South Bramwith YW 85
South Stainley YW 83
speech communities 3, 48–51, 68, 89, 183, 188–9, 199–200, 205
Spondon Db 82
Stainborough YW 83
Stainburn Cu 83
Stainburn YW 83
Stainforth (Lower Strafforth) YW 83

Index 247

Stainforth (West Staincliffe) YW 83
Staining La 83
Stainland YW 83
Stainmore We 83, 114 n. 44
Stainton L 83
Stainton (Upper Strafforth) YW 83
Stainton by Langworth L 83
Stamford Bridge, battle of 160
Stancill YW 83
Standroyd La 83
Stansfield YW 83
Staunton Harold Lei 83
Stenigot L 83
Stenwith L 57 n. 3, 84
Stonegrave YN 57 n. 3, 77, 84
stone sculpture 3, 15–16, 56, 125
Stony Middleton Db 80
substratum influence 206–9
Suebi 122, 124
Sunday Letter see Carta Dominica
Sutton Hoo 30
Svebdegg 126
Svipdag *see* Svebdegg
Swanage Do 111
Swanscoe Ch 57 n. 3, 66 n. 13, 79, 84
Sweden/Swedes 105, 108, 122 n. 56, 124
'switching-code' 43–6, 51, 60, 64–8, 89, 95–6, 100, 109, 181–3, 199, 203
Swithun 136
syncope (ON) 35, 37, 40

Tacitus 134
Tatham La 79
Tathwell L 86
Tebworth Bd 5
Terfinna land 106, 109
Tettenhall, battle of 113–15
Thornby Nth 74, 84
Torworth Nt 84
trade 8–9, 29–30, 41, 103–5, 137
treaties 4–6, 110
Trūsō 91, 106 n. 27

Ubbi 128
Uhtred 5
Úlfljótslǫg 133
'Unstable *i*' (OE) 23

unstressed syllables 36–7, 40, 65, 199–200
Upphaf allra frásagna 157
Urchfont W 114 n. 43
Urmston La 85

Vendel Period 29–31
Venus 131–4
Verner's Law 38
Vistula 106 n. 27
Vita Ædwardi Regis 186
Víðarr 123–5, 126 n. 60, 127, 135
Vortigern 110
Vulcan 133
Vǫlsunga saga 147

/w/, loss of (ON) 40, 62
Wainscarre Nt 81
Waldere 106
Wales 49
Walmsgate L 77
Waltheof 154, 189 n. 7
Wareham Do 111
Warthill YN 84
Watton YE 85
Wealhstod (a monk) 165
Wealhstod (a bishop) 165
Wear, River 141
Wedmore So 4
Wednesfield, battle of *see* Tettenhall, battle of
Welbeck Nt 71
Welbourn L 73
Welburn (Bulmer) YN 73
Wendish 148
Wendland/Wends 93, 106, 108, 148
Werburg 4
West Melton YW 80
West Saxon dialect 27, 34–5, 39, 60 n. 5, 107, 172, 193
West Scrafton YN 87
Westsæ 106, 109
Wheatcroft YW 79
Wheatley YW 79
Whitby YN 49, 187
Whitby, Synod of 164, 170
Whixley YW 199

Widsith 29, 102, 104–7, 124
Wight, Isle of 120
Wigston Parva Lei 84
Wihta 123–4
Wihtgils 123
wills 6, 118, 174
Wine 164
Winestead YE 84
Winksley YW 85
Winnibriggs L 73
Wintringham YE 79
Wippedesfleot 110
Withcall L 85
Withern L 85
Witland 106 n. 27
Witta 123–4, 126 n. 60
Woden *see* Óðinn
Worcester Wo 7 n. 4
writs 192–3
Wulfila 21–2
Wulfstan (a seafarer) 90–5, 97–101, 103–5, 182

Wulfstan I (archbishop of York 931–56) 112
Wulfstan II (archbishop of York 1002–23) 7–8, 90, 128–39, 171–2, 174, 192
Wægdæg 123

Yanwath We 76
Yatehouse Ch 76
Yelvertoft Nth 75
Yngvars saga viðfǫrla 147
York YE 76, 112–13, 116, 128, 138, 140–1, 152, 159–60, 195
York, church of St Peter 5
York Plays 210
York, St Mary Castlegate inscription 190

Þórr 129–43
Þunor *see* Þórr

Öland 107–8

Ǫrvar-Odds saga 147–8